Advance Praise for *The Conspirators*

"Al Martin's book, *The Conspirators*, is a shocking and insightful exposé of Bush family crimes. Martin, a former Bush family insider, recounts numerous instances of deceit, fraud and other financial illegalities perpetrated by members of the Bush family and their associates through a mountain of dummy corporations and arms-length cut-outs."

"He reveals that Iran-Contra had little to do with fighting Communism and a lot to do with siphoning spectacular amounts of wealth to a small circle of powerful insiders."

"The author also outlines how scores of minor 'players' in the Iran-Contra fraud have subsequently died under mysterious circumstances in what he says was (and is) an ongoing cover-up of massive wrong-doing orchestrated at the highest levels of government for decades past."

"The book turns on its head the publicly accepted - and often media reinforced - misconception that individuals enter politics and government service to benefit the nation. On the contrary, Martin shows how the only real motive is to serve their own interests by lining their own pockets to the detriment of the American taxpayer."

"Martin's book deserves be widely read and acted upon."

— David Guyatt, author *The Secret Gold Treaty*

"The book is tremendously important. One of the best exposés of Bush Family crime to come along in many years."

— Jeff Davis, Tom Davis Books

"Just finished reading Martin's book. It's a mindblower. In the last chapter, he presents a credible scenario as to what conditions may precede the doomsday scenario of a national emergency martial law police state."

"Hopefully 'business' is still too good to mess up a good thing. It brings the cliché 'too big to fail' to mind. If it ever looks like the principals are about to take the big fall – look out."

— Phil Segrave

THE CONSPIRATORS
SECRETS OF AN IRAN-CONTRA INSIDER

AL MARTIN

The Conspirators:
Secrets of an Iran-Contra Insider
By Al Martin

Copyright © 2001 by Al Martin

Al Martin Raw: Criminal Govt Conspiracy
Web site: http://www.almartinraw.com

ISBN:0-9710042-0-X

Book and cover design by
Uri Dowbenko

National Liberty Press, LLC
Printed and bound in the United States of America

To order additional copies,
Call toll-free 1-877-776-9004

CONTENTS

AL MARTIN: THE MAN WHO STILL KNOWS TOO MUCH
BY URI DOWBENKO

Al Martin is the man who knows too much.
About US Government fraud at the highest levels.
About Iran Contra.
And about the conspirators who continue their dirty work.

He's a self-described fourth level player, just below George and Jeb Bush, and he has first-hand knowledge of the dirty deals and scams that never stopped.

And why is this story still important? Because these frauds are ongoing (they just roll them over) and they continue to cost taxpayers billions of dollars a year.

In the past, Lt. Cmdr. Al Martin, US Navy (Ret) has testified before Congress for the Kerry Committee and the Alexander Committee, which investigated the illegal operations of the so-called Iran-Contra Affair.

The book you are about to read is an astonishing true crime story that has been too hot for prime time. In fact, Al Martin's story is an unprecedented exposé of high-level government crimes, cover-ups and scandals.

It includes eye witness accounts of US Government-sanctioned narcotics trafficking, illegal weapons deals, and an epidemic of securities fraud, real estate fraud, banking fraud and insurance fraud by high-level government perps.

These criminal perpetrators are members of the cryptocracy, those who rule from the shadows of government, a secret bureaucracy which wields the powers and resources of the federal government, but which often operates outside the chain of government command. Former Assistant Secretary of State Elliott Abrams called it "a shadow government in the United States." In Al Martin's words, "it's a Government Within a Government, comprising some thirty to forty thousand people the American Government turns to, when it wishes certain illegal covert operations to be extant pursuant to a political objective."

Because of what he's seen first hand and experienced, Al Martin has been in hiding, a whistleblower targeted by these very same bureaucrat perps.

"Iran-Contra" is itself is a euphemism for the outrageous fraud perpetrated by government criminals for profit and control. Offhandedly, this inaccurate term entered history as shorthand for the public scandals of illicit arms sales to Iran coupled with illicit weapons deals for Nicaragua. The real story, however, is much more complex.

When George Bush, Bill Casey and Oliver North initiated their plan of government-sanctioned fraud and drug smuggling, they envisioned using 500 men to raise $35 billion.

When Iran-Contra finally fell apart, they ended up using about 5,000 operatives and making over $350 billion in covert revenues.

One of Al Martin's primary roles was as a fundraiser for the bogus "War Against Communism" in Nicaragua. His expertise as a finance specialist served "The Cause," how Oliver North termed the enterprise of raising cash for secret illicit operations.

After he retired from the Navy, Al Martin's life went into the fast lane as a black ops specialist and Office of Navy Intelligence (ONI) officer. In his book "The Conspirators," Al Martin tells the facts that have been ignored or covered-up for over 15 years, ripping the covers off the sleaziest secrets of the US Government power elite.

Because of his failing health, Al Martin has decided to go public and tell the whole story of the Iran-Contra Conspiracy. His book is an unprecedented revelation of the secret world of the US Shadow Government, a first hand account of his own personal involvement with Iran-Contra scams

Since he has worked directly with members of this criminal cabal, Al Martin states unequivocally that both the Republican and the Democrat Parties were and are complicit in illegal fundraising and money laundering.

His book *The Conspirators* is a secret history of the 20th century, an exposé of outrageous proportions, and a truly uncensored version of what really goes on in the back rooms of *realpolitik* brokers and their gofers.

Al Martin tells facts and names names, which no one has dared write before. He describes the hidden side of Washington in a astonishing story of true conspiracy that is breathtaking in its sweep.

Imagine a "system" in which insiders use government agencies and programs as their own private piggy bank, like a criminal privatized public sector, and you can begin to understand the highest levels of corruption and criminality in the USA.

This is what Al Martin calls "How the Real World Works."

THE CONSPIRATORS
SECRETS OF AN IRAN-CONTRA INSIDER

AL MARTIN

"In government, the lie has many fathers, whilst the truth remains an orphan."

— Thomas Jefferson

Chapter 1

CONFIDENTIAL FILE: ALEXANDER S. MARTIN

- Born 5-19-54, Oberammergau, West Germany, Federal German Republic.
- Mixed German and American parentage.
- Returned to United States 09-Aug-1957.
- Graduated Masconoma Technical School, 16-May-1972.
- Full ROTC training then available at high school level.
- Graduated with certificates in electronics and communications equipment, as well as a Level 05 Certificate in Russian Languages.
- Subject joined the United States Navy, 19-May-1972.
- Sent to China Lakes Naval Air Station to complete basic training and for further training in electronics and communications.
- Subject MOS - 16-Sep-1972.
- At subject's request, TDY'd 03-Oct-1972 Naval Communication Center, Saigon, South Vietnam.
- Remained in South Vietnam theater until cessation of naval and air hostilities on 27-Aug-1973.
- On 04-Sep-1973, subject again, and on request, TDY'd Subic Bay, Pacific Theater of Operations Naval Command Center.

- Discharged honorably United States Navy 19-May-1976.
- Immediately thereafter joined United States Naval Reserves, Active Status.
- Remained United States Naval Reserves active status doing two tours.
- Transferred and relisted, inactive service United States Naval Reserves, 19-May-1984.
- Retired United States Naval Reserves 19-May-1988 at the Reserve Officers Rank of Lt. Commander.

After my discharge from active naval duty service in 1976, I moved to Cuzco, Peru, and set up a business with a childhood friend, George W. Carver III, son of then CIA Deputy Director, George W. Carver Jr.

The business dealt in alpaca, llama, and vicuna, but was actually a cover, as a "G" for the State Department.

My assignment was to gather intelligence on Russian military operations in Peru. At the time, Peru was officially pro-Moscow. It was armed by Moscow and had about 4,000 Russian army advisors in the country.

I remained in the country until September 9, 1977, the coup of Gen. Hector Bermudez and the installation of civilian President, Fernando Terry. At that time I returned to the United States, initially settling in Miami.

While in Peru, I became acquainted with numerous CIA field agents and support personnel, then being run out of CIA's Lima station. These included Deputy CIA Station Chief Eugene S. Barlow, more commonly referred to as "Buzz" Barlow, whose claim to fame was that he had secretly recruited Vladimiro Montesinos, a Peruvian army officer, who then in turn developed an intelligence network that informed on Russian Army and Soviet KGB movements within Peru.

An interesting footnote to this is that eight years later, Montesinos would become a double agent working for the KGB. He was being run by then Assistant Deputy KGB Director, Major Yuri Shvets, whose cover was Commercial Trade Attache for the Soviet Embassy in Washington.

Barlow would play an important role in Iran-Contra, particularly in the post 1983 environment and would finally finish up his career as a senior FBI agent at the Tulsa field office.

Subpoenaed before Congress in 1987, Barlow either refused to answer, or answered "I don't know" a total of 117 times when asked about his Iran-Contra role.

In 1978, I met Lawrence Richard Hamil, a Department of Defense shadow player, a hanger-on as many are, who wait for profitable covert operations.

His father was the well-known Harry J. Hamil, former senior Defense Department policy analyst of their southern desk before his death of natural causes in 1984.

Hamil and I and others including Frank Snepp, Jack Terrell, Harry Aderholt, Landon Thorme, Duke Rome, and a host of other players in the shadows of Washington, became involved in a scheme in 1979 to traffic in American Express credit cards in Argentina on behalf of the American Express Corporation.

At that time, the United States had placed a short-lived financial embargo on the country of Argentina in an attempt to pressure the military junta there.

I received twenty dollars for every American Express Card delivered to waiting customers in Argentina.

You may remember that the scandal was broken by the *Washington Post* in 1980. They showed that there was extensive CIA involvement in the operation and that, in fact, the CIA had actively cooperated with other United States financial institutions to evade the financial embargo placed on Argentina at the time.

Through 1980, I also became involved with Mr. Hamil and others in illicit transactions to evade the Dominican sugar blockade.

In the late 1970s, I became involved with Lt. Col. Jack Terrell, Brig. Gen. Harry Aderholt, Lt. Col. Landon Thorme, and Lt. Col. Duke Rome. All would become major Iran-Contra participants three or four years later.

Landon Thorme, for instance, was very close to Jeb Bush. He acted as a corporate straw man for Jeb Bush in a lot of Bahamian shell corporations formed around Bush's principal artifice called IMC (International Medical Corporation) then directed by the infamous Miguel Recarey, who fled the country in 1985.

In 1984, at the request of Lawrence Richard Hamil, I formed several corporations in Florida, chiefly among them, Southeast Resources, Inc.

I also established offices in Miami, ostensibly to act as a primary marketer for Hamil's series of corporate shells, collectively known as the Gulf Coast Investment Group.

The shells were formed primarily to legitimize the flow of funds between wealthy individuals and right-wing Republican investors who wished to support Iran-Contra.

Oliver North called it "The Cause." Secord called it "The Enterprise" and by June 1984, it was just starting to get off the ground.

Obviously it was not legal for these individuals to contribute money to an illicit and illegal covert operation of state. Therefore they needed a legitimizing factor, which is what Hamil and I provided.

In July 1984, I had a meeting with Richard Secord and Larry Hamil in Miami. There I was extensively briefed about Iran-Contra operations and was allowed to review voluminous CIA white papers concerning Operation Black Eagle drafted in 1983.

Very quickly I understood that Iran-Contra (or the euphemism "Iran-Contra") was a ruse to ostensibly arm an envisioned 50,000 man guerrilla or "Contra" army in Nicaragua, which would act as a bulkwark against the increasingly powerful Sandinista regime.

The Sandinistas by that time had built up an army of 120,000 men and were being extensively equipped by the Soviets.

From mid-1984 through the end of 1985, the Gulf Coast Investment Group's operations and its subsidiaries were rapidly expanded to include not only the marketing of fraudulent limited partnerships, real estate limited partnerships, oil and gas, etc., but also to include money laundering, securities fraud, bank fraud, insurance fraud, and the laundering of proceeds from State-sanctioned narcotics operations.

Since I began to understand the increasing risk of staying in business with Mr. Hamil, he and I parted ways on February 10, 1985.

Hamil was becoming increasingly a risk at that time. He was conducting operations that he was never authorized to do, and there became a point when, very simply put, the Agency would not cover for him any more.

Consequently on May 5, 1985, with my help, Miami Field Office FBI Special Agent Ross Gaffney took Mr. Hamil into custody at the Bahia Mar Marina in Ft. Lauderdale, Florida.

My first direct knowledge of CIA-sponsored narcotics trafficking came during a March 3, 1985 policy and planning meeting at the FDN, the Nicaraguan Government In Exile, then located in Miami. It was headed by President Adolfo Calero and financed by the CIA.

At this meeting, Oliver North, Fred Ikley, Nestor Sanchez and others laid out North's plan to increase narcotics operations by establishing new narcotics trafficking out of Honduras, which would flow through Swan Island (an island off the coast of Honduras controlled by the US Defense Intelligence Agency) and then would inflow to Cap Haitién, Haiti, and from there into the United States, principally through the port of New Orleans.

At that time, I saw entire schematics for operation and was advised that Francois Duvalier and Washington lobbyist Ronald H. Brown (later Commerce Secretary Brown) had helped Col. North meet with Duvalier and discuss the arrangements.

When these arrangements were completed by April 1983, I was informed, when in an FDN policy and planning session, that Col. Jean Paul, then commanding officer of the Dessiline Battalion of the Haitian army, would be the new contact man for narcotics operations in Haiti.

Later on, the largest quantity of cocaine trafficked were through these sea-borne operations.

The Director of Security for those operations out of Swan Island was none other than Deputy Defense Intelligence Agency Director for Carribean, Central, and South American Theater Operations — Frederick C. Ikley.

In 1988, it was estimated by the Hughes Commission that in a two year period about 50 tons of cocaine moved through this channel.

Unfortunately for Col. North, by 1986, Colonel Jean Paul of the Haitian army (now Gen. Jean Paul) wanted an increased share of the revenue compared with what he was originally being paid — $50,000 per ship that he cleared from the port.

In 1986, Jean Paul began to secretly contact certain leading liberals in Congress, principally Ron Dellums. He began leaking information to Mr. Dellums, information which later wound up in Sen. Kerry's hands.

Three days before he was to be subpoenaed in 1987, Gen. Jean Paul was poisoned to death with a bowl of pumpkin soup.

It was fed to him by none other than his mistress, Lucille, who later became the wife of Lt. Gen. Prosper Avríl, Haitian Army Chief of Staff.

In 1987 during the Kerry Commission hearings, when there were demands by the Senate Foreign Relations Committee, chaired by Christopher Dodd, to investigate the murder of Jean Paul, within three days of the call for said investigations, Lucille Avríl was assassinated.

Then Robert Bennett, brother of Michelle Bennett, wife of Jean-Claude Duvalier, attempted to sell information to congressional investigators. Just as quickly he was found dead in a fire in one of his warehouses in Port-Au-Prince, Haiti.

To conclude on the topic of CIA narcotic distribution through Haiti — the one individual I've left today in a position to talk is Maj. Michel

François, former commanding officer Haitian police department of Port-Au-Prince.

Maj. François was indicted in 1989 for narcotics trafficking and was arrested recently in Honduras. He is quietly being held there on an extended basis prior to extradition to the United States.

The United States requested his extradition from Honduras through the Department of Justice extradition section.

At the same time, the US State Department, at the insistence of the CIA, has pressured the Honduran government not to extradite Maj. François.

The likely conclusion to this affair will be that Maj. François will be quietly liquidated prior to ever being extradited to the United States.

Throughout the remainder of 1985, my operations continued, this time under the direct authority of Maj. Gen. Richard Vernon Secord.

My relationship with Gen. Secord began to deteriorate in the summer of 1985 due to my increasing nervousness about my exposure and operations, should they ever be made public.

This culminated in a meeting on Thursday, December 19, 1985, in Miami between Oliver North, Richard Secord, myself and my private investigator, Steven Dinnerstein.

At that time, we discussed my being paid the remaining $200,000 that Richard Hamil owed me with an additional $50,000 to be paid the following week.

We were to establish a meeting in my office where Hamil would appear and would be paid a certain sum of money. In exchange, he would give back to Col. North certain documents North wanted to retrieve from Hamil, after Hamil was scheduled to be liquidated.

I was to immediately leave the United States and arrive at a safe house then established by Col. North in St. Martin.

Unfortunately, Hamil discovered the intent of the meeting a day before it was due to happen and the meeting was scrubbed.

At that time, I was effectively on the outside looking in.

In February 1986, I was informed that I was a co-conspirator and also a target of a bill of indictment against Lawrence Richard Hamil, proffered in the Miami district, alleging bank, securities and wire fraud.

On February 16, 1986, I had a meeting with Jeb Bush at his office at 1390 Brickell Avenue in Miami to discuss the context of my grand jury testimony.

At that time, Mr. Bush informed me that my attorney, Michael Von Zamft, would be contacted with further instructions.

In fact, my attorney, Michael Von Zamft, was contacted directly by then Attorney General Ed Meese with instructions for his client — me — to invoke national security privilege for refusal to answer all questions in said grand jury.

On Friday, March 21, 1986, I did in fact appear before a Miami grand jury and was, in fact, questioned by the infamous and sinister Assistant United States Attorney William Richard Scruggs, then chief of political liability control and suppression for the Miami US Attorney's office, then headed by Leon Kellner.

In fact, I refused to answer all questions on national security privilege. An in camera, ex-parte hearing was held before the day judge, Judge Eugene Spellman, which had been arranged in advance by Attorney General Meese and then Deputy Attorney General George W. Terwilliger.

In that meeting, I dictated ten pages of secret testimony which was sealed by Judge Spellman.

In ten days, the government then appealed to the Federal 11th Circuit, in Atlanta to overturn the seal. The seal was dissolved four days later.

Oddly enough, the government made no effort to act upon the overturn and demand the information.

It was later discovered that a copy of the transcripts had been spirited out of the judge's office in cooperation with the illicit help of his secretary Judy, who also worked part time as a secretary for Jeb Bush at the Dade County Latin American Republican Club.

Participating in this scheme with the judge's secretary to illegally secret a copy of my transcript from the judge's chambers were the infamous, sinister, and dreaded bagmen of the Department of Defense, Lt. Col. John Berglund and his aide, Maj. Karl Wahl, formerly seconded to the 407th Intelligence Unit of the 16th Expeditionary Force, Southern Command.

I continued to retain relationships with local Miami federal agencies, principally the FBI, the Drug Enforcement Agency and Customs until the collapse of Iran-Contra the day after Thanksgiving 1986.

In fact, I was invited on Thanksgiving Day to go the Miami Field Office with Mr. Dinnerstein to search certain files and aid in a large shredding operation, which took place in the Miami Field Office that day. I was then informed that similar shredding operations were occurring in both Drug Enforcement and United States Customs offices on that day.

The next day, Attorney General Ed Meese gave a national address and told the American people that we got a problem and it's called "Iran-Contra." It was an effort to put a simple spin on the operation, that it was simply the diversion of 40 million dollars in Iranian weapons profits to support the Contras.

In 1987, I switched sides, as it were.

Initially I began to cooperate with the Kerry Commission until I realized that chief committee investigator, Jack Blum, and his staff, Jack Terrell and Ralph Maestre, were being paid by the CIA to suborn the Kerry Commission investigation. They were also being used as a front to elicit information from potential witnesses for threat assessment.

Unbeknownst to my superiors, I realized the temerity of what later would be called Iran-Contra as early as March 1985. I understood that if Iran-Contra was to ever be made public that the Agency would need many scapegoats.

Unfortunately for me, I elected to align myself with the Democrat-controlled investigating committees in the 1987 to 1991 timeframe. I had cast aside the classic Washington dictum that those who tell the truth about their government die with their personal reputations in disgrace and their personal finances in ruin.

From 1987 to 1991, I cooperated with every Democrat investigating committee in Washington investigating Iran-Contra and later investigating Iraqgate, BCCI, BNL, etc. from the early stages of the Kerry Commission hearings in 1987 to the Tower Commission, the Hughes Commission, and the Alexander Commission. This finally ended in 1991.

Despite the 1.6 million pages of testimonies, depositions, affidavits, and interrogatories accumulated by these committees, not one shred of the truth was ever revealed to the American public.

Of the 1,300 witnesses, subpoenaed, deposed, interrogated before these committees, 413 have since died under clouded circumstances.

Regarding Barry Seal. I was aware of Barry Seal as early as 1979 since Mr. Seal and Mr. Hamil had a personal and business relationship.

Early on in 1980, Hamil began laundering money that Seal was accumulating through his illicit narcotics trafficking activities.

In 1983, as a matter of fact, Mr. Hamil and Mr. Seal set up a fraudulent oil deal in Arkansas called Trinity Oil. This later was to involve Larry Nichols, former marketing director for ADFA, the Arkansas Development Finance Agency, although Mr. Nichols is very reticent to mention it today given his current predicament.

Until 1984 I thought of Seal as little more than an early, mid-level CIA doper, one of the increasing legions of CIA dopers at that time.

Tosh Chumlee, whose father was Colonel Michael Chumlee, Mickey Toliver, and other notorious CIA dopers had just gotten involved. Barry had already been involved for some time.

On September 11, 1984, I was extensively briefed on the meeting between Oliver North and Senior CIA Operations Office head Duane C. "Dewey" Claridge about cementing Seal's relationship with the CIA for "sanctioned" narcotics operations.

I was also aware of the extensive 2,500-page debriefing of Seal on May 23, 1984, undertaken by the Department of Justice to sanitize Seal's CIA connections at that time.

Agents involved in that interrogation were later to become infamous in the post-Iran-Contra environment and charged with participation in a variety of cover-ups — Bill Kennedy and Ernie Jacobson of the FBI, and Tom Cash, then Director of the Miami DEA office, who acted as a paymaster in some cases for Barry Seal.

However, I did not become extensively familiar with Seal's operations until January 1985, due to tape recordings I have with Betsey Wright, then Governor Clinton's chief of staff, and Governor Clinton's senior counsel at that time, Bruce Lindsey, Raymond Young (more commonly referred to as "Buddy" Young), Dan Lasater, Patsy Thomasson, and Winston Bryant, then Attorney General of the State of Arkansas.

The following is the summarized transcript of tape recorded phone conversations occurring on Wednesday, January 9, 1985, concerning information received on that date as to the whereabouts of Larry Hamil who was arriving at Miami International Airport on a Southern Air Transport air charter from Washington on his way to Little Rock via Miami.

Larry was scheduled the following day to pick up a large amount of cash in Little Rock, Arkansas. He was to meet with Bruce Lindsey, Raymond Young, then Assistant CIA Deputy Director Clair George, and Oliver North on that day.

The person who is most able to provide more information is Betsey Wright. A call was made to Betsey Wright in the Governor's office in Little Rock. She was friendly but would provide little direct information, suggesting that Buddy Young should be contacted pursuant to the relationship with Larry Hamil and Barry Seal.

Here's a summary of transcripts (Thursday, 10-Jan-1985)

- Received a call from Barry Seal who stated that he received word from Betsey Wright concerning my wanting to know the location and whereabouts of Lawrence Hamil.
- Asked Barry if I could record call. He said, "all right."
- Barry Seal confirmed that the federal government and a number of states were well aware of Larry Hamil's whereabouts and activities, the private confidential group where his activities were originally based at Mena, Arkansas airport.
- Barry Seal promised that if Larry Hamil was involved in unauthorized fraud that he would be stopped and that Barry Seal would keep me further informed.
- Further he said that any monies that Lawrence Hamil had owed any other players in "the group" would be returned in full.
- If any problem continued, call Betsey Wright back and ask to have Buddy Young call me.

Record of meeting, February 11, 1985, Little Rock, Arkansas involving Clair George, Dewey Clarridge, Oliver North, Barry Seal, and Larry Hamil.

Clair George, by the way, is one of the overall connections in all this. The relationship between Barry Seal, Dewey Clarridge, and Oliver North is well known and has been well documented.

However, to this date, Barry Seal's relationship with the CIA's chief of authorized narcotics operations, Clair George, has not been well documented nor publicly revealed despite the fact that said documentation is not that difficult to obtain.

It is interesting to note at this juncture that pursuant to the renowned scenario where Barry Seal had recording cameras ensconced in the rear bay of his personal Fairchild 123 Aircraft, whereupon landing in Nicaragua to disembark and unload narcotics — the photographs and videos that were later used by Ronald Reagan in an effort to inculpate the Sandinista regime in narcotics trafficking — what was not revealed by the administration at that time was the fact that the CIA had a ringer within the Sandinista Ruling Council, namely Council member Thomas Borgé.

To continue a condensed summary of Barry Seal at this point, it was obvious to me that by September 1985, Barry Seal was becoming a problem due to extensive prior ongoing federal investigations by uncontrollable aspects in the FBI into his operations.

By December 20, 1985, the decision had been reached by William Casey to have Barry Seal liquidated.

The enaction of that decision was left to Oliver North and Richard Secord pursuant to a meeting on the afternoon of December 19, 1985 and December 20, 1985 here in Miami, where in fact Oliver North and Richard Secord met with William Von Raab, then Customs Director.

There was also a telephone conversation with Regional Customs Director, now recently retired United States Customs Commissioner, George Weiss, FBI field office head, William Weld, and DEA Miami head, Tom Cash.

Secord made the arrangements for the liquidation of Barry Seal upon meeting with Jim Langton, then President of Southern Air Transport and Bill Mason, then Vice-President of Southern Air Transport.

A $50,000 contract for liquidation of Seal was given to two individuals, Raoul Herrera, and the infamous Bernardo "Bernie" Tamayo, who is now serving a life sentence in Angola State Penitentiary, Louisiana for being the trigger man in the hit.

What has never been publicly revealed is that after the assassination of Barry Seal on February 10, 1986, the government tried to put out the spin that Tamayo and Herrera were Colombian hit men dispatched by Fabio Ochoa.

In fact, they were not dispatched by Fabio Ochoa, nor were they even Colombians.

Southern Air Transport has always been sensitive to the fact that both individuals were former Southern Air Transport employees and had worked as aircraft mechanics for Southern Air Transport only a year earlier.

Tamayo confessed to the crime and received a life sentence without parole.

Herrera is still challenging his conviction.

Tamayo has never talked, never admitted the truth, and for certain reasons regarding his family, will never reveal the truth.

It's a dead end for anyone to explore that avenue.

However, Tom Spencer, Counsel for Southern Air Transport and personal counsel for Richard Secord, continues to threaten to sue any public agent and any media outlet that even mentions that Tamayo and Herrera were former Southern Air Transport employees.

He even challenges anyone to prove that, insofar as records indicating their employment with Southern Air Transport had long since been destroyed.

Unfortunately for Mr. Spencer, while under my employ, private investigator Mr. Dinnerstein was able to get copies of their Southern Air Transport employee identification cards.

In conclusion, Iran-Contra was very simply a ruse.

The ruse was to arm a 50,000 man army in Nicaragua by means of sanctioned trafficking in cocaine, by means of trafficking weapons, and by means of the intricate and complex network of State-sponsored, State-organized, and State-protected fraud.

It was fraud of every nature.

- Fraud perpetrated upon savings & loans and commercial banks.
- Fraud perpetrated on securities firms, and insurance firms.
- Fraud perpetrated on the Internal Revenue Service through a variety of illicit tax shelters.

Such a scheme had really never been devised and frankly it was not envisioned in 1983. It was an operation that simply got out of hand and, at its peak in 1985, involved over 5,000 individuals.

The essential concept was to refinance and to replenish the coffers, of what constitutes, as then Assistant Secretary of State Elliott Abrams said publicly, "a Shadow Government in the United States," a Government Within a Government, comprising some thirty to forty thousand people that the American government turns to when it wishes certain illegal covert operations to be extant pursuant to a political objective.

It's been estimated by the Kerry Commission, and re-estimated by the Hughes Commission, that the US institutions and individuals were defrauded out of $5 billion to $7 billion dollars.

Most of the money was guaranteed by the US Treasury.

It's money that the taxpayers of the United States will ultimately have to pay.

Chapter 2

THE NATIONAL PROGRAMS OFFICE AND OPERATION SLEDGEHAMMER

I N OCTOBER 1983, Operation Black Eagle was reformulated from Operation Eagle. It began with the appointment of Oliver North as Chairman of the powerful and then still secret National Programs Office (NPO).

CIA Director William Casey thought this was necessary since the NPO had extremely secure storage, transportation and air routes within the United States as well as in the Caribbean and the Central and South American theaters. Such secure facilities would be necessary for the envisioned trafficking in the quantities of cocaine and weapons that Casey felt would be necessary.

These sites included such renowned places as Iron Mountain, Texas, the airfields outside of Medford, Oregon, the airfield in Joplin, Missouri, etc.

Iron Mountain, Texas, by the way, was extensively written about in the media during the late 1980s and the early 1990s. In fact Rebecca Sims, the noted Iran-Contra journalist and former accountant for Bobby Corson, came the closest to understanding what it was all about, before she hit the brick wall.

In terms of policy management, Casey formed a series of inter-governmental agency Restricted Access Groups (RAGs). Ultimately three such groups were formed. The top Restricted Access Group 1 was Vice President George Bush — as it was decided that all narcotics, weapons and money operations vis-a-vis Iran Contra, would be consolidated under the office of the Vice President.

Also included in these Restricted Access Groups were then Vice Presidential National Security Advisor, Col. Donald Gregg, then Deputy Secretary of State Lawrence Eagleburger and Assistant Secretary of State Elliott Abrams, who was in charge of the Inter-American Affairs Office (an office which served in no other capacity except being a propaganda tool for the Nicaraguan Contras), Richard Armitage, and Assistant Secretary of State, Bernie Aronson.

In the Department of Defense, the RAG group included Assistant Secretary of Defense, Frank Carlucci, Assistant Secretary of Defense Richard Stilwell, and Casper Weinberger himself.

In the CIA, besides Casey, there was the infamous Deputy Director of Operations, Clair George and Assistant Deputy Director of Operations, Alan Fiers.

Later in Restricted Access Group 3, in terms of CIA involvement, there would be included various CIA Station Chiefs, such as the infamous and sinister Joseph P. Fernandez, the Costa Rican Station Chief.

The names involved in the Restricted Access Group would change as these men changed positions in government — from 1983 through 1986.

When Frank Carlucci left the Defense Department to become Presidential National Security Advisor and Bobby Gates became Deputy Director of CIA, Gates supplanted Carlucci within Restricted Access Group 2.

When Gates's nomination to become Director later failed, Gates was put back into Restricted Access Group 1, when he took over from Carlucci as Presidential National Security Advisor.

At the peak of Iran-Contra operations in the spring of 1986, there were approximately 1,000 direct Government employees involved — from Cabinet Secretaries all the way down to Special Envoys.

A good example of a Special Envoy who was involved was Bill Walters, son of famous ambassador Vernon Walters, who operated under then Deputy Assistant Secretary of State, Michael Kozak. Walters was Special Envoy to Panama for illegal and covert operations acting as a liaison between Panamanian G-2 and Elliott Abrams's Inter-America Affairs Office.

During the Iran Contra years (specifically from 1983 to 1986), a wide variety of contingency operations were developed.

The most sinister of these, in my opinion, was Operation Sledgehammer.

I heard North discuss it extensively during one of the FDL meetings in Miami in the fall of 1984. Sledgehammer was actually being put together when North was appointed Chairman of the NPO.

I didn't realize until late 1984 that there was a double agenda in North being so appointed. It was not only for the secure transportation and storage of weapons and narcotics. The facilities of the NPO were also being used and reactivated for their communications capability, in terms of weapon sites that would be used by US armed forces.

Sledgehammer was essentially a contingency operation to institute a putsch against the United States Government (with the tacit support of said Government) should knowledge of Iran-Contra operations become publicly disseminated.

The feeling was that if people were to know the quantities of narcotics and weapons being dealt and the enormity of State-sanctioned fraud against US banks (and other financial institutions which taxpayers ultimately guarantee), there would be such a reaction among the people that in order to divert public attention, it might become necessary to institute a putsch having the tacit agreement of the Reagan Administration.

I know this sounds draconian, but that was the level of concern in those years.

These NPO facilities were used as storage sites for advanced communication equipment, for instance, that would be necessary for the control of cities by US armed forces.

There were some speculative media pieces done on Operation Sledgehammer in the late '80s and the early '90s, but it was nothing substantial. The few documents regarding Sledgehammer that had leaked out in late 1986 and early 1987 wound up in the hands of attorney Paul Wilcher, for example.

And we all know what happened to Wilcher…

As a matter of fact, Danny Casolaro actually wound up with some of them, but unfortunately he was liquidated before he could do anything with them.

Bill Moyle from *Jane's Defense Weekly* also obtained some of these materials. Three days later he was found hanged by his own necktie inside a closet in his hotel room in Santiago, Chile, while investigating the famous Chilean arms dealer, Carlos Cardoen.

Another well-known journalist I knew at the time who had received some genuine information regarding Operation Sledgehammer was Keith Wickenham.

Keith received certain materials from a certain party about ten on the morning. He drove his automobile home to take a shower and get cleaned up and go back to his office.

About an hour later, when he was done, he got back into his automobile. When he turned on his ignition, it blew up — with him in it.

The police ruled his death, or the car explosion, to be an "accidental vapor explosion."

The local investigation was quickly closed and a few months later, all the files were shredded.

Another well-known journalist who obtained materials about this operation was Steve Perry. He got them in Washington, secreted them in a safe deposit box in the First National Bank of Washington and took a holiday. It was a little holiday he had scheduled to go ice fishing in upstate New York.

The second day there, Mr. Perry fell through the ice and promptly drowned.

When the executor of his estate opened up the safe deposit box, there was nothing there.

I apologize when I said we all know what happened to Paul Wilcher.

Wilcher was a famous liberal attorney in Arlington, Virginia. Actually he lived in Manassas, but he practiced in Arlington and had a condo there.

His firm represented many people like me who had been on the short end of the Iran- Contra stick when everything fell apart.

In the event that you're not familiar with the story, Wilcher was simply murdered.

His beaten and naked body was found sitting on his own toilet seat in his own condominium.

The police — a man and woman police officer, arrived at the scene very early — when in fact his killer was exiting the building. But they didn't make the connection at the time.

A few days later, they did make the connection.

And when they made the connection through an artist rendering as to who it was, the CIA saw a copy of that artist rendering too.

The two police officers were quickly put on paid leave and they used up all their vacation and benefits. Then they were allowed to retire early with enhanced pensions.

Suddenly a few weeks later, bank accounts appeared for both of them at the Nassau, Bahamas branch of the Royal Trust Company of Canada.

The two police officers are now comfortably retired in the Caribbean living under assumed names.

(When Bill Casey headed the Agency, he would remark privately that his sense of honor was such that "American police officers should not be liquidated unless absolutely necessary.")

Regarding Operation Sledgehammer — all those who ever attempted to publicly disseminate any genuine documents or information have now been liquidated, some 36 people in all.

Wilcher, by the way, was murdered by a guy named Eddy Castille, who is employed by Department 4 (Domestic Wet Operations, or DWO) of the Agency. He's one of their shooters.

Castille inspires so much fear within the community that the very mention of his name in context with what he does has proven to be a death sentence — or at least a sentence of substantial pressure, harassment and intimidation.

The well-known Iran-Contra attorney in Texas, Dave Parker, is a notable example of what happens to people who ever mention Castille's name.

Former Army CID investigator Bill McCoy told Parker to keep his mouth shut when Parker was disseminating information about this guy.

After Parker's office was bombed, after his house burned down, after his car was blown up and after he was beaten up three or four time — he got the message.

He has never mentioned the guy's name publicly again.

Another interesting transaction was the famous KGB document purchase of 1991, which was arranged by none other than Dick Armitage and Frank Carlucci.

When Frank and Dickie left the Government, they immediately went to Moscow and opened up an office of the Blackstone Investment Group.

Although it was supposed to be an investment office, it was essentially a conduit for money coming out of Washington to purchase KGB documents.

In 1991, an enormous sale from the KGB files was consummated for $36 million.

It always struck me as somewhat humorous that the sheer volume of documents purchased was so large that it took the entire cargo bay of an Southern Air Transport C-130, which was used to fly the stuff out of Moscow.

The purchased documents were a real grab bag of what would have been very politically damaging documents, especially for Republicans in the United States — had they ever been made public.

They included very early Vietnam files concerning CIA mischief in Vietnam, then compiled by probably the greatest southeastern Soviet intelligence expert the KGB ever had, Colonel-General Nikolai Chernugin. In fact, everything the KGB had on Iran-Contra, Iraqgate and a real host of other problems was also purchased.

It's interesting to note that the only general in the KGB who objected to the sale (now chief of their North American Desk) was the very loyal and patriotic General Alexander Karpov.

Included in this deal, by the way, was a package (let's call it a travel package) wherein over 300 KGB generals and colonels were allowed to enter the United States and were provided with very comfortable homes, mostly in northern Virginia.

Most KGB generals now get a check for $12,000 a month from the Agency.

KGB colonels get $8000 a month plus a panoply of favors.

Most of these guys are now in the import-export business. They have offices in and around McLean, Virginia.

It's also interesting to note that four former KGB generals have import-export offices in the same building in McLean where Oliver North has his office.

How easy it is to purchase the silence of others with the appropriate-sized slice of the American Pie.

The reason I mention this? It's an interesting case study in the way things work and the decisions men make.

For his loyalty to the Soviet Union, General Karpov will soon retire a broken — and financially broke — man in the run-down dacha he owns in the Crimea.

On the other hand, a KGB general who cooperated by keeping his mouth shut is already retired in a very comfortable brick colonial home in Silver Springs, Maryland. He also has a Mercedes Benz and a golf course membership.

Back to Iran-Contra. Let us take a look at the Department of Justice role in Iran-Contra. More specifically, let us examine its political liability control and suppression function.

In an effort to insulate Ed Meese from the more tawdry affair of liability control and suppression, the S-1 (Suppression-1) function of the

Department of Justice was put in the hands of his subordinate, Deputy Attorney General George W. Terwilliger.

This Terwilliger is a real piece of work. His equally sinister and dreaded henchman, Lowell Jensen, is now a federal district judge in California.

Terwilliger, by the way, is now a senior partner in the Washington DC law firm of Woods, McGuire, one of the repositories for nasty right-wingers in waiting (the ultimate repository being the Heritage Foundation).

Included in the Suppression Control Unit of the Department of Justice (which, of course, is a secret unit of the Department) were what I used to call the Sinister Bobbsey Twins — Associate Attorney General David Margolis, then Chief of Domestic Criminal Operations, and the equally sinister Mark Richards, then Chief of the International Crime Section.

The function of these people was to prosecute those who had talked too much — or who might talk too much in the future — such as the way I was prosecuted in 1986, although unsuccessfully.

The Suppression Unit in the Department of Justice is so powerful it reaches into all agencies.

This Unit maintains control features into all politically sensitive US Attorneys' offices that were involved in Iran-Contra — Miami, Tampa, New Orleans, Atlanta, etc.

In Miami, for instance, the Control Unit's hand-picked boy was the powerful, infamous, dreaded and sinister William Richard Scruggs, who is still an Assistant US Attorney there.

In West Palm Beach, it was Jay Lewis, who would prosecute politically sensitive narcotics cases, such as the Jack DeVoe case.

These were cases where people had actually trafficked in narcotics on behalf of, with the complicity of, or at least with the acquiescence of the Agency.

The people had now become politically expendable. And there was a whole route maintained for people like me who got prosecuted in the aftermath of Iran-Contra. Tremendous resources were devoted to these prosecutions too.

The people who were rather mid-level in the Department of Justice within the Suppression Group at the time are now senior officials.

A good example is Lee Radek, an Associate Attorney General and also the head of Justice's Public Integrity Section.

Public Integrity? What a joke that is.

The Public Integrity Section of the Department of Justice, by the way, is full of ex-CIA players.

At the time, Lee Radek's assistant was Deputy Associate Attorney General Bobby Muller. Bobby was forced out of the Department in 1992 for having a big mouth. He was an alcoholic and he fancied himself a Republican cocktail circuit dandy.

The problem is that in the Beltway, Bobby would get half in the bag — and in an effort to be humorous — would run his mouth off about what people had said. He would do it when there were members of the press around.

It was a riot the stuff that Bobby would say.

Bobby was the one who forced that comment out in June 1992, the public comment George Bush made to Sarah McClendon about Iran-Contra.

When McClendon asked George about Iran Contra, George Bush said, "Sarah, if people ever knew what we had done, we'd be chased down in the streets and lynched."

It was also Bobby who reiterated what Bob Dole had said when Bob Dole was half in the bag.

I myself was not ten feet from Bob Dole during the Reagan re-inauguration dinner in January 1985, which was held inside the Watergate Hotel because it was so goddamn freezing outside.

Record snow. Record cold temperatures in Washington.

Bob Dole was half smashed.

Frank Carlucci was there. Armitage was there. The whole gang, the whole cabal was there.

And Bob Dole said, "America. Land of the Naive and Home of the Provincial. Thank God."

I think the final nail in Muller's coffin was that stuff he gave *Mother Jones* Magazine, an article called "Shredded Justice" by Mary Fricker and Steve Pizzo (1991) about Attorney General Billy Barr.

Muller had said that Barr would go around to the 6th floor of the Department of Justice building.

That's where all the shredders are.

And Billy would call himself, "Billy 'I Never Saw a Document I Didn't Want To Shred' Barr."

The infamous Richard Scruggs rose to prominence in the media since he directed the last kidnapping under the Reagan-Bush political kidnapping policies which ended in 1991.

They would kidnap people, foreign fugitives, who knew too much.

The last kidnapping was the renowned Israel Abel. Finally the Costa Rican government said, No More.

Mr. Scruggs, an Assistant US Attorney, is under indictment in Costa Rica for felony kidnapping, yet he continues to serve in the Department of Justice.

The Department of Justice continues to this day to deny the Costa Rican extradition request.

In fact, there are over 17 senior officials still serving in the Department of Justice, who are under indictment in foreign countries for breaking the laws of those countries, yet they are protected by the Department of Justice to this day.

These are guys like Scruggs, or former US Attorney Leon Kellner and former US Attorney Stanley Marcus (respectively now a senior law partner and sitting federal judge in California).

You can't imagine the human misery they've created.

The number of people falsely incarcerated — not because of what they did, but because of what they knew.

The people who were killed because of these men's fervent wantonness to control liability.

It really should be exposed.

Besides the *Miami Herald,* no one has ever made a serious attempt to do it. And they were very quickly shut down.

In 1993, Spencer Oliver attempted to present the secret Amnesty International Report stating that there were over 1,200 US citizens wrongfully incarcerated because of what they knew about Iran-Contra.

Unfortunately, it got destroyed before it could be disseminated outside Congress. But Spencer's still got a copy of that report.

Another person who would be valuable for Republicans who want to use Iran Contra against the Clinton cadre would be Andy Leff.

In the early 1990s, Andy was the head of the DNC Press and Research Office. It was his job to conduct an investigation of Iran-Contra on behalf of the DNC.

Leff was one hell of a good investigator. He was also very friendly with Maury Waas, a freelancer who wrote for the *Washington Times* and the *Wall Street Journal.*

Maury was one hell of a competent investigative journalist. I met him several times and liked him.

Ron Brown had ordered an investigation of Iran-Contra in an effort to embarrass Bush and others in the upcoming election. The problem was that Andy found substantial connections between Ron Brown's Iran-Contra role, as well as Bill Clinton's and a host of Clinton Cadre members' roles in Iran-Contra too.

He wisely kept it secret from his immediate DNC superior, Dan Carroll. But he would leak this information out to Maury. He would package it up into stories.

What happened is that Carroll got wise to what was going on and figured that this information was coming from Leff.

Andy Leff left his office on a Friday night — this was late 1991 — and over the weekend, unbeknownst to him, his office was raided by Dan Carroll and a special team from the DNC.

They discovered what he had found out about Ron Brown and Clinton and other Democratic involvement in Iran-Contra.

All his investigative files were shredded.

The locks on his office door were changed.

When he came in on Monday morning and went to his office, his own secretary said she didn't know who he was.

Leff immediately knew what was coming. He went to Dulles International Airport. He didn't even go back to his own apartment. He got on the first plane and got out.

He currently lives in hiding in California. He's frightened of his own people — with justification, I think.

But I'm one of the few people who knows how to reach him, and I think he would be more interested in getting involved again because he wants some revenge.

In the aftermath of any illegal covert operation which collapsed and became public, Iran-Contra is the most egregious and notorious.

When an operation collapses, people like me get put through a three-tiered strainer. We'll call it the "A," "B," and "C" strainer.

The "A" strainer is for people who were two rungs of the ladder above me — guys like Major General Richard Secord and Major General John K. (Jack) Singlaub.

These are the people who are on the right side of the door of liability when it slams shut. They are the ones who get their "briefcases" and they will always live in great financial comfort and security, just going along — endlessly committing fraud and endlessly being protected from the consequences of it.

This is something that Richard Secord continues to do to this day.

The bulk of the people involved in such an operation are put through the "B" strainer.

The "B" strainer is where people are pressured, harassed, intimidated, discredited, bankrupted and sometimes imprisoned on false charges, forced into exile in an effort to maintain the deniability of their superiors and to legally discredit them before any potential congressional committee, or any court proceeding in which they might testify, or give any deposition on someone else's behalf.

The "C" strainer, which is the minority — in which usually one in ten people are put through — is death.

Those are the people who were simply down on the ladder. They were not trained intelligence people. They found out a few little kernels of something that nobody wants revealed. And these people are considered unreliable, so they are simply done away with.

As we mentioned, more than 400 people out of the 5000 involved would be in that category.

On the rim, between "A" and "B," there are always some limbo people — like me. There are only two or three dozen of us left.

These are people who were not quite high enough on the proverbial ladder to get their "briefcases" and get taken care of when the door of liability gets slammed shut.

Yet they know too much.

They would be too much of a problem if a serious effort to discredit them, ruin them, or imprison them were to be extant, since it would give people like me a platform.

It would again focus the spotlight on us.

It would give us a platform, or a soapbox as it were, from which to speak.

And that is something that we must be denied at all costs.

The handful that's left — people like me — naturally this handful gradually diminishes as time goes by, simply through attrition or through a variety of changing circumstances.

However we are stuck in a never-ending state of limbo.

It's called being in the proverbial jack box from which we cannot crawl out.

Essentially that's the way we will live the rest of our lives. We're never going to be invited back on the inside.

We will always be monitored or watched in some fashion.

As a few years go by, as in this case with the collapse of Iran-Contra, I have settled into a zone of understanding with my antagonists.

I know there is a line in the sand for me. If I cross that line by talking too much, I am punished.

Or I am suddenly arrested. I've been arrested 17 times in 10 years.

Suddenly I'll be arrested again on something out of the blue that no one ever knows anything about.

I'll spend forty or fifty days in some country jail under an assumed name.

I'll be kept away from a telephone. I will be kept in very uncomfortable circumstances.

And I don't really get out, until word gets out of my circumstances and then there's some pressure from my friends on Capitol Hill.

And finally I'm let out.

But the message is sent.

Through constant arrests and constant intimidation and pressure, I have learned to survive and to know where my personal line in the sand is.

When information gets out en masse and it's quickly disseminated, it gives me some protection. However, it is an absolute fantasy that public attention gives one protection. It doesn't.

The only way it does is if it's disseminated quickly. In other words, a surgical strike is made with what one knows. One does all the talk shows back to back. Then one can get some protection. But that's more easily said than done.

And it doesn't alter one's circumstances. I can do all the talk shows, but they won't pay me any money. I could appear in every newspaper I wanted, but that doesn't change my circumstances.

I have to garner funds to get back into the woodwork and the only way that is ever going to happen is through someone who has an interest in what I know, for whatever purpose — whether they want to publicly disseminate it or use it for some sort of lever.

Anyway I'm going to put together some list of precise operations — paramilitary, illegal covert operations, narcotics and weapons operations, fraud and money operations, money laundering operations, and so on.

The only thing I can do off the top of my head is based on my sense of what the public is interested in knowing.

One of those things would be to look at Iran-Contra, to look at the 5,000 people involved and to ask —

- What happened to those people?
- What were the circumstances of the 400 who were murdered?
- What are the circumstances of the 1,200 of those 5,000 who were incarcerated?
- Were they incarcerated for what they know and not for what they may have done?

- What happened to the 500 at the top?
- What are their circumstances today?
- Are they living in comfort based on their illicitly gotten gains?
- What fraud do they continue to commit?
- How has that fraud taken on a new form?
- How has trafficking in weapons taken on a new form?
- And overall, how has this affected the American people? In other words, what has been the cost to the American taxpayers to bail out institutions, brokerage firms, banks, savings and loans, insurance companies, even some quasi-governmental agencies, which were in severe distress because of the fraud these 5,000 committed?
- How many billions of dollars did it cost the taxpayers to bail these institutions out?
- How many billions of dollars of revenue was denied the US Treasury because of certain narcotics and weapons transactions and a whole panoply of other transactions, like illegal partnerships, illegal securities deals, and so on?

I think that the one thing the American people are interested in is — what did it cost them?

They don't give a shit who made what really, or what was done, or the weapons or the narcotics.

Sure they have some sizzle. But that's all they really have.

The meat of it?

What did it take out of the American people's pockets?

That's something the American people are always interested in.

Also on the broad canvas, what's been overlooked is the KGB involvement in Iran-Contra — what the KGB knew, the amount of information they accumulated.

You have to look at KGB involvement in Iran-Contra over a much broader period of time — from Soviet intelligence activities in the United States until the early 1990s.

You have to look at how that information got sold back to essentially the same people in Washington who committed the mischief.

The other area to look at is the 500 at the top, most of whom are still in government, by the way, to look at what they did, what happened to them, how the cover-up worked, how they were able to orchestrate a cover-up, and where they are now in government.

It would show people how little has actually changed.

The control mechanism is still in place.

This would be an excellent way to demonstrate how political liability spreads and how it crosses party lines vis-avis Iran-Contra, Iraqgate, BCCI, S&Ls and so on.

Chapter 3

OLIVER NORTH: THE MONEY LAUNDERING DRUG SMUGGLING "PATRIOT"

FIRST I'D LIKE TO DISCUSS illegal money raising and money laundering during the Iran-Contra period, specifically from the 1983 to 1986.

Back to Operation Black Eagle, September-October 1983.

Part of this operation was envisioned beyond the narcotics and weapons aspect. It was the huge amount of money that would be necessary for such an operation, since the arming of the Nicaraguan Contras was only a ruse.

However, as an offshoot of this operation and starting in late 1983, Oliver North and others established a series of corporate entities.

They were mostly 501c3 tax exempt foundations, forums, institutes, etc. for the purpose of raising illicit money.

That is where soft money contributors from civilian sympathizers could be washed through this type of an artifice. Then the cash would simply be bled off.

You will notice the number of artifices Oliver North formed in the Republican Party, the RNC at the time, with words such as "Eagle," "Liberty," "Heritage." These were very popular names.

The American Eagle Foundation, first formed by Oliver North and Jesse Helms, is a 501c3. It was later to become known as the Eagle Forum, which is a large organization headed by Lynne Cheney.

Its parent is the Eagle Foundation, which by the way, just bought a seventy-percent interest in Regnery Publishing.

That's why Regnery can't publish any more books about Republicans.

Anyway, included in these artifices were other North-controlled entities such as the American Liberty Foundation.

The RNC had a separate deal called the American Eagle Association, which was for people who contributed $10,000 a year in soft money.

This was the famous deal where they got the little plastic card, like a credit card or membership card, with a number on it. It included an 800-number that rang in a basement cubicle in the White House.

North had a gal that staffed the phone all the time. That was always a hot seller.

We solicited many, many $10,000 donations for that. Through my own marketing corporation, I received a fifteen-percent commission.

By January-February 1985, through the Miami policy and planning meetings of the FDN, which Oliver North would often attend, our goals were quickly being met. That is, the original money goals as laid out in the July 1984 memorandum between Donald Gregg, then Vice Presidential National Security Advisor, and Oliver North to eventually be able to reach a billion dollars a month in fraud.

That number was rapidly being reached.

We used existing RNC operations such as GOPAC to raise illegal money, or money that would in turn be used for an illegal purpose.

These are the years when Pete DuPont still chaired GOPAC.

And I still have a list to this day of GOPAC contributors who we would put the arm on to contribute to a North-Secord (Richard Secord) controlled entity.

They were more than happy to contribute to it in exchange for the favors they received.

The fraud — and when I say fraud — I am talking about the whole ball of wax — illegal fundraising, illegal bank loans, illegal security transactions, fraudulent insurance transactions, etc. There are about nineteen classifications of state-sponsored fraud in all. It all began in this fashion in late 1983. By 1985, we were absolutely booming. The level of fraud was simply incredible.

Later when the first substantive audits were done by Comptroller of the Currency, Robert Ludwig (in his secret memorandum to George Bush), he was actually concerned that we collectively (I'm talking about 2,000 out of the group of 5,000 that operated at the time) were beginning to seriously undermine US savings and loans, commercial banks, insurance companies, security firms, etc. There were huge quantities of money that were being bled off in fraudulent transactions and loans that would be defaulted on, stock swindles, etc.

Restricted stocks would be transferred to a variety of Swiss banks or certain security firms, wherein letters of restriction would be surreptitiously removed pursuant to US SEC Reg. 14 after which the said stock would be illegally resold.

Anyway, in that memorandum of the Comptroller of the Currency and a subsequent secret memorandum from the Office of Thrift Supervision, there was some genuine concern that we were weakening the nation's financial system.

This was 1986, when the economy itself was already weakening. Interest rates were rising. The Reagan deficits, now by 1986, had grown to over $400 billion annually. Consequently, all this really came to a head in 1987.

It was later secretly commented on. The only person who ever had the balls to say anything about it was then southeastern regional SEC Commissioner, Charlie Harper, who had formerly been the Miami District SEC Commissioner.

He was the only one to publicly ever say anything about this. Of course, after he said that, Charlie was quickly bumped up the ladder, and he never said anything again.

The fraud in question operated in a pyramid.

This pyramid was originally designed in 1984 by Oliver North and later redefined with the influence of Jeb Bush and his brothers, Neil and George Jr.

At the very top of this pyramid there was authorized State-sponsored and State-sanctioned fraud, using political organizations and foundations illicitly, using them illegally in a tax-exempt capacity, and then illegally siphoning off the money to support a covert operation, which in itself was illegal.

Underneath, there were people like me, essentially subcontractors who developed a series of corporate artifices, usually oil and gas, gold bullion or gold mining deals, aircraft brokerage deals, real estate deals, all of the old right-wing favorites for the surreptitious and illegal generation of money and to defraud banks and so forth.

These were banks that were sympathetic, of course. In other words, the banks knew that they were being defrauded.

You couldn't simply defraud a bank that was not inside the circle, so to speak.

In July 1984, I was approached by the infamous Lawrence Richard Hamil, who was then operating under the direction of Richard Secord.

Hamil had already set up a series of thirty-seven corporations, all using the word "Gulf."

It was very common.

- Gulf Coast Investment
- Gulf Oil and Drilling Supply, which was in a partnership with Jeb Bush.
- Gulf Realty, which was another joint partnership with Neil Bush.
- Gulf Offshore Trust Corporation, a joint deal with George Bush, Jr.
- Gulf Asian Corporation, a joint venture between us and Prescott Bush, the Vice President's brother, and his son, Wally.

Wally owned a securities firm in Phoenix, called J. Walter Bush Securities.

As a matter of fact, the firm was in the Lincoln Savings and Loan Plaza. He had a good deal with Charlie Keating. They did a lot of business with the Lincoln Savings and Loan. Keating would provide financing for illegal securities deals — deals that existed nowhere but in a file drawer.

(Coincidentally, J. Walter Bush Securities was located in an office directly opposite the World Anti-Communist League office, the infamous front organization founded by General Singlaub.)

In exchange, the bank got notes and stock, which eventually wound up being worthless.

The fraud was segregated. For example, Jeb Bush's real forté, when it came to fraud, was oil and gas drilling, oil and gas fraud, real estate fraud, mostly commercial real estate fraud, à la that Broward Savings and Loan scandal, in which they lost three or four million dollars because of Jeb.

And the list goes on.

Neil, of course, was almost exclusively real estate. These included all of those Gulf Realty deals. This is the same Gulf Realty Corporation of the late 1950s, which was originally a CIA proprietary that got cut loose in the 1970s and lay dormant for a while until Neil and his two partners, Bill Walters and Ken Good, picked it up and instituted a tremendously complex web of land fraud that stretched across Florida, Texas, California, and Connecticut.

It was a really intriguing web of land fraud.

The Boca Chica Development, the Destin Country Club Development — these were all deals that were designed to be frauds.

They went down the tubes. Ultimately they were bailed out with public money to the tune of $780 million apiece.

There were about 100 such projects in all which were ultimately bailed out by some public guarantee institution.

It wasn't necessarily the FDIC or the FSLIC, but in some cases, very esoteric public guaranteed funds were used to bail these deals out.

George Jr. naturally specialized in oil since he controlled the Bush family oil portfolio including Harken Energy stock, Tidewater Development stock, and Apache and Zapata stock.

These were all deals where George Sr. had formerly been on the Board of Directors. Now George Jr. was on the Board of Directors, since Sr. as Vice President couldn't have that capacity.

Harken Energy was a classic fraud.

The stock still trades on the AMEX at five or six dollars a share. It's been pumped up recently because there's a new fraud going on with those Bahrainian leases that Richard Secord originally had ten years ago.

The stock will shortly collapse back to two dollars again, as soon as everybody gets out.

A lot of Republicans will make money on the deal.

You think, for instance, that the fraud doesn't still go on today. It does.

A recent example of this fraud is Bre-X Minerals on the Vancouver Stock Exchange.

George Bush was on the Board of Directors and made about $40 million in the deal through stock he never paid for.

Former Secretary of State Henry Kissinger made $12 or $13 million on the deal.

George Schultz made money on the deal.

Joe Clark, former Prime Minister of Canada, made money in the deal.

It's just another example of the continuation of the original fraud, which links back to Iran-Contra.

I remind everybody that Iran-Contra is the genesis for so much of the fraud that exists today. In some cases, not even the corporate names have been changed. Their jurisdictions may have been changed, but the people behind the deals are all the same.

Anyway, I set up a corporation in Miami in 1984. I didn't even have to disguise it. It was just a regular Class C Florida corporation called

Southeast Resources, Inc., which did nothing other than market the product of other people.

It did not generate any of its own product. It was simply a marketing company. It had marketing contracts for illegal product, illegal limited partnerships, illegal loan syndications, and so forth.

I was in a very good position to see a very broad range of fraud, since at one time in 1985, I had over 300 investment products in-house.

And these not only came from the Bush Boys or Richard Hamil, but in some cases I marketed a deal called Trinity Oil and Gas, Ltd., which was a collaboration of Barry Seal, Richard Hamil, Larry Nichols and a few others, as I have previously mentioned.

Barry Seal is conventionally described — and conventionally pigeon-holed — as a drug smuggler, but he was much more.

There's much more to this man than simply drugs. His money laundering in corporate operations is an area which has never been touched.

If anybody ever wanted to do a serious work on Seal, you have to look at this area.

By 1985, I was personally raising about $3 million a year through Southeast Resources.

Of course, I was only one guy out of two thousand. What I mean is that I don't have any special claim to fame on any of these deals.

However, an interesting capacity I became involved in was passing along money to certain politicians in states where we had marketing operations, which was part of the routine.

This was part of the system of the fraud — that the money would get passed on to Republicans, particularly Republican governors, or Republican members of the House and Senate in certain states where we had operations.

A good example of this (about which I testified to the Kerry Commission in 1987) was passing along money to the husband of then Governor Martha Lane Collins, Republican of Kentucky.

Her husband, Dennis the Dentist, was a dentist on the Board of Directors of First National Bank of Frankfort, Kentucky.

He, himself, later got indicted for fraud, with Jake Butcher and his brother in that National Bank of Frankfort and the Union Planters Bank in Nashville deal.

That was a good-sized fraud — about $80 million. Of course, Dennis the Dentist made out pretty well. He never spent any time in jail or anything. And Collins was absolutely protected.

Another guy I passed money to (actually it was to his aide) was then Republican Governor Thompson of Illinois.

I was in Chicago regularly because many of our contributors were in Chicago. Richard Hamil and I would meet regularly with the governor's aide in the bar in the Whitehall Hotel on E. State Street in Chicago and pass some envelopes — $20,000, $40,000 at a time.

Those are just two examples. But another way that Republican members on the Hill were paid off was this — they were given limited partnership interests for nothing. Granted, these limited partnership interests were fraud and they weren't worth the paper they were printed on.

But ultimately (Porter Goss is a prime example of this) Porter was given shares in the Destin Country Club deal, which was all a fraud.

What happened was the bank, City Commercial Bank of Sarasota, Florida, which was in the loop, ultimately bought back the shares from him — even though they were worthless.

It was one way of getting Porter money.

The same thing was done for former Representative Paula Hawkins. Hawkins profited enormously from these schemes.

You can see by the pattern of Republican congressmen, senators, and governors that they were all in Iran-Contra states — states where Iran-Contra activity was extant, like Texas, Florida, Arkansas, Kentucky, Illinois, California, Colorado, and so on.

There was some effort to investigate this in 1987. As a matter of a fact, it was the Tower Commission that first began to notice all these connections because of Hayden Gregory, the General Counsel. He was a real bright guy, but Tower had his own vested interest in Iran-Contra through his disguised interest in the infamous Houston Energy Partners, which had been controlled for years by Jim Baker.

Before the Tower Commission could complete its investigation, however, Senator Tower died in a mysterious plane crash near Brunswick, Georgia. It should be noted that the first contingent of supposed NTSB investigators on the scene were actually CIA agents posing as NTSB investigators. Tower's personal briefcase also somehow mysteriously vanished.

George Bush has an interest in Houston Energy Partners.

Lloyd Bentsen had an interest in it, and it still exists to this day.

Houston Energy Partners, Ltd. owns a lot of Texaco and Pennzoil stock that was given to them for nothing.

In some cases, these deals were done years ago. These were frauds that were done by George Bush's father, Prescott Sr.

In other cases, they go back as far as the late 1940s.

But in the 1980s, the management of these corporations knew some of these deals had to be finally repaid.

That required initiating new fraud to repay old fraud, which is the same continued pattern from the 1980s until today. That is exactly the recycling of money that goes on. Old fraud eventually has to be bought out from the fruits of new fraud.

The pressure has continued, particularly since Bush has left office. It's one of the reasons the man is taking Prozac.

Another reason is his sons are all under some sort of pressure because they cannot or have not been able to generate sufficient fresh revenues from new fraud to pay back old fraud.

This was discussed *vis-a-vis* the Sumitomo situation, the Daiwa Securities deal and so on.

Bush Sr. attempted to get into a fraud in Nevada with what is commonly known as the Peruvian Gold Certificate Fraud. These certificates are now controlled by the Durham family and the Hellenic Corporation and Cosmos Corporation in Nevada.

Bush was able to obtain some of the original certificates and hypothecate them. Interestingly enough, the Treasury Department very quietly created a loophole saying that these certificates were valid again — when in fact they had actually been declared canceled years ago.

The contact person, who made all this happen in Nevada, is still there. She was there ten years ago. She was the person to see in Nevada for Republican sponsored fraud — the Secretary of State, Frankie Sue DelPapa.

She is George Bush's hand picked person in Nevada. Since Bill Miller is retiring, most likely Frankie Sue (unless someone goes after her) may be the next governor.

But, let me tell you, she had some balls. I mean, she would go directly into corporate files, and actually pull out original documents and have them forged and transferred without any of the corporate officers of said corporation even knowing about it.

Suddenly assets would wind up being surreptitiously pledged to bank loans. It's a little like the Wild West or something.

When people would complain about it in Nevada, Miller would do nothing. Nothing would ever be done about it.

Just a couple of years ago, Secord and Brigadier General Heinie C. (Harry) Aderholt screwed Mac Ponder out of $11 million in Texas Ponder Oil.

Old Mac (you know he's a nice old guy) tries to go out and complain about it. But the only thing Ponder got was his life threatened and nothing was done.

Covert Action Quarterly did a substantial article on the subject in an effort to draw attention to it.

So people think this is old news. It isn't. It continues to this day.

Nobody will do anything about it, and it's very unlikely that anybody will ever do anything about it.

Anyway, to give you a specific example of how it worked at the time — I marketed some of his Gulf Coast Investment Group oil and gas limited partnerships to Richard Hamil.

It was supposedly based out of Kentucky. And naturally on paper, everything looked perfect. The oil wells existed.

Sure, they were old limestone pumpers that pump one barrel a day. But, hey, they were suddenly available, generously provided to us with the support of Armand Hammer, who was a large contributor to the causes of Oliver North.

And he was willing to do whatever it took. Suddenly these one-barrel-a-day pumpers were pumping eight hundred barrels a day — on paper.

The Kentucky state-certified geologist, a guy named Jim Kelly, who, by the way, was related to Richard Secord — he certified everything. Later, he got decertified over allegations of fraud.

And everything was beautiful — down in Warren County, Kentucky, Crock County, Knox, that whole oil region in Kentucky.

Kelly eventually wound up going to jail over it. But that's only because he got greedy and talked a lot.

But anyway, people would "invest" in a limited partnership. They were offered $10,000 units. We had it all arranged.

They got two-for-one write-offs, of which was common in the pre-1986 tax reform days.

All our "investors" were in the fifty-percent tax bracket.

They would invest $100,000 and get beautiful-looking limited partnership certificates and documents that looked wonderful with an absolute guarantee that they'll be a write-off.

They would be paid out in "royalties" over a period of, say, twelve months, or eighteen months at the most.

They would receive during this time, half of their money back.

At the end of this time, the partnership in question would go into liquidation.

They would receive another three or four cents on the dollar and they would get to write off the balance of their investment — two-for-one.

Since all these guys were in the fifty percent tax bracket, after tax they came out whole. They hadn't lost any money.

As a matter of fact, they were always ahead just a little tiny bit when you figured in the tax considerations. They had already been thrown a little sweetener.

And the real sweetener was the favor they got with Oliver North.

These guys were patriotic — mostly doctors, lawyers, good solid Republicans. They supported "The Cause." They could not contribute to "The Cause" directly, legally, so people like us offered them a vehicle in which to do it.

Half, from 40% to 50% of their money, would be slowly bled off to a group of North-Secord controlled entities, probably the most famous among them being Intercontinental Industries based in Costa Rica.

It was the only artifice that was ever actually mentioned publicly, in which some details were released during the Kerry Committee hearings.

Nothing was ever discussed about Secord's personal corporate entities — the Stanford Group of Companies, Stanford Overseas Technologies, Stanford Investment, Ltd., and so on.

Anything with the name of "Stanford" in it was Secord's personal deal.

Richard Secord, Brigadier General Harry Aderholt, Col. Bobby Anderson, Col. Robert Steele — these were also all guys who would hang around Southern Air Transport all the time.

Another thing I wanted to mention — Ludwig's career was essentially ended at Comptroller of Currency when he surreptitiously gave a copy of that classified memorandum to Bob Dockery.

Bob Dockery was an excellent Democratic investigator and I talked to him extensively. We did a lot of business together.

He worked for Chris Dodd when Chris was Senate Foreign Relations Chairman.

So Ludwig leaked that memorandum, wherein he stated his opinion of CC, that certain banks such as Texas American Bancshare, Inc., MCorp, Allied Bancshares, Great American Bank and Trust of Palm Beach (that was Marvin Warner's deal) had been taken down under the weight of fraud, i.e. unrepaid Iran-Contra generated loans. And when he leaked that, he was out. That ended him.

Bobby Miller got appointed as temporary Comptroller of the Currency for a little while and he absolutely cleaned the place out.

Bobby shredded everything when he got there. Later, everything got shredded out of OTS.

It's interesting to note the connection between some of the old crowd at OTS and the RTC, the Resolution Trust Corporation and Bill Seidman.

Bill has made a big reputation now as an economist and market prognosticator.

But what the RTC did was commit fraud — a fraud compounded on a fraud.

In the liquidation of Lincoln Savings and Loan, certain members of the Board of Directors of Lincoln Savings and Loan were able to hide certain assets of Lincoln Savings and Loan to prevent the bondholders and various shareholders and creditors from getting hold of them.

There's another interesting aspect to the collapse of Lincoln Savings and Loan.

Look at the $800,000 home Singlaub owns outside of Phoenix, in a very, very exclusive subdivision by the country club.

It was listed originally at $800,000. He paid $160,000 for it.

All these houses are on a cul-de-sac. On one side of the cul-de-sac is Jack Singlaub's house. In the middle of the cul-de-sac, Richard Secord owns a home. On the other side of the cul-de-sac, George Bush owns a home.

And the mortgage holders? Lincoln Savings and Loan.

Another example of everybody scratching each other's back would be Richard Secord's land holdings — the land he owns around Greeley, Colorado. It's very prime land, and it's not developed. I mean, the land's $100,000 an acre.

Secord's land literally goes as far as the eye can see.

It was a default out of none other than Silverado. Richard Secord got to pay ten cents on the dollar for it.

Suddenly the original mortgage papers all get put through the shredder from the previous holder.

The bank simply writes off the money and puts the paperwork through a shredder.

Knute Royce tried to talk about this and Peter Keitel and John Solomon, when John first got to AP but they hit the brick wall real quick.

I just wanted to mention Iran-Contra sympathetic banks in Miami.

They included:
- Bayshore National Bank
- Eagle National Bank
- Capital Bancshares
- Ocean Bank
- Sunshine State Bank

I could go on and on. But these were all banks that understood what was going on. They understood they were participating in a fraud.

Bayshore Bank was one of the first I had dealt with.

As a matter of fact, that was the first bank I had dealt with because Richard Secord introduced me to Tony DiConcerti. DiConcerti was the Chairman and Secord had borrowed through Barbara Studley. He fronted Studley into a bunch of loans — Secord and Aderholt. Ultimately they defrauded the bank out of about $13 million.

Then Bayshore Bank finally went into liquidation.

To avoid having to disclose anything, Eagle National Bank stepped in and quickly took over Bayshore. It was within a matter of a couple of days.

There was never any public disclosure of Bayshore's bad loans. At the time, Eagle National Bank was owned by Jose Antonio "Pepe" Cabrera-Sarmiento, who also owned the Banco de Colombia. He bought 80% of Eagle National Bank from Burt Kanter.

Burt Kanter still owned 20%.

Eagle illegally lent millions, and I mean millions, to people like me, and Richard Secord, and Harry Aderholt, and a list of other people.

All of these loans got defaulted on.

One of the reasons Eagle was used was because they had a very confidential wiring arrangement with the Banco de Colombia for funds — to get funds out of the United States.

You could do it very quietly and in size with them — because Sarmiento's one of the big fourteen big names in Colombia.

And Walter Greenberg is another one of the fourteen Colombian names. Wally also had an interest in the Banco de Colombia.

Wally then recirculates some of the money to buy office buildings in Miami.

My own office building, the Bayshore Office Building, on 4770 Biscayne Boulevard was a Greenberg building. Anyway, it's complex.

One of the reasons no one — other than Rebecca Sims and a few others — has ever wanted to go after it is because it is a tedious, complex, intricate web of fraud in a pyramid.

At the top of that pyramid, there are people like George Bush and a few others like Oliver North.

But Oliver North doesn't even belong on the top of the pyramid.

George Bush is at the very pinnacle of that pyramid.

I don't know if anyone would ever want to divulge the resources necessary to put all this together — the time, the labor, the cost — the millions of documents involved in connecting the dots. It would be an enormously costly task.

And certainly, it's one of the reasons nothing has ever been done.

The narcotics and weapons have the sizzle. But that's not where the real meat is.

The meat is in the fraud. That's what costs the American taxpayer. It wasn't narcotics or weapons.

Here's an interesting and humorous example of how we would compound a fraud upon a fraud upon a fraud and so on.

I have a recording of a conversation I had with Jeb Bush. And naturally he didn't know he was being recorded. But what Jeb would do (Jeb was a sharp cookie and still is a real sharp cookie) since he knew we were taking banks down the tubes (I'm speaking in the collective sense now since there were 2,000 people involved) is mention in this conversation (and he mentioned this to a lot of other people too) is say, "Hey Al, you gotta short the stock of MCorp. It's going down the tubes. We've taken it down the tubes."

At the time MCorp common stock was trading about three bucks a share. You couldn't short any of it. It was all out. All out of the box. Nothing to short. But the preferred stock, which was trading about eight dollars — you could still get shorts off.

What Jeb does then is he borrows a million dollars from MCorp just as it's going down the tubes. He uses that million dollars to short MCorp preferred stock, which ultimately winds up going down to zero, and then doesn't pay back the loan after he was involved in originally taking the bank down.

I can't tell you how profitable that was and how many times we shorted the stock.

We did this with Allied Bancshares, Texas American, Great American Bank and Trust, and Silverado.

We did this on their preferred stock. Obviously we knew the banks were going to fail because it was "we" who were causing them to fail.

We would then use the bank's money which we illegally borrowed from them to short their own stock and then in turn not pay back the loan, or pay back the loan at thirty or forty cents on the dollar when it got in the hands of the FSLIC.

Because the entity we used to borrow the money would then declare bankruptcy and liquidate fraudulently.

So only thirty or forty cents on the dollar had to be paid out. It became a fraud, compounded on a fraud, compounded on a fraud.

Other notable Republican Iran-Contra profiteers at the time were Henry Hyde, for instance. I already mentioned Porter Goss.

But Henry was recently censured by the House and fined a lot of money. $300,000… or $800,000… I forgot the number, but it was six figures.

Naturally, very little was ever made public about it.

There was some talk one day, the *New York Post* did a little thing on it, and that was the end of it.

But Henry had gotten involved in a bunch of illegal partnerships with us that borrowed a lot of money from Oak Brook Savings & Loan in Illinois and the Key Bank in New York. Henry was on the Board of Directors at one time with D'Amato, Alfonso D'Amato's brother.

And Key Bank was taken straight downhill.

Henry had short positions in both their stocks.

He used the banks' own money to sell their own stock short, having participated in the fraud that took the banks in question down the tubes.

And later on, D'Amato's brother, who is an attorney, Louie, got indicted. He also wound up getting indicted into a murder-for-hire scheme. He was looking at about twenty-five years in jail.

So he spends eight months in jail.

Suddenly the guy that actually pulled the trigger on a contract killing winds up slipping on a bar of soap in jail and he dies.

The depositions and affidavits, interrogatories he had done previously suddenly disappeared.

Real interesting deal.

But D'Amato, through his brother's connections, made a fortune in illegal Iran-Contra profiteering. He is very weak. To this day, D'Amato could be gone after. If anyone wanted to sink D'Amato, it's very doable.

Of course, I can't picture anybody wanting to do it.

To round out the list of Republicans, there's Rick Santorum of Pennsylvania, who was very young at that time.

When he was still Congressman Santorum, he profited immensely through that ISC scandal (International Signals and Controls) in Scranton, Pennsylvania.

You might remember the deal. Gordon and Jacobson ran it. And Gordon wound up going to jail. Jacobson quietly left the country and now lives in Israel.

But Santorum profited quite handsomely off that deal as did Arlen Specter.

That's why Billy Turpin, Deputy Inspector General in the Justice Department, former Chief of the Federal Office for Labor Racketeering in Philadelphia, is still looking at Specter.

He's got a collaboration with Andrea Volks. Andrea is now the Senior Assistant United States Attorney in Philadelphia for their fraud division. And Andrea has been wanting to go after Specter for a long while.

They just busted Allen Teal for running out in those Salt Lake City's securities scams for the ninety-second time. They've tried and tried to turn Allen Teal to talk about Turpin and others he had done business with in Pennsylvania and Colorado.

But so far, they've had no luck in doing it. But they're trying.

The only Democrats, by the way, that I can think of off the top of my head that could still be hit with Iran-Contra profiteering would be David Pryor and Dale Bumpers, and of course, Aphernon and Shelby.

Shelby's out of Alabama, and they could both be whacked with Iran-Contra profiteering.

If someone wanted to go after Clinton, they'd go after Pryor and Bumpers because of that phone call, which tips their hands that Pryor and Bumpers had knowledge of Iran-Contra — what was going on, including knowledge of narcotics trafficking in Mena, Arkansas.

If you want to go after Pryor and Bumpers or go after Clinton through Pryor and Bumpers, the way to start would be with that conversation, which is fully documented and available for sale.

If somebody wanted to sink Ron Dellums, that's also doable. It's only because I still got part of the Control Files I was given in 1985.

I never had all of them. I know it's been speculated, but I just had thousands of pages. These are the famous so-called Secord Control Files, which is the way we did business at that time.

Obviously we knew that what we were doing would ultimately fall apart and there would be public hearings and so on, and we knew that key Democrats would have to be controlled.

Consequently Control Files were established in the early 1980s with the help of the CIA. That's how I know so much about Dellums' personal narcotics use, his problem with women, his problems with some of his financial dealings and so on.

David Boren — I'm very familiar with his homosexual proclivity, and how the CIA caused him to be set up in that 1984 trade mission trip, where those pictures were taken with that seventeen-year-old boy.

That was all a set-up deal, but it absolutely controlled Boren.

You know the Gonzalez deal — when his gray Lincoln got riddled with bullets outside of his Washington townhouse. After that Henry wasn't a problem any more. He's an old man. He figured it wasn't worth it — trying to tell the truth.

I'd also like to briefly mention international cooperation on Iran-Contra with our allies. I've always liked, but wasn't really involved, with our British friends at MI-6 and their aid to us, vis-a-vis one of their cut-outs, the infamous, sinister, and renowned Churchill Matrix Corporation.

That was an MI-6 deal and their personal hand picked boy was Paul Henderson. This became public in 1988. In that lawsuit, the criminal action in London, where MI-6 finally had to admit that it was one of their cut-outs and that in fact it had been used for illicit weapons transactions, and that in fact Henderson was one of their guys.

After they made those admissions, any further look at Churchill Matrix got shut down in a hurry. One of the reasons is because of Mark Thatcher's connection to it.

Churchill Matrix kept financing Mark Thatcher deals.

Mark was a young guy, but these were the go-go 80s and his mother was Prime Minister, and he figured he could do whatever he wanted.

I have a picture of him with Oliver North. I mean, he got very involved with us at one time. He liked the fast life. He liked to do drugs. He was big into racing cars. He liked women, and he raised money for us among loyal Tories in England.

That money would then got funneled through Churchill Matrix. until it later became revealed what Churchill Matrix was doing — vis-a-vis illicit and illegal armament shipments in the Middle East.

Other corporate artifices in the mid and late 1980s that were helpful to us were the Univac Missile Corporation of Germany and Ryan Meyer Chemicals of Germany. Ryan Meyer was the one that built those chemical facilities in Libya.

It has to be looked at separately — the international connections into Iran-Contra — because there are crossovers. It is the very same corporations, cut-outs, chemical manufacturers, weapons manufacturers and so on that then reappear two or three years later, post Iran-Contra, in what now is known as "Iraqgate."

But it's the same names and faces from the past. And it's the same profiteering. There was just a different list of scapegoats. The routes were the same — that old route from the United States, South Africa, Israel route, that trans-shipping route that had been used in Iran-Contra was exactly the same route that then gets used in what is now called Iraqgate. This is how the new runs into the old.

During Iran-Contra, one of our prime suppliers of arms (how Secord did all the weapons transactions on behalf of North) was a company called Trans World Armaments of Quebec City. It was owned by the infamous Emmanuel von Weigensburg.

This is publicly detailed in the so-called Lake Resources civil lawsuit (United States v. Richard Secord) in an effort to recover that $13 million bucks that sits in the Union Bank of Switzerland.

Anyway a recent news story had three guys arrested attempting to sell helicopters to Iraq, military helicopters being supplied by Trans World Armaments of Quebec City.

The helicopters were US military helicopters.

That was the whole scheme with Trans World Armaments.

The Defense Department would sell them brand new US military items and they would list them as used.

They would sell them for very cheap prices to Trans World. Actually they would sell them very cheaply to the Canadian army. The Canadian army would then turn around and sell them to Trans World at somewhat marked-up prices.

Trans World would then turn around and sell them to Richard Secord using money that we had defrauded to get these weapons to other places in the world that we wanted these weapons to go to.

But you may know how this Trans World Armaments deal broke open in Canada. And how Joe Clark made money. It was the Brian Mulroney connection, and it was a much bigger scandal in Canada than it ever was here.

THE CONSPIRATORS

Chapter 4

"DO NOTHING" JANET RENO & IRAN-CONTRA SUPPRESSION

J ANET RENO WAS FIRST appointed in 1981 as State Attorney for Dade County, Florida. At that time, the state government was heavily Republican. She was personally recommended for the job by then candidate for State Controller's Office, Gerald Lewis, who himself would become known for his Iran-Contra activity five years later.

Reno, once ensconced in her new position, immediately began to surround herself with some of the old Republican cronies from south Florida including Kathy Rundle, Jay Hogan and Dick DiGregory, who was later moved to the Miami US Attorney's office in 1984 as a political liability control specialist.

The first two years of her tenure as State Attorney for Dade were uneventful. It wasn't really until late 1983, when Iran-Contra activity was getting geared up in south Florida that Reno began to come into more prominence.

The original deal, of course, was politically sensitive cases, Iran-Contra connected cases, and cases that dealt with narcotics, weapons or fraud that could not be handled by the US Attorney's office in Miami (then controlled by US Attorney Stanley J. Marcus) would be kicked down to the state level.

The potential defendants would be re-indicted on the state level where a trial was much more controllable because there was no national security exclusion blanket. Also, of course, state trials did not generate the publicity from national media outlets that federal trials did.

Reno's role as State Attorney became more important for a while after Stanley Marcus was forced out of office under pressure in late 1983. Afterwards he was appointed the federal district judge in the 9th district of California — a district where it was anticipated that there would be Iran-Contra activity, particularly narcotics.

This was part of the scheme leading up to the most egregious Iran-Contra activity — to appoint US Attorneys to federal district judgeships as control features. They would then in turn make sure that certain Iran-Contra sensitive cases were heard in their court.

You saw this time and time again in all of the sensitive districts — Dade County, West Palm Beach, Tampa, 3rd District of Tampa.

You see this in the 1st District of New Orleans, 2nd District of New York, 9th District of California, 10th District in Denver, and so on.

Marcus, by the way, was succeeded in his position by Leon J. Kellner, who was confirmed without any problems into the office at the end of 1983.

It was at this time that the control unit feature was put together, that is, where Janet Reno would control Dade County in terms of Iran-Contra politically sensitive cases.

Jay Lewis was promoted in West Palm Beach to Senior Assistant State Attorney there. You saw the commonality between the way the US Attorney's office in Miami and the Dade State Attorney's office worked, and the US Attorney for West Palm Beach, and the way the West Palm Beach State Attorney worked in terms of bouncing down politically sensitive cases.

They were always being handled by the same state attorneys or assistant state attorneys, always being heard in the federal jurisdiction by the same federal Republican-appointed judges or the same elected Republican state circuit judges.

As an example of what I am talking about — if one were to review Iran-Contra politically sensitive cases, say, from 1984 to 1990, in the 1991 and 1992 period, one would see the same consistent pattern.

Let us take, for instance, the US Attorney's office in Miami. All politically sensitive, Iran-Contra politically sensitive cases, would be heard by one of two judges — either the chief federal district judge, Lawrence King, now retired, or the cases would be held by the newly ensconced Republican judge Fred Marino.

In some cases, when there was an overload, the cases would be bumped up to the retired judge, Claude Atkins, a solid Republican. The defendants were convicted in every single Iran-Contra sensitive case heard by these three federal district judges.

On the state level, during the government's motion to close a trial under national security procedures — when they started to get overturned regularly by the 11th Appellate Circuit in Atlanta — which was still loaded with Carter appointees by the way — the cases in question (and there's three or four hundred of the prominent ones) would then get kicked down to the state level.

Reno would prosecute, but she would repackage the charges. Everyone would cry about estoppel, but because of that state federal loophole, there was nothing they could do about it.

Reno would prosecute the cases, always using the same Assistant State Attorney, Chet Zerlin, an Assistant State Attorney in Dade County. In turn, some three hundred cases would be heard by the same judge, Richard Gersten, a well-known right-wing Republican in Dade County, a man, who made no secret of his personal friendship with everyone from Oliver North to Jeb Bush.

In other words, defendants who knew too much about Jeb Bush or Oliver North usually didn't have much of a chance of being exonerated in his court.

This was at the peak of Iran-Contra activity in 1985, also the peak of such activity in the three big Florida jurisdictions where most of the CIA-sponsored narcotics and weapons trafficking occurred.

Janet Reno had such a place of prominence as a state attorney for Dade County that when Ed Meese made a visit to the US Attorney's office in Miami on August 9, 1985 for a briefing, he brought Lowell Jensen with him. Jensen was later also made a federal district judge.

By the way, Janet Reno, a state attorney, was actually invited to a classified briefing at the US Attorney's office with the then Attorney General of the United States, along with the US Attorney from Miami, Leon Kellner and, of course, William Richard Scruggs, then Senior Assistant US Attorney in Miami, who also performed the S-1 function in that office.

S-1 is the political liability control and suppression unit that exists within each US Attorney's office as well as the Department of Justice.

At that meeting, it was decided that more and more criminal cases scheduled to be held in the federal jurisdiction would now be bumped down to the state level.

By August 1985, Meese, Terwilliger, and Bobby Muller, etc. at the Department of Justice were having an increasingly hard time plugging all the holes in the dike.

There were too many people in the media who were getting a piece of what was happening and beginning to figure it out.

Certainly, those who figured it out first in the media were those who wrote for papers in areas where there was a large amount of Iran-Contra activity. Miami was chief among them.

Dave Lyons of the *Miami Herald* was well known for his cutting edge stories about Iran-Contra, even before it was called Iran-Contra.

Warren Richie of the *Sun Sentinel* was another. Ray Locklear used to be the head investigative reporter, and Ray is now the editor of the *Tampa Tribune*.

These guys had a sense of what was going on. They knew that people were being railroaded in court because they knew too much, and they would regularly write about it. They would show up with mini-cam recorders at the Miami International Airport, taking pictures of Southern Air Transport aircraft, and so on.

Therefore it was decided that many cases would now be heard on the state level — to keep them out of the limelight. The reason? You don't have people from the *Washington Post* and *New York Times* covering state trials like you do federal trials.

In this 1985 period, particularly the summer/fall of 1985, Janet Reno had had a separate problem *vis-a-vis* the famous Frank Fuster case. This made the national headlines at the time. They had committed enormous resources to find Fuster guilty, and he was ultimately found guilty.

The attorney who represented him, Michael Von Zamft, was a famous national security attorney. He was principally one of the very few national security attorneys who specialized in defending Iran-Contra people.

Reno was nervous that the Fuster case was going to blow up in her face. And, of course, there were all of the unusual dealings she had with Fuster's wife, Ileana. She let Ileana out of jail, making sure she wasn't sentenced to any jail time. She also made sure that Ileana got deported later to Honduras where nobody in the media could find her.

Reno also made the deal to arrange for money to be delivered to Ileana in Honduras.

There was an interesting article in the *Herald* about how this girl living in some dirt-poor tenement in Honduras was able to pay $28,000 in cash for a Ford Bronco and where the money came from.

When Lyons got onto that story, it was shut down in a real hurry. That's how sensitive this case was.

Had it blown up in their faces, it would have been discovered what the state attorney did in order to try to indict Fuster — all the secret little deals that were made. Illegal wire taps. Illegal mail intercepts. Illegal. Illegal. Illegal.

Reno was sensitive to this at that time, and, frankly she needed some help from Washington, which she got.

In 1985, DiGregory went from the State Attorney's office in Dade to the US Attorney's office in Miami.

As a matter of fact, it was DiGregory that put together the case against Noriega. DiGregory would have regular briefings with Reno as to what was going on *vis-a-vis* sensitive Iran-Contra cases within the Miami US Attorney's office.

In 1986, when everything began to fall apart *vis-a-vis* Iran-Contra, things became very sensitive in terms of maintaining the cover-up.

Then along comes the most sensitive Iran-Contra narcotics case of all, Jack Raymond DeVoe. Of course, there were some subsidiary cases around that, Tony Fernandez and Bill Blakemore, Billy White and those guys. But DeVoe was the central character. Fernandez and the other people were really just a side show.

That DeVoe case started out as a federal case. Then it got kicked down into a split jurisdiction between West Palm and Miami. Jay Lewis naturally was appointed as the lead prosecutor on the case. DiGregory handled the case for the US Attorney's office and acted as advisor to the State Attorney.

Janet, herself, acted as the prosecutor on the Miami end of the case. I don't have to rehash the DeVoe case to explain how much of a sham it was.

Sam Pennington was lead defense counsel on the case. Sam had been formerly been General Counsel of the CIA. The other defense co-counsels were of course, Norman Brownstein and Jim Natali, also former CIA counsels.

DeVoe was ultimately convicted and sentenced to 220 years.

He spent seventeen days in jail before he was quietly allowed to leave the United States.

The last I heard — he was living in India of all places.

I know that Fernandez spent a little more time in jail, but he was let out and now lives comfortably in Honduras in the witness protection program.

That was a common tool in those days to hide politically sensitive people — within the witness protection program, particularly in Guatemala, Honduras. It's still done to this day.

Michael Palmer, another Iran-Contra drug figure, is also living under very comfortable circumstances in Honduras in the federal witness protection program.

Reno's office also had knowledge of Iran-Contra inspired bank fraud that was going on in south Florida. Part of the challenge came from within the infrastructure of the State of Florida, including Gerald Lewis, the powerful Comptroller of the state, who happened to be Marvin Warner's second cousin.

And we all know who Marvin Warner is.

The Great American Bank and Trust ultimately cost the US government — it wasn't huge money — but it was three to four hundred million dollars.

And Reno's office could have stepped in and prevented that early on. For political reasons, they purposely did not do so, as they did not attempt to prevent or prosecute anyone involved in the collapse of Bayshore Bank, or Orange Bank, or Ocean Bank, or a variety of other banks within her jurisdiction which collapsed under the weight of unrepaid, illegal Iran-Contra connected loans.

By 1987, during the Kerry Commission hearings, Janet Reno had accumulated the nickname within the Miami press corps as "Do-Nothing Janet."

It was so obvious. It had become so transparent what she was all about — prosecuting some politically sensitive cases and making sure the right state attorney and the right judge heard it.

In some cases, the defendants had attorneys that did everything to suborn their own defendants' cases.

Von Zamft is an absolute classic example. John Luongo, Neil Lewis, and other very well known Miami attorneys, who all had their own affiliations with the Republican Party, in turn would represent people who just didn't have a chance from the get-go.

They were usually given alternatives right before the trial began. "Give us some information you've got that we want." "Keep your mouth shut about other things," and so forth.

But "Do-Nothing Janet" — that's what the *Miami Herald* always used to call her.

They went after her to no end, and that's why she would not begin investigations of banks that were failing, or of certain corporations in the greater Miami area controlled by the CIA or airline companies that were committing illegal arms trafficking. She had the authority because they were in her jurisdiction. She had the authority at least to investigate them in terms of Miami transactions. None of this was done.

She was roundly and consistently criticized as to why certain cases that connected to certain Republicans under the umbrella of Iran-Contra were not being looked at.

Anyway, to bring this up to date, that's all in the past. Since she was appointed Attorney General of the United States, nothing has changed. She was appointed for the original reason of being a control feature.

And whom did she bring with her to be her Associate Attorney Generals?

Hogan, of course. And, Kathy Rundle took her place. But she brought guys like Hogan, DiGregory, and Scruggs — although Scruggs still remained at the US Attorney's office.

You can see how quickly — after she got cleared as Attorney General — she got Richard Scruggs out of the US Attorney's office in Miami and made him Chief National Security Advisor to the Attorney General.

The reason that was done, by the way, was twofold. One, Scruggs had been the best political liability control guy the Republicans ever had. Let's put it that way. You think, oh well, it's a Democratic administration, but as you know, political liability cuts both ways.

It was still necessary to control things from the past. The other principal reason why Scruggs was given a sub-cabinet position was so he would be immune from the Costa Rican extradition warrant for his Costa Rican indictment.

Costa Rica formally requested Scruggs's extradition from the United States on a charge of kidnapping, a violation of Costa Rican national sovereignty. This was the kidnapping of Israel Abel, discussed previously — the last political kidnapping undertaken by the Reagan-Bush political kidnapping policy which ended in August 1991.

In other words, you have to kidnap cocaine traffickers who had connections to the CIA from foreign soil to prevent them from talking.

Abel was the last guy to get kidnapped. He's currently doing twenty years in the Georgia State Penitentiary.

Another premiere incident was that of Paul Wilcher in 1993, when Wilcher wrote that now famous ninety-nine-page letter. Three weeks later, Wilcher was murdered. Then suddenly Stephan Von Metzger and Rolf Elmquist — all those guys from that old [CIA] proprietary TKF Engineering and Trading International — suddenly they write letters to Reno.

They're all dead. My own opinion is that I wish somebody would actually write a book or do something serious about Reno. A whole book could be written about her.

An awful lot of people have suffered because of Janet Reno. People have been killed. Eight to nine hundred people incarcerated — not because of what they did, but because of what they know. And although she was just a mouthpiece and did what she was told from Washington, nonetheless, she's the one that did it.

Janet Reno should be exposed because she continues to do it. Those who tried to tell the truth about what we knew, *vis-a-vis* state-sponsored misdeeds in the Iran-Contra period, have suffered greatly at her hands.

Perhaps it's not exactly fair to say it's because of her — because she's just doing what she's told — nonetheless she's the one out front.

Another interesting point here is the relationship she had as the Dade State Attorney's office with the Miami police department, the Metro Dade Police Department, and the Miami OCB, Organized Crime Bureau.

They didn't trust her because they understood what was going on. They understood even in 1987-88 what was going on. And I always found it interesting that, for instance, the Metro Dade Organized Crime Bureau would specifically not share information with the State Attorney about politically sensitive people that they were targeting.

Omar Elesquary is absolutely the classic example — and his brother John. His real name is Juan, but he likes them to call him Johnny. They were after Elesquary. They knew the CIA was protecting him. They knew Elesquary had worked for the DGI (Cuban Intelligence Service), and he came over in the Cuban boat lift.

He knew that Elesquary was being worked both sides of the dangle by the DGI. They knew his brother's connection with an art gallery. His brother owns a famous art gallery right in the heart of Ponce de Leon Boulevard in Coral Gables. And they knew that it was being used as a front for weapons.

They purposely would not share this information with the Dade State Attorney because when they had shared information before about others, for instance, when they attempted to investigate the Orca Supply Company, they were immediately shut down.

This was also true in this time frame of the Metro Dade Police Department. When they were to investigate the famous murder of Don Aronow, they purposely didn't share information with the State Attorney.

When Rolando Sotes was murdered after Sydney Freedberg botched that interview and went public with it and actually caused the guy to be murdered, the Metro Dade homicide detective, that Sgt. Fernandez, had found out what the CIA connection was and he turned up dead in a canal in the back of his house in the Hialeah, Miami lake. That death was ruled an "accidental" drowning. He did everything possible to pressure the Metro Dade Police Department from halting that investigation in Sotes's murder because of where that connection went.

Rolando Sotes, after all, had been a partner of Felix Rodriguez.

Johnny Elesquary and his wife were stopped driving their Lincoln Continental down Key Biscayne Drive. The trunk of the car was opened to reveal a load of sophisticated automatic weapons with silencers and laser guiding sights. Instead of being arrested, the trunk was closed. The officer in question put in a report and then he got a call back Janet Reno's office. They were allowed to drive off with a trunkload of unregistered automatic weapons with silencers on them.

Reno attempted to pressure, to obfuscate, to destroy documents in politically sensitive cases, cases connected to the CIA, cases connected to some Iran-Contra activity, and cases that would hurt prominent Republicans.

You may remember another interesting case which was nationally prominent — the murder of the Miami lawyer. Three hundred kilograms of cocaine was found in his basement.

Initially Janet Reno said there was no cocaine found in his basement. Then it was twelve kilograms. Then it was something else. And then suddenly the cocaine disappeared.

When they got a search warrant for Tony Fernandez's wife — the State Attorney's office got a search warrant for her apartment in the Alexander Building on 53rd & Collins, Miami Beach, five million in cash was found in a hidden wall safe behind a big picture on the wall.

Suddenly the next day, this woman is allowed to leave the United States with the five million intact.

Chapter 5

CLASSIFIED ILLEGAL OPERATIONS CORDOBA AND SCREW WORM

N EXT I WILL DESCRIBE several operations and, more importantly, their entrails — from the 1983 to 1986 time frame. The first operation is the infamous and renowned operation known as Operation Cordoba Harbor (March 1985).

I first learned of the existence of this operation in the first bi-weekly policy and planning session of the FDN in March of that year.

Present at this meeting were myself, Jeb Bush, Oliver North, Lt. Col. Samuel C. Watson, ADC to the Vice-Presidential National Security Advisor, Frederick Ikley, then Chief of Caribbean and Central American Theater Operations for the Defense Intelligence Agency, and his hench-man, the infamous and sinister Lt. Col. John Berglund, who had been seconded to the DIA from the 407th Intelligence Unit, 16th Southern Expeditionary Forces, then commanded by Lt. Gen. John Galvin.

You may remember that the general, when questioned in deposition two years later in the Kerry Commission, claimed that he did not know or did not recall anything about Iran-Contra — 133 times.

Also present in this meeting were President in Exile, Adolfo Calero, his younger brother and chief bagman, Mario Calero, and Nestor Sanchez. There were some others, but I didn't make notations who they were. I didn't know everyone.

In this meeting, North laid out the plan. He had a white paper and the charts, graphs, and blueprints to lay out a plan to mine Cordoba Harbor, the principal eastern port of Nicaragua, in an effort to destroy Soviet and East Bloc shipping that was secretly bringing in weapons to the Sandinista government.

This operation (I found it rather interesting) called for the use of then state-of-the-art Titan Mark 4 Sea Mines, which could be controlled by satellite communications.

The operation would be to lay down these mines at the bottom of Cordoba Harbor, which is a rather deep harbor. These mines could later be activated as hostile shipping, came into the harbor and the mines literally can be targeted through magnetic resonance imaging right to the hull of a ship and caused to detonate.

The resources that would have to be committed to this operation included resources of the Defense Intelligence Agency and required clearance from a Restricted Access Group 1. That's why Watson was there to report the minutes of the meetings to Donald Gregg, then Vice Presidential National Security Advisor.

North gave a contract for military style pontoon boats to Don Aronow Marine. Aronow had also, only weeks before, been given a contract through Oliver North, surreptitiously, to build five gun boats for the Panamanian Navy.

Aronow did not have the ability to manufacture the type of pontoon boats that they wanted. He, in turn, gave the contract to a man in Ft. Lauderdale, who ran a boat building business that specialized in military application pontoon boats. This man was also an arms merchant specializing in different types of naval warfare systems. He used the alias John Anderson, but his real name was Roger E. Moore.

You may remember recent revelations about Mr. Moore's connection to the Oklahoma City bombing — vis-a-vis his gun shops in Arkansas. This is a good example of how these operations still have entrails into the present.

Anyway this operation was actuated, I believe, on March 12, 1985. The pontoon boats were being built. The mines, of course, could not be purchased from US inventory. They had to be "wrapped around." A so-called wrap-around transaction was Maj. Gen. Richard Secord's specialty.

In fact, what happened was that the mines were sold to Defcon Armaments, Ltd. of Lisbon, Portugal from US inventories. They, in turn, sold them back to Stanford Technologies Overseas, a cut-out controlled by Richard Secord.

Some of this, by the way, the US government has admitted.

Referring to the 1991 civil suit, United States v. Richard Secord, Civil Division, 1st Eastern District of Virginia, File #1202-A, otherwise known as the infamous Lake Resources Lawsuit, the government makes astounding admissions about how arms transactions worked in Iran-Contra through various European and even eastern European arms dealers. How Secord purchased weapons from them. Where the money came from and so forth.

In this lawsuit the United States government admits that Secord was its agent and admits that it ordered Secord to break the law on behalf of the United States government. It's very interesting reading, about fifty-seven pages, filed in the Eastern District in Alexandria.

Anyway, the mines were in fact obtained. The pontoon boats were being built. The resources in Nicaragua already existed vis-a-vis Eden Pastora. I can't imagine whose idea it was to put him in command of the local operation. It later proved to be a mistake.

This operation, like many other operations, was actually never effectuated although the mines and physical plant and security had been arranged.

In fact, in the eleventh hour, in May of 1985, there was a leak out of the Contras. The Sandinistas became aware of this. The leak came from Eden Pastora, who purposely leaked the information because at that time, he was extremely pissed off about the CIA not giving him as much money as they had previously been giving him.

So he purposely leaked this to the Sandinistas and the whole thing went down the tubes. In terms of some of the entrails of this operation, Operation Cordoba Harbor was extensively discussed during the Kerry Committee hearings and much of it was made public, not all of it, but much of it.

Certainly what was behind the scenes, what happened to this operation was not made public, but it is interesting to note that it is really this project which was tied to the Panamanian gun boat transaction with Aronow Marine.

Oliver North had given Aronow five million dollars in cash as a down payment on these five Panamanian gun boats.

Aronow then took another million dollars from him for the pontoon boats. He only paid Roger Moore $350,000 of that.

What North was not aware of, and what he should have been aware of, was the very deleterious financial condition at that time of Aronow Marine. It was virtually bankrupt.

All the monies that North had given Aronow were simply used to prop up Magnum Marine for another two years. The gun boats in question were never built.

North later became absolutely livid about it. It was this situation which led to Aronow's murder in Miami.

You may remember some of the details that were made public.

A dark brown Lincoln Towncar.

Four men with sunglasses with Uzis with silencers on them.

Aronow got machine gunned in the parking lot of his own office building when he was attempting to get into his car.

Of course, this murder, like so many others at the time, was conveniently blamed on unknown Colombian drug lords.

Boy, was that an excuse that we heard time and time again, particularly towards the closing days of Iran-Contra when "liabilities" were being cleaned up.

This was actually a sanitation team which had been sent from Department 4 of the Central Directorate — otherwise known as the Domestic Wet Operations Division of the CIA.

The guns (four silenced Uzis were used) came locally.

It's interesting to note that the guns were supplied locally, in Miami by the infamous Johnny Elesquary, who is the older brother of the infamous, absolutely infamous Omar Elesquary, code-named "Casper" at the time.

John Elesquary and his wife, Betty, ran a very upscale art gallery as a cover in Coral Gables, right on Ponce de Leon Circle in Coral Gables, Florida.

The odd thing was when these guns were being delivered, Elesquary had a brown Lincoln Towncar, which was also described as a brown Lincoln Towncar from which the men came who assassinated Aronow.

He was stopped by the Miami police for speeding on Key Biscayne Drive. A search of his car revealed these four machine guns included with a group of weapons in the trunk — sophisticated stuff with laser sightings and silencers .

Instead of arresting him and confiscating the weapons, a supervising Sergeant of the Miami Police Department named Raul Fernandez showed up.

The long and short of it was that he was not arrested. The weapons, obviously illegal, were not confiscated. And he was allowed to go on his way.

It's interesting to note that a year and a half after this — Fernandez knew he had a little piece of something and he was part of this something we have not discussed — but he was part of the, shall we say, Iran-Contra team within the Miami Police Department.

Anyway, Fernandez attempted to extort North about a year and a half later with this. He had filled out a police report. He just hadn't filed it. And he wanted $250,000 for it.

Nine days later Fernandez was found floating in the canal behind his house in Miami Lakes. His death was ruled an "accidental drowning," and the report that he had made was never found.

Operation Cordoba Harbor was also an interesting example, as later proved in the Kerry Committee hearings, of how North would personally become involved in raising money from very well-heeled Republican right-wingers and fervent anti-communists.

Money for this operation, as a matter of fact, was raised from the Bass family and the Hunt family in Texas.

Richard Bass gave Oliver North five million in cash in a briefcase.

The Hunt brothers gave him another two million in cash in a briefcase.

That is one part of Oliver North that tends to get overlooked as time goes by — his personal involvement in raising illegal monies for illegal covert activities from right-wingers.

It was left to us — his minions — to raise all the fifty and hundred thousands, but North would get personally involved for two million or more.

The next operation I would like to discuss was Project Donation West (July 1984), West indicating the western part of the United States.

That idiot, John Maddis from the Kerry Committee, that attorney that bird-dogged for them in Miami, never understood what the "West" even meant.

He thought it was somebody's name. It wasn't. It meant the western United States.

Anyway, Project Donation West was a money operation.

These operations we're discussing are being divided the three classical ways —

1. Drugs, 2. Weapons, 3. Money. Weapons also included paramilitary operations.

This is a money operation. Project Donation West was a huge operation at the time. Operation meaning it was covert and illegal.

This was the establishment of Major Gen. John K. Singlaub as titular head of western theater operations — western United States theater operations — vis-a-vis the raising and supplication of the covert revenue stream to Iran-Contra through his artifice, the World Anti-Communist League, which, interestingly enough, had offices in the Lincoln Savings and Loan complex.

As a matter of fact, their offices were directly next to J. Walter Bush Securities. This is all interconnected.

Anyway, the World Anti-Communist League was set up. Singlaub was ensconced as its head, ostensibly to raise money to support various Republican politicians and others who harbored anti-communist views. It was supposed to push an anti-communist political agenda, of course, which never happened.

They sent out a bunch of flyers and letters to make it look like that's what they were doing. But that's not what they were really doing. Most of the $183 million odd dollars they raised directly from the public. Later they could only actually account for about $3 million of it.

Anyway, in this operation in July 1984, I had not yet been invited to the policy and planning sessions of the FDN, nor do I think that this would have been specifically discussed there.

It was actually Gen. Secord that gave me the run-down on this operation of setting up the Western Fraud Channel, as he called it, which I think is a good way to consolidate it.

In this channel, under the guise of the World Anti-Communist League, numerous limited partnerships were set up — as a matter of fact, hundreds of them at one time.

By the way, when you talk about Iran-Contra bank fraud, securities fraud, insurance fraud, you have to delineate the fraud, and then you delineate it by billions of dollars and banks and corporations and how it worked and so on.

What makes this project particularly interesting is that this established the original insurance fraud channel — something that has not been thoroughly discussed. Bank and securities fraud has been discussed ad nauseam. But this was the more discreet insurance fraud channel, which ultimately generated about $350 million of ill gotten revenue, defrauding insurance companies — with their cooperation, of course.

The first insurance company involved in this scheme was the giant firm AIG, or American Insurance General.

You need only look at who the chairman and board of directors were at that time to understand that they were complicit to this deal.

The first insurance fraud to be committed was the famous aircraft diversion scheme, in which Terry Reed actually became involved, in a very small way, with his own airplane.

But, Singlaub had appointed a guy to run the aircraft insurance fraud which would later expand into luxury motor yachts insurance fraud.

It was a guy named Mitch Marr, an Israeli citizen. I have no idea what his real name is. I'm sure it's not Mitch Marr, but that's how he was known and that's how he was later described before different congressional committees.

In September-October 1984, Mitch came to my Miami office. He was making rounds and visiting all the guys who were helping out, as he used to say. He told me about the scheme in which people could donate aircraft for tax write-offs. For an aircraft that was worth $100,000, you could get a write-off for $300,000 absolutely guaranteed. It would pass scrutiny.

They could donate the aircraft to a subsidiary, a 501c3 subsidiary of the World Anti-Communist League, and then the World Anti-Communist League would take some of the aircraft and turn them over to others.

They would turn them over to DeVoe Airlines, Rich Aviation, Southern Air Transport, Polar Aviations, Southern Air Cross, on and on and on, to use them for narcotics trafficking. These were aircraft that were suitable this. Aircraft that was not suitable for doing so would be hidden in a variety of hangars in the western United States, principally in Joplin, Missouri.

This is the one part of this operation that Reed knew about — the Joplin, Missouri deal where a lot of the aircraft got hidden and then were claimed to have been stolen.

American Insurance General would simply pay out the claims – hundreds and hundreds of them. There were millions of dollars of claims involved. And the reason this part of the scheme fell apart was because the ATF inadvertently came across the tremendous amount of aircraft that they realized had been declared stolen in these hangars in Joplin, Missouri.

They weren't looking for them. They were actually looking for something else. But this is an odd circumstance of how often these operations would become exposed.

The ATF immediately brought in the DEA. This was DEA agent Brad Ayers who tried to talk about it publicly and then was taken down afterwards. Later he became famous for having found the cocaine residue on the Southern Air Transport C-130.

Anyway they realized the aircraft was stolen, but this was never publicly revealed at the time. It was not publicly revealed until quite a few years later.

As a matter of fact, it required a phone call from George Bush himself to prevent this operation from being exposed at the time. Obviously, it wouldn't look good since one of his sons was on the Board of Directors of American Insurance General at the time.

Anyway, that's how Donation West — and a lot of other limited partnerships and real estate limited partnership deals — were set up with Lincoln Savings and Loan. They were all fraudulent. All those Phoenix developments never existed, other than as a piece of paper.

The luxury motor-boat, or motor-yacht, fraud which Marr would later proffer in June of 1985 was very similar. Luxury motor-yachts could be donated to a tax-exempt subsidiary of the World Anti-Communist League for huge tax write-offs.

Those motor boats which were considered to be in good enough shape were used for narcotics trafficking. The others were taken out someplace in the Bahamas and sunk.

After the donation had obviously been made, the insurance claims would be put in for them. Often there were fidelity and guaranty instruments on these boats — insurance fidelity, F&G instruments written by a subsidiary controlled by the World Anti-Communist League in the Bahamas called the British American Marine Trust Company, Ltd. which existed in a file drawer in Jack Singlaub's office.

It's also interesting to note that the British American Trust had an office in Ft. Lauderdale, Florida. Singlaub, unfortunately, put a guy I knew in charge of it. I told Singlaub not to do it, but he did it anyway.

His name was Jerry Chenault. Jerry was like Richard Hamil. He was like hundreds of other guys who were no more than confidence men.

They're just old time con men with some government connections. They hang around in the shadows of Washington, waiting for the next illegal covert operation to become extant so they can get involved and use it as an excuse to rape and pillage and line their own pockets, knowing that they can get away from it.

That's exactly what Chenault did. He began to sell a lot of bogus fidelity and guaranty instruments through this insurance company which really didn't exist. It did exist, but its capital in turn, was financed by the

Imperial Bank of Montserrat, an offshore banking deal also set up by Singlaub, which was, in turn, guaranteed by worthless notes from Lincoln Savings and Loan.

Anyway Chenault began peddling these things to all sorts of people and it just created an awful lot of problems.

Chenault got himself indicted and threatened to spill the beans.

When Chenault was getting in his car one morning for one of his court hearings (he lived in a very exclusive section of Ft. Lauderdale), the car blew up — with him in it. It was ruled a "vapor explosion," by the way. But that's the way that liability ended.

When the FBI, which was out of the loop, went to Chenault's office, they found every document shredded and every tape magnetized.

There weren't even any fingerprints in the place.

Another individual that Singlaub became involved with through the World Anti-Communist League — another old time government connected scamscateer — was the infamous Dr. Robert Adler, an old con man who lived in Tampa, Florida.

He formerly associated with Ray Harvey and Maury Strong and Larry Freeman, the old CIA Tampa guys.

Anyway, Adler had set up a bunch of schemes known as the Eagle Investment Group, which were all Costa Rican offshore mutual funds.

A lot of these were farming or agricultural deals, set up under Section F — that agricultural exemption which later on fell apart.

The money was diverted into Singlaub's coffer and Adler's son went to jail for about seven years.

Adler himself pled guilty because he was quite old at the time. He got about eighteen months probation. But Adler, to hedge his bets, had secretly spoken with Spencer Oliver, the famous Democratic congressional investigator in Washington, and he was due to meet him.

Spencer was secretly coming to Tampa to see him. The day before Spencer arrives, Adler suddenly died of what was called an "accidental dose of barbiturates."

No autopsy was performed. His body was cremated before his family was even informed that he had died. A very common circumstance. Several hundred circumstances like that happened.

Regarding Project Donation West — there were many other interesting connections including that big Connecticut real estate fraud deal that involved Jeb Bush. He was the general partner. It also involved the Destin Country Club development with Neil Bush which all fell apart.

Seventy-eight million dollars of money was missing. It involved several Republican members of Congress including Peter Goss.

The next operation we are going to discuss is Operation Screw Worm, which you may have heard about, if you are an Iran-Contra aficionado.

This was May 1986, and Operation Screw Worm was the last and largest of the so-called CIA guns-for-drugs operations actuated during Iran-Contra.

What this entailed was moving the primary air and sea channels from Miami, southern Florida and Georgia into New Orleans and other points west.

By this time, the summer of 1986, the Miami channel had become too well known.

There were leaks about it in the press. Guys from the *Miami Herald*, UPI and API would hang around Southern Air Transport hangars in Miami airport with video cameras. Simply put, the situation was becoming untenable.

Therefore, in Operation Screw Worm, it was decided to move everything to what was called the "Western Corridor" from what had been the "Eastern Corridor."

This was when the New Orleans channel was established. Part of what precipitated it was the breakdown in the relationship with Lt. Gen. Reuben Mata, then chief of staff of the Honduran army, Maj. Gen. Hector Bermudez, then chief of staff of the El Salvadoran air force, and the death (it was actual natural causes) of Maj. Gen. Richard Stilwell, later to be Assistant Secretary of Defense Richard Stilwell. His father was the famous general.

When he died in May of 1986, his henchman, the infamous and sinister John Carter, could not take over the channel. They could not maintain the security of the Guatemalan corridor any more as it had been before.

That was principally due to the fact that President of Guatemala, Gen. Ephraim Rios Montt, a fervent supporter of George Bush and a fervent anti-communist, began to understand, as other generals in the Central American theater understood, that things were unraveling. They wanted to cover their ass and they wanted out.

At this time there was suddenly all this activity in Panama. Elliot Abrams and his deputy Michael Kozak, a special State Department envoy, Bill Walters from Narcotics were suddenly there, G-2 Security tremendously beefed up and so on.

That's because Panama would now have to be used exclusively in lieu of the Guatemalan air corridor. They would have to fly stuff out to the west and along the Mexican coast and so on.

Screw Worm was the last and the largest. It envisioned (which actually did happen for awhile) a tremendous expansion of "authorized" narcotics trafficking. I mean, a tremendous expansion.

North had set up the time in May 1986 of the first biweekly policy and planning session of the FDN, and this absolutely astounded me. Fred Ikley was there. Don Gregg, himself, was there. The usual cast of characters, Manuel Diaz, Nestor Sanchez.

But North envisioned an increase of 50,000 kilograms a month, which absolutely astounded me.

And Jeb Bush, I think correctly, voiced concerns that had already come into play —that the Agency was dealing in so much cocaine, importing so much cocaine that the street value of it was becoming depressed. This had already happened.

In 1985, cocaine was commanding $30,000/kilogram.

By 1986, it had dropped to $15,000/kilogram and was continuing to drop.

But North felt it was important to raise the revenue, so there was going to be a tremendous increase in importation.

In Operation Screw Worm, all of the air routes were substantially beefed up.

This was when Southern Air Transport was added some maximum cocaine and weapons capacity, air transport capacity.

Almost an entire fleet of then 735 aircraft were now committed to the operation. All of its divisions were now committed when it controlled Evergreen Airline — that was committed. Polar Aviation was committed. Even right down to little tiny four airplane divisions like the little key division in Puerto Rico called Yakez Air Link controlled by a guy, one of their people named Oswaldo Gonzalez.

This was to become very important later on because Gonzalez was the first guy to spill the beans on it to Congress when he was secretly deposed in Miami. He wouldn't even go to Washington.

This guy was scared shitless about his own survival. He knew what had happened to everyone else that had talked. Anyway, Gonzalez did in fact spill the beans on it and was actually put under subpoena, a Congressional subpoena.

Unfortunately Gonzalez wanted to fly back to Puerto Rico and he had to move some money, or he had something to take care of before he came back to the United States to testify.

He flew his own airplane and the airplane never made it to Puerto Rico. It was never found. It simply disappeared along with Oswaldo Gonzalez. It is assumed that the aircraft is now 10,000 feet at the bottom of the ocean.

The sea routes were also beefed up — the reason why Ikley was there. The narcotics sea routes out of Swan Island, Honduras up to Haiti.

By the way, this is primarily where the big increase in narcotics trafficking would come — through the sea routes. I mean, we're not talking about speed boats — we're talking about freighters.

It is interesting to note at the same time how everybody on the southern end of this deal — our so-called allies among the Central American right — were getting nervous because they knew what we were doing.

It was simply becoming unmanageable. And the liability was so enormous, I mean, if the American people had found out...

Even today, if they ever found out the enormity of what we were doing, there'd be hell to pay.

But Gen. Mata of Honduras became real nervous about having a tremendous increase in sanctioned narcotics operations through Honduran territory. That's part of the reason, by the way, that Swan Island was used. It was speculated there were some very sharp people in Congress who wondered — why suddenly move Honduran operations to an island that is a hundred miles off the coast of Honduras, although it's a Honduran possession?

It's because Mata didn't want such huge narcotics operations on Honduran soil. He also wanted substantially more money deposited to his Swiss account which North simply was not prepared to give him. He had met in April (I have notes of the meeting) with Jose Fernandez, a very close North aide, CIA station chief in San Jose.

Mata wanted a whole lot more money — like a million, two million dollars a month more for his continued cooperation. And North wasn't prepared to pay it.

You may remember that Mata was secretly indicted after that, indictment unsealed, raided by US troops, and US troops in Honduras illegally raided his house.

Anyway the long and short of it is that Mata was killed.

Any documents he had were never found. The money that he had accumulated (it was known he had an account in Geo Bank) was never found.

Gen. Bermudez was later killed in a car accident.

By the way, as an adjunct to Operation Screw Worm, this also led to this Haitian problem with Colonel, then Brigadier General Jean Paul.

Jean Paul, obviously, had to be informed that there was going to be a substantial increase in freighter traffic insofar as he controlled the Dessiline battalion and supervised and controlled the port of Cap Haitién.

Suddenly Gen. Paul wanted a whole lot more money as well.

Duvalier himself was smart enough not to interfere. He was fine with what the deal was for him. But Paul wanted a whole lot more money and, this led to his death shortly thereafter, Brig. Gen. Jean Paul was murdered by poisoned pumpkin soup, given to him by Avríl's wife, with whom he was having an affair at the time.

Avríl later became the military leader of Haiti in the wake of the collapse of the Duvalier regime.

Anyway the whole thing became a debacle — but it was all secured.

The thing about Operation Screw Worm which made it very sinister and egregious and the reason why it was so focused on by a little clique in Congress that did have an understanding of what was going on is that a lot of people died to make it happen.

People who were nervous, people who were leaking stuff out — a lot of people died and that became a problem for Jack Brooks. When Jack became aware it, Henry Gonzalez became aware of what was going on. It became a problem. And they started to hammer on it.

This led to Gonzalez being shut down when Gonzalez's car was machine gunned in front of the townhouse he owned in Washington.

After that, Gonzalez never went after it again.

Out of all the Iran-Contra projects and operations of which there were maybe 350 or so (50 to 60 that I'm intimately familiar with) it's interesting to note that Operation Screw Worm, in the aftermath of Iran-Contra, became absolutely the most sensitive operation of all because of the egregiousness of the liability.

There was a huge effort to control it, to control the political liability aspect of it, in the ensuing Iran-Contra cover-up. Any time any of us talked about it, we were immediately incommoded in some fashion — pressured, harassed, intimidated. Something would happen to us.

You will see this also happened, not only to Iran-Contra players, but people in the mainstream media who attempted to write articles about it — or go after it. They were also incommoded in some fashion, or pressured, or harassed, or intimidated, or discredited.

Jonathan Beatty of *Time Magazine* is an absolutely classic example. Knute Royce, Peter Keitel — these were all big names.

Brian Barger. It was Screw Worm that ended Brian Barger's career as a mainstream media guy.

Bill Moyle attempted to do a *Frontline* piece concentrating on this operation, and this is what the force did — it knocked him out of the box.

When Rob Parry continued to push it, he suddenly found he couldn't make a living as a journalist anymore.

Anyway — enough of Screw Worm for now. It would take hours and hours to actually go through all of it, all the people involved, the money, everything.

I gave you three projects or operations. I could discuss many more. These are just three out of fifty-six or fifty-seven, of which I can speak intimately.

Of course, I've done this with very little reference to my own notes and logs. I have to do it that way. This has given you a thumbnail sketch off the top of my head.

I wanted to mention something else that is an interesting sidenote. There was a little print item in Knight Ridder and others picked it up, that Thor Hansen had finally been arrested crossing from Denmark into Holland and was due to be extradited to the United States on a cocaine charge.

Thor Hansen (you would have to be very familiar with Iran-Contra to recognize the name) is a very interesting character. He's a Dane, a Danish national, and he was involved with the leaders of a very right-wing Danish motorcycle club gang in the early 1980s.

He spreads out, becomes the leader of other European, politically right-wing, European motorcycle gangs — guys that gravitated to the leather jackets and the German WW II helmets and that type of thing.

Then he came to the United States and became involved with the Hell's Angels. They knew who he was, and he was looking for a link-up between certain right-wing factions within the Hell's Angels and the right-wing factions in the European motorcycle gang — skin-head, Nazi helmet, jack-boot types.

Thor, through a strange combination of circumstances, had some friends in the Haitian exile community in Miami. He lived in Miami for a time and I got to know him pretty well.

Oliver North got to know him and he liked him too. Immediately he liked his politics, liked what he could do for Oliver North and others.

Thor, unfortunately, became involved in a plot to overthrow the Duvalier regime in 1983. He was in my office with the whole plan at one time, trying to sell this plan to Oliver North.

This was late 1983 when Ollie first come into prominence. Ollie said, "No way. We got a deal with Duvalier. He does what we want. And there's no way we want to see this guy overthrown."

North tries to dissuade Hansen, so he tells him, "You get the Hell's Angels." North already knew that there were many right-wing sympathizers within the Hell's Angels, particularly in the California chapter, and also in Arizona, the Southwestern and even Northwestern chapters where they were strong.

So Hansen becomes an intermediary between Oliver North and the Hell's Angels and works out a deal to distribute Company coke, as it were, principally in California but also throughout the southwest and northwest.

And it became a very, very lucrative deal.

Unfortunately, what happened later is that Hansen inadvertently got arrested — the idiot. He got stopped with sixty kilograms of cocaine in the trunk of his car.

Everyone immediately has to deny knowledge of this guy. He just stupidly got stopped, and he wasn't worth protecting.

I know Ollie himself told me later on that it simply wasn't worth protecting this guy. So, he gets nabbed with sixty kilos of Company coke in the back of his car in Miami and some people think North set him up. He didn't. It was inadvertent. It was an odd circumstance. He had failed to turn on his right blinker when he turned right or something. It was really an odd thing.

So normally, for sixty kilos, you're not going to get bail, but $300,000 bail was arranged for him. He went before Fred Marino, the Republican federal judge. North made sure that most guys that he wanted to get out on bail went to the right Republican judges in the first federal circuit.

Anyway, Hansen skipped bail. And North said, "Look, you're now on the outside looking in. Nothing we can do for you, so you get the hell out of Dodge."

And so he left and went back for Europe. It was purposely understood that he became like Miguel Recarey, like Israel Abel, like so many others.

Yes, he was officially wanted by the United States — but unofficially he wasn't. He lived rather openly in Europe for years.

We're talking about something that happened twelve years ago. Then suddenly, this guy's arrested after all these years, and he's going to be extradited back to the United, back to Miami. And everyone is sitting around, scratching their heads, wondering why this guy gets arrested.

The reason Hansen was suddenly arrested is because he was much brighter than people ever gave him credit for. I always thought he was bright. I know Oliver North and Jeb Bush and other guys thought this was a dummy, just a right-wing, blockhead. But he wasn't. He was no dummy. Particularly when it came to documenting what he was doing and tape recording other people's conversations and getting copies of documents that he saw. And unbeknownst to anybody, he had a big pile of this stuff hidden away.

He had started to leak some of this to Rich Paxton at the *Washington Post*. I'm sure Rich would deny this as Rich always denies everything to protect his source. But Rich worked with Jerry Knight at the Post for a long time on Iran-Contra stuff. Some of the stuff he was leaking implicated Jeb Bush in his knowledge of CIA sponsored narcotics trafficking in the mid 80s in southern Florida.

Interestingly enough, Hansen gets arrested. He's going to be extradited. Two days after Hansen is arrested, Jeb Bush declares for the second time, publicly declares his intentions to seek the gubernatorial candidacy for the Republican Party in 1998 in Florida.

In other words, Hansen had to be shut down, and he was. I believe he will be brought into Miami. He controls a lot of information that people don't want coming out. Particularly now that the power has shifted, the curve is shifting in Washington.

The Democrats would love to deal with this guy Hansen. And what's going to happen is this guy will secretly be brought back to the United States. A time will be declared for his extradition. He will be brought quietly back to Miami. He will be held incommunicado. He will be made a deal he cannot refuse. And he will quietly disappear into the very special witness program the way DeVoe has disappeared into it and the way Mike Palmer disappeared into it.

I don't mean the FBI's witness protection program.

I mean the Department of Defense's witness protection program, which many people don't even know exists — but it does.

The Department of Defense maintains a very secret witness protection program. It also involves the Internal Security Department of the State Department. Anyway, Hansen, two months from now, will be living comfortably, God knows where, just as DeVoe was sent to India.

Palmer is in Honduras. I know that. But he is one of perhaps the fifty or sixty individuals who simply knows too much. He has the material well hidden and he is still well enough. He still has not been discredited to the point that he would not be believed. So he'll be comfortable and he'll be gone.

And the Democrats looking to deal with this guy will simply never know what happened to him.

Later on I want to give you a preview of other topics, for example, the US Forestry Department diversion of C-130's and A-10A Thunderbolts.

You may remember the incident where six of these C-130's wind up being sold into Libya through Egyptian agents. Ed Wilson and Frank Terpil and Richard Secord brokered the deal. And this is the deal that led to Wilson's downfall to cover everybody else's ass.

Ed will spend the rest of his years in the federal pen.

Frank Terpil and Richard Secord will live the rest of their lives in great comfort and security.

The Egyptian general and the Egyptian colonel that brokered the deal from the Sooner Defense Corporation of Florida, the maker of missiles — when that went bankrupt, those two Egyptian officers had connections into that.

They wind up getting arrested, and then suddenly, they're not arrested.

Then suddenly they're back in Egypt.

Then suddenly they got diplomatic immunity. And then in an effort to look for someone to disgrace in that Sooner Defense deal, suddenly the four star general, Wallace Nutting, is put under the gun.

But Wallace is an heir to the Nutting Furniture fortune, and he had the resources to fight back. And he fought back.

And then there was the downfall of Sooner Missile Corporation, Sooner Defense Corporation. Then it suddenly was all shut down. All the indictments shut down. What remained of Sooner Defense was sold to Rafi Eitan.

Nutting finally got his reputation back. And that's just another topic that I can discuss because I got hired as a consultant by Nutting's defense attorney, so I'm familiar with it.

Another case is the Sarkis Soghanalian case — the arms merchant who continues to reside in jail and probably always will. His subordinate, Gerard Lachinian also has another very interesting case.

Lachinian is out of jail. He made a deal. He keeps his mouth shut. He lives comfortably. And he's still in the weapons business.

That's a case the *Miami Herald* went after hard. They understood what the deal was.

However, the Knight Ridder newspapers (when they got too close to it) Dave Lyons got shut down in a hurry, when they found out the connection between Lachinian, Gen. Rojas and Oliver North and the other connections as well.

Chapter 6

THE DON AUSTIN DENVER HUD FRAUD CASE

S TEVE DINNERSTEIN SENT ME a copy of the most recent proposed case sheet known as a "Proposed Case Financing Sheet," dated 09-08-97. It's put together, not as a narrative, but in memorandum form. Here's how it reads:

PROPOSED CASE FINANCING 09-08-97
I. SUBJECT: Donald Austin, MCC, Denver, Colorado.
II. LOCATION & DISPOSITION: 10th FJC "Denver"
Case originally heard by FDJ Z. Weinshank.
Reheard by FDJ E. Barnhill.
Prosecuted by AUSA Mike Norton "Denver USAO."
Case ended 6-7-91 in guilty verdicts.
7 counts MBW Fraud.
21-year sentence proposed by FDJ Z. Weinshank.
Current PLCF handled by a USA B.
Calfman PIS DOJ "Washington D.C."
This is what these initials mean.

"MCC" — Metropolitan Correction Center
"10th FJC" — Federal Judicial Circuit
"FDJ" — Federal District Judge
"AUSA" —Assistant United States Attorney
"USAO" — United States Attorney Office
"MBW Fraud" — Mail, bank and wire fraud
"PLCF" — Political Liability and Control File
"PIS DOJ" — Public Integrity Section Department of Justice
I. Type of Case: Iran-Contra sensitive.
Proposed financing: COLA $15M for three-stage to recovery.
Proposed risk of capital: nil.
Estimated return on investment $300-400M.
("M" means thousands)

Estimated time to 3-stage completion: 120 days in current political environment.

I should explain what three stages means because it's not self-explanatory in this letter. You'd have to be in the loop to know.

Three-stage recovery means this is a typical three-stage case. The guy is currently in jail. First stage, he has to be gotten out of jail. Second stage is to make sure he stays out of jail through the right legal and political moves. Third stage is recovery of funds.

Next section of this sheet is entitled "Comments."

Dinnerstein's has asked me to paraphrase his comments for security reasons. The reason why is that it is a sensitive case. In the comments, Dinnerstein points out that this is the very last of the Iran-Contra sensitive HUD cases in Denver yet to be resolved.

He points out that the resolution of the case is made easier by the impending indictments of Federal District Judges Zita Weinshank and Ed Barnhill and former Assistant United States Attorney Mike Norton. The charges are obstruction of justice and conspiracy.

These indictments should be forthcoming. He points out that he has spoken with Assistant United States Attorney Barbara Kaufman at the Public Integrity Section (that's Lee Radek's office by the way) at the Department of Justice in Washington.

Kaufman is desperate to control the political liability of this case and make sure that this is resolved the right way.

What that means to imply is that they're looking for a deal.

Kaufman mentions to Dinnerstein, who mentions in these comments that an earlier proposed solution had been a memorandum from Kaufman to Margaret Love, head of the PBF, the Presidential Pardons Board. She's the head of it. And that had been earlier discussed — giving this guy an outright pardon and approaching him directly with a deal.

But that had been scrapped, as it was considered that this guy wasn't familiar enough with the liability he represented to be approached with such a deal.

In fact, Kaufman welcomes Dinnerstein's involvement as an interlocutor, you could say. I'm reading some of this into it because this thing is written for somebody that really understands what it is that's being discussed.

I am not only paraphrasing it, but I'm also doing a little interpretation for you. Dinnerstein proposes and Austin and his counsel, David A. Parker of Dallas, Texas, has agreed that in exchange of $50,000 financing commitment stage three — in three stages in other words — $50,000 financing commitment from someone who will enjoy 25 percent of any and all recoverable sums pursuant to the Austin matter.

Dinnerstein states that upon preliminary investigation, it was discovered that $1.6 million was imminently recoverable pursuant to HUD insurance guaranteed premiums that were paid but never recorded at the time.

This, by the way, is the essence of the bribery, conspiracy and obstruction against the federal district judge.

I'll have to explain some of the background of the Denver HUD situation so this makes sense.

Dinnerstein says "$1.6 million imminently recoverable. "

Another $400-800m is probably recoverable pursuant to residual equities of property that Austin and the Austin Corporation owned and that are still intact.

Dinnerstein also mentions in the comments that he has a meeting on the 18th with Lee Radek himself, who's an old friend of Steve's, to discuss the political disposition of this case.

Regarding Denver-HUD-Iran-Contra profiteering, I've got to give you a little background for this to make sense. There was a scenario of fraud conducted through the HUD office in Denver, when Samuel Pierce was head of HUD and became part of Iran-Contra profiteering, dissipation, illegal transfer of funds, and so on.

A number of billions were involved.

The center of these frauds was HUD, namely the HUD office in Denver.

How the fraud worked was by having Iran-Contra connected individuals such as Austin involved. Austin however didn't really understand the bigger scheme.

That's the reason he's still in jail, while his partner, James Grandgeorge is not in jail any longer, despite having received a similar sentence.

The way these schemes work is to form real estate companies and incorporate licensed mortgage brokers into them. These then act as pass through agents for HUD loans. They're also used in the solicitation of guarantee agents.

Very simply, projects would be defaulted on or the same mortgages would be applied for. There'd be two, three, and four first mortgages from HUD on the same properties which would then, in turn, guarantee equally fraudulent bank loans usually through Silverado.

Monies then would be siphoned off, and ostensibly, this was just part of a much larger fraud that we have discussed. It was one item out of a thousand that was a channel fraud meant to raise a certain amount of money over a period of time, due to the continuation of illegal and covert activities.

But, obviously for this to work, there have to be Republican judges involved, as well as Republican US Attorneys and Assistant US Attorneys. This includes Gale Norton, former Attorney General of the State of Colorado and current US Secretary of the Interior, who can also be indicted for various malfeasances.

The reason Dinnerstein says it's so easy is because Zita Weinshank and Ed Barnhill, both Republican appointed judges, are part of the original scheme.

In this case, what Austin and his attorney didn't realize (he had a high-powered attorney who was not politically savvy and didn't understand the politics behind this case) was that Austin had to be discredited when the thing fell apart.

He and Norman got a twenty-one year sentence. I think Grandgeorge got a nineteen year sentence. The original deal should have been: they serve three or four years and that was it. They would be released.

How they're normally released is either their cases would be reversed on appeal, purposely reversed on appeal, and then not refiled.

Or in some cases, they would be taken out by the Department of Justice and essentially released.

The Department of Justice only has to claim that the inmate is cooperating with a sensitive federal investigation, and that way, they can be kept out forever really. There is no time limit. They can be kept out forever. And that is usually only done, when they want further control on an individual. In this case, it wouldn't have been necessary.

I know certainly that the Austin case somewhat baffled the US Attorney's office, the Department of Justice, in terms of why this guy Austin didn't make moves earlier to get himself out — or to even approach them to discuss it.

The reason why is because he didn't understand enough of his own situation at the time. He didn't understand the bigger picture, didn't understand the politics, didn't know what to do, and had an attorney that didn't know what to do.

It wasn't until the last thirty days when I got involved in it that things started to happen.

And now this guy Austin will get out of jail.

Getting him out isn't any problem. That can be done in two weeks. That's simply filing a motion to get him out pending appeal.

The government will ask for no bond, and the long and short of it is the original case will be overturned very quickly. It won't even have to be heard, as a matter of fact — the minute these judges are indicted and the original US Attorney who prosecuted the cases is indicted (that's if the government will elect not to appeal which is good cover for them)

Austin's attorney, Parker, is competent. He doesn't understand, but he's competent at least. We've told him what he has to do to file the right motions to recover, which is all that's got to be done.

The government's simply looking for something to hang their hat on. Therefore Austin has got to make at least the right moves, both in criminal and civil courts.

Dinnerstein also estimates in this memorandum that Austin himself (since a copy of this is going to Austin's counsel) will eventually wind up with approximately a million dollars in his pocket after all percentages are paid out and after all recoveries are exhausted.

The only thing Austin has to do is forget, keep his mouth shut, and he will be encouraged to, perhaps, relocate in the Caribbean, where he does own a piece of property. He still owns a condo there.

This guy was able to keep some assets after this debacle. However none of those assets are liquid. He couldn't raise any money off of them. That's why he's in this predicament.

However, I suspect that Mr. Austin will be happy with the arrangement. A million dollars. He's a sharp operator. It's enough to start his life over and everyone else involved in this case — everyone will make money — and Ms. Kaufman.

That's how you have to talk to this woman. You can't call her Barbara or "Miss" or "Mrs.", it's "Ms." Kaufman. She will get what she wants which is the end of the political liability of this case, and the political liability control file that is currently extant can be retired.

You might also be wondering where the money is coming from that Austin's going to recover.

Austin is clearly entitled to XYZ sums. Where the money comes from, by the way, is from pools of money that were originally and quietly set aside by the Department of Justice as these schemes were beginning to collapse in the 1988 to 1991 time frame.

The money already exists in a pool that is just simply held quietly and off the books so to speak.

I suspect there can't be much money left because of the seventeen Iran-Contra sensitive HUD cases Dinnerstein and I have been involved in.

There's already been a lot of money paid out, and to my knowledge, Austin is the very last.

So I suspect there can't be much money left in the pool.

However, of course, there is an advantage to being the last guy left and that is that the Department just wants to clean it up.

If this guy, is in fact (as I believe he is) the last guy to be incorporated into a Liability Control File at the Department, then not only can they close the file on this guy, they can close the file on the whole channel.

The whole thing is shut down permanently, which is another reason they want to move this case along. As you can well imagine, this comes along at a good time for Austin because of things that are going on beyond his control at the Department of Justice pursuant to what we have discussed — mainly the bigger conspiracy control is beginning to unravel.

Although Austin is just a tiny cog in the wheel, it certainly creates a good environment for him to deal — now that he's got people handling it that actually know what to do and know who to contact, and have made deals before.

There's going to be a lot of people that are going to make money in this case — the guy that comes up with the money to finance it, people who handle it, Austin himself. Everybody's going to make money.

And the Department of Justice is going to get what they want.

Chapter 7

BUSH FAMILY FRAUD AND IRAN-CONTRA PROFITEERING

D URING THE IRAN-CONTRA years, principally 1983-86, there was a State-sponsored pattern of fraud undertaken by members of the Bush family and members of the Reagan regime, and powerful Republicans in the shadows of Washington.

This, of course, has been extensively written about and reported, albeit in a rather chopped-up fashion, in the past.

The impression that a serious student of Iran-Contra fraud would have is that Iran-Contra created an environment combined with the swinging 1980s for members of government to commit fraud — bank fraud, securities fraud, real estate fraud, insurance fraud, brokerage fraud, a whole panoply of fraud.

However, if one were to gather the probably five hundred to one thousand articles that have been written about this fraud individually, one would conclude that it really was just isolated.

Or it was something that certain individuals took to commit on their own initiative.

Next, I will attempt to prove and otherwise illustrate to the reader my contention that this was a State-sponsored pattern of fraud with a specific agenda.

The mainstream media has not wanted to connect these dots in the past, although as we have discussed before, many individual journalists, even well-known journalists have attempted to write more sweeping articles.

Certainly Sydney Freedberg has when Sydney was with the *Wall Street Journal*. Her successor, Ed Pound, at the *Wall Street Journal* attempted to do the same.

There were other people in the media who were very interested in Iran-Contra related fraud, and they did write substantive articles about it in the past — Frank Bass of the *Houston Post*, George Williamson of the *San Francisco Chronicle*, Scott Shepherd at the *Atlanta Constitution*, Jay Epstein at the *Philadelphia Inquirer*, Jerry Knight and Rich Paxton at the *Washington Post*, Paul Rodriguez at the *Washington Times*, Doug Franz, formerly with the *Los Angeles Times*, now with the *New York Times*.

I know all of these men very well, and they have all written substantive articles concerning individual transactions, corporations, partnerships, but their editors have always prevented them from any effort to connect the dots, as it were, into what a potential reader would believe was a pattern, or an organized activity, sponsored by and protected by the Government of the United States.

Regarding the Bush family, I think it's best that we start with Jeb.

After all, Jeb is the member of the Bush family that I know the best. I have met him personally on many occasions. I've talked to him and had the most business dealings with him, particularly in the 1985 time-frame, when fraud was really at its absolute peak.

We've divided Iran-Contra into money, weapons and narcotics. So now we are concentrating on the money angle. The reason, by the way, I have such extensive first-hand knowledge of Jeb Bush's financial activity in this time frame is because fraudulent transactions would often be discussed at the bi-weekly policy and planning sessions of the FDN in Miami.

Also, business transactions would be discussed at the Dade County Latin American Chamber of Commerce and the Dade County Latin American Republican Club, chaired respectively by Jorge Mascanosa and Jeb Bush. I was an active member of both and I attended meetings regularly.

Also, I marketed Jeb Bush product. Many of his deals, particularly on the real estate side, were put together as either limited or general partnerships.

In some cases, his deals got wrapped up into others which became small public companies — commonly known in those days as a Regulation D, or Reg-D, filing under US Securities Statutes 501 to 505 — occasionally a statute, S1, S3, or S18 deal.

These are all common euphemisms used in the securities business to describe different types of legal filings.

The real differentiation is how many shareholders, how many shares can be outstanding, how much capital could be raised, what the requirements are to maintain a market in the shares and so on.

I raised money for Jeb Bush deals both in terms of partnerships and in terms of private placements, or in terms of — which was very common and very popular in those years — backing a company with assets into a so-called penny shell. That is a publicly traded corporate shell that had no assets. The stock traded for perhaps a few pennies on the pink sheets.

It would be more interesting to concentrate on some of the more exotic, esoteric, or arcane fraud committed by Jeb Bush.

Some of his fraud has been reasonably well detailed, even in the Miami and Fort Lauderdale press, for example the $4 million fraud against Broward Federal Savings and Loan in Fort Lauderdale, Florida.

It has also been extensively documented — how he committed the fraud, how he was able to avoid the consequences of the commission of said fraud and so forth.

Broward Federal Savings and Loan ultimately wrote off $3.85 million worth of Bush Realty loans, which were essentially fraudulently obtained, since the assets were all doubled and tripled in value surreptitiously on paper and substantial misrepresentations were made in the obtaining of those loans and obviously those loans were fraudulently obtained.

Broward Federal Savings and Loan never made any real effort to recover the money. One has only to look at the then-prevailing Board of Directors of said institution to discover why.

One fraud I would like to talk about, which I think is interesting and actually more sinister, is Jeb Bush's involvement in a company in Key Largo known as the Marine Research and Development Corporation, Ltd. of Key Largo, Florida.

How Jeb gets into that, by the way (and this was a mystery until I helped Lyons at the *Miami Herald* with his piece on it) is because Jeb was general partner in the Boca Chica Development in Boca Chica, Florida.

There were actual investments by the Bush Family Trust in that Boca Chica Development, which is a very large development that includes the lodge, the townhouses and the marina complex.

Ultimately, in that Boca Chica deal, Jeb defrauded $9 million out of The Great American Bank and Trust Company, then headquartered in West Palm Beach, Florida, and owned by Marvin Warner.

The Great American Bank and Trust was one of the very first Iran-Contra banks of any size to fail, specifically under the weight of unrepaid Iran-Contra related loans.

They ultimately had to write off a $9 million bridge loan in that deal.

The Marine Research and Development Corporation of Key Largo, Florida, was essentially (and this is going to sound a little farfetched) nothing more than a shell corporation — a proprietary cut-out of the Hungarian Intelligence Service.

I know this sounds a little way out, but we must remember the very good article, in 1988 by Sydney Freedberg in the *Wall Street Journal* about this company with my help, identifying the two principals of this company as Hungarian intelligence agents in the United States.

At that time, even though Sydney was given great literary license in that 1988 piece by the *Wall Street Journal* (this was right on the cusp as she was transitioning out of the *Wall Street Journal* into the *Miami Herald*), they refused to allow her to connect Jeb Bush to the deal.

This would have absolutely opened a Pandora's Box, and they knew it.

The Marine Research and Development Corporation was run by two Hungarian intelligence agents which she identified in the paper. Their controller was Imre West, who's real name is Imre Vida.

He himself controlled a very important Hungarian intelligence cut-out in the United States known as Northwest Industries, which had substantial business dealings with Oliver North and Richard Secord, especially Richard Secord.

Northwest Industries had a very large relationship with one of Secord's principal artifices, the Stanford Technology Overseas Corporation, Ltd., which was at one time registered in the Bahamas.

When Sydney confronted Jeb with this article in 1988, he admitted that he had a small relationship with the Marine Research and Development Corporation of Key Largo only because that corporation and his Boca Chica Development had land borders in common.

Boca Chica Development did lease some lands and some water rights to this Marine Research and Development Corporation.

Jeb publicly claimed that he did not know who these two Hungarian intelligence agents were — he'd never met them and never heard of them.

That's an out-and-out lie, and I can prove it.

I know who both of these men are.

I have a photograph of these men with Jeb Bush having his arm around one of them. It was taken at a dinner of the Biscayne Club on one of the evenings of the bi-weekly Friday night dinners at the Biscayne Towers Club.

Anyway, Marine Research and Development Corporation supposedly did shellfish research and artificial shellfish farming habitat.

They also conveniently had (and this is how they get into a much bigger connection) a rare, hard-to-get, and very unusual license, wherein they had six trawlers, a combination of fishing trawler/research boats. These were about sixty-seventy-eighty foot steel boats. I was even aboard one of them at one time.

At any rate, they had a very unusual license, wherein they could actually travel to Cuba and back again because they had a deal with the Cuban government for artificial lobster habitat.

In the 1984 incident, when these boats were moving very freely and surprisingly unmolested by the U.S. Coast Guard from Key Largo to Cuba (the Port of Mariel more specifically) and making the round trip, on the trip back, these boats would be brought very close to the Turks and Caicos Islands.

Now, in the 1984 incident, one of these boats developed some sort of mechanical trouble and drifted into Turks and Caicos waters. It was duly boarded by a police patrol boat of the Turks and Caicos government to render assistance, whereupon a substantial quantity of cocaine was discovered in the holds of this boat.

And it was substantial — seven or eight hundred kilograms.

Naturally, George Robinson, then Prime Minister of the Turks and Caicos Islands, who as you will remember was to later himself get indicted for cocaine trafficking to shut him up, decided he was going to keep the cocaine.

And George was very quickly contacted by Clair George, then Deputy Director of the CIA, who wanted the cocaine back.

George was essentially holding the cocaine for ransom.

The long and short of it is that Robinson attempted to take the cocaine into the Bahamas, and he was going to have Eddie Bannister and Nelson Rolle, where Nelson Rolle represented him.

Both Eddie Bannister and Nelson Rolle were Bahamian members of Parliament. Nelson was also a private practice attorney. He had an office on 37 Bay Street in Nassau. You may also remember they were both indicted.

But when they did, in fact, attempt to make a deal to give back this cocaine for a fee to the CIA, Bannister got himself seized off that sports fishing boat, and Rolle was baited into a meeting in Miami where he was arrested.

These guys were indicted and prosecuted for cocaine trafficking.

And they got pretty good sentences, twenty to thirty year sentences.

Nelson Rolle, Eddie Bannister and George Robinson are now out of prison after serving five or six years — one of those quietly let-out deals by the FBI, where it will be claimed for the rest of their sentences that they are aiding and investigating an ongoing investigation of the FBI and so on, when, in fact, they're back in the Bahamas and the Turks and Caicos Islands respectively.

And the story never ends. I also have ancillary documentation of how the Parliament of the Turks and Caicos Islands got its arm twisted in order to lift the Prime Minister's immunity, so that he could be prosecuted in the United States — the money that changed hands, who was involved, where the money came from.

Marine Research and Development Corporation also offered a series of limited partnerships, and one of which I marketed supposedly for the production of underwater shellfish farms type of deal.

Anyway, it was all bullshit, believe me.

The reason why this MRDC is such a key component is that its limited partnership was also used as the bait in the infamous and sinister bait-and-switch political control mechanism of investment deals, which were offered to investors targeted within the ranks of senior Democrats on the hill.

When I say this is the bait part — all the investors got their money back plus a profit out of this MRDC deal — but they were not allowed to invest any more than two hundred thousand dollars.

It wasn't envisioned for someone to invest millions into this deal because it was a bait deal.

Some would put in a hundred thousand dollars. They were going to get back a hundred and thirty thousand and walk away with a sweet taste in their mouth.

Then they would get switched to a different deal that was completely bogus.

And they would get leveraged and financed up the yin-yang, signed on fully recourse notes, and the plug would be pulled out of them.

A good example of this is Congressman Bill Alexander.

One of the principal broker/dealer marketers in the limited partnerships of Marine Research and Development Corporation was Jeb Bush's cousin, Wally, Prescott's son, who controlled the firm known as J.Walter Bush Securities.

Also, marketing these deals were different divisions of the National Brokerage Group, then controlled by the infamous MDC Holdings.

They were shut down later and they were controlled by Allen Teal. Allen recently got himself re-indicted — in part, thanks to my help in 1995 — for running a string of securities firms that were essentially boiler room operations out of Salt Lake City.

They do not have the Republican Party political protection that they had ten or twelve years ago. But it was all a fraud. The limited partnership was a fraud. The securities firms were frauds. It was a fraud, compounded upon a fraud, compounded upon a fraud. It was essentially just money laundering.

Anyway to get back to Congressman Alexander. He just bought a few units, twenty thousand dollars worth of the deal.

I know. I sold it to him. And he got back twenty-five thousand dollars.

And he was very happy, you know.

Then, of course, what happens is he gets switched into that Boulder Property Limited Partnership deal. There were seven of them. Boulder Property Limited 1, Limited 2, Limited 3, and so on. And it was an out-and-out fraud.

Alexander bought three million dollars with of it. He signed three million dollars worth of fully recourse notes, and the plug was pulled out from under on that deal.

Alexander was forced into bankruptcy. And he was also the force of that, the manipulation of the bankruptcy. The way it ultimately came out for him, it was pretty good.

He didn't get pressed that hard, as long as he backed away from certain Iran-Contra investigations.

Now, who else got hooked into the Marine Research and Development deal for the sweet taste was Ron Dellums of California and Steve Solarz of New York.

David Pryor and Dale Bumpers also became investors in the deal.

I also have extensive documentation about powerful Democrats on the

Hill who bought into this deal, got a sweet taste, and then got transferred into other deals for much larger amounts of money that all had the proverbial plug pulled on them.

Anyway, enough on the Marine Research and Development Corporation.

I have some notes I made when I was helping Freedberg, but this is a deal that you could literally write a separate book about it. And you could plug Jeb Bush into every part of their operation.

I could illustrate how Jeb got paid for his involvement with Marine Research and Development Corporation.

How he got kick-back commissions on bogus security and partnership deals.

How he got certain concessions on property owned by the Marine Research and Development Corporation.

I can prove that he knew who the two individuals were.

Another deal I was involved in with Jeb was the Gulf Oil and Drilling Supply Corporation, which had formerly been a CIA cut-out that was left dormant. This was part of a package.

As we sweep into the end of 1983 into 1984, there were literally a thousand or more dormant cut-outs of the Agency, which were essentially existing as little more than shells in a counsel's file, in Bobby Beckman's file drawer.

Beckman was deputy general counsel for the CIA at that time. The Gulf Oil Drilling Supply Company relates to fraud that had previously been committed by Jeb's father, George Sr.

It even goes back into George's father, Prescott Sr.

This is the so-called bogus Argentine oil and gas leases that Jeb's grandfather had once owned. That's how old this fraud is.

Believe me, oil and gas fraud is a real old fraud in the Bush family.

Even my former partner, Hamil, bought leases from Jeb that were totally worthless.

Suddenly, they could be made to look worthwhile, as was commonly done in those days. Anyway a tremendous amount of money was raised for this deal: three or four hundred million dollars. It was a lot of money. And there was almost no oil left in these things.

Some of these wells were old pumpers, and the one-barrel-a-day specials, give them a shot of acid every ninety days deal.

But anyway, we're not going to get into it. That is something that we could look at separately — the fraud committed in that deal — which members of the Bush family profited, what banks got hurt.

Citibank and Chase Manhattan both got hurt in that deal.

Merrill Lynch got hurt in that deal.

But, of course, very early on, Don Regan was Chairman of Merrill Lynch.

You know, there was a reason why he went from being Chairman of Merrill Lynch to Presidential Chief of Staff.

Another deal I wanted to mention, although it's smaller in nature, it was only a $30 or $40 million fraud.

Jeb was on the Board of Directors of the Orca Supply Company of Coral Gables which was an active (not a former cut-out) an ongoing cut-out of the Agency at the time.

It was managed by the infamous Lt. Col. Jack Terrell, otherwise known in Congressional hearings, as El Flaco. Not his code name.

That was something he was called south of the border because Jack is six foot four and probably weighs a hundred and fifty pounds.

The Orca Supply Company supposedly dealt in oil field service equipment when, in fact, it actually surreptitiously dealt in weapons.

And Jeb was on the Board of Directors and was paid ten thousand dollars a year.

As it was, he got paid a lot of ten thousand dollars a year for being on a lot of board of directors of a lot of, shall we say, shadowy little companies.

Not necessarily the largest, but the most notorious and publicly known deal that Jeb Bush was involved in was IMC, the International Medical Corporation with his partner Miguel Recarey.

Jeb got hammered with this deal in 1990 and 1991, when Recarey fled the country and it ultimately cost the government about $350 million that had to be written off because of this deal.

Jeb would rightly point out that he was only a director of the corporation and in fact owned a medical subdivision shell corporation registered in the Bahamas which is technically true.

However, it's interesting to note how Miguel Recarey himself was able to flee the country for Venezuela, three hours after a warrant was issued for his arrest, and he winds up being driven to Miami International Airport in a car owned by the Bush Realty Corporation of Miami.

As a matter of fact, it was George Fernandez that drove him in the car, obviously before George was murdered. And he took a private plane, by the way, at Miami International Airport, the flight of which had been listed as a flight for Bush Realty.

And Recarey was allowed to live rather openly in Venezuela for a couple of years, until the *Miami Herald* and the *Wall Street Journal* started to hammer away on this IMC deal.

This was probably the closest that Jeb Bush ever got connected in the media with illicit Iran-Contra profiteering and how much it cost the Treasury, how his father became involved, his father's relationship with Miguel Recarey, and really how the whole deal was worked out to allow Recarey to get out of the country.

Recarey then joins the list of about two dozen other guys who, by the late 1980s, are officially sought by the United States government on various bills of indictment, but unofficially not wanted for political motives.

Jeb also profited quite handsomely in HUD loan fraud.

Jeb was certainly part of that whole equation. And documents I have put together would indicate that he and other members of his family ultimately cost HUD about $135 million dollars.

Anyway, this is enough for Jeb for now. I want to get on to Neil Bush, insofar as I did have some direct business dealings with him — along the same lines I had with Jeb, raising money for him, in other words, marketing his product.

Neil's principal artifices were the Gulf Realty, various Gulf Realty Limited Partnership deals — Gulf Realty Associates, Gulf Realty. There are twenty or thirty things that he controlled with his partners, Ken Good and Bill Walters, whom I actually know better than Neil — with the name Gulf Realty.

This is what was picked up from the old Gulf Realty in the 1950s, which at one time was a large, shall we say, boiler room real estate operation in Florida.

It was one of the very early boiler room operations in Florida in the 1950s, selling land to the unsuspecting. But they did do, originally, some legitimate projects. All those Coral Ridge and Coral Springs projects. Those were legitimate at one time.

Anyway, Gulf Stream Realty had been essentially dormant at one time until Neil picked it up. It was another case of a picked up dormancy of what had been an earlier fraud to create a new fraud.

I had raised money for a real mixed bag of Neil's developments — principally that development, the Destin Country Club, what later became known as the Destin or infamous Destin Country Club deal.

Ray Locklear at the *Tampa Tribune* broke this open. Ray is now an editor. He was promoted upstairs to prevent him from writing about any more Republican involvement on a personal recommendation of Porter Goss, no less.

I want to mention Porter to some degree as an example of how senior members of Congress — he's senior chairman now of one of the finance subcommittee — made a fortune in terms of illicit Iran-Contra profiteering at the time.

Essentially along the same lines, a lot of Republican members made money, that is, leveraging themselves into deals, getting these interests for nothing or near nothing. Borrowing money on them. Then defaulting on the loans. Then going back to another artifice to have the loans picked up from a friendly source to pay off the ill-gotten fruits of the first loan.

But Porter made a lot of money. For a nickel-and-dime Congressman, he made $12 or $13 million dollars in these deals illicitly.

Bob Graham even became involved in this deal with that acreage he swapped out into one of the Gulf Stream properties which, in turn, got incorporated into one of Swissco Management deals.

Swissco Management was controlled by Carlos Cardoen. Anyway, that Destin Country Club deal — we drew that one out pretty good. And documents indicate that it ultimately cost the United States taxpayers about $78 million dollars.

Neil had also become extensively involved in the Topsail Development Group, Ltd. of Pensacola, that twenty-six thousand acre parcel from the Ball Estate where George Ball's signature winds up being forged.

And who's the secretary in this deal, the one that transports the papers, that executes the conveyances? None other than Barbara Studley.

By the way, in the media, for press purposes, this deal is what later gets known as the "St. Joseph Paper Land Deal," which was one of the, if not *the*, largest real estate frauds, ever committed in the United States.

The Bushes would have been exposed in this deal and taken down. George Bush never would have survived the political scandal, if this whole deal had not been bailed out by Coca-Cola, with that $150 million dollar loan that Bob Goizueta personally approved.

Bob Goizueta, former Chairman of Coca-Cola, died awhile ago of natural causes. I made some effort to determine if that's right, and natural causes was correct. He had cancer and he died.

But Bob was a huge supporter of George Bush and the Republican party. Coca-Cola had quietly helped bail out some of these deals in the past.

When they allowed all that land in Belize (the 45,000 acres Coca-Cola owned in Belize, including some very choice coastal lands) to get wrapped and re-rolled into that loan, which the Banco de Popular Santa Domingo branch headed, it was all European bank money that came into that deal.

But that's what bailed this deal out — the $150 million that Coca-Cola used to bail it out. And they ultimately lost it. They had to write off $60 or $70 million because of it.

Credit Lyonnais had to write off $60 million. Credit Lyonnais, as a matter of fact, had attempted to complain about this deal. That was in 1991-1992, when Credit Lyonnais itself was having problems, bogged down by the weight of unrepaid Iran-Contra lending. Some of it was for just tremendous amounts of money.

The *Economist* and the *Financial Times* of London tried to get into that to some extent when Paul Sappan (and Paul was one hell of a good investigative reporter, particularly when it came to political kind of fraud) wrote that series of articles on Credit Lyonnais, and Credit Lyonnais' rather close relationship with the Bush family and other senior Republicans in this country and how much money it had cost them over the years. Anyway, we're getting far afield. We're supposed to be talking about Neil Bush.

So I have pretty well documented not only my involvement, but the involvement of others, in these Gulf Stream real estate deals. Hamil was extensively involved in them. And they ultimately cost the American taxpayers $432 million by my calculation, which I think is about right.

I know that when Henry Gonzalez chaired the House Banking Commission, they had privately estimated $418 million. Naturally, they could not publicly release it.

When they attempted to publicly release it, you may remember Henry Gonzalez wound up having his silver Lincoln Towncar machine-gunned to send him a message. And the message was received. And Henry's an old man, and he understood the reality that you simply cannot tell the people the truth, particularly about something like this.

Because where does it stop? Somebody would get the idea this might be connected to something larger, which in turn is connected to something larger.

And as Henry had said to me personally, it simply is not politically possible to tell the people the truth about the Bush family.

But it has to be done in a chopped-up fashion — individual frauds, individual corporate artifices, and $20 million was lost here, $30 million was lost there.

Aren't these bad guys? Well, we'll see. My book's going to change that. My book will test the theory that you cannot tell the truth.

The only thing is, how do you do it in a book without turning it into an encyclopedia?

Other activities of Neil I have extensively documented are of course, his relationship with Silverado, and how much he ultimately cost Silverado, which was more than $2 billion by the way.

The Boulder Property limited partnerships when they all collapsed cost $750 million dollars in losses alone. Alone. That's just one deal.

We're not talking about the M&L Development deal.

You throw into that the losses they suffered because of MDC and M&L Development and all of those fraudulent deals with Ryder Homes, and Pulte Homes where there were millions written off and land that they never even owned to begin with.

The Gloryhole Mining deal in Colorado — there was a $150 million written off with that.

I mean, the fraud is simply enormous — to try to comprehend these numbers and the egregiousness of it.

But the funny thing is and the reason why Neil, I think, didn't get as lambasted publicly as he could have is because Neil personally never made all that much money himself in any of these deals.

When Iran-Contra came to an end, when this bullshit came to an end, which was not 1987 (I mean, the Iran-Contra profiteering really did not come to an end until 1989) Neil had only made $3 or $4 million for himself, some of which he had to spend in attorney's fees and other things.

But anyway, I know there's some perception that Neil's got an offshore account that's well-stuffed. I simply don't think he has.

I think when we get down to doing Neil individually — I only have between a thousand and fifteen-hundred documents relating to him.

I didn't do as much business with him. And I was by no means aware of all of his deals or activities. I was aware of twenty or thirty of them that I had some direct involvement in.

I know the most about Jeb since I had more involvement with him. I raised more money for his deals, a greater variety of deals. In some cases, I had an actual third-party equity interest in them through Southeast Resources, Inc., interests in some of Hamil's deals, principally that Gulf Stream Limited Partner Associates, series III.

But let's get on to George, Jr.

George, Jr.'s specialty was insurance fraud.

We all have our specialties. Jeb is sort of a mixed, what I always called a mixed specialist, that is, Jeb likes any kind of fraud — banking, security, real estate, oil and gas, gold bullion, aircraft brokerage.

The whole panoply of all the old right-wing favorites for the surreptitious production of covert revenue streams.

Neil was much more in the real estate end of the fraud. But George, Jr — I would classify as an insurance fraudster, in terms of his Iran-Contra profiteering.

By that I mean that he profited quite handsomely from all those bogus claims in that scheme that was originally developed by Jack Singlaub for the so-called missing aircraft and luxury yacht scam.

Singlaub started it under the auspices of the World Anti-Communist League, Inc., which as we've mentioned before, had its corporate headquarters in Phoenix, in the offices next to J. Walter Bush Securities in the Lincoln Savings and Loan Plaza.

We've described this fraud before, how it worked. It wasn't all that big of a fraud. Frankly, I know AIG claims about $15 million, but I think it's a little more, either $18 or maybe $20 million.

AIG never made any effort to recover the money because this was AIG's corporate contribution to Iran-Contra. Look at who the Chairman was and the Board of Directors of AIG at the time.

You know, we tend to look at corporate contributions as being very simple.

Oliver North goes to see Peter Coors and Coors gives him $2 million dollars in a briefcase.

Or old Mrs. Graham of Texas gives him $2 million in a briefcase. And that's their contribution.

But corporate contribution is similar to Coca-Cola.

Republican-friendly corporations can't simply give money for an illegal, covert purpose of State. However, they can funnel money in other ways.

How does an insurance company do it? By paying off fraudulent claims of property that is claimed to be stolen, which in fact has not been stolen.

It's simply been moved to somewhere else. To an undisclosed location.

I do have extensive documentation about it, mainly because I had marketed part of this so-called tax shelter part of this thing for Mitch Marr.

Mitch was the national chairman for brokerage activities of the World Anti-Communist League, and Mitch used to come to Miami and Fort Lauderdale all the time trying to drum up people who were willing, sympathetic Republicans, who were willing to donate expensive, private aircraft and expensive yachts and get ten times what these things were worth as tax deductions.

And then, of course, the boats wound up in North Andros Island in a little facility there with the names changed and the numbers changed. And the planes wound up at hangars from Boca Raton to Joplin, Missouri with changed numbers and such.

But that deal, you know, it was a fraud envisioned to raise $20 million dollars or so, which is about what it did. The principal insurer who took it on the chops, of course, was AIG.

In some cases, insurance policies had to be switched to AIG. American Insurance General (AIG) was the largest in the country then, and American Reassurance, more commonly known as American Re and their subsidiary General Re, were all controlled by very sympathetic Republicans.

There hasn't been a lot written about George, Jr. in terms of his Iran-Contra profiteering because it didn't involve that large a number. He did have some direct involvement and certainly profited from the Lone Star Cement fraud, the Sooner Defense Development fraud, the MK Industries fraud, (that was the MK Trucking Fraud deal that all the Bush family profited by).

But these frauds weren't in the hundreds and hundreds and hundreds of millions of dollars. They were all in the tens of millions of dollars type fraud.

There was a much more limited number of people that got hurt by that. None of these deals that George, Jr. was involved in ultimately really got charged back to the American public, through some route, some public financing to which some guaranty authority was obligated and so on and so forth.

As we had previously estimated, George, Jr.'s fraud during Iran-Contra only ultimately cost the American taxpayer $10 to $13 million dollars — nickels and dimes in the greater scheme of things.

How George, Jr. can be more directly inculpated is because he is a much more powerful functionary and is listed in many more documents for the Bush Family Trust. He is the only one of the sons with an absolute and full power of attorney and this includes their primary asset, which is not part of the Bush Family Trust.

Bush Family Trust has very little assets. The last public declaration in 1992 that George Bush, Sr. made was showing they only had $17 million in assets.

That's because the crown jewels are not in it.

The crown jewel of the Bush family is their interest in the rather secret and gigantic Houston Energy Partners, Ltd.

We only need to look at who the other partners are — ranging from the late John Tower to the still-living Lloyd Benson to get an idea of just how large of an entity it is and how big of a fraud it has been over the years.

Anyway, I would say something about George Jr., but I would stick to what I knew about first-hand, which really isn't much.

I would use him as an angle to develop insurance fraud. I'm breaking this down into categories of Iran-Contra fraud within terms of a State-sponsored operation in terms of Bush family and other powerful Republicans' profiteering.

And that would be a good angle to get into insurance fraud. It was my interrogatory that forced the government to drop the insurance fraud charges against Terry Reed in 1990.

I have a letter from Kathy Robinson who was the Assistant United States Attorney for Kansas City indicating that it was, in fact, my interrogatories that made the government make the decision to drop the case. Interestingly enough, they only dropped it if Reed and others would agree to a seal not to discuss it.

But let's get on to George Bush, Sr.

I probably have the most about George Senior, only because of my relationship with his children in a legal and financial nature. I do have substantive documents on George Sr.'s Lone Star Cement Fraud and his involvement, in other words, how he profited. Also, the MK Trucking deal and the Sooner Defense deal.

Within defense contracting fraud, I've never even bothered to organize all the documents. I have so much of it, as a matter of fact, particularly within the Loral Group, which as you know for years has been one of their principal holdings.

But I've got so much on the Loral corporate fraud and fraudulent transactions with Martin Marietta and then how that bounces back to Sooner Defense that, frankly, I haven't even organized all of it.

They're in bankers' boxes and rough files. And I have banker box upon banker box upon banker box full of documents describing their fraud.

I also have a lot of documentation pursuant to George, Sr.'s involvement in fraudulent deals surrounding Zapata and Apache Energy.

I have a lot of stuff with him in Harken Energy, also including a lot with George, Jr. in Harken Energy. That's another possibility. But again, these weren't large frauds. They were little security frauds, the fraudulent diversion of monies in those bogus Bahrainian leases when they temporarily ensconced Richard Secord to be their Middle-Eastern Director for Bahrainian Operations which existed in a file drawer.

What that Bahrainian deal came down to was George Bush, Sr.'s close friend, former Saudi intelligence chief and major Iran-Contra figure, Ghaith Pharaon. That was just a donation to Iran-Contra by the Saudi government. And that's what the bogus Bahrainian lease deal effectively comes down to.

It wasn't much — $38 million, something like that.

Secord received about $3 million for his own pocket. Harry Aderholt was thrown a bone out of the deal. It was no big deal really.

I also want to discuss an overview of Bush family fraud, ala Iran-Contra profiteering. I want to mention other Republican fraud and Iran-Contra profiteering such as Henry Hyde's bogus deals with the Oak Brook Savings and Loan in Illinois, Key Bank of New York — that was $800,000 of fraud.

Interestingly enough, Henry Hyde has within the last twelve months, quietly been censured by the House, although that censure was not made public.

The House Operations Committee absolutely agree with my numbers, when I said approximately $800,000 that Hyde had defrauded from those two institutions which is exactly what they say in that censure.

I'd like to discuss Bob Dole but that's not a lot of money that Bob made in Iran-Contra profiteering, frankly, $3 or $4 million. It really isn't a whole lot.

I'd like to stick to, let's say, a dozen senior Republicans, who are still senior Republicans, by the way. And the few millions they made here and there at the expense of the public purse *vis-a-vis* their involvement in Iran-Contra fraud

Also, within this brief overview on Iran-Contra fraud, Bush Family and senior Republicans, I'm going to blend into this the so-called "Control Files" that Richard Secord once had in his possession.

You may remember they're so named because of Secord's famous comment, "If a Democrat doesn't have a problem that we can control him with, we'll create one for him."

That's an interesting issue that I'd like to delve into — the concept of an organized control mechanism that was coordinated by both elements of the CIA and the NSC to essentially set up senior Congressional Democrats, who might be a problem later on in any subsequent Iran-Contra investigation.

And there are some notable instances.

How Henry Gonzalez got the arm put on. You know, his car was machine-gunned and the townhouse bombed.

How Ron Dellums got set up with that cocaine matter.

How David Boren got controlled in that 1984 agriculture trade mission trip to Cuba, of which I have an affidavit from Bill Alexander insofar as he was a member of the Agriculture Subcommittee at that time and attended the trip. And he knew quite a bit.

I was surprised at how much he knew about how the CIA had successfully compromised Boren in that photograph, when Boren was attempting to keep his own homosexuality quiet in a very heavily Christian district. A new conservative Democrat in a heavily Christian district.

But I would like to delve into the Control Files more extensively.

How Steve Solarz got a control mechanism put on him the same way Bill Alexander did.

It was a financial control mechanism. It was — either you're going to be bankrupt, or we'll keep you out of bankruptcy.

Steve Solarz talked to me and Dinnerstein (Dinnerstein's known him since they grew up together). I really don't know because I only met Steve Solarz a couple of times. You remember that Steve Solarz, when he was still in Congress, was one of the guys who substantially pushed the Iraqgate investigation in 1989 and you see how suddenly he got turned off like a goddamn light switch.

He backed away from that and back-pedaled after pushing and pushing and pushing it. The reason why is that some old recourse notes were dusted off of a shelf and stuck in his face and said, "You're going to pay these recourse notes or you're going into bankruptcy, or you're going to keep your mouth shut."

And he elected to keep his mouth shut. As a matter of fact, when he left Congress, he was paid back. He was given some choice positions with six-figure lifetime incomes and Steve's just not interested in talking about it anymore.

Frankly, I don't blame him. He's had enough of it.

The final thing I'd like to mention is that I intend to incorporate the series of 501c3 tax-exempt foundations started by Jesse Helms and Oliver North, i.e. the bogus nature of them.

Some of the fraud committed by these tax-exempt shells, controlled by Ollie and Jesse — they really just lent his name to it and received some kickbacks. It wasn't much, 4 or 5 or $600,000 a year for two or three years. But some of the transactions were so blatantly illegal as to be humorous.

Next I'll include salient highlights of the President's brother, Prescott Bush, Jr.'s Iran-Contra fraud activities.

Also his son, Wally's fraud, as well as an overview of the father Prescott, Sr.'s fraud. Then I'll include a compendium of fifty years of Bush Family fraud which will be entitled "The Legacy of the Bush Family: A Vortex of Fraud."

Chapter 8

INSIDER STOCK SWINDLES FOR "THE CAUSE"

I WOULD LIKE TO EXPLORE in further detail both Bush Family and Republican-related Iran-Contra fraud and illicit profiteering and to give more specific examples.

In terms of banks, I would like to use as an example three major Texas lending institutions which were very prominent in Iran-Contra fraud and were, in fact, taken down by this fraud.

These were Texas American Bancshares, then chaired by Bobby Corson, Allied Bancshares of Texas, then chaired by the infamous Walter Mischer, and thirdly, MCorp.

They were the three largest savings and loans and/or commercial banks in Texas in the mid-1980s.

The combined losses in these institutions totaled some $5 billion. By 1988-89, these banks were, in fact, insolvent.

Mischer and Corson were later investigated by various Congressional committees as to the nature of unrepaid Iran-Contra loans. In some cases, these were some of the few groups of institutions where the CIA was directly involved.

These institutions had lent money to the CIA in the past, which incidentally is against the CIA's mandate, but it was done, nevertheless, due to very tight Republican control of these three institutions.

In fact, by 1989, it was determined that the CIA had borrowed for illegal, covert operations some $350 million from these three institutions. It also failed to repay that amount. These banks were involved principally in fraudulent Iran-Contra related profiteering — real estate loans, oil and gas ventures, illegal securities transactions, etc.

I'll give you an example of what we used to call the "Double Fraud Scam." It was late in the game, about 1987-88. As mentioned previously, Iran-Contra officially collapsed on the day after Thanksgiving 1986, and certainly the entrails of its fraud continued and still continue to this day.

It became apparent that these banks were failing and the very same individuals who were causing these banks to fail (by not repaying loans) were Jeb Bush and George Bush, Jr.

We can cite specific examples of oil and gas loans and real estate loans in which they were involved that were fraudulent to begin with — but in the so-called Double Scam, this was essentially an inside stock swindle.

I will use MCorp as an example, wherein a corporate artifice could be formed by Jeb Bush, let's say. Money could be borrowed from MCorp. The money would then be used to short (sell short, in other words) MCorp's stock.

When the stock plummeted, the shares would be bought back at a large profit, and the original loan itself would be defaulted on through the marginal, corporate entity that originally borrowed it, which most likely existed nowhere except in an attorney's file cabinet.

The money garnered from both the defaulted loan and the profit from the short sale of the stock would then be used for a variety of purposes: 1) for personal enrichment, and 2) for Republican donations.

I will give you a specific example of this, although it's a very small amount of money in comparison. In late 1987, it was obvious that MCorp was failing. MCorp common stock was trading at about three dollars a share.

Unfortunately, you could not get any shorts off. In security parlance, that means you could not sell any of the stock short, insofar as all the stock was out of the box, meaning that the market-makers in said stock did not have sufficient shares to cover shorts.

However, you could still sell short MCorp preferred stock, which was then trading at about eight and a half dollars a share. What I did (as a matter of fact, Jeb Bush introduced me to the loan with certain provisos about where parts of the proceeds were to go later on) is that I formed a separate shell known as Mar-Tech Industries. I borrowed $85,000 from M-Corp through Dean Witter. Through the accounts that Mar-Tech controlled at Dean Witter, I was able to short 10,000 shares of MCorp preferred at varying prices between $8 and $8.50.

Within three or four months, M-Corp preferred shares had fallen in value to $3.

I then covered my 10,000 shares between $3 and $3.50 a share, making approximately $50,000 profit.

I then proceeded to dissolve Mar-Tech and defaulted on the original $85,000 loan, after having made two interest payments.

I now had $135,000 in total profits, as you loosely describe $85,000 illicitly obtained from a fraudulent bank loan, or a bank loan that I obtained under fraudulent circumstances, plus $50,000 garnered through the short sale of said stock, essentially using the bank's own money to short the stock and then defaulting on the loan.

Others did this in much larger quantity than I ever did. I was just given these little trades because it got to the point you couldn't consolidate.

Jeb Bush was particularly concerned and I know that George, Jr. was concerned. I don't know that directly from George, Jr., but I do know in my discussions with Neil that his brothers were concerned about the congestion of corporate artifices borrowing money and shorting the stock.

Anyway, with $135,000, I was asked (and this was the original condition on which I was given the trade) to donate one-half of my proceeds. And I did proceed to donate some $65,000 dollars, which I have records of, to a variety of Republican-controlled election/political institutions.

This is similar to what we had done in 1985-86. Now we were using a different type of fraud — securities fraud, instead of the normal real estate, or oil and gas, or gold bullion, or aircraft brokerage fraud.

Anyway, I donated $20,000 to GOPAC from these proceeds in 1988. This was when Pete DuPont still controlled GOPAC, actually right on the cusp before Newt Gingrich controlled it.

And, as we have described before, GOPAC was an infamous Republican artifice for taking surreptitiously and ill-gotten monies and dividing them up amongst Republican candidates.

I also donated money to several 501c3 tax-exempt organizations, which had previously been formed by Jesse Helms and Oliver North and which Jesse Helms still controlled. These, of course, were illegally formed.

All of the money that went through them was illegally garnered. They were named The American Enterprise Foundation, The American Eagle Forum, The American Institute of Freedom.

Usually what happened with these monies is they wound up getting filtered into other Republican-controlled entities, such as the giant Heritage Foundation.

In some cases, they went back to the 1988 Reagan-Bush re-election campaign through The American Eagle Foundation.

The American Eagle Foundation was formed in 1984 for $10,000 contributors. That was the scheme that we had previously talked about wherein you've got your little membership card for $10,000 a year with a toll-free 1-800 number that rang into a cubicle in the White House basement. That was Oliver North's deal. He was the one who came up with the concept. He was the one that formed it. The girls who manned the phone were actually NSC secretaries, including, by the way, Fawn Hall.

Anyway, these three institutions were extensively investigated by the so-called Tower Commission in 1988, headed by Senator John Tower. The general counsel of the committee was Hayden Gregory. I knew Hayden quite well and he had asked me for certain materials that I had and I freely gave them to him.

Of course, it was like the fox guarding the hen house — John Tower being the leader of the old Texas Republican club investigating Texas institutions wherein Republican fraud had happened.

However, Hayden Gregory, the general counsel of said committee, had put together very hard-hitting reports about these three institutions and the whole nature of Iran-Contra Republican fraud and profiteering.

This was the report that was contained in that aluminum briefcase that John Tower was carrying with him when his plane crashed outside the airport in Brunswick, Georgia in 1988. And, of course, the metal briefcase in question was never recovered.

It's intriguing to note in this case that three hours after that crash happened, a so-called team of FAA inspectors arrived from Washington. It actually turned out to be and I have documentation regarding this incident that the FAA inspectors were actually gentlemen from the Department of Defense.

Anyway, that report was history.

There was only one other copy, and Hayden Gregory had it. Gregory was out of town, in New York at the time. Before he was even informed that Tower's plane had gone down and Tower had been killed, the one other complete copy of the report he had in his office mysteriously disappeared by the time he got back to his office the next day.

There were some excerpts, some portions of that report that survived, that John Tower's daughter, Penny, got her hands on and had begun to leak some of the stuff out to the *Atlanta Constitution*, more specifically, to Scott Shepherd.

That was very quickly stopped as Penny stopped leaking the material and disgorged possession of the material.

I have a copy of the mortgage for Penny's home.

The next day it was duly recorded in the Registry of Deeds of Norcross County, Georgia where she lived, that the $85,000 balance on the mortgage on her house had been paid in full, from an off-shore entity, a Netherlands Antilles corporation.

It was the Netherlands Antilles Corporation duly entitled the Tri-Lateral Investment Trust Group, Limited, with officers unknown.

Of course, during this time, both Walter Mischer and Bobby Corson had been deposed by said Tower Commission. Mischer didn't give up that much and invoked the Fifth Amendment — or said he didn't remember, a lot of the time. But Corson did give up a lot. He said far more than he should have.

Hayden Gregory, recognizing the sensitivity of it, immediately placed said deposition under seal.

Of course, this means absolutely nothing because it wasn't three hours later before the White House had a copy of it.

When Corson was subpoenaed subsequently by the Hughes Commission to be asked questions about his deposition regarding fraud at Texas American Bank of Commerce, he died of a sudden and convenient heart attack three days before he was to arrive in Washington to talk to Congressman Hughes.

Bobby Corson had maintained a file in the den of his own home, containing all the records and notes and such that, to wit, formed the foundation of his deposition before the Tower Commission.

His son, Bob, Jr., attempted to do the same thing that John Tower's daughter had done. That is, young Mr. Corson started to leak information to The *Houston Post*, mainly to Frank Bass.

After a few leaks, Mr. Corson, Jr., of course, being a loyal Republican and a member of the Texas State Republican Committee, duly disgorged the documents in exchange for which the next day there appeared a fifty-seven foot Chris Craft, in a marina, in the Bahia Mar Marina in Ft.

Lauderdale, with the title in his name, indicating that there were no encumbrances, liens or mortgages on said luxury yacht.

After some investigation by Mr. Dinnerstein, it was discovered that said yacht had been formerly a donation to the Charitable Educational Division of the World Anti-Communist League, then still controlled and still in existence by General John K. Singlaub.

I'd also like to interject at this point the infamous case of the Peruvian Gold Certificate Scam, engineered in 1988 by George Bush, Sr.

George, himself, was involved, and so was his counsel C. Boyden Gray. Helping in this fraud was George's personal friend and very loyal Republican scamskateer, then Nevada Secretary of State, Frankie Sue DelPapa.

Frankie, as a matter of fact, will probably be making a gubernatorial bid in Nevada, now that Bill Miller is out of the scene.

But this is the famous case of that Peruvian gold certificate which was one of the unusual gold certificates issued by the Trans-Continental Agreement between the United States and certain South American countries in 1875, wherein the United States Government agreed to support certain South American countries which were then in some financial difficulty, including Peru.

The United States Treasury issued a limited number of high-value gold certificates based on its own deposits. Simply put, these were were then hypothecated by South American central banks, which could then be used to borrow bullion against the U.S. Treasury.

Almost all of these certificates were redeemed in 1913 and 1914. However, one certificate was left outstanding, which it's believed was an oversight at the time. These certificates were compounded in perpetuity, that is, they had no limitation.

The interest was payable in gold and compounded in perpetuity. And the compounding of said gold payment was accrued at a fixed price of twenty dollars an ounce.

Now what happened, therefore, is that this one remaining certificate consequently became worth a fortune.

Although it had been technically listed as canceled by the United States Treasury after the expiration of the redemption period in 1914, George Bush was able to get a waiver (as he knew he would, given his position) a waiver from the U.S. Treasury, indicating that this was still a valid and negotiable instrument.

Bush knew if he could get his hands on this instrument, it would be worth a fortune to hypothecate, which is exactly what happened.

This certificate, through a long series of transactions, ultimately winds up in the hands of a retired Secret Service agent, Mr. Durham, who at one time, as a matter of fact, had worked with one of George Bush's Secret Service security details.

Through some underhandedness, Bush was able to garner control of this instrument through essentially out-and-out fraud committed by Frankie Sue DelPapa regarding a Nevada corporation, which had been formed by Mr. Durham and others to hold this certificate and the rights thereunto, called the Cosmos Investment Corporation.

DelPapa essentially switched all the officers and principals and directors of the Cosmos Corporation into another corporation that had been formed by George Bush and some others known as the Hellenic Investment Holding Group, Limited.

It was absolutely a blatant fraud.

Durham subsequently died. His widow tried to pound the drum on this thing for a long time, but couldn't get anywhere with it. Simply put, the mainstream media that had been interested in this thing considered it too old and too conspiratorial to touch.

But I have a lot of the documents. Dinnerstein got involved in this and he discovered what had happened.

It's interesting to note the route that this certificate takes once it gets in the hands of George Bush. It winds up getting hypothecated at both Sumitomo and Daiwa Banks in Tokyo. It is re-hypothecated at Jarlska Bank of Copenhagen. Re-hypothecated again through the Greek National Bank.

Papandreou was still in power. Papandreou and George Bush Sr. had been involved in many marginal business transactions involving the surreptitious hypothecation of gold bullion at the Bank of Greece through the Union Bank of Switzerland and Credit Lyonnais in France and Bank Paribas.

Of course, I was not directly involved in any transaction relating to this. I was subsequently asked — Dinnerstein and I — to become involved for a certain fee on the owner's behalf in this matter.

A separate book would have to be written about it, for it goes to the very heart of the great right-wing cabal — the way everything works and what it's all about. It exposes transactions that are decades old, transactions that were frauds in themselves.

You can see through the continuation of this deal a pattern where new fraud has to be committed to pay back old fraud and so on.

I think what frightened the mainstream media is the incredible sums of money that are involved. And ultimately, a Peruvian gold certificate turned out to be the seed or germination of a series of transactions that ultimately forced Daiwa and Sumitomo to create fictitious trading losses in order to cover losses incurred in a series of fraudulently obtained, politically related loans.

Anyway, this is simply so big. I would perhaps just briefly mention it, only because I have such precise detailing of it. But I would not attempt to connect the dots into the vortex of the way everything works and what it's really all about.

It's simply too big, and it would immediately be looked at as something conspiratorial, which, of course, has always been the Republican line in an effort to discredit anyone.

It was only in recent years, in 1995, that I was again retained by representatives of the original owner, or his widow, should I say, in an effort to negotiate with Bush or to see if they wanted to do anything about it insofar as they effectively absconded with said instrument.

So I talked to an attorney who had previously represented me in Miami, Neil Lewis, who is very closely aligned with Republican interests in Miami and is a personal friend of both Neil and Jeb Bush. I told Neil the circumstances. And he said, "Give me a couple of days and I'll get back to you."

And he did, in fact, talk to Neil Bush. After a few days, Neil Lewis got back to me and said that the Bushes feel that there are so many layers of protection between them and this transaction that nobody will ever be able to uncover it and they simply did not wish to deal.

So, that ended that, because it would obviously take enormous resources to fully uncover this fraud. And to actually challenge the perpetrators of the fraud would require resources certainly beyond that of the average individual.

In front of me, I have a banker's box loaded with original lists of all of the clients of Richard Hamil's Gulf Coast Investment Group and all of the sub-clients of Southeast Resources, Inc., which was my own company at the time. It has totals of all of the monies "invested" in fraudulent limited partnerships, both oil and gas, real estate and others, along with the disposition of those sums, including certain sums that were paid to GOPAC, and in some cases, certain sums that were paid through another corporate artifice directly to candidates — $20,000 to then-Republican Governor Martha Lane Collins of Kentucky 1986 re-election campaign,

$20,000 in cash to one of then-Republican Governor Thompson's of Illinois election people.

I have details of when the money was given and things of that nature, although it would be unusual for money to be given directly.

Normally, the money, as I said, was given to GOPAC. It was given to some Republican-controlled, illegal, tax exempt artifices, or in other cases, monies directly from the accounts of Southeast Resources were simply wired to the Costa Rican corporation of Intercontinental Industries SA, which maintained a bank account at the Banco de Popular in Santo Domingo.

This was an account controlled by Oliver North and Richard Secord and was one of the principal accounts that was used for the laundering and garnering of illicitly gotten monies through illegal transactions supposedly in support of the Nicaraguan Contras.

I would mention another $20,000 in cash donation to the 1986 failed re-election bid of Paula Hawkins in Florida. Hawkins was essentially forced out of office under Iran-Contra connected scandals.

Further in this box is substantial documentation regarding our transactions with Swissco Management Group of Miami controlled by the infamous Carlos Cardoen. It detailed his extensive illegal property transactions between Senator Robert Graham in an illicit, illegal, surreptitious tax-exempt foundation, then controlled by Swissco Management.

Swissco Management's offices were raided in 1992 by the FBI. Carlos Cardoen, despite being under indictment by the United States for Iran-Contra arms trafficking, still lives comfortably in his home base in Chile.

When there were some Congressional demands for this material, particularly of what remained of the Alexander probe (Congressman Charlie Rose and the Government Affairs Sub-committee had demanded some of this documentation), it was discovered that the Miami field office of the FBI had inadvertently mislaid the documents that it had seized.

I also see some documents in the bottom of the box on the Sooner Defense case.

I think it was terrible that the Bushes attempted to lay blame for certain fraud committed by the Sooner Defense Corporation onto the shoulders of one of its directors (whom I personally liked), the renowned retired four-star general, Wallace Nutting.

That was the Nutting Case in Tampa involving the Egyptian general and the Egyptian colonel. It was a fairly well covered case.

Nutting got out of it, though, when sufficient documents were garnered to prove certain other involvements in said fraud involving Mischer, George Bush Jr., Jeb Bush and others.

I would like to make note of a 1988 letter I have in my position sent from then-Secretary of Defense Dick Cheney to then Attorney General Richard Thornburgh wherein the Secretary of Defense asks the Attorney General to stop an investigation of Loral Industries and E-Systems.

Both are major defense contractors in Texas. Both are publicly traded corporations in which the Bush family has substantial interests.

This investigation had been started by the Attorney General's office under allegations of Iran-Contra weapons-diversion programs involving both corporations.

Loral and E-Systems (E-Systems in particular) have had a long affiliation with the CIA over the years. There was a 60 *Minutes* piece done in 1993. 60 *Minutes* had contacted me about information on the piece concerning an aircraft diversion scheme instituted by E- Systems. Actually it was instituted by the CIA, but E-Systems had an involvement in it.

Next to the E-Systems properties was a little tiny corporation with some hangars, known as CZX Productions, Ltd.

60 *Minutes* didn't even know what CZX stood for, by the way. This is a scandal where the CZX affair had been worked on extensively by one of the best Democratic Congressional investigators, Tom Strzemienski.

This was during the time when Tom worked for the Government Affairs Sub-Committee, which Charlie Rose, Democrat of North Carolina, had chaired at one time.

CZX, by the way, stands for Casey, Zumwalt, X Files, and it is one of the deepest, darkest, most sinister and treacherous of all Iran-Contra operations.

Some of it has been made public. This was not only a diversion of weapons, but an artifice in which the names of problem people — people who knew too much — were kept. It also involves a related operation, a cover-up operation ongoing at the time by the Office of Naval Intelligence, this operation being handled by the infamous, sinister, dreaded, and powerful Vice Admiral Lawrence Pauley.

It also involved Admiral Henderson, Admiral Garrett and others. Garrett later became Secretary of the Navy.

Anytime that anyone has ever tried to press this issue, you see the powerful reaction and the resources that are garnered to push them back, particularly through the Office of Naval Intelligence.

When I mentioned and got involved in CZX because I happened to have some material which I obtained through working on something else with Steven Dinnerstein (although I was aware of CZX at the time), it really didn't have anything to do with me.

I just happened to have some information on it. Admiral Pauley apparently was distressed enough to come to Miami and engage in a quiet meeting with certain parties regarding me. There was that level of concern.

And certainly after this time, things went worse for me. I was further discommoded. Let's put it that way. They sent me a signal to stay out of it.

But CZX Productions (and I will mention this in the book) — about a dozen people died because of it.

And to keep it quiet, I would guess, a dozen more are wrongfully incarcerated because of it. "Wrongfully incarcerated" means they are incarcerated much less for anything they did and much more for something they knew.

Chief among those wrongfully incarcerated is Ed Wilson — the infamous Ed Wilson. His former partners, Frank Terpil and Richard Secord, made out pretty well because they knew enough to keep their mouths shut about it.

But what broke this thing was when suddenly six C130 Hercules transport aircraft (formerly belonging to the United States government) wind up on a satellite photograph taken over Lybia.

It relates back to the Sooner Defense case, as Sooner was used as a transit artifice because of Sooner's connections with the South African government. The connection is made through this Egyptian army colonel and general who came to the United States. They wind up getting themselves indicted. Anyway, this is a whole separate story.

As always, we get the problem, how in the hell do you condense all this in what's going to be a manuscript of a reasonable length?

I have so much material, and I've never really organized it all because it's such a job. And I've never really had to organize it all until now. And I am digressing certainly from Iran-Contra fraud.

But I did want to mention more covert operations, more covert entities and connections. I do intend to spend some time on what I feel has been an overlooked part of Iran-Contra in terms of illegal, covert operations, and that is the involvement of the Office of Naval Intelligence, principally through one of its cut-outs — the infamous Evergreen Airlines, which was used in the so-called Iran-Contra Guns-for-Drugs Program.

Evergreen Airlines principally flew in the western corridor. Its home base was in Medford, Oregon and related to this, I will also mention the case of the Wa-Chang Trading Company scandal of Albany, Oregon.

That was the so-called Zirconian Scandal which involved Dick Brenneke. He was up to his ears in it. And it involved the infamous Roy Reagan of Hammit Valley Aviation.

Hammit Valley Aviation had formerly been a proprietary cut-out of the CIA. This includes my knowledge of it at the time of my involvement (1984-86) and my subsequent knowledge of it.

I have subsequent knowledge of it because often people who got hurt came to me and/or Steven Dinnerstein to get involved for a fee in helping them get some redress which would garner further details on something I already knew something about.

Anyway, Evergreen was ultimately thrown into bankruptcy and there was a bankruptcy-related civil fraud case against Evergreen which reveals a lot of information that one of my old cohorts, Major Gary Atel filed.

Atel is probably the leading expert, not only Evergreen Airlines, but the ONI/CIA connection as it relates to Iran-Contra, which has always been a very sensitive connection.

Atel had asked me for certain information regarding Hammit Valley Aviation that I gave him.

The only reason I had it was because of Richard Secord. Secord had been so heavily involved with Hammit Valley and he personally knew Roy Reagan.

Consequently, I had some copies of letters between Secord and Reagan (Regan is how you pronounce his name.)

Also, I would like to get this down as a matter of record. I intend to publicly reveal for the first time all that I knew about Eugene Hasenfus and the circumstances surrounding the shooting down of his aircraft, something I have never done before.

Of course, I know much more about Hasenfus than Hasenfus does, especially what Hasenfus was involved in. So does practically everybody else.

What Gene Hasenfus didn't realize is that when the Soviets made him an offer of a million dollars to defect, when he was sitting in that jail in Managua, it occurred to him that the only thing he had ever done was kick stuff out of the back of airplanes.

So why was the Soviet government prepared to offer him a million dollars to defect and prepared to get his wife, Sally, and his then three children out of the United States quietly?

What Gene didn't realize was that he was going to get used not only for propaganda, which he suspected, but as a pawn, or a chip, in a much larger geo-political game at the time.

Everyone seems to forget the timing of this.

Look at the timing when his aircraft was shot down.

Look at the timing of the Reykjavik summit in 1986.

Look at the allegations that Gorbachev was making. He was licking his chops at being able to ram CIA narcotics trafficking down Reagan's throat

That's why they wanted Hasenfus so desperately — to back up information that had been received by the KGB's Washington Station at their embassy.

My old pal, Major Yuri Shvets, who wrote the book *Washington Station* was muzzled to a huge degree about writing this. He only mentions a little bit about what Gorbachev had said at the summit regarding CIA narcotics traffic and Reagan's response about laughing and saying, "Oh, yes. We've been doing that for years."

But the KGB knew that they had some steak.

The documents are the steak, but they needed sizzle. And Hasenfus would have been that sizzle. A living, warm, breathing body standing up and saying, "This is what we were doing. And these are who my superiors are."

That's why they were so desperate to get him. It was unknown to Hasenfus.

He will never have any idea of the desperate measures undertaken by Casey, North, Elliott Abrams and others to get him out of that jail in Managua and back in the United States.

I will reveal some of the desperation of those measures. But, again, this is a subject matter I think more fitting for a whole separate book.

Elliott Abrams tried to act cool after Gene went down and Sally, Hasenfus's wife, had called Elliott Abrams and Elliot gave her $10,000 in a paper bag. This would later come back to haunt Gene, when he attempted to proceed with that civil suit against Southern Air Transport et al. in 1990.

But Hasenfus and his wife and others of his defense counsel, and the defense counsels of Cooper and Sawyer in that trial have no idea of what went on, the desperate measures behind the scene, the people that died because of it, and the documents that were shredded because of it.

But I will reveal some of this. Not all. I don't think it's wise to reveal all, nor do I have the space to do it.

After Hasenfus was shot down, in that two or three week subsequent time period, it had been assumed (of course, I knew differently even at the time) that the earnest measures taken by North and others, Casey and the panoply of people that were involved in Iran-Contra (Assistant Secretary of State, Bernie Aronson and then under-Secretary of State, Larry Eagleburger, Assistant Secretary of State, Richard Armitage — the whole cabal), that the reason they wanted to get Hasenfus back so badly was because he potentially threatened to reveal the entire Guns for Drugs Operation a little earlier than they wanted it revealed.

They knew it was going to get revealed anyway. But they wanted time. They needed another nine months or so to institute a good tight cover-up of it.

That wasn't the real reason such desperate measures were taken. The desperate measures were taken, not because of what he might say to the press in Managua or any other international press, but to keep him out of the hands of the Russians and to prevent him from winding up in a press conference in Moscow.

That's why such desperate measures were undertaken.

As we've discussed it, I feel sorry for Gene, but when he got back, he was naive and thought that he was part of the team and that's what he was told.

Elliot Abrams said, "We'll take care of you. And monies owed you will be paid."

That was all a lot of horse shit.

Gene should have known it. And ever since, Gene has essentially misplayed his hand. And the reason he's misplayed his hand is his timing. He has not revealed things when they should have been revealed. He's withheld information when it should not have been withheld. And the reason this is the case, by the way, is because Gene never had an understanding of the bigger picture in which he had suddenly become thrust.

If he had an idea of the bigger picture, and if he had the brains to handle things differently, he would not wind up being now a member of the Iran-Contra fucked, refucked and double-fucked.

Another connection, or crossover connection, when we cross over from weapons, narcotics and fraud, I am going to discuss is my knowledge of something that has not been written about publicly.

That is the deep old Brazilian connection into George, Sr. and others — a very deep and very dark connection of which very little has been mentioned. Only once publicly to my knowledge, in an article in The

Wall Street Journal, has George Bush, Sr.'s connection ever been mentioned to a very sinister and very wealthy Brazilian financier named Amaro Pintos Ramos.

Some of what I know involves the illicit transfer, not only of weapons, but also of nuclear materials.

I imagine that's one reason that nobody has ever wanted to to look at this. It involves a large amount of fraud. All types of fraud. Oil and gas, bank and securities fraud. Everything.

It also involves the illicit sale or attempted illicit sale of nuclear materials out of Brazil and certain transactions that — not only was the Agency involved in — but George Bush himself was involved in.

And I don't think anybody has ever wanted to link George Bush — although linking him to Iran-Contra fraud, knowledge and profiting from cocaine and weapons transactions — I don't think anyone has ever wanted to link him to the transfer of certain nuclear materials and components.

But that is something that I intend to do.

Further, I intend to reveal the connection between George, Sr. and Jeb, and these Brazilian transactions through the International Signals and Controls, Inc. of Scranton, Pennsylvania.

This was the infamous story with Mischer, Gerwin and Jacobson.

There was another corporation in Virginia which was a cut-out, not International Signals and Controls, but International Systems and Components. Separate. A different company altogether. They have often been mixed up.

But I will explain the difference and how certain materials left this country and went elsewhere.

Anyway, let's get back to Iran-Contra fraud. I had intimated previously that I would like to spend more time on Prescott Bush, the Vice President and later President's brother, and Wally, his son and their Iran-Contra fraud.

So I will use the one example with which I am most familiar, an example that has been, to some degree, publicly revealed.

That is Prescott Bush's so-called $5 million Korean Swindle, which involved his partner, Alphonse D'Amato's brother, the attorney.

That fraud, although small, is a good example of how Prescott used the family name to commit his own little series of petty fraud. During Iran-Contra, it didn't amount to much — $20 or $30 million.

Wally's ability to commit certain securities fraud, particularly at

Merrill Lynch, and get away with it was due to the control feature that existed at Merrill Lynch. Even after Don Regan left to become Chief of Staff in the Reagan Administration, Ray Birk was his successor, and Ray was very friendly to the old Republican cabal. He was also very sympathetic to Iran-Contra.

Consequently, Merrill Lynch was used for certain illicit transactions. And this so-called $5 million Korean swindle is a good example of that, of the use of power to cover up something.

What makes it more sinister is the fact that somebody was murdered because of the swindle.

Yes, the money was ultimately returned, but that wasn't until after somebody in Korea threatened to start to talk.

And someone in this side of the world got murdered because of it. As you may remember, that murder got pinned temporarily on D'Amato's brother.

And D'Amato was facing a twenty-five year to life sentence.

Through a series of missing evidence and forgetful witnesses, he winds up spending three months in jail.

Prescott specialized in Korean and Japanese fraud because of the old Republican connections that existed between the Japanese conservative and Korean and Republican parties here.

I'm going to make a blind reference and use Prescott Bush to get into it — why it was always necessary to have a Republican control guy as ambassador to both Japan and Korea.

You see how quickly (after Donald Gregg was essentially forced out of his position as Vice Presidential National Security Advisor because of Iran-Contra allegations) he ultimately winds up becoming Ambassador to South Korea.

There's no mystery as to why that happens. It really has only been in recent years that that whole money connection between Korea and the Republicans here fell apart.

And I believe the former Korean President, General Ro Tae Woo is under a death sentence. Of course, it will be commuted. But there are hundreds of millions of dollars missing from the Korean Treasury because of it, which mysteriously wound up in Republican coffers here.

Anyway, I will try to condense that into what I intend to say about Prescott and Wally. I also want to make note of my knowledge of the Republican and Democratic party crossovers into certain transactions and to certain artifices, particularly some large foreign banks. The

Industrial Bank of Indonesia, for instance. The Hong Kong and Shanghai Bank, their branch in Hong Kong.

And of course, I will bring in the whole Arkansas matter, and I will build the bridge. As I've always said, Arkansas is where political liability vis-a-vis Iran-Contra crosses party lines. And I intend to show that bridge, both in context of narcotics, weapons, and money transactions.

Next I am going to build that bridge into Republican/Democratic political liability crossovers in Arkansas, vis-a-vis Arkansas-related Iran-Contra weapons, narcotics, and monies operations.

I will talk about my knowledge of Governor Bill Clinton, Betsey Wright, Bruce Lindsey, Buddy Young, Patsy Thomasson, Dan Lasater, Web Hubbell, Hillary and Rose and Hubbell Law Firm, and Stephens Investment Group.

I did a lot of business with Stephens. I did business with Lasater. I was familiar with what was going on at the time.

I have extensive 1985 tape recordings of gubernatorial aides, Bruce Lindsey and Betsey Wright discussing Oliver North's operations in Arkansas.

They can't say that they didn't know about them — and their efforts to manipulate the Arkansas State Police on behalf of the Republicans.

And we will discuss, of course, my knowledge of then U.S. Attorney, Asa Hutchinson, Republican U.S. Attorney in Little Rock, and the cover-up that was instituted by them and the Little Rock Office of the FBI, vis-a-vis Iran-Contra operations.

We'll talk about everything in Arkansas from Barry Seal to Max Mermelstein and their connections. "Fat Max" Mermelstein is certainly an overlooked connection in Arkansas.

But although the focus of this book is principally Republican in nature (it has to be because that's what was going on when I was involved), I would also like to mention the Democratic crossover.

Some people may consider this news old, but I would like to draw the entrails to this day. How some mysterious deaths on the Democrat side of the ledger are directly related to the entrails of Iran-Contra operations.

This would be a good point in the book to show that certain things that happen today had their genesis in Iran-Contra activity in the mid-1980s and that certain entrails of that activity are still ongoing to this day.

In this Democratic/Republican liability crossover, using Arkansas would be an excellent way to portray the relevance of said information

115

today. How people are still dying because of this information. How people are still being incarcerated because of this information in an effort to discredit them.

I will also mention here the extent of my knowledge insofar as I was involved with so many, both Republican and Democratically controlled investigating committees, in the 1987 to 1996 time frame.

Also to use several illustrations where Republican-controlled committees were dying to get into Arkansas and use Iran-Contra activities in Arkansas against Clinton and others, but could not do so because they could not gerrymander out Republican liability and, therefore, they couldn't use it.

I have a tape-recording of a very interesting conversation I had with Bob Dole's campaign manager about this subject in the last Presidential campaign.

You can easily see the Republican reaction in attempting to use this kind of information.

I also wanted to mention that I have been assembling a condensed compendium of Israeli involvement in Iran-Contra, principally centering around my knowledge of the activities of the infamous Michael Harari with subsections about Ari Klein.

It would be principally about Harari and certain meetings Harari had with both Oliver North and Manuel Noriega, and even one meeting with George Bush himself and Assistant Secretary of State Elliott Abrams, and then-Deputy Assistant Secretary of State Michael Kozak.

These are detailed transcripts of meetings involving the Panamanian G2 and security for narcotics shipments and weapons trans-shipments through the South African corridor which Harari arranged.

I'm going to mention a little bit about the US/South African/Israeli connection into Iran-Contra and how that worked through South African military intelligence which was then under the command of General Magnus Milan.

But I'm not going to dwell on this because — *where does it all stop?*

I do want to mention an important weapons and narcotics channel, so you can clearly see the involvement of the Israelis in Iran-Contra, which I think has been much overlooked.

People talk about Israeli involvement in Iraqgate, but there was substantial involvement, not only through Michael Harari, but others and even the influence of the great Rafi Eitan, himself, during Iran-Contra and how this related to the liquidation of Amir Nir and others.

It's important to show the relationships and to show that a lot of people died to cover this thing up and to cover up the knowledge of this relationship.

Essentially it was to cover up Michael Harari's activities.

I'm also going to reveal for the first time much more extensive knowledge than what people have commonly presumed about Amiram Nir, in terms of that July 29, 1986 meeting at the King David Hotel in Jerusalem, which George Bush attended and how that sealed Nir's fate.

Also to be discussed will be how Nir's wife, who is an American, was treated by Israeli intelligence after Nir's death.

THE CONSPIRATORS

Chapter 9

CORPORATE FRAUD, STOCK FRAUD AND OTHER SCAMS

S O FAR, WE HAVE ATTEMPTED to illustrate Iran-Contra vis-a-vis the breakdown of three specific areas — namely, narcotics, weapons and fraud. Returning to fraud, we will examine individual transactions and individual companies, as they related to the overall pattern, an organized pattern, of State-sponsored fraud under the guise of what is now known as Iran-Contra.

The first deal I would like to speak about is the infamous Trinity Oil and Gas Corporation, founded in 1984 by Barry Seal, Lawrence Richard Hamil and Larry Nichols.

Trinity Oil and Gas was designed to be a fraud similar to all other oil and gas frauds at that time.

Not unlike Jeb Bush's Gulf Oil Drilling Supply Company.

Not unlike Larry Hamil's Gulf Coast Investment Group and LRH Associates, etc.

We will examine what these frauds had in common, how these frauds related to each other, and ultimately where the money went.

Trinity Oil and Gas was perhaps a little different. Its purpose was perhaps a little different. It was not only designed simply to be a fraud, but also as a vehicle to launder Barry Seal's money — money that Barry Seal was earning from his narcotics activity.

Barry Seal, of course, has been extensively discussed in public before, but usually only in the context of narcotics. His involvement corporate-wise, or in fraud, is really an overlooked area.

Anyway, Trinity Oil and Gas — to get its base of operations, similar to Gulf Coast Investment Group — purchased a bunch of old, beat out, one-barrel-a-day pumpers, two-barrels-a-day pumpers.

These were principally in the sand tar pits outside of Bartlesville, Oklahoma.

Most of the assets that Trinity Oil and Gas started with to construct the fraud were assets that it had purchased from the old Sterling Oil of Oklahoma and the old Lyric Energy of Oklahoma, both which had been publicly traded companies on the NASDAQ prior to this time and had unfortunately busted out with the decline in oil prices in the early 1980s.

Again, the scheme was similar.

You take the one or two-barrel-a-day, fifty-year-old pumpers that are given a shot of acid every three months, and you make it appear that they're pumping four hundred to eight hundred barrels a day.

Of course, how you make that appear is by your runs and logs. In this case, Hamil, once again, turned to Hess Oil, a division of Marathon Oil, then owned by Armand Hammer.

We have discussed before how Armand Hammer allowed certain divisions — oil and gas divisions, suppliers, distributors — that he owned to be used to commit fraud.

I guess, you could say this was his contribution to Iran-Contra and to Republican sources.

Anyway, as they had done with Gulf Coast Investment Group and with Gulf Oil and Drilling Supply Company, Hess had given false runs and logs, making it appear that in fact Trinity Oil was pumping five hundred times the oil that it was actually pumping.

And one would say, "Where are the cash deposits? Where is the cash flowing through Trinity Oil and Gas accounts to match this supposed oil production?"

Of course, where it was coming from initially was Barry Seal.

Barry Seal was simply using this as a device to launder money.

After July-August 1984, Trinity Oil and Gas, under the auspices of Larry Hamil, became something larger, a newer entity, and an entity to actually defraud people.

As we have said before, we're using the term "defraud" loosely.

Actually people invested in Trinity Oil and Gas Limited Partnerships, who wanted to contribute to "The Cause" as Oliver North referred to Iran-Contra.

But obviously a private citizen could not simply contribute to an illegal activity of government, ergo another artifice steps in, namely Trinity Oil and Gas.

Monies are siphoned off accordingly. It was very similar to the way monies were siphoned out of Gulf Coast Investment Group and Gulf Coast Oil and Drilling Supply.

You would notice that all three of these companies tended to use either Hess or Marathon as their pickup agents in the field.

They also tended to use the infamous Orca Supply Company of Coral Gables, Florida, supposedly to purchase oil well equipment.

Orca Supply Company was a CIA cut-out that had been dormant. It was picked up again and was run through the Iran-Contra period by the infamous Lt. Col. Jack Terrell, aka "El Flaco."

What was different about Trinity Oil is that it is one of the very few Iran-Contra deals one can point to wherein money was siphoned off in both directions, politically speaking.

Not only did money go to Republicans, but it also went to Democrats in the State of Arkansas.

Trinity Oil and Gas is an excellent example to illustrate how important the State of Arkansas was (and the Democratic substructure in Arkansas was) to overall Iran-Contra operations.

For instance, Trinity Oil and Gas was legally formed and its general counsels were the Little Rock Law Firm of Rose and Hubbel. As a matter of fact, it was one of Web Hubbel's own accounts wherein he was counsel.

You will see that others within the Board of Directors of Trinity Oil are Dan Lasater and Raymond "Buddy" Young. Invoices, by the way, would be faked to make it appear that Trinity Oil and Gas was actually purchasing materials from the infamous Brodex Manufacturing and Global Associates.

Certainly, we remember these artifices from the past. Freddie Lee Hampton, Calvin Edwards, George Rebb — all of the Mena players.

Also, what should be mentioned — and I think it's very unique to Trinity Oil and Gas was its relationship with Seth Ward of Ward Manufacturing.

Same old scheme. Faked invoices for materials that were supposedly purchased, that were in fact never manufactured or delivered.

Brodex Manufacturing, Global Associates, Ward Manufacturing and so forth were receiving $20,000 - $40,000 a month. That type of thing. It was essentially money being bled out of Trinity Oil and Gas.

Of course, records subsequently revealed that Trinity Oil and Gas was making substantial contributions to GOPAC, as well as to individual Republicans. It had also made contributions to the Democratic State Party Committee in Arkansas.

Regarding Trinity Oil and Gas, there was Jeb Bush's involvement with it *vis-a-vis* his own oil and gas fraud, the Gulf Oil Drilling Supply Company.

Trinity Oil and Gas purchased Argentine and Brazilian oil and gas leases for about $30,000 or $40,000 per lease from Gulf Oil Drilling Supply.

Of course, these leases were effectively worthless.

Gulf Oil Drilling Supply obtained these leases originally from Zapata. They bought these leases for a dollar each from Bush-controlled Zapata Oil, which had held these leases for some time. But they were tantamount to worthless.

Suddenly these leases are effectively given from father to son and they wind up in the hands of the Jeb Bush-controlled Gulf Oil Drilling Supply Company.

Gulf Oil Drilling Supply Company hypothecated these leases, borrowed money from these leases with numerous Iran-Contra friendly banks in the Miami area, principally Capitol Bank.

Later they would default on these loans, and when Brazilian authorities got word that these leased areas were being used for fraudulent purposes in the United States, Brazilian authorities mounted an investigation.

It was a half-assed investigation, but it was enough for Jeb Bush to disgorge. He didn't want anything more to do with these leases, so consequently he sold them to Trinity Oil and Gas, which again made the same claims that Gulf Oil Drilling Supply Company had previously made. They said that these leases were, of course, fabulously valuable, when in fact, they were tantamount to worthless.

To further illustrate the Arkansas connection to Trinity Oil and Gas, it should be noted that the general counsels with the law firm of Rose and Hubbel — their bank was another infamous Arkansas Iran-Contra bank, Twin Cities Bank of North Little Rock, Arkansas.

The officer there, later a director of the bank who handled the account, was the infamous Jonathan Flake. Flake was the one who helped Seal and Hamil put together limited partnerships and syndications, while the bank provided bridge loans.

Also, in general partnerships of oil production, proved up production (which they didn't have, but they simply made it appear that they had), interests were sold by, of all people, Dan Lasater.

Flake, by the way, was an officer and director of Twin Cities Bank of North Little Rock — a key figure in Iran-Contra fraud in Arkansas.

Flake was involved in numerous oil and gas scams and bogus real estate limited partnerships that the bank also marketed and/or financed. He was also involved with numerous U.S. congressmen.

In all of these bogus oil and gas deals or bogus real estate deals that Congressman Alexander, Congressman Solarz, Congressman Dellums and others got hurt, the common factor is Twin Cities Bank of North Little Rock Arkansas and its senior loan officer and later director, Jonathan Flake.

A precise example of Flake's involvement would be that Twin Cities Bank of North Little Rock was both a submarketer through its securities division as well as a financier in terms of holding non-recourse and fully recourse paper on bogus limited partnerships.

However, Flake was directly involved in the marketing and subsequently financing of the fraudulent real estate investment trust known as the Boulder Property Limited Series of Partnerships.

It was through these partnerships that Congressman Alexander lost about $3 million. Now Alexander didn't actually lose the $3 million. He didn't have it to lose. But he was forced to default on the debt and forced to declare personal bankruptcy because of it.

Later we will again touch on Twin Cities Bank of North Little Rock, Arkansas, and see how that bank is a key element in the so-called Denver Daisy Chain.

Through this bank, it can be seen that Neil Bush was a substantially larger Iran-Contra fraud and Iran-Contra profiteering player than the public has been led to believe because there is a direct connection between Silverado and Twin Cities Bank of North Little Rock.

That connection exists through Phil Winn of the Winn Group in Denver and his partners Leonard Millman and Steve Mizel, as well as Millman's company, MDC Holdings, a publicly listed company and its then brokerage subsidiary, the National Brokerage Group.

These are all infamous Iran-Contra artifices, but we are going to explore in the Denver Daisy Chain and make the connection between the Denver frauds and how that filters through Arkansas. This is an area which has not been extensively researched in the past.

Moving on to the infamous Gulf Oil Drilling Supply Company — this was Jeb Bush's favorite oil and gas fraudulent artifice. Many of these Iran-Contra frauds would borrow names from large existing well-known corporations, such as "Gulf."

You will see in virtually every oil and gas fraud in Iran-Contra the word "Gulf" is used.

However, it is commonly and correctly presumed that the word "Gulf," as in Gulf Coast Investment Group and its subsidiaries refers to the southeastern United States region, meaning "Gulf," which is the common presumption.

In the case of Gulf Oil Drilling Supply — Jeb Bush's deal — it referred to the Arabian Gulf. This is not commonly known publicly, but it really should be.

It's rather obvious when one looks where Gulf Oil Drilling Supply Company supposedly did business.

Its principal foreign office was in Bahrain, which was headed by, of course, Richard Secord.

Gulf Oil Drilling Supply of Miami, New York and Bahrain was, I believe, a more sizeable fraud than has been publicly thought in the past.

When one adds up total losses taken by banks and security houses, it is in the $300-$400 million range, so it is what I would consider to be a medium to larger size fraud.

The fraud was rather simple.

Richard Secord arranged through then Vice President George Bush Sr.'s old friend, Ghaith Pharaon, the then retired head of Saudi intelligence, for Gulf Oil and Drilling to purchase from the Saudi government oil and gas leases in the Gulf which were effectively worthless.

As you know, most Gulf Oil production is onshore and not offshore.

The reason is that it is very expensive to extract offshore.

And, of course, these leases would be dummied up, then prettied up to make them look like they were just worth a goddamn fortune.

The leases again would be hypothecated or borrowed against in some other fashion, again, through Intercontinental Bank or Great American Bank and Trust of West Palm Beach, which subsequently failed under the weight of unpaid Iran-Contra loans.

Marvin Warner was the chairman of that bank.

Also, in the case of Gulf Oil Drilling Supply, there was some moderately large international lending to that company. As you would suspect, it was principally out of the old George Bush friendly banks — Credit Lyonnais and Banque Paribas, which, combined lent $60 million dollars to Gulf Oil Drilling Supply, which, of course was defaulted on later.

It has always been my personal opinion that the reason the Kerry Committee, the Hughes Committee, the Alexander Committee, and other Iran-Contra investigating committees on the Hill as well as some people in the media shied away from Gulf Oil Drilling Supply (and why there is so little known about it publicly) is because it directly relates to the great conundrum.

The minute it is seen that Gulf Oil Drilling Supply had relationships with Credit Lyonnais, Banque Paribas and others — that puts it in a whole different much higher realm.

The old George Bush connections of deep old fraud is something that everyone in the media and on the Hill is frightened of because — if you started with Gulf Oil Drilling Supply and investigated it to its logical conclusion, you get into that whole bigger picture where there is multi-billion dollar fraud — something no one really wants to look at.

And Gulf Oil Drilling Supply is very difficult to segregate, to look at it as one individual company, or one individual fraud, or a series of frauds because it's really much more than that — and it taps into a much larger pre-existing fraud.

However, I would certainly recommend that it be pursued, since I have substantial information about Gulf Oil Drilling Supply (I did business with them and with the Orca Supply Company).

In some cases, I repackaged the worthless leases into other partnership deals. But I do have substantial information about it.

There is a lot more information available about Gulf Oil Drilling Supply than is commonly presumed, because when Iran-Contra unraveled the day after Thanksgiving 1986, there was a big effort to classify documents concerning Gulf Oil Drilling Supply.

There wasn't any effort made to hide them under correct analysis that no one would want to get into the deal and really pick it apart for fear of that big bugaboo — for fear of getting into the bigger picture of the deep old frauds.

It should also be noted that Gulf Oil Drilling Supply also retained banking relationships with the Bank of Greece, Union Bank of Switzerland, and Jarlska Bank of Copenhagen.

One need only look at who was on the Board of Advisers of Gulf Oil Drilling Supply to see what the fraud was all about — essentially the old cast of characters.

Ghaith Pharaon was on the Board of Advisers.

Andre Papandreou, the former Prime Minister of Greece, was on the Board of Directors.

Marcel Dassault, Jr., the old man's son, was on the Board of Advisers.

And, of course, we see these names again and again in Iran-Contra frauds as these names surfaced ten and twenty years earlier in other type of Bush-orchestrated frauds.

To get back to Trinity Oil and Gas — I wanted to mention something that's been completely overlooked. Trinity Oil and Gas was a publicly listed company for a short period of time on the pink sheets.

It was a deal that was done in part through Meyer Blinder (Blinder Robinson Securities in Denver) as well as Atlantic Securities, Balfour McClain Securities, Singer Island Securities.

All of these companies had the same ownership through the National Brokerage Group of Denver.

Trinity Oil and Gas was backed into a shell which was then pumped up. The stock traded as high as a dollar before the deal collapsed.

But returning to Trinity Oil and Gas – it's a good example of what I would list as a pass-through fraud, that is, a nuts and bolts fraud.

The company is started as a fraud to legitimize flow of funds from Iran-Contra sympathizers to the hands of Oliver North and Richard Secord and others. Then it would pass into the hands of the political parties and the various members of the Bush family who had financial interest in Trinity Oil and Gas vis-a-vis the connection between Trinity and their own corporations.

What I mean by "pass-through" is not only was the oil-and-gas part of it a fraud (to defraud banks and securities firms), but you then back it into a public shell — start it out at three or four cents a share and pump it up to a dollar.

That is simply another way to exploit the fraud.

We have taken an oil and gas fraud, moved it into a banking fraud, then into a securities fraud. It's called squeezing every last penny of fraud out of the initial fraud, which is not directed toward anything else.

In the Florida connections (during 1983 to 1986) I was friendly with Charlie Harper, then the SEC Commissioner from Miami.

I used to see Charlie. Charlie used to go to a lot of Republican functions. Charlie was also a team player, and when I mentioned the Trinity Oil and Gas, and Gulf Oil Drilling Supply, Charlie said that those were on his "red flag" list — personally provided to him from his superiors in Washington. These were deals that he was not to look at or investigate.

Subsequently, in my 1987 testimony before the Kerry Committee, I had mentioned this to Jeff Goldberg, then Counsel for John Kerry's office, and they approached Harper.

Harper immediately denied that such a list existed, and three weeks later, of course, Charlie was promoted to Regional SEC Commissioner in Atlanta.

Of course, at this time, Mr. Harper was also unable to explain where the money had come from for him to purchase a $350,000 vacation home in the out islands and where the money had come from for his sailboat and his Cessna 210 airplane.

He had always claimed that he was an honest public servant, living on his salary of $68,932 a year.

It should further be noted that when the Kerry Committee attempted to ask then-Florida State Controller, Gerald Lewis (the cousin, by the way, of the infamous Marvin Warner) and later subpoena him as to why he had not investigated certain security transactions and businesses ongoing in Florida such as the Gulf Coast Investment Group, Trinity Oil and Gas, and the Gulf Oil Drilling Supply Company, the comptroller promptly resigned his position and elected to take an extended vacation in his luxury Caribbean home, which he purchased for the equivalent of ten years his public salary.

Chapter 10

THE TRILATERAL INVESTMENT GROUP FRAUD

I'D LIKE TO DISCUSS another infamous Iran-Contra cut-out — the Tri-Lateral Investment Group, Ltd. This was another offshore corporation formed early in 1984 by Larry Hamil which included, as either its officers, principals, or directors, Richard Secord, Oliver North, Jeb Bush, Gen. Aderholt, and the infamous, sinister and dreaded Col. Robert Steele.

Steele, by the way, now runs a business in McLean, Virginia called Outsource Computers, Inc., whose soul contractee is the National Security Agency.

Anyway I wanted to use the Tri-Lateral Investment Group as a good example of one business which incorporated all phases of the old right-wing favorite frauds, i.e. oil and gas, real estate, gold bullion, aircraft brokerage, security and banking fraud, insurance fraud. They were all wrapped up into one.

What Tri-Lateral would do in real estate, for instance, would be to form various fraudulent real estate investment trusts, which didn't exist as anything more than paperwork in somebody's file drawer. They would take out leases on the land, build a few models, get bridge loans, rehy-pothecate the bridge loans and so forth.

The net result is that in the end, the project would collapse, and $20 or $30 million would disappear.

But on the real estate end of transactions, Tri-Lateral is interesting for its involvements in a very infamous fraud — the Topsail Development, Ltd. Fraud of Pensacola, Florida.

This was the famous diversion of 22,000 acres in central Florida, which was financed by original bridge loans from the American Bank and Trust of Pensacola, Florida, which at that time was owned by BCCI.

It seemed odd at the time, but this was not known until some years later. People thought it was odd that BCCI would own a little nickel and dime commercial bank in Pensacola, but it was essentially to launder money and to provide bridge financing for Iran-Contra profiteering.

In 1988, the American Bank and Trust of Pensacola, Florida collapsed under the weight of unrepaid illicit Iran-Contra loans. The Topsail Development deal was the largest real estate fraud ever committed in the United States. It was ultimately bailed out by the Coca-Cola Corporation through those Belizian transactions.

Tri-Lateral Investment Group had become involved in that transaction *vis-a-vis* the leases that Tri-Lateral held through Larry Hamil on 45,000 acres of coastal Belizian property.

But all it ever was – was a first right of refusal and tenuous leases. The land was never actually owned by Tri-Lateral. The loans, by the way, the $9 million in bridge loans to purchase the lease on those lands, came from Great American Bank and Trust of West Palm Beach.

Marvin Warner personally approved the loans. I was involved in several meetings. I was sitting there, as a matter of fact, when Marvin Warner met with Hamil and Secord and others to discuss the bridge loan.

Naturally, this $9 million was never paid back, but that was the intent.

Simply transferring money from the bank into other people's hands ostensibly for "The Cause" which we all chuckled about, as everyone knew that it was essentially going into other people's pockets.

As history recounts, of course, Great American Bank and Trust also failed in 1988 under the weight of unrepaid illicit Iran-Contra loans, to the extent of about $156 million that wasn't repaid.

In terms of oil and gas, Tri-Lateral also had an interest in Gulf Coast Investment, Ltd., which held a lot of marginal oil production and lime-stone production in Tennessee, Kentucky, and Oklahoma.

The old one-a-day pumper routine. In oil terms, what's known as the Knox in Clay County, Kentucky that extends up around Olney, Illinois. These are all beat out one-a-day pumpers, one-barrel-a-day, two-barrel-a-day pumpers that have been around for fifty years.

Hamil made them look like they were simply pumping thousands of barrels a day. What Tri-Lateral would do was to take its supposed proprietary interest in Gulf Coast Investment Group and make it appear that this proprietary interest was worth a lot more than it was.

It would then hypothecate that interest to commercial loans, principally out of Citibank. It would then purchase with this money Citibank's securities, mostly Citibank bonds.

I remember the large amount of the coupons in 1993 that Tri-Lateral held with money it was lent by Citibank.

The notes would then be held at Merrill Lynch, where they would be margined out. Then the money, again, would be put into something else, usually a bankers acceptances, often at Chase Manhattan.

What I'm trying to say is that you start with $100,000 and at the end of a series of frauds that $100,000 is essentially turned into a $10,000,000 house of cards, of which perhaps $5,000,000 in cash was actually extracted before the whole house of cards falls down.

As I've said before, what made this possible is that all the financial intermediaries, banks, brokerage houses, or security companies, were all determined "Iran-Contra friendly."

Again, essentially it was transferring wealth from a bank, from a brokerage, from investors, from one pocket to another.

Another reason I wanted to mention the Tri-Lateral Investment Group is that it was deals concerning the Tri-Lateral Investment Group which eventually forced the downfall of Richard Hamil in May 1985.

When Hamil was transferring all that cash out of Union Bank of Switzerland (in so many of these frauds I was involved with or familiar with or marketed or whatever) Union Bank of Switzerland was invariably the butt end of the fraud.

In other words, it was the last place a fraud was hypothecated. It was where the final cash would be extracted.

You can pretty well see that the United States government admits that in its famous Lake Resources civil suit against Richard Secord, which was filed in 1991.

The government makes the admission, that during this 1983 to 1986 time frame, it had funded a variety of frauds on behalf of Richard Secord and that Richard Secord was its authorized agent.

In fact, they admitted that the CIA had had a longstanding relationship with the Union Bank of Switzerland and that many powerful Republican interests also had a longstanding relationship with the Union Bank of Switzerland.

The problem was that UBS was always supposed to be made whole in the end. As I attempted to describe these frauds before, the last agent had to be made whole. The last big agent in this case was UBS.

Unfortunately, Richard Hamil and Richard Secord did not make UBS whole — all that money that Hamil transported in physical cash they laundered through Zurich.

Hamil would board a plane. He would fly to Curaçao. The money would get deposited at Banque Z in Curaçao, and then the money would be re-transferred to a Banque Paribas branch in Belize City.

People tried to trace that down before and they found out there isn't any branch there.

Well, yes there is. It's not incorporated in Belize, however. It's an offshore branch of Banque Paribas Panama Branch.

This was the ultimate deep repository for Secord and Hamil, where the money ultimately got skimmed off, which ultimately accumulated to about sixteen and two-third million dollars, as I later identified in a whistleblower complaint to the government and to the Treasury Department.

The Treasury Department duly informed me that they had found about sixteen and two-thirds million dollars in the account.

I had known in 1985 the account had contained about eight million dollars. And I didn't know what transactions had been committed after that time, or how much that account was ultimately worth.

I would add a personal note here. This was another whistleblower complaint that I got screwed out of. I had been promised and I still have the letter, as a matter of fact, from the Treasury Department's FARCO (Foreign Asset Recovery Control Office) then under Rich Newcomb that I would receive a $623,000 finders fee for the identification of that account, which the United States government subsequently froze.

However, I was then informed that under that 1986 Administrative Whistleblower Act, that there were pre-existing claims or pre-existing information, about which, of course, the Treasury Department doesn't have to tell you what they are or anything.

I have complained bitterly before about the holes in that Whistleblower Act that you could drive a truck through.

I've never known anyone who's identified a surreptitious account that's ever received a finder's fee that they're supposedly entitled to by law.

The Tri-Lateral Investment Group, Ltd. is also one of the deals (one of the very few deals, perhaps only a few dozen deals in that era by this group of guys) that you could connect Jeb, Neil, George, Jr., Prescott, and Wally Bush. All five — you can put in the Tri-Lateral Investment Group, Ltd.

You can put Neil in it *vis-a-vis* Tri-Lateral's dealings with Neil's Gulf Stream Realty.

Then you back up a step and put Neil Bush into Tri-Lateral Investment Group's dealings with the Winn Financial Group of Denver run by the infamous former Ambassador to Switzerland, Phillip Winn.

You can put George, Jr. in the deal *vis-a-vis* the Tri-Lateral Group Ltd.'s fraudulent relationship with American Insurance General (AIG), of which George, Jr. was a part through the same series of fraudulent fidelity guarantee instruments issued on behalf of Harken Energy from American Insurance General. Tri-Lateral Investment Group then sold bogus oil and gas leases to AIG.

This is a direct fraud that George, Jr. profited to the extent of (not a lot) about $1.6 or $1.7 million. But it was a clear out-and-out fraud.

Finally, I want to make note of the Tri-Lateral Investment Group because I think it's worth noting that it was allegations of receiving illicit campaign donations from the Tri-Lateral Investment Group which ultimately led to the defeat of Republican Senator Paula Hawkins in 1986.

Tri-Lateral Investment Group (in terms of gold bullion fraud, another old right-wing favorite for the generation of illegal, covert revenue streams) was also involved in that 20,000 ounce transaction that Larry Hamil and Richard Secord did.

I use Larry and Richard Hamil interchangeably but the man's real name is Lawrence Richard Hamil. In various public documents and in congressional testimony, he is often referred to as either Larry Hamil or Richard Hamil.

Anyway, Hamil had in conjunction with Richard Secord (using a letter of recommendation from Jeb Bush) borrowed money from Citibank to buy 20,000 ounces of gold bullion from Deak Perrera in New York.

The said bullion was then transferred to the Royal Trust Bank of Canada, actually its branch in Nassau, the Bahamas.

The bank then issued a bonded warehouse receipt, as it is entitled to do. The Nassau branch of the Royal Trust Bank of Canada is authorized to issue bonded warehouse receipts. The said bonded warehouse receipts

— at the price of gold at that time was perhaps $7 million worth of bullion.

The said bonded warehouse receipts are then rehypothecated back here in the United States through a variety of Iran-Contra friendly institutions.

Ultimately, Hamil and Secord hypothecate the same 20,000 ounces of bullion thirteen times. At thirteen different lending institutions. This is one of the oldest tricks in the book. The gold bullion trick.

I mean this was Jack Terrell's original scheme. This was a scheme that had been used in the 1970s by the CIA — the hypothecation of gold bullion in ten different places.

Of course, those deals all fell apart in the end.

By the end of 1986, all those deals fell apart. And as usual, the bank simply wrote off the money — about $2.3 million. It was about a $2.3 million loan issued by Bayshore Bank and Trust of Miami, Florida and this was certainly one of the lynchpin loans which involved Jack Singlaub.

Gen. Jack Singlaub was the one that got the money. Of course, this was probably the straw that broke the camel's back, which caused Bayshore Bank to fail.

The reason why the media doesn't like to go after it is because it is cumbersome and tedious. But you can see how one fraud started out with two Iran-Contra players — Larry Hamil and Richard Secord. And yet, you can see all the way through the transaction of these frauds how others benefitted.

In this case, it was Gen. Singlaub. And the common denominator in so many of these frauds is Jeb, Neil, George, Jr., Prescott, and Wally Bush. There have been very few that have made a real effort to put all this together.

One thing that's interesting to note here is why Lawrence Richard Hamil continues to be so hot today — to this day in fact.

Why is it he can never be found?

Why is it he is either in jail or out of jail?

When he's in jail, there are never any records that he's ever been in jail.

Why is that he's still both protected and punished by certain people in the government?

What are the texts of his old and deep relationships with the Department of Defense and the Department of Justice and so forth?

The principal reason why? Just examine his frauds.

Look at all the people involved (who are still in office today, or seeking a higher office, or in certain agencies who have been promoted) in Hamil's principal group of frauds: Gulf Coast Investment Group, Tri-Lateral Investment Group, LRH Associates, Trinity Oil and Gas and a few others.

There's perhaps six at the very top of the list of all the hundreds of corporations that he's formed.

But look at the people who can be hurt, and, in some cases, who have been hurt. Look at those involved. Look at the number of Republican Congressmen and Senators that profited from these illicit deals within the Iran-Contra time frame of 1983 to 1986.

And look at how many of them are still in power today.

They are much more powerful than they were then.

Certainly Henry Hyde, now Chairman of the Judiciary Committee, in recent years was quietly, non-publicly censured by the House and fined $835,000 as a final resolution to that Oak Brook, Illinois real estate scam and the hypothecation scam at Key Bank of New York. That was directly related to his involvement in LRH Associates.

Porter Goss was also quietly reprimanded by the House, secretly you could even say, since anybody who has ever tried to obtain information about Hyde's or Goss's reprimand has never been successful in obtaining any documentation of it.

Goss was reprimanded and fined $365,000 by the House Ethics Committee, the internal component of it. But Goss made a fortune.

It was in the millions that Goss made through the Destin Country Club Development Group, through the Topsail Development Group, through his surreptitious investments in Zapata, and Apache, and Tidewater, and Harken Energy. That was the Harken Energy stock fraud. It really is tremendous. And it is directly related to the reason why Hamil continues to be such a bone of contention and such a sore spot for the government and for many in the government to this day.

In late 1995, when I was in my most recent difficulty with the FBI and was incarcerated, Jesse Helms intervened on my behalf and pressured Janet Reno. Consequently I was let out of jail and not further pursued.

You don't think Jesse Helms did that out of the goodness of his heart, do you?

It's because when I was in jail, I called Paul Rodriguez at the *Washington Times* and gave him more information that he had been pestering me about for a long time.

The *Washington Times* (Paul Rodriguez more specifically and his friend, Jamie Dettmer) had pressed Jesse Helms about all the money that he and Oliver North had skimmed out of those big series of 501c3's in the mid 1980s — the National Eagle Forum, the National Freedom Alliance, and the whole panoply.

You'll see it's all common language that Oliver North used when he formed these things. But millions were taken out of these supposedly tax-exempt organizations illicitly and Helms profited by them, and Pete DuPont profited by them as did various members of GOPAC.

Helms didn't help me out out of the generosity of his heart.

It's that I rattled his goddamned cage.

And I threatened to reveal more information about that.

And to this day, when a reporter calls up Jesse Helms and throws up Oliver North or Larry Hamil's name in his face, he turns white as a god-damned ghost.

Now as we get into larger and more intriguing Iran-Contra frauds, I want to mention my involvement with the infamous Churchill Matrix Group, Ltd., which had operations in London, Paris, and Brussels.

Its United States operations were headquartered in, of all places, Columbus, Ohio. Churchill Matrix was supposedly engineering and industrial components. It had a relationship with the infamous TKF Engineering & Trading International, Ltd. of Santa Barbara, California. It also had a relationship with the equally infamous International Systems and Components (not to be confused with International Signals and Controls of Scranton, Pennsylvania).

International Systems and Components Corporation of McLean, Virginia, also had offices in Dallas, Texas.

In that Churchill Matrix deal, it was later discovered that the entire thing was an MI-6 British intelligence front, which unraveled in 1991 in those big series of trials in London, when Paul Anderson was finally forced to admit he was a British Intelligence agent and that in fact the whole deal had been an MI-6 operation put together at the request of the CIA during Iran-Contra to surreptitiously get certain components to Iraq, which the CIA wanted to be gotten to Iraq.

The only reason the deal fell apart and became public is that in this country Mark Thatcher got listed as a co-defendant in the original indictment.

Finally, his mother, then Prime Minister Margaret Thatcher, decided to preempt the US action by pulling the plug in London and forcing the MI-6 to admit what it was.

That's the only reason, by the way, that the whole deal fell apart — the Mark Thatcher angle.

What British Intelligence was trying to hide at the time was the connection between MI-6, the Agency, and Carlos Cardoen.

Had Thatcher been forced on the stand, he would have spilled the beans about Carlos Cardoen, and that was the link that both the Agency and MI-6 wanted hidden at the time.

Chapter 11

LAWRENCE RICHARD HAMIL: THE US GOVERNMENT'S CON MAN

N EXT I'D LIKE TO explore the background and various dealings of the infamous Larry Hamil.

He was born Lawrence Richard Hamil in Rockville, Maryland on November 16, 1944, the firstborn child of Harry and Virginia Hamil.

Harry Hamil was a thirty-two year veteran of the Department of Defense, retiring as a senior policy analyst on their Southern Desk.

The Southern Desk was a military policy desk involving the Caribbean, Central and South America.

Virginia Hamil worked for many years as a secretary at the National Security Agency. It should be noted that before her retirement, Larry's half-sister, Nancy, also was a secretary at the National Security Agency. And during the Iran-Contra years, she worked directly in the Director of the National Security Lt. Gen. William Odom's office.

Larry Hamil has used so many aliases during his lifetime, that actually very little is known about his early life. He attended but did not graduate Georgetown University in the early 1960s. In 1966 he had a brief marriage which resulted in the birth of one daughter, Samantha.

The father Harry Hamil passed away in 1984 of natural causes. Hamil's mother, Virginia, had left Rockville upon retirement and took up residence in West Palm Beach, Florida.

The earliest of Larry Hamil's business dealings comes from the late 1970s, when Larry and other parties, one of them being his longtime friend and associate, Martin Cohen, became involved in a scheme to smuggle American Express cards into Argentina.

In the late 1970s, a financial embargo was put on Argentina by Washington in an attempt to pressure the military junta there out of power.

The American Express Corporation turned to the CIA, who turned to all the players in the shadows of Washington, including Larry Hamil and his erstwhile sidekick, Martin Cohen, to conspire with American Express to smuggle American Express credit cards into Argentina contrary to this financial embargo.

Hamil got paid a hundred dollars per card.

They took the cards down there by the thousands. It was a rather large operation.

The *Washington Post* finally discovered this operation and the CIA connection in 1980. American Express was rather severely fined and the CIA was substantially embarrassed, but, of course, denied all knowledge of it.

The next illicit business transaction that I am aware of that Larry was involved in was only a year after, in 1980, during the infamous Dominican Sugar Embargo, when the United States was attempting to pressure the military government of then Raphael Trujillo out of office.

One way of doing this was to embargo Dominican sugar. Hamil became involved in a series of transactions to surreptitiously transport sugar out of the Dominican Republic at a substantially reduced price and to disguise that sugar through Jamaica and Haiti, where it was sold at a tremendous profit.

It's sketchy. I don't know all the people he was involved with in this conspiracy. I do know that one of the people he was involved with was the infamous Frank Snepp.

Frank had just retired that year from the CIA and was looking for little things to get himself involved in since Hamil made a substantial amount of money in this endeavor.

I know that he lost a substantial sum of money when the government froze some of his accounts in late 1981. I don't know how much of the money he was actually ever able to retain.

The next illegal transaction Mr. Hamil got himself involved in was in 1982, during the so-called Falklands War.

It was a scheme in which he and Marcel Dassault, the famous French industrialist and Amaro Pintos Ramos, Brazilian industrial shadow player, longtime CIA ally, and longtime George Bush friend, attempted to smuggle into Brazil, transport across the border and sell Exocet missiles to the Argentinian government, which proved to be the most effective weapon Argentina had against British warships during that campaign.

The Argentinians were desperate during that conflict to get their hands on more of those missiles. They were willing to pay whatever it took — ten or twenty times the normal price one of those missiles fetched on the open market.

I don't know what quantity of missiles were smuggled in. I think it was a very small number, perhaps thirty or forty missiles.

My impression though was that the profit was in the millions from that transaction.

Later on during the Iran-Contra period, from 1983 to 1986, Hamil would continue to transact a lot of business with Marcel Dassault and with Pintos Ramos.

Pintos Ramos is one of the common connections that Hamil had with George Bush, Sr.

And it was the common connection that he had with all the Bush sons. That's how he knew the sons before Iran-Contra came along.

For a point of reference, Dassault Industries in France is the largest French defense contractor. It makes jet fighters and missiles for the French government and for export.

If Larry Hamil were to be categorized, he would wear the label of one of the legions of quasi con men with government connections who wait in the shadows of Washington for the next illegal, covert operation of state to come along from which he can profit.

And he's not the only one. There are legions of these guys. It just so happens that Larry Hamil is probably king of the hill wearing this moniker.

Prior to the beginning of Iran-Contra operations in 1983, Larry knew about Iran-Contra, or what later became known as Iran-Contra, as early as 1981. Larry actually had physical copies – voluminous documents, thousands of pages — of the original CIA white papers on Operation Eagle, as it was formulated in 1981 by Bill Casey.

It was always a mystery to people how Hamil obtained these documents.

How he obtained them was through Dewey Clarridge.

Hamil and Dewey go back a long way into all sorts of fraudulent, shadowy mischief.

Hamil subsequently became quite friendly with the infamous Clair George, who a few years later was to became a Deputy Director of the CIA. Other friends of Larry's within the Agency were Assistant Deputy Director, Allen Fiers, and Costa Rican Station Chief, Jose P. Fernandez.

The reason why Hamil was let in so readily to these operations and the reason he was allowed to commit fraud and to profit by it — he did serve some useful purpose in terms of money laundering and his absolute specialty. It was hiding money and secreting money. Both were very valuable commodities and valuable skills for the Agency.

He was looked on very kindly by Bill Casey. He knew Bill Casey. He had known Bill Casey most of his life. Bill Casey and his wife and Harry and Virginia Hamil had played bridge for years. They knew each other. And Bill Casey knew what Larry was, but he also knew that Larry could be helpful in certain ways.

Therefore, if Larry wanted to make a few million fraudulently in what was already an illegal operation of the CIA, it didn't make any difference to Bill Casey. Of course, to say it didn't make any difference to Bill Casey is rather a broad statement.

The actual *quid pro quo* between Hamil and the CIA always seemed to be to me (and Hamil pretty much said so) that he could pretty well do what he wanted providing he was helpful to them when asked and providing that his individual frauds did not expose or embarrass the CIA.

Of course, eventually by 1985, it was his frauds that *did* threaten to expose the CIA and *did* threaten to embarrass them.

So consequently, Hamil's position changed from being on the inside to being somewhere between being on the inside and being on the outside.

In August of 1983, when Operation Eagle was dusted off the shelf, reformulated as Operation Black Eagle, and put into operation, Hamil was involved almost from the get-go.

Hamil immediately set up a series of thirty to forty shell companies, domiciled both domestically and offshore, mostly involving oil and gas, banking transactions, gold bullion, brokering transactions, real estate — all of the old right-wing favorites for the generation of illegal, covert revenue streams.

Hamil's principal artifices were the Gulf Coast Investment Group and everything around it that had the word "Gulf" in it.

Initially he had even wanted to pick up the old Gulf Realty out of west Florida, but Neil Bush wanted that for himself. So Neil and his partners, Bill Waters and Ken Good, picked that up.

Hamil always felt kind of nicked on that. That's why Neil, in order to smooth the waters, let Hamil get into Gulf Realty frauds via an artifice that Hamil had created called LRH Associates and Gulf Coast Limited Partnerships, his principal real estate fraud artifice.

And you will see that both Gulf Realty (Neil Bush's Gulf Realty) and Hamil's Gulf Realty Limited Partners were involved in that fraudulent Destin Country Club development deal.

Subsequently, they were involved in the fraudulent Boca Chica development deal. And ultimately they were involved in the largest real estate swindle ever enacted in the United States, the Topsail Development Limited deal out of Pensacola, Florida, which involved the swap of 26,000 acres in Florida for land in Belize.

The business commonality during this period of time between Larry and Jeb Bush came through Larry's Gulf Coast Investment Group and Larry's, as well as Barry Seal's and Larry Nichols's, partial control of Trinity Oil, as we have discussed.

But, the commonality between Jeb Bush and Larry was in a series of both onshore and offshore bogus oil and gas lease swindles. Also, there was some commonality in some of the banking fraud between Jeb and Larry. In a careful study, you will notice that both Jeb and Larry tended to do business at the same banks and tended to know the same Directors, all at the same banks, Iran-Contra friendly banks.

Larry's connections with George, Jr., have always been considered rather nebulous. People have never been really able to put it together. It's not as obvious as his connections with Jeb and Neil. But the real connection is between American Insurance General (AIG) and that series of frauds instituted by Jack Singlaub in the World Anti-Communist League, when he had Mitch Marr and Barbara Studley acting as front people for him. And that is the real connection with George, Jr, because George, Jr. got a piece of that through an interest in a Dallas-based oil company that he controlled.

There is also some commonality between Larry Hamil and George, Jr. *vis-a-vis* Harken Energy and Zapata and Apache and Tidewater Corporations, insofar as Larry was involved in various stock frauds surrounding those companies, and in which George, Jr. and George, Sr. both profited.

Larry was also very close to the partners of the infamous Houston Energy Partners —Don Regan, James Baker, Lloyd Bennett, and John Tower. He had known these guys for some years because his father had known these men.

Larry was never short of being able to boast about himself. Part of his own downfall was his mouth. He would say how he was a member of the old Texas Republican drinking club, of which John Tower was the *de facto* leader.

But it is really John Tower who introduced Larry to Walter Mischer and Bobby Corson. You can imagine how Hamil took those introductions to the biggest S&Ls in Texas and proceeded to rape and pillage them in a series of oil and gas and gold bullion frauds.

Later, Larry, Jeb, and George, Jr., all participated in (I wouldn't call it a swindle, but I would call it certainly) a marginal transaction in terms of borrowing money from those banks to short the stocks of those banks and then defaulting on the loans. Of course, the banks ultimately failed. Stocks went off the board almost for pennies.

And, I wouldn't call that an out-and-out stock swindle, but it was certainly a fraud. We all benefited quite handsomely from it. Jeb and George, Jr. made a fortune from it. Neil had a substantial short position in Silverado. And when Silverado collapsed, Neil made $3 or $4 million, and then of course, never repaid the loan.

To begin with, he had borrowed the money from Silverado. They were in unique positions. They knew that these banks were failing and were going to fail under the weight of unrepaid Iran-Contra/CIA loans.

It was later revealed in The *Houston Post* that the CIA had borrowed from and had used the three big banks in Texas — Allied Bancshares, Texas America Bank and Commerce, and MCorp. And in the end, the CIA ultimately defaulted on about $350 million worth of loans.

Others of Hamil's close friends in the government at that time were National Security Adviser, Frank Carlucci.

Hamil used to meet Frank quite often in Florida at the Ocean Club for lunch. This is at the same time when Frank Carlucci exposed himself by being seated at the same table with the infamous CIA doper, Jack DeVoe.

What a mistake that was. I don't know how they allowed that to happen, but someone took the photograph.

Bobby Gates got wrapped up into the same problem with that townhouse, exactly the same deal when he allowed himself, the then Deputy Director of the CIA, to be photographed through a security camera in the lobby with the infamous Carlos Cardoen.

At the State Department, Hamil's principal friend there was Larry Eagleburger. "Fat Larry" — we used to call him.

Larry Eagleburger had also known Harry Hamil for a number of years. As a matter of fact, it was Harry Hamil (this is a very little known fact) that got Eagleburger his first job in the State Department some years ago. Larry Eagleburger then rose to the position of Under Secretary of State.

Larry was also very friendly with the Assistant Secretary of State, the infamous Richard Armitage. Armitage would consistently act to protect him at the State Department.

Although Armitage was Assistant Secretary, he was also Chief of the Internal Security section of the State Department, which had consistently acted in concert with the CIA and other parties to authorize narcotics trafficking. This has been mentioned in the press. It's been written about before, i.e. Armitage's role in narcotics and his knowledge of it.

Carlucci and Armitage are now in business together at the Carlisle Group.

It was really because of Hamil's personal friendship with Don Regan that he was able to commit all that securities fraud through Merrill Lynch.

Merrill Lynch would lend him good quality securities (Citicorp bonds, things like that) but they were actually financing the inventory of this stuff in his corporate accounts.

He wasn't paying for any of it. He was paying for it with bogus cashier's checks from the British American Insurance Trust Co. of the Bahamas, which was an offshore bank that he controlled, which was also bogus.

They would post bogus fidelity and guaranty instruments to Merrill Lynch, backed up by a standby letter of credit, which was actually a good standby letter of credit from American Insurance General.

Of course, it was all a fraud.

American Insurance General would never pay any claim. That was the deal. It was just to stand his collateral against a marginable position in Citicorp bonds and high quality securities that Hamil would then use to rehypothecate at other institutions.

Ultimately, Merrill Lynch had to write off some money because of this. It wasn't much, $2 or $3 million. But they did ultimately get stuck with it. And, of course, Hamil's relationship with Merrill Lynch fell apart when Don Regan left as Chairman and Ray Birk came in.

Another friend and business partner of Hamil's was the infamous Marvin Warner.

Marvin Warner and Larry Hamil were partners in a lot of bogus real estate deals being run through ESM Securities. The bridge money for these deals was coming out of Marvin's bank in Florida, the Great American Bank and Trust, which was headquartered in West Palm Beach. It ultimately failed as well with losses to the taxpayers of about $170 million. But you will see them in partners in a whole variety of deals through ESM.

As a matter of fact, it is one of the real estate deals financed through ESM through Ohio State Savings that gets rehypothecated at the Glen Brook Savings and Loan in Illinois.

This was the deal that Henry Hyde became involved in when Henry wanted his piece of the Iran-Contra pie.

The interesting connection is that Henry Hyde, subsequent to this, introduced Hamil to Key Bank of New York. Hyde knew everybody at Key Bank because of his friendship with Alphonse D'Amato, and Alphonse's brother, Louis, the lawyer, who was the general counsel at Key Bank.

Louis, you may remember, subsequently got himself into trouble, and was close to being charged with murder. He ultimately served eight months in jail.

Anyway, it was transactions at Oak Brook Savings and Loan in Illinois and Key Bank in New York, for which Henry Hyde was secretly censured by the House later on, wherein Henry Hyde admitted he had illegally profited to the tune of about $850,000 in certain bogus real estate transactions.

The connection between Hamil and Porter Goss was through Jeb Bush.

Jeb kept letting Congressman Porter Goss into all of his deals — the crossover transactions that he had with his brother, Neil, in those bogus Gulf Realty Developments.

Porter consistently had an interest in all of these deals that collapsed. The difference, of course, was that he actually got to sell his interests, before the deal collapsed.

Porter made a lot of money during the Iran-Contra period.

Henry Hyde and Porter Goss are just two examples.

We could go on and on with Republican Congressmen and Senators who profited vis-a-vis Iran-Contra fraud. It's not limited, by the way, to Republicans. There were some Democrats like Senator Graham who profited quite handsomely through that Swissco Management fraud, the tax-free land swap he arranged for himself with Carlos Cardoen and Swissco Management.

When the FBI finally raided Swissco offices, the Senator's documents were conveniently missing from the evidence they collected.

Anyway, that's another whole story that would require another ten hours just on that fraud.

By 1985, Hamil was violating the mandate that was given him and, by extension, given to me as his partner in 1984 from Gen. Secord.

The mandate was quite clear. Part of it was that Larry was not to commit frauds on individuals. That would become messy and hard to cover up, which is precisely what Hamil did. In his greed, he wanted to squeeze every dollar he could out of his perceived protection from Washington.

Hamil then proceeded to commit fraud on unauthorized individuals.

The original Gulf Coast Investment scheme was supposed to be strictly an artifice that would legitimize the flow of funds from sympathetic Republicans to "The Cause," as Oliver North calls it. To "The Enterprise," as Richard Secord called it. To "The Government Within a Government," as Assistant Secretary of State Elliott Abrams would call it. That's what we were doing.

Of course, being a private individual, you could not donate money to an illegal, covert operation of state. But you could have an intermediary.

You buy bogus oil and gas interests, which essentially become used as a laundering device to get the money to Oliver North and other parties.

The problem with Larry is that we were given lists of selected wealthy Republicans who wanted to do this. Larry went outside of that list and started to raise money from unauthorized people. And consequently, this created a problem.

By late April or early May, it was obvious that something had to be done about Hamil, and, of course, something was done.

On May 5, 1985, Hamil was arrested by the FBI in Miami. He was on his boat, *The Capital Delight*, at the Bahia Mar Marina in Ft. Lauderdale.

Finally the much vaunted FBI agent of Miami office, Field Agent Ross Gaffney got his man.

But their incompetence frankly borders on hilarity. They went to the wrong boat and arrested the wrong man.

Hamil was right in the next pier, in the next dock, ten feet from them in his bathing suit looking at them, waving at them.

And they didn't realize it. Ross Gaffney didn't have a photograph of Hamil and didn't know what he looked like.

Larry's last transactions that I knew about during this timeframe came in April of 1985, when he was at Union Bank in Switzerland, where he did a lot of business. He was delivering $432,000 in cash to Banque Z in Curaçao and was depositing it into one of the accounts of the infamous Intercontinental Industries SA, controlled by Oliver North and Richard Secord.

Before we go further in this, it should be mentioned that not all of Hamil's dealings were with Republicans.

How Hamil got involved in Arkansas (this has been another question that people have always wanted to know) wasn't just through the Trinity Oil and Gas deal.

It also wasn't simply through fraudulent securities transactions with Stephens Investment Group.

And it was not simply through bogus banking transactions at Twin Cities Bank of North Little Rock, Arkansas.

In fact, Hamil acted as a Republican bag man in Arkansas. He used to transport money for the Agency for operations in Mena. He would transport a large amount of physical cash in a briefcase.

One of the things that Larry was often used for was a courier of cash.

That's how Larry becomes so involved and so intimately knowledgeable about Buddy Young because he met Buddy Young.

He and Buddy and Barry got into Trinity Oil. They then, in turn, got Danny Lasater and Patsy and Harry Thomasson into transactions.

Larry set up more bogus corporations in Arkansas, of course, through the Rose Law Firm — and Hubbell acted as general counsel.

As a matter of fact, Hillary, herself, was the counsel on several of these bogus corporations, including the sinister Trinity Oil and Gas deal.

Bruce Lindsey, then deputy to Governor Clinton, and Betsey Wright, then the Governor's personal secretary, knew precisely what Hamil was doing in Arkansas. They also knew his itinerary — whom he was meeting and the amounts of money that were involved.

It was obvious that they were being briefed on Oliver North's Guns-For-Drugs operations in Arkansas. And it also became subsequently revealed through further conversations that Attorney General Winston Bryant was also familiar with this.

As a matter of fact, when Bill Duncan was with the Attorney General's office, it was Bill who leaked the word out to Col. Tommy Goodwin, the Commander of the Arkansas State Police.

Goodwin got on the phone to Governor Clinton. He was all pissed off because he was not being kept informed of all the CIA narcotics and weapons transactions in the state.

Clinton says he's well-advised of it, and that it's an authorized operation of the US Government. And that was a key problem — that conversation.

By the way, Goodwin had an internal taping system. He taped all of his calls. That tape was one of the three tapes out of the infamous series of forty, during the FBI sponsored break-in of Goodwin's office.

It was when Asa Hutchinson, then US Attorney in Little Rock, Republican, ordered the Arkansas State Police Commander's office be broken into, and three tapes were stolen out of the forty tapes that he had regarding this matter.

One of the tapes taken was that conversation.

Tommy Goodwin went out and tried to tell people about it.

And subsequently he suffered a heart attack.

In September 1985, Hamil's original bill of indictment was about a foot thick in terms of documentation. He was indicted on a variety of counts, mostly mail fraud and wire fraud.

The indictment was reamended, reamended, and reamended until finally a foot thick stack of documents, as filed in September 1985, wound up being a one-inch thick stack of documents by 1986.

Hamil, ultimately, plead guilty. He was sentenced to forty-five years or something. And then began the great Hamil odyssey of being in and out of jail all the time, which persists to this day.

I would estimate that the man has probably spent (I would guess) six of the last thirteen years actually incarcerated in this continuous in-out, in-out, in-out.

First he's in jail someplace. Then he's in another jail and another jail. He was transferred thirty-two times in six months between penal institutions — always under assumed names. Or he wasn't there. Or there was no record of it.

But this continues to this day. For instance, one day Hamil would be in the Desoto Correctional Facility in Florida or the Hudson Correctional Facility.

Two days later, he'd be seen in Zurich, Switzerland. Or he'd be seen in New York, or Washington in the company of Department of Defense officials.

Then a week later, he'd be in some other penal institution.

This yo-yo persists to this day. This is the ultimate conundrum about Hamil. I can understand why people would want to protect him because of what he knows.

But in that case, it would be more logical, simply to eliminate him. I mean, that would be the obvious step.

As discussed before, on December 20, 1985, Oliver North simply wanted to liquidate him. That would have been the obvious, quick and easy solution.

There's got to be something that keeps this guy alive, and frankly I don't know what it is. Maybe it's because he's created documents. I know that North was never able to get the documents he wanted to recover from Hamil, so that is a possibility, but someone protects this guy from on high.

His protection comes from more than the Department of Defense, and it is somebody very high who acts to protect him, even in this recent subpoena that Hamil received from the House Judiciary Committee.

First, the Department of Justice says they've never heard of Larry Hamil. They don't know who he is. After he's subpoenaed, suddenly National Security blocked to prevent his testimony.

Anyway, these are the questions that need to be answered. The problem is that anytime anyone has ever pushed the Department of Justice, or the Department of Defense, or the Department of State, or the Agency (not so much the Agency because they have more natural defenses, i.e. they just deny everything) about Hamil, doors immediately close. Red flags go up. Beads of sweat form. Documents are shredded. Reporters who ask questions suddenly go missing.

People who cause those questions to be asked are suddenly harassed, pressured, intimidated, surveilled upon, sabotaged and suborned in every possible manner.

The key questions to be asked? The Department of Justice claims they don't know him, yet they institute a national security block to prevent him from testifying, while is a convicted felon.

Why does he still carry a very high security clearance at the Department of Justice?

Why is it every time he travels he goes in a private Lear jet owned by the Department of Defense?

Why is it that when he was staying at a very expensive, very luxurious condo in Palm Beach at $6,700 a month rent, why was the rent being paid by the Department of Defense?

What is it about this guy? And that is a real conundrum.

The major publication reporters who have looked into this, like Brian Barger and Karen Burns, Peter Collins, Dave Allen, even Gloria Borger — look what happened to their careers.

When they made serious attempts to investigate Hamil, they were all burned.

Collins, Burns and Allen were all kicked out of ABC for it.

When Dave Allen went after it a second time, he was thrown out of CNN.

When Aaron Rostom at ABC looked into it, he was thrown out of ABC.

I don't know what happened to Brian Barger, but Brian looked into Hamil and said he wished he'd never looked into Hamil.

He dropped doing Iran-Contra stuff, and now he's doing nature documentaries.

When Rob Perry, Bill Moyer's associate, on *Front Line*, looked into it, Bill said, "You've got to stop this. I'm getting too much heat."

And he had to leave the editorial investigative staff of *Front Line*.

Another example is that investigative reporter at *The West Palm Beach Post*. I've forgotten her last name. But her first name is Linda. She wanted to go after Hamil with a vengeance. She had a pretty good understanding of who Hamil was. She had discovered a treasure trove of documents about Hamil. She said, "This will end George Bush." It will change the way history's going to look on the then recently expired Bill Casey. " Man, was she excited.

Two or three days later in Ft. Lauderdale, she's suddenly found dead out in the middle of the swamps of the Everglades, bound and gagged. The police discovered her apartment had been rifled, and the documents and tapes that she had were missing.

Well, that ended that.

As we've said in the past, dividing Iran-Contra into the major three areas — narcotics, weapons and fraud — Hamil's been consistently put into the fraud category. And that's true. That's where he belongs.

However, people have consistently overlooked his involvement in weapons transactions. Not that they've overlooked it, but nobody's ever really investigated that in the media.

Hamil was quite friendly with the infamous Canadian arms trafficker, Emmanuel von Weigensburg, who controlled a company called Trans World Armaments, Ltd. in Quebec City.

Hamil had flown there to facilitate a weapons transaction with the government of Iran involving F4 Phantom fighter spare parts that von Weigensburg was buying from the Canadian Air Force.

It was obvious that the transaction was authorized, since at the time we also met two members of the Royal Canadian Mounted Police External Intelligence Unit, which is no longer in existence.

It has now been repackaged as CEPIS — the new Canadian Intelligence Unit.

This is one story that an entire separate book could be written about How those two RCPM Intelligence agents later disappeared.

How they suddenly reappeared under new names in the Caribbean with multi-million dollar bank accounts, living quietly on the beach, and drinking piña coladas.

That's another whole story that *The Toronto Star* attempted, but then very quickly backed away from because of pressure from the conservative government of Joe Clark.

A good starting point for investigative journalists to look at Hamil *vis-a-vis* illicit and illegal Iran-Contra weapons transactions is to review that so-called Lake Resources civil lawsuit (US v. Richard Secord) filed September 21, 1991, Civil Division 1202-A, 1st District, Eastern Virginia, in Alexandria.

That famous lawsuit was used by a lot of investigative reporters. The government admits that Secord was its agent and admits that Secord acted illegally at the orders of the American government *vis-a-vis* weapons transactions.

If you look at what the government states about all the various weapons brokers in Portugal, Czechoslovakia, and all these countries, you'll see it reads like an exact itinerary of Hamil's travel plans at that time.

It's an excellent place to start, and I would recommend that lawsuit for any investigative journalist.

Of course, any investigative journalist who's interested already has a copy of it, insofar as it's one of the very few times that the US Government makes admissions of wrongdoing *vis-a-vis* Iran-Contra.

You can actually tell, in reading this lawsuit, what Iran-Contra was all about, that Iran didn't have anything to do with it, really. It was *all* Contra.

This was really only meant to be a thumbnail sketch. There are many unanswered questions about Larry Hamil that I think will remain unanswered due to the fear that people have of attempting to find out who is behind Hamil.

What is the complete story? Where was he? What did he do with regards to the frauds, the money, and the weapons?

Ultimately I cannot tell you who is the top dog behind Larry Hamil. I don't know. And I think anyone, who might have known or might have discovered it, is now dead.

And that sort of sends a message. Consequently nobody to date has made any herculean effort to find out who is behind Hamil.

Top investigators have even said to me — "There's no amount of money that I would take to make a frontal assault to find out who's behind Hamil."

Chapter 12

US GOVT. DRUG SMUGGLING, ILLICIT WEAPONS SALES AND WHOLESALE FRAUD

S O FAR, I HAVE TRIED to describe a compendium of Iran-Contra activities. These have been commonly divided as 1) Narcotics, 2) Weapons, and 3) Money.

Money refers to fraud.

Narcotics refers to illicit narcotics transactions directed by certain U.S. Government agencies.

Weapons refer to the illicit sales of weapons which the US Government wanted to transfer, even though these transfers were clearly in violation of the law at the time.

We will also explore in greater detail all three areas of Iran-Contra, producing a compendium of Bush Family Fraud, *vis-a-vis* illicit Iran-Contra profiteering.

The Bush family has been heavily involved, especially George, Sr., George, Jr., Jeb, Neil, George's brother Prescott, and Prescott's son, Walter.

We will also explore in detail the infamous M&L Industries fraud, involving Robert Josephs of Denver, as well as the Bush family's role in that fraud and their profit.

Other Bush Family Frauds include the so-called Lone Star Cement Fraud, involving Lone Star Industries of Texas, the Loral Defense Corporation Fraud, the E-Systems Corporation Fraud, the Marriott Missile Diversion Fraud, the Sooner Defense Missile Diversion Fraud, and a whole host of other diversions, frauds, stock swindles, including Zapata, Apache, Tidewater, and Harken Corporations.

We will also attempt to produce a complete compendium of Bush Family Fraud, *vis-a-vis* Iran-Contra, and to add up the numbers — what these frauds actually cost the American taxpayers in terms of failed financial institutions and in terms of monies that came from the public purse to bail out these banking, securities, and insurance institutions.

Rest assured, the numbers are in the billions.

We will limit discussion of fraud to Iran-Contra related fraud with respect to the Bush family. Some of these banking corporations involved include Kingsdale Bank, Beach Federal Savings and Loan, the Worthen Banking Group, and the Stephens Investment Corporation.

Also there was fraud specifically targeted to help certain Democrats within Arkansas, then Governor Bill Clinton and the Tyson Chicken Diversion Fraud, which is much larger than commonly believed and the Arkansas Bestway Trucking Kickback Diversion Fraud.

Some of the corporate entities, by the way, are publicly listed companies, which have since changed their names.

Arkansas Bestway Freight is now known as AmeriFreight. But you will clearly see how then Governor Bill Clinton profited from a diversion of fees being paid Arkansas Bestway Trucking to crate weapons from Ft. Campbell, Kentucky into Mena, Arkansas. These weapons were then flown south, and conversely narcotics were flown the other way — Oliver North's much renowned Guns-For-Drugs Program.

The complete Arkansas Democratic Party infrastructure at that time was well aware of it through its knowledge and involvement in the chain of command of Iran-Contra activities in the State of Arkansas.

There will be much attention paid to Clinton minions, such as Betsey Wright, Bruce Lindsey, Winston Bryan, and Col. Thomas Goodwin, then commander of the Arkansas State Police.

We will also juxtapose the involvement (in terms of a conspiracy to suppress knowledge of this) of certain Republicans in the state, such as the then renowned Little Rock U.S. Attorney, Asa Hutchinson, who now sits on the House Judiciary Committee, and who with its Chairman, Henry Hyde, has attempted to block every effort to reinvestigate these matters again.

We will also show the consequences that key members of Congress who have acted to initiate investigations have suffered — Sen. Kerry, Congressman Hughes, Congressman Alexander and others. We will show what happened to their political careers and what happened to them financially, and how they were pressured to not look at certain Iran-Contra matters in their investigations.

We will also look at the political and personal fortunes of certain members of Congress who acted to block Iran-Contra investigations— and how their fortunes rose because of it.

In terms of sanctioned Iran-Contra narcotics operations, we will zero in on Arkansas and narcotics operations in Arizona, Oregon, and New Orleans, Louisiana.

We will look at the diversion of narcotics trafficking from the Southeast Corridor to the Northeast Corridor, since I have substantial information about this. We will also piece this together, so the reader can understand, the entire route these narcotics took as well as who was involved and the extent of US Government involvement in both the air and sea routes.

We will also discuss in greater detail the Haitian sea corridors for transporting cocaine and we will see the huge amount of monies involved — who profited by it and who still has much to lose by this information being exposed today.

We will also explore what happened to many key witnesses due to be called before Congressional committees and the clouded circumstances under which they died.

In some cases, they died just a few days before they were to testify, or were to submit for depositions, or had intended to submit affidavits, or be questioned for interrogatories, etc.

I think a very complete picture can be drawn about the 400 people, mostly American citizens, who died because of what they knew and not because of what they may have done.

It is also my intent to look at examples of the 1,200 American citizens currently incarcerated in federal institutions serving long-term sentences related to Iran-Contra narcotics activity, as well as fraud and weapons activity.

We will see exactly why they are incarcerated, what happened to them, and the unusual circumstances at their trials, the invocation of "National Security" surrounding their trials.

And we will also look at the so-called "A Team," a set of people, including Jack DeVoe, Tony Fernandez, and other narcotics traffickers who were operating with the direct sanction of the US Government.

We'll see how well they were treated. Certain individuals faced two hundred year sentences.

Then the Iran Contra Crime Era (1983-1986) moved into the Iran-Contra Crime Coverup Era (1987-1993) and I think this is equally important.

The acts committed by government to cover up these matters were equally egregious, if not more so. This is the period when the bulk of the people died, when the bulk of documents were shredded, etc. I certainly think it is important to show the shift in focus from the perpetration of the acts into the mechanics of how they were covered up

For the reader, it's important to be able to draw the conclusion that is mine — that the conspiracy to cover up these activities was as great as the conspiracy to perpetrate them.

The story of BCCI (Bank of Credit and Commerce International) is also important to show how large a role it played in both Iran-Contra and Iraqgate activities. This was money laundering and fraud of unimaginable proportion. It has been commonly presumed that BCCI's central involvement came in Iraqgate. That is completely untrue.

BCCI was formed in 1978. From the time of Burt Lance, it had substantial Iran-Contra involvement.

BCCI is also a good example to show Democratic Party involvement in Iran-Contra and how certain individuals in the Democratic Party profited.

There will also be an overview of what is commonly known as Iraqgate — who profited, where the money went, what it was all about, and the separate conspiracy that was orchestrated by the US government and other governments to cover it up.

Iraqgate involved a wider conspiracy to cover up than Iran-Contra did originally in terms of international involvement. We will see the British and German governments' involvement in an effort to protect their interests and cover their own political liability.

We will further illustrate the so-called Capitol Hill Control Files that existed (1983 to 1986), wherein certain parties around the Reagan and Bush Administration, including Richard Secord, Bill Casey, Bobby Gates, and a host of others, acted to pressure certain members of Congress who were considered hostile.

"Hostile" meant that they might institute some action to investigate matters relating to Iran-Contra. Over 42 members of the House and Senate were controlled financially and sexually.

I'll also go into my personal file on whistle-blowers in government and those not in government, with salient highlights such as Peter Viednicks of Customs, and Brad Ayers of DEA, and what happened to them and others when they attempted to blow the whistle on Iran-Contra drug trafficking activity.

How whistle-blowers' lives were absolutely destroyed by the Government. How every subterfuge was employed to discredit them, to disgrace them, to ruin them, and to bankrupt them.

It's a pretty sordid tale, and it should be told.

The Viednicks case is particularly egregious. The man's immediate superior was the infamous, sinister and dreaded George Weiss, who would eventually rise to become Customs Commissioner of the United States. He participated in incriminating, inculpating, and doing everything possible to destroy his own subordinate.

His reward? Weiss steadily advanced from local to regional Customs Commissioner and ultimately to Customs Commissioner of the United States. Then he was ultimately forced out by his own past, in that series of articles in the *Washington Times*, in which I had a hand. I thought it was important for the sake of justice to see that Weiss was forced out. And he was.

We will illustrate several examples of how government whistle-blowers were discredited, intimidated, pressured, harassed, suborned by their own superiors, and what the superiors' reward was.

There's a direct correlation that can be drawn. As we have spoken before, the genesis of so much of today's mischief making in Washington is grounded in what has been termed Iran-Contra. In fact, continuing conspiracy and continuing coverup has its genesis in Iran-Contra activity.

Regarding the 1992 election, we will show the secret deal that Perot was essentially was forced to make in June of 1992, and we will discuss the infamous document shredding in the final days of the Bush Administration.

Then we will proceed to 1993-94, the actions that the Clinton Administration took to cover up its own Iran-Contra exposure, and to continue to discredit people, and the files that they inherited, the Control Files, they inherited from the Bush minions.

This was the reason why the Clinton Administration held over an unusually high — over 1,100 — number of Bush people in key positions within the Executive offices and federal agencies.

We will see that Clinton did nothing to extradite 17 senior members of government who are wanted in various foreign countries for violating their laws regarding Iran-Contra activities.

We shall also explore in detail the continuation of the Bush political kidnapping policy which continues to exist to this day, despite Clinton denials to the contrary.

Next, we will look at the 1996 Democratic Campaign Conspiracy, money laundering, illicit contributions from foreign governments, and the so-called Chinese Connection will be fully detailed.

As I mentioned before, these Chinese, Indonesian, and Southeast Asian connections are essentially nothing more than old Republican connections brought forward into a Democratic Administration for the purposes of extracting money. But the protocols and understandings and the transfer of technologies remain effectively unchanged underneath the surface.

We'll also make a complete review of all the people that I was involved with. We'll focus on, perhaps, the top fifty or sixty — where they are now, and what has happened to them. It will be a clear illustration that those who talked did not fare very well, those who participated in the original acts, and those who participated in the ensuing conspiracy to cover them up and how wealthy they have grown — and how comfortable they are now.

We will also touch upon the secret arrangements between the Soviet government as it was collapsing and the American government, the dissemination of information from the KGB and the Eastern European Intelligence files to the United States.

We will discuss the transfer of people, senior KGB officers, who now live comfortably in the suburbs of Washington, D.C.

My principal motivation in completing this project is the hope that it can be used to exact some measure of justice.

Chapter 13

US GOVERNMENT SANCTIONED DRUG TRAFFICKING

L ET US EXPLORE IN GREATER detail US Government involvement in Iran-Contra narcotics trafficking.

Since 1985, a good researcher can find evidence in many forms — in criminal lawsuits, depositions, affidavits, as well as testimony before various congressional investigative committees. There were even admissions in newspaper articles in the London Times.

In fact, there is now a substantial body of admission by the United States government that it "acquiesced" to certain narcotics trafficking during the Iran-Contra period from 1983 to 1986.

However, when the government states "acquiesced," I would maintain that this "acquiescence" is tantamount to actual authorization.

The term "acquiescence" would imply that the government simply turned a blind eye. But when one looks behind that word and what the government's actions were, as well as what is already known as a matter of public record, these are not acts of "acquiescence."

They are much more proactive, and they are tantamount to a conspiracy by the United States Government to traffic in narcotics for the purpose of generating ongoing covert revenue streams.

US Government sponsored criminal activities include 1) the appointment of CIA and FBI personnel to have direct contact with narcotics traffickers, 2) the manipulation of US Customs to ensure certain aircraft and ships were not inspected, and 3) the maintenance of secured shipping routes and narcotics storage facilities by the United States military.

Let's examine for a moment specific examples where acquiescence and a proactive policy tend to butt heads, as it were.

First, there is an established chain of command within the CIA and other government agencies with respect to narcotics trafficking with the involvement of then Deputy Director Clair George, his subordinate Assistant Deputy Director Allen Fiers, his subordinate Dewey Clarridge, and certain foreign CIA Station Chiefs such as the infamous Joseph P. Fernandez, Station Chief of Costa Rica.

Of course, these names are well known and this chain of command has now been publicly detailed in a variety of forms.

- The involvement of Oliver North in the CIA-sponsored narcotics chain of command,
- The involvement of senior FBI personnel,
- The creation of a separate quasi-agency in 1983 (the so-called Vice Presidential Task Force on Drugs) so that Customs offices in the southeast United States would ensure that certain air and sea traffic was not intercepted or searched,
- The maintenance both in the United States and in Central and South America of secure facilities for the transportation and storage of narcotics under the auspices of the U.S. military.

A prime example of this is US military control of the Panamanian G-2, particularly from 1985 to 1986 in order to maintain certain airfields and storage facilities for the transshipment of narcotics to the United States and, conversely, for weapons flowing the other way.

These are not the activities of "acquiescence." Rather, these are activities of US Government sponsorship. And this sponsorship continues in the post-Iran-Contra era after 1986.

A good researcher could easily establish a pattern of what happened to well-known narcotics traffickers who were caught and sentenced and given rather stiff sentences. After all, twenty, thirty, or forty year sentences are not uncommon.

The US Government was doing this on purpose to dissuade anyone from making a connection between itself and the defendants.

A good example of this would be four Bahamian State Ministers who became deeply involved in CIA-sponsored narcotics trafficking with respect to the Bahamian Connection, which involved the recently deceased Lyndon Pindling, Prime Minister of the Bahamas at the time.

The four ministers in question are Nigel Bowe, Eddie Bannister, Nelson Rolle, and George Robinson. These men ultimately received (as it's a matter of public record when they were tried during the 1986-88 time frame) twenty or thirty year sentences.

But when the media spotlight, or the Congressional investigation spotlight, was turned off these cases, these men served between two to five years of their actual sentences.

Their motions for sentence reductions were quietly approved *ex parte*, and they were quietly allowed to leave the United States. In exchange for this, they have never publicly talked about their involvement in Iran-Contra narcotics trafficking again.

This largesse regarding federal sentencing was extended to defendants from the highest ranks, like Jack DeVoe, down to individual narcotics traffickers such as the infamous Tosh Chumley and Mickey Toliver, who both received very long sentences, but in fact served very little time.

There is an interesting common theme that runs through all CIA-connected narcotics traffickers of this period.

These included men who were prosecuted — from Jack DeVoe to Barry Seal, Tony Fernandez, Bill Blakemore, Roberto Ruiz, Donald Raulerson and his son, Don, Jr., who virtually controlled CIA narcotics trafficking in Georgia. There are about fifty-four names in all, but the one common thread that runs through all these supposed defendants is the connection of their defense counsels to the government.

Every defense counsel that was involved in defending these gentlemen was a former employee of the CIA.

When I say "former employee," I mean as an attorney, a former CIA counsel, or a former Department of Defense counsel, or a former National Security counsel, etc.

It's one of the common themes that exists in every single case. The more prominent the narcotics trafficker defendant in question, the more prominent was his counsel's relationship with the Agency.

DeVoe's lead counsel was James Pennington, a former General Counsel of the CIA. His co-counsels included James Natali and Norman Brownstein.

Brownstein is a former senior Department of Justice counsel. Natali is also a former CIA counsel.

Another common thread that runs between the senior narcotics traffickers is that they all controlled their own airlines.

DeVoe controlled DeVoe Aviation.

Barry Seal controlled Rich Aviation.

Gus Connors controlled Connors Aviation and so forth.

Also, from the small carriers all the way up to Southern Air Transport — the civilian defense counsels of these corporations, those who represented civil matters for these corporations, were also all former attorneys from the CIA or the Department of Defense or some other federal agency.

Southern Air Transport is a glaring example of that. Robert Beckman, a former CIA Deputy General Counsel, and Tom Spencer, a former Department of Defense Deputy Counsel were senior counsels to Southern Air Transport.

I would like to insert an interesting story which illustrates the connections of defense counsels to the government and these narcotics traffickers.

This is the story of the death of Gus Connors.

Gus Connors controlled Connors Aviation, and his attorney was the infamous Phil Bronner of Miami, a former CIA counsel who represented numerous small airlines with narcotics trafficking implications.

Connors died under suspicious circumstances. He died about five minutes after exiting the US Attorney's office in Miami. He died in the middle of the street, as a matter of fact. He was crossing the street downtown, and it was clear that he had been physically beaten, that something had happened to him.

When he entered the building, he was fine.

When he left the building, his face was puffy and swollen and he was black and blue and had abrasions.

It's clear that something happened to him in that building when he was asked to talk. Of course, later he walked out of the building and after he walks about thirty feet, he proceeds to die of what was determined on his death certificate to be a heart attack.

His body was cremated four hours later — before his family was even notified.

Dave Lyons at the *Miami Herald* was one of the first investigative reporters to know what happened. That's only because he was downtown at the courthouse. He was eating lunch where a lot of the reporters eat — directly across from the U.S. Attorney's office — and he saw what happened.

He immediately tried to go to Gus's office to talk to Gus's secretary to try to get copies of some documents.

He was at Gus Connors' office, which was near Miami International Airport, where most of these airlines maintain their offices, either right on the airfields or directly off the airfields.

He got there in seventeen minutes.

When Dave Lyons got to Connors' office, Phil Bronner was already in there. He had dismissed Connors' secretary and was jamming files from Connors' file cabinets through a shredder.

He denied Dave Lyons any access to the property. This was later brought out in articles by Dave Lyons about what had happened.

It's an interesting connection — just how close these so-called former CIA counsels were to their former employers with respect to the representation of certain narcotics clients.

Another way the government "acquiesced" to these narcotics operations was by effectively allowing them to launder vast sums of money through Iran-Contra sympathetic banks in south Florida.

They allowed enormous sums of money to leave these banks for accounts in Central America, the Carribean, South America, and so on.

Banks like Eagle National Bank, which was 80% owned by the Banco de Colombia, the central bank of Colombia, were allowed to maintain a confidential cable arrangement with their main bank in Colombia. They were completely unfettered. There were no forms to be filled out. Nothing.

These transactions would be in the millions of dollars deposited in Eagle National Bank, then sent down to banks in Colombia and elsewhere.

It is true that the chairman of the bank, Jose Antonio "Pepe" Cabrera-Sarmiento, did eventually take the fall and was convicted of money laundering. He received a fourteen year sentence, of which he served very little.

At the time the Chairman of Eagle National Bank, Burt Kanter, was very much involved with laundering money. I know. We used to sit and talk about it at lunch. I was a substantial client of Eagle National Bank at that time, as was Jeb Bush and all of his minions.

But Kanter was never looked at. Abel Holtz, the chairman of Capital Bank in Miami, was supposedly investigated for links to narcotics trafficking and money laundering but again, nothing ever became of it.

As we've discussed before, in the narcotics end of Iran-Contra, there were perhaps 500 principal players involved.

When I say "principal players," I mean agents of the United States Government, agents of foreign governments (Panama, Haiti, Cuba, Belize, and so on), the narcotics traffickers, their defense counsels, who were essentially acting as quasi-government agents, and bankers who were also acting as quasi-government agents.

There are about 500 notable names. And this would be a book in itself. Iran-Contra narcotics trafficking would be a book in itself.

I don't intend to devote too much more time because it is simply so extensive. However, we can talk about what happened to all of these 500 people in the post-Iran-Contra environment — what I would call the cover-up period from 1986 to date.

Of these 500 individuals, about 200 have died under suspicious circumstances. The others are in exile, or they have made all sorts of deals.

Some are living quite comfortably at the largesse of the U.S. government.

Former Haitian President Cedras is a good example of one who's living comfortably.

Also one of the most overlooked governments involved in this is the government of Cuba. There's been much said, much written, and much already known about the Panamanian and Haitian governments' involvement. But there's been very little said about Cuban government involvement.

More specifically there was the direct involvement of Fidel Castro's brother, Cuban Defense Minister, Raul Castro, who was essentially the chief contact or conduit (whatever word you want to use) for CIA narcotics trafficking in Cuba.

Specifically, it was at the Isle of Youth, which is a small island off the Cuban coast. It used to be called the Isle of Pines in Battista's days. It had, of course, been a Carribean stronghold for the CIA for narcotics trafficking.

There is much information in the public domain about CIA activity at the Isle of Pines which goes as far back as the 1950s. The only time this was exposed publicly was when renewed attention was put on Robert Vesco.

However Vesco wasn't simply hiding in Cuba. He was acting as a defacto Station Chief for the CIA there.

When he lived in great luxury at the Havana Yacht Club, he was meeting regularly with Raul Castro. It was Vesco who originally leaked that information to the *Miami Herald* about CIA activity and CIA's closeness with certain members of the Cuban government. This actually led to the execution of General Arnuldo Ochoa, a very sordid incident.

Ochoa simply knew too much, and it was felt that Ochoa may have been at risk of defection, which he certainly was.

As a matter of fact, the Cuban government knew that he intended to defect. Their only real concern was that if he did defect, he would be going straight into the hands of a Democrat controlled investigating committee at the time.

With what he knew about the Cuban government's involvement with the CIA regarding narcotics trafficking, that would have been a real problem.

Consequently, he was set up and subsequently executed on the personal instructions of Fidel Castro.

In this time frame (1987-88) which was the real beginning of the Iran-Contra cover-up, closely following the murder of General Arnuldo Ochoa, there was the murder of Lt. General Reuben Mata, then Chief of Staff of the Honduran Army.

He was "shot while resisting arrest," while his home was being raided by US soldiers. It wasn't even Hondurans. It was an operation mounted by Oliver North himself, which Oliver North has never denied publicly.

The old Latin standby of "shot while resisting arrest" was used as the reason why the General did not come out of his residence alive and why all of his personal files in his home were looted.

By the time the Honduran Police got there, there wasn't one scrap of paper left in the house with any writing on it.

Also, after this assassination, there was the assassination of the infamous Haitian Colonel, Jean Paul, who later had become Brigadier General Jean Paul, Commanding Officer of the Dessaline Battalion.

He was Oliver North's direct contact in Haiti.

Jean Paul controlled the Haitian port of Cap Haitién, which became a principal transshipping route on the sea lane narcotics trafficking operations instituted by Ollie North in late 1985, when the air trafficking was getting too publicly revealed.

This was a time when reporters were hanging around Miami International Airport with camcorders. It was then decided that narcotics trafficking operations would shift more and more to the sea routes. This involved Swan Island off of Honduras, which was controlled by the Defense Intelligence Agency at the time.

There was a period of time during these cover-up years that you will see many murders and suspicious deaths of people involved in these operations.

If these people had talked, there would have been real problems.

There was the case of General Mata and also General Jean Paul, who was murdered by Lt. General Prosper Avríl's wife, Lucille. She was the one who actually made him the poisoned pumpkin soup which killed him.

Lucille herself was murdered three days later. Her body was found in an abandoned warehouse in Haiti controlled by George Bennett and his partner Ronald Harmon Brown, the late Commerce Secretary.

There was a period of time when there were a lot of murders close together. That was because there was a concern that this was the transition time between the Kerry Commission hearings and the Hughes Commission on Iran-Contra.

Congressman John Hughes was a pretty bright fellow. I had worked for him and tried to help him as much as I could. And he had a real good understanding of all this. He was going to subpoena a bunch of people.

And that's another interesting note, which is often overlooked. Of course, it's overlooked because the access to the information isn't always available. But if you see the subpoenas issued (or subpoenas that were intended to be issued) by the Kerry Committee, the Hughes Commission, the Alexander Commission and so on, and even Independent Counsel Lawrence Walsh, and then you see how closely they relate to people who were murdered at the time, and just how many people were murdered on the eve of being subpoenaed by a congressional investigating committee, it becomes quite a revelation.

Bill Alexander tried to make this public in 1992. He had a wonderful list prepared. He had the support of both Congressman Jack Brooks of Texas and Congressman Charlie Rose of North Carolina.

The *Washington Post* and the *New York Times* would not touch it with a ten-foot pole.

It would be quite a job now because this area has not been examined seriously by anybody in four or five years, neither in the press nor in Congress.

It would be quite a substantial job of pulling all this information together which is a matter of public record in some form, let alone all the information that is not a matter of public record. But certainly, it's doable.

As I mentioned recently, there is a much increased willingness in the media now, even the mainstream media, to go after this. There was a recent London Times article and the people at the *New York Times* and *San Francisco Chronicle* who have been calling around on Capitol Hill lately trying to dig through old records.

There is a new willingness to go after this stuff now and to actually put it in print.

Another case which cane be used as an illustration is the largest of all the CIA-connected narcotics cases — the Jack DeVoe case.

It's commonly called that because Jack DeVoe was the central defendant — although there were, as the indictment reads, a whole panoply of defendants, including virtually all of his partners: his principal partner, the infamous, sinister and dreaded Michael K. Smith, Tony Fernandez, Bill Blakemore, and Bill White.

The defendant list just goes on and on, but the principal defendant was DeVoe.

DeVoe was indicted and he was represented by a total of six different attorneys, including Pennington, his lead counsel.

DeVoe was actually convicted and sentenced to 220 years.

He served 17 days in jail then quietly left the United States. He was last reported in India. But that information is old and I don't know how correct it is anymore.

Michael Palmer is currently living low, although luxuriously, in Honduras.

Fernandez was subsequently killed. After his conviction he was subpoenaed by Lawrence Walsh's people, but before the FBI contingent could talk to him, he was killed.

One of his motor boats exploded with him in it.

It was ruled an "accidental" fuel leak.

Blakemore was killed in an airplane crash a few days later in the Bahamas. He had his own Cessna, a twin Beach Baron Model 410, which supposedly ran out of fuel and crashed on a remote archipelago in the Bahamas.

I don't remember off the top of my head without referring to my records, but I can tell you that no less than four other defendants in that case subsequently died under clouded circumstances.

The common thread among all these deaths is that they were going to be subpoenaed, or they had leaked information out to the other side (to some newspaper, or Congressional investigative committee, or the Independent Counsel's office) in the vain thought that perhaps that this would protect them.

In fact, everyone knew that leaking information to the other side simply led one to being, at the very least, discredited, and inconvenienced, or, at the worst, it led to one's own death.

There had been many journalists in the 1990-94 timeframe who have attempted to go back through court records to look at these cases and have met with every possible obstacle.

The DeVoe case is a good example. It generated 60,000 or 70,000 pieces of paper in the criminal proceedings. Some of these materials are still under "National Security" seal.

Even though these documents are supposed to be publicly available, the government has gone through every effort to obfuscate where these materials are in court records, where they've been sent to, or whether they're in reserve document storage facilities.

In come cases, they are sent to other agencies under blind files. It is not as easy as you'd think to gain access to public materials anymore unless you knew the routine where these files were sent.

Palmer is a good example.

When Dinnerstein was hired by a third party to look at Palmer a second time in 1995, all of Palmer's court records (this was a West Palm Beach federal jurisdiction case) turned out to be in a federal courthouse in Detroit under a file of a Mr. Smith.

That's the way it goes when you try to track down this information. Of course, if you don't know where the information is. or if you don't know the current file numbers, Freedom of Information Act requests are tantamount to useless because you have to have the precise file numbers.

These points only touch on the effort the government has made to obfuscate materials that should be properly, and constitutionally are, in the public domain. This obfuscation is enough to defeat most journalistic efforts.

The government knows full well that in our new era of bottom line corporate journalism, no media outlets, either electronic or print, will allow the investigative reporter the time and resources to actually mount a thorough search for these documents.

If they cannot obtain them quickly and cheaply, they won't go after the story — because they can't. Their editors won't allow the expenditure of time or money. The only way this would ever be put together in book form, for example, would be to hire somebody like Steve Dinnerstein as a full time employee to do nothing but hunt down these records and get copies of them. It would literally be a full time task for probably a year or more — and it would not be a cheap or easy.

This government obfuscation program, regarding public information is not only done by the Department of Justice, other federal agencies and certain state jurisdictions, but also by Congressional obfuscation.

It's something that people don't like to talk about — Congressional obfuscation of public materials.

Before Congress changed hands in 1994, many Congressional investigative committees controlled by Democrats, such as the House Oversight Committee, then chaired by Charlie Rose, or the Banking Committee, then chaired by Henry Gonzalez, had investigators who worked for these committees.

There was Tom Strzemienski, Dennis Kane, John Cohen over at the Judiciary when Brooks controlled the Judiciary. These men had substantial quantities of hard-to-find public information put together.

Unfortunately, when these committees changed hands, these men were all thrown out under various guises to keep their mouths shut in exchange for a government paycheck and a pension.

Then, when these committees became dominated by Republicans, all of this stuff, tremendous amounts of material, was shredded. That was done in order to make it difficult to reassemble the material.

If all the collected material is shredded, if the investigators who collected it are precluded from talking about it for fear of losing their employment, then you have to go out and put it back together again by hand.

It's not an easy task, although, it would be simpler for Dinnerstein because he has thousands and thousands of pages of these materials in his own files. He does not have tens of thousands of pages, but he does have thousands of pages.

Also he knows other investigators, particularly other private investigators, who were hired on the side by various committees. Even Larry Walsh's Independent Counsel's office accumulated a lot of these materials and may still have them. If you know all the people who investigated this thing outside of normal government channels, that's the first place to look for materials.

All the investigative reporters, in the last ten years or so, who have written pieces on this still have materials left. It's easier for Dinnerstein because, in many cases, he aided these people — or I aided these individual reporters in writing these articles.

In other words, I have a list. I know who all the reporters are. And I know the text of the articles they wrote, what information they had garnered at the time.

That would be another direction to move. There are ways to speed it up and make it a little cheaper to do this, but it would require somebody with the knowledge to do so.

As always, there are still key individuals who are willing to talk for the right price. This always exists in the wake of any covert operation. But you have to know who these people are, which means you have to have had intimate knowledge of how all of it worked at the time, who all the players were, what happened to these people, and what are their current circumstances.

There are a few people besides Dinnerstein and myself who have that kind of information.

For instance, one of the people who would be willing to talk for the right price is Robert Bennett. He's been making noises all along that he would be willing to cooperate with somebody for the right price.

Robert Bennett is George Bennett's son and Jean-Claude Duvalier's brother-in-law. Duvalier married Michelle Bennett and Bob is Michelle's brother. He is a fount of information when it comes to CIA narcotics operations in Haiti.

He's also a fount of information about Ronald Brown's connection with the Duvalier regime and how Ron Brown profited by that connection.

Also Robert Bennett can put Ron Brown, Virginia Madsen, General Avríl, and President Duvalier together like no one else.

This investigation leads to a chain of events which ultimately winds up in the attempt to intimidate Congressman Gonzalez. His car was machine-gunned in front of his townhouse in Washington — and it's an episode that no one likes to talk about anymore.

There is a direct chain, and Bennett is a fountain of information about it.

Another thing I wanted to mention was a relationship that Jack DeVoe had with the infamous, sinister and dreaded National Security Advisor, Frank Carlucci.

Carlucci exposed himself too much in his relationship with DeVoe.

There's even a photograph that was taken of them together. In the future, I'd like to examine what happened to all of the journalists and Congressional investigators who tried to put this relationship between Carlucci and DeVoe together. As you may well understand, none of them fared too well.

As we have discussed, the subject of Iran-Contra narcotics trafficking is just one of the three legs of Iran-Contra.

I think it's important that some members of government be exposed.

If — and when — George Bush, Jr. is elected in 2000, he will quickly put back all the old gang in positions of power — the *de facto* cabal as it were. Guys like Frank Carlucci, Assistant Secretary of State Richard Armitage, and Assistant Secretary of State Elliott Abrams are bound to make a come back — and that would prove very dangerous for people like me.

Then the Bushes, their minions and the cabal would be in a position of near total control again. People like me would become very inconvenient.

I don't think we would simply be pressured, intimidated or harassed any longer. I think that George, Jr. and Jeb would seek some sort of a final solution.

There are so few of us left that the real question is — what difference would it make if another 50 people died under clouded circumstances — when over 400 have died already?

It's nothing but a drop in the ocean.

I intended this to be an overview of CIA-sponsored narcotics trafficking during Iran-Contra, which can be later discussed in greater detail. My intent was to pull individual cases, take a look at the defendants, their connections to the governments and what happened to those defendants.

I also think it's important all throughout this book to show — "Here is the text of the original conspiracy called Iran-Contra, and here is the text of what happened in the post-conspiracy/cover-up years" — to make the circle complete.

How many people died to protect what information, to protect whom, how much information was destroyed, what happened to both the conspirators and conspiratees, and what the likelihood is in terms of exposing information that has yet to be exposed.

This is certainly where I'm going to be headed when we talk about the third leg of Iran-Contra activity — namely CIA-sponsored narcotics trafficking.

To this end I will limit what I have to say about the original conspiracy to what I knew either firsthand — or what I was directly involved in.

The ensuing cover-up, of course, has to be a little more third party, since I was already on the outside looking in. Therefore, I cannot really speak firsthand of the cover-up.

Certainly I know what happened because of what happened to others and because I know how it affected me. As part of the conspiracy and the cover-up, we will also be discussing not only the individual narcotics traffickers, but all the little nickel-and-dime narcotics airlines that were involved as well, culminating with a more exhaustive review of Southern Air Transport, the King of Narcotics Airlines.

Also I want to look at what happened to various federal prosecutors in the Department of Justice, those who were charged in maintaining the lid on Pandora's Box in the Iran-Contra narcotics cover-up, how these individuals were promoted, how they did thereafter, and how their careers blossomed beyond their wildest expectations.

One of the non-governmental individuals I want to focus on, regarding Iran-Contra/CIA narcotics trafficking, is the person I know the most about — Jeb Bush.

Although Jeb has only roundabout connections through his associates to Iran-Contra narcotics trafficking, they are worth exploring and setting down on paper because Jeb Bush can be put in a sequence, in chains of events, which ultimately lead to the deaths of people who know too much, which lead to the incarceration of people who know too much, and which lead to a whole lot of misery and really egregious acts.

Jeb is a good place to start — if one is going to look at the Bushes.

At least, he is, for me, because I know the most about him. I think it's important that Jeb's role in Iran-Contra be more fully explored.

Although there have been a lot of individual newspaper articles written about the subject, there really hasn't been much written about Jeb Bush and Iran-Contra narcotics trafficking.

We need to look at Jeb and his relationship with Southern Air Transport, his relationship with a group of attorneys around this entity who also represented him, and his direct employment of several Iran-Contra foot soldiers, men such as Manny Perez and Manny Diaz, attorneys such as Michael Von Zamft, others like George Morales who worked for Bush directly at the time.

What happened to these guys?

Morales was murdered the day before he left prison. I think it's important that Jeb be exposed so Jeb never rises again — at least not in terms of national power.

I've been asked in recent months by my own attorney and by several journalists and former investigators – aren't I concerned about the election of Jeb Bush as Governor of Florida and the re-election of George, Jr. as Governor of Texas?

But I'm really not concerned — not for my own safety anyway. They've made it pretty plain (at least Jeb has done so through his attorney who has talked to my attorney and so forth) that their only intentions are to keep me in the jack box and to make sure I don't cross that imagined line in the sand.

They, all of the Bushes, do not want to refocus the spotlight on their own Iran-Contra past. One indication of their supposed "goodwill," as they like to put it, is that some people like Gene Tatum have been taken care of.

They have finally received their "briefcases." In other cases, the Bushes have made it known that they are trying to extend the olive branch to some, perhaps me included. I don't know.

They've made some noises in that direction. However, this is just a foot dragging process to keep people like me quiet until what they hope comes to pass — that George, Jr. becomes the next President of the United States.

Then they can effectively put together this cabal again. And then, there will be no further deals. People like me will simply become inconvenient and ultimately disposed of in some fashion. In the interim, I am not frightened. Yet now is the time to act.

Now is the time to try to expose these people before they have a chance of getting back into power. And there is renewed interest in the media to do so. There is a renewed interest in Congress to do so.

Of course, that interest is always politically motivated. And that interest is always looking to be gerrymandered with the proverbial political scalpel. But nonetheless, it acts as a platform.

One must remember that in this book, which is a 100% non-fiction work, there will be new revelations in every page. It should be the most explosive Iran-Contra book ever written. And it could change the way people look at these Iran-Contra figures to ensure they never rise again politically speaking, which is my real goal.

In a final summary, we will continue to discuss Iran-Contra/CIA narcotics trafficking, the government principals involved, the private principals involved, and the airlines involved. We will discuss the air and shipping routes in greater detail. We will also discuss Oliver North's Guns-For-Drugs Operations out of Mena, Arkansas. And we will discuss Mena operations where political liability crosses party lines. Politically that becomes a different ball of wax for Clinton and his minions. But that's where we're headed.

Chapter 14

THE CHINESE CONNECTION: US WEAPONS AND HIGH TECH GRAFT

T HE FINAL REPORT of the Congressional Select Committee, chaired by Christopher Cox of California, has been released. His co-chairman, Nelson Dix of Washington, is a Democrat but essentially controlled by Republican interests, who's very close to the defense industry within the State of Washington.

They have released this Cox Report, wherein they mention that illicit transfers of high technology American weapons in exchange for political money have been going on for over twenty years.

Of course, they just mention it as a matter of state policy.

In their draft report, they mention only two defense contractors — Loral and Hughes Electronics. The only reason these two were mentioned is because they have already been previously exposed *vis-a-vis* the illicit transfer of high technology weapons to China.

However, no mention was made of political money in exchange for Department of Commerce permits allowing these defense contractors to export weapons and technology. Furthermore, no other defense contractors were mentioned in the draft report of the Select Committee.

This report will now go over to the Defense Intelligence Oversight Committee, which is investigating criminal matters *vis-a-vis* this very same subject pursuant to subpoenas said committee issued to high-ranking military personnel in and around the Redstone Arsenal in Huntsville, Alabama.

What the Select Committee has claimed in their findings is that the relationship *vis-a-vis* technology transfers of weapons has existed for approximately twenty years.

That is approximately correct, by the way.

They also mention the importance of Pakistan and Israel and a few other nations in this trade. However, they fail to tackle the subject from the very beginning.

So, for the purposes of this discussion, we will have to consistently digress so that the reader can understand the geopolitics of the relationship between the United States and the People's Republic of China, particularly from 1977 to 1979, when these illicit technology transfers began to occur.

What the report fails to include is the original importance of Pakistan as a surrogate arms merchant for the United States in 1978, the beginning of this period.

We must now remember the time frame and what was happening at that time and the United States geopolitical and geomilitary policy then *vis-a-vis* both the Soviet Union and the Peoples Republic of China.

You may remember that in 1977, President Carter delinked the United States from Taiwan by withdrawing diplomatic relationship with Taiwan, ostensibly to seek an increased trade relationship with the China. At the same time he extended, in a confidential protocol, certain military guarantees to Taiwan.

This was walking a fine line, and President Carter knew that it was an immensely unpopular decision, particularly within conservative quarters where Taiwan had been considered a traditional ally of the United States. This had particularly been true in Republican administrations of the past.

At the time Prime Minister Ali Bhutto of Pakistan, whom the United States had initially supported, began to waver *vis-a-vis* the protocols he had established with Washington in exchange for both economic and military aid.

In late 1977, Bhutto began a rapprochement with India and a rapprochement with the Soviet Union taking the traditional Pakistani policy, a regional economic, political economic, and military policy, in absolutely the opposite direction of what it had traditionally been. In other words, Pakistan had been a *de facto* political, economic and military vassal state of the United States, which it was then and still is today.

Ali Bhutto, in doing this, perhaps failed to appreciate the power of the CIA in Pakistan at the time — and continuing to this day.

The CIA has substantial assets in Pakistan. At that time, in late 1977 and early 1978, the CIA was very influential and very closely aligned with the Pakistani military.

As Ali Bhutto increasingly began to ignore the wishes of the United States, *vis-a-vis* U.S. theater policies in the Indian sub-continent, the CIA quietly started to encourage the Pakistani military, then under the command of Chief of Staff, General Zia el Haq to institute a coup d'etat against the Ali Bhutto administration. It would be a coup d'etat that the United States would secretly support.

As history recounts, the coup d'etat was undertaken.

When Zia el Haq came to power, one of his first official acts at the covert urging of the United States, was to put Ali Bhutto on trial for treason.

Ali Bhutto is history now, as he was promptly hung.

His daughter Benazir, who was politically popular in Pakistan at the time was exiled to England.

It should be noted that the CIA has used England in the past as a political dumping ground for those it wished to see exiled.

Zia was ensconced in power, and his power not consolidated by the spring of 1978, he proceeded to do his masters' bidding in Washington, and immediately reversed Ali Bhutto's rapprochement policies.

He immediately stopped the warming of Pakistani relationships towards India and the Soviet Union. He immediately reinstituted a very hard line, both politically and militarily, against India and the Soviet Union. And he immediately began to thaw out the previously close relationship between Pakistan and China.

One of the points of putting General Zia in power was to restore the balance of power in the Indian sub-continent *vis-a-vis* United States and China geopolitical policy.

Since Zia was a right-wing dictator, he would reinstall a pro-western, (secular in name only) democracy, which is essentially what he did in Pakistan at that time.

Zia contained Muslim fundamentalism by force of arms. He readopted an extremely close relationship with the United States for public consumption, but the real underlying truth was that Pakistan was a *de facto* vassal of the United States in every way possible. It could not survive without United States money.

So, once again, as had been done previously, Pakistan acted as an arms merchant between the United States and the People's Republic of China. In other words, high technology weapon exports were being sent to Pakistan.

Then Pakistan was essentially re-exporting these exports to China, sometimes by itself, or through using African or Israeli intermediaries.

At the same time, the double impact of this policy was that since Zia was, in Washington's eyes, the golden-haired boy of Pakistan, and we were able to act in a more overt fashion in terms of arming Pakistan.

Washington did, in fact, sell billions of dollars worth of weapons to Pakistan — all on credit of course. The same scheme has been used before.

Pakistan didn't have any money and it never has had any money.

The US government provided credit for large scale purchases of weapons from U.S. defense manufacturers, and issued quiet credit guarantees, disguising these guarantees among various quasi-government agencies, such as OPIC, CCC and the Export-Import Bank.

A little mini-scandal was ultimately created in the 1980s, when the policy once again shifted to the CIA-backed Benazir Bhutto and her People's Party in a coup d'etat against General Zia. Of course, the first thing Benazir Bhutto did when she took her father's place after an eight-year gap, was to have Zia hanged.

But, anyway, it's necessary to skip around to make this thing continuous.

Back to 1978 — the balance had been restored in the sub-continent *vis-a-vis* our interests, namely that India, although technically a non-aligned state and the second power of the non-aligned association of states, was in fact a Soviet satellite.

India was financed by the Soviet Union. They received all of their arms from the Soviet Union. In the United Nations, they would consistently vote with the Soviet Union. Although they maintained the facade of independence and paid lip service to the west, they were in fact a *de facto* Soviet state.

Pakistan was very pro-United States. Having been extensively armed by the United States, it resumed its theater political and military position by being hostile towards India and keeping India in check.

It was also hostile toward the Soviet Union and moving once again closer to the People's Republic of China, particularly the People's Army and the Public Security Bureau (PSB).

These events relate essentially to earlier doctrines — doctrines that had originally been discussed in 1971 when Nixon first broke the ice with China with his meeting with Zhou Enlai.

These were later consolidated into a CIA policy in 1973, which literally became known as the "Colby China Doctrine." It was realized that the United States and China had very similar, global geoeconomic, geopolitical and geomilitary global interests vis-a-vis the containment of the Soviet Union, and that the policies were so close that the language that was often used publicly was extremely similar.

Colby's concept was to contain Soviet expansionism in all spheres simultaneously by supporting opposite factions.

The public pronouncements by China were almost exactly the same thing, except as the Chinese would be very cute and use the word "hegemonism," as in to contain Soviet "hegemonism."

"Hegemonism" is just nomenclature for "expansionism."

As we go forward to 1979, we again see a shift in theater politics, particularly on the side of the Soviets.

The Soviets had by now invaded Afghanistan, and this was a direct threat to United States interests within the geopolitical balance in the Indian sub-continent.

The Soviets made it known that they were looking for India to move much more openly toward the Soviet camp. In order to entice India to do this, the Soviet Union began giving India thermonuclear weapons technology.

Naturally, when the CIA became aware of this, which was only within a year or so, Pakistan would also have had to have this technology.

The CIA was frightened of even covertly giving this technology to Pakistan. They, in turn, asked China to give thermonuclear weapons technology to Pakistan, which China gladly did. They saw it in their best interest, since they had traditionally looked at Pakistan as a buffer state between themselves and India.

Now, with the Soviet Union making a bid to expand their influence in the Indian sub-continent and threatening to introduce larger scale weapons systems in Afghanistan, China suddenly became extremely close to Pakistan.

At this time, the United States became increasingly nervous vis-a-vis

Soviet expansionism, so in the 1979 to 1981 period, high-technology weapons transfers, as well as shipments of the actual weapons to the People's Republic of China were stepped up.

It was these high technology transfers that essentially allowed the People's Republic of China to build a military satellite system as well as a military spy and intelligence gathering satellite system, something they had been unable to do before.

The United States considered this a "stabilizing" factor.

The People's Republic of China was way behind the eight ball in terms of satellite development.

Both the United States and the Soviet Union had extremely well developed military satellite systems, so they could view every square inch of each others' territory. In some ways, this acted as a mutual deterrence and mutual compliance.

China, lacking this technology, was constantly suspicious of the Soviet Union.

It was feared in the United States that China, on only a perceived provocation, could very readily actually launch thermonuclear weapons at the Soviet Union because they did not have the technological means to enter into any type of a mutual deterrence with the Soviet Union.

Therefore, we looked at it in terms of macro-geopolitical and geomilitary interests to see China have these types of high technology systems.

The further coincidental benefit to this was that it made billions for U.S. defense contractors.

This was particularly true in the early 1980s. And the more billions that U.S. defense contractors could make surreptitiously, the more millions of those billions would get donated into Republican coffers.

There was still a geopolitical interest in doing this, but starting around 1981 that became increasingly skewed as the Chinese began giving more and more millions to the Republican National Committee.

There are some further connections that go way back and exist to this day that should be mentioned because they are germane to other policies of the 1980s, even to Iran-Contra.

This is the traditional connection between the United States, the South Africans, the Israelis, and the Pakistanis — and later the Iranians. The Iranians didn't become part of this equation until about 1985.

As I mentioned before, the Chinese had been giving thermonuclear weapons technology to the Pakistanis, but what the Pakistanis wanted was missile technology to go along with that — something the Chinese were sorely lacking.

This was particularly true with the so-called theater nuclear weapons delivery systems. The Pakistanis weren't interested in strategic systems. They were interested in theater systems. And theater systems were something that the Chinese had not devoted a lot of effort to developing.

The Chinese principal interest had always been the ability to project thermonuclear power within a strategic theater of operation, not a specific regional theater. They didn't face any real threat in terms of a regional theater.

Therefore, starting about 1981, when Reagan first came to power, with the consent of the United States, the Israelis started to give Pakistan missile technology, particularly short-range and medium-range missile technology, as well as the technology to affix thermonuclear warheads to missiles, which is a much more sophisticated technology than equipping a missile with a conventional or even a chemical warhead.

A thermonuclear warhead on a missile is a whole different ball of wax. And where did it get the missile technology? Pakistan got the missile technology from Israel.

And Israel got the missile technology as a technology transfer from South Africa.

The South Africans, of course, originally got the technology from the US.

That whole connection starts between the United States and the South Africa. It had been commonly presumed by the Soviet Union, and incorrectly presumed, that it was the United States which covertly transferred thermonuclear weapons technology to Israel, which allowed Israel to build thermonuclear weapons of its own.

Of course, Israel did not have thermonuclear weapons capability fully developed and deliverable until 1976.

The South African already had thermonuclear weapons in 1972 as well as the ability to deliver them, at least on a short-range basis.

South Africa, though, was a different case. They were much less interested in missile applications and much more interested in low-yield thermonuclear artillery shells, particularly 155 mm and 175 mm thermonuclear artillery, five-kiloton yield artillery shells.

The United States had previously provided the South Africans with this technology, particularly as it related to artillery shells or extremely short-range thermonuclear weapons systems, such as the Lance Missile System, a very good portable short-range missile system that carries either a five- or ten-kiloton thermonuclear warhead. They are rather accurate, cheap to produce, with a simple guidance system. This was what the South Africans were looking for.

This again related to an earlier policy, wherein the United States was extremely concerned about the white South African government's viability.

The obvious mathematics made South Africa inherently unstable. Four million white people and eighteen million black people — both sides hating each other. These kinds of numbers always frightened the United States because the United States wanted to absolutely ensure that the South African government would remain white, would remain pro-western, and would remain essentially under joint United States-British political control as it did for years.

Also the United States wanted to ensure that its supplies of strategic minerals (all of which it got from South Africa) would remain intact — materials such as rhodium, tritium, and strontium, particularly strontium-90, cesium-230, mercury-240.

These are strategic minerals that are found in very few places in the world. The two principal places they are found naturally occurring is in South Africa and in the Soviet Union. They are all important components (chromium is another one) for the construction of thermonuclear weapons.

The United States was concerned that the South African government remain stable so that its supply of these rare minerals would remain stable and available.

Were there to be a radical black administration, or were the white government to be overthrown and a left-wing black administration be installed (which might become chummy to the Soviet Union) — this was a real concern in the 1970s.

It would be seen as a real problem to the strategic interest to the United States. Therefore, the United States gave South Africa thermonuclear weapons technology, concentrating on what the South Africans needed.

Namely, the South Africans' internal interest was the ability to eliminate (with the use of low-yield thermonuclear weapons) large numbers of blacks quickly.

If one looks at the demographic situation in South Africa, one sees that those eighteen million blacks aren't simply spread across the country. They tend to be concentrated in large numbers in small areas.

There are large quasi-cities, or quasi-slums, or camps (whatever you want to call them) and there was the subsequent institution of the South African "Homeland" policy, which essentially set aside small independent states for blacks.

But to make a long story short, the policy of the South African white governments had been traditionally to concentrate as many blacks as possible into the smallest area possible, and to make these areas as far away from the white population (and the white industrial centers) as possible.

This way they would be much easier to contain and much easier to eliminate, particularly if one had thermonuclear weapons.

As I mentioned earlier, it's necessary to digress in order to understand the whole policy *vis-a-vis* China because it starts with other countries and other concerns which filter into China on both regional theater and strategic levels.

To conclude on South Africa — a second reason why we provided the South African government with thermonuclear technology was for South Africa as a *de facto* vassal of the United States to act as a bulwark against potential Soviet expansionism in Africa, particularly in the border states around South Africa — Namibia, Zimbabwe, and Mozambique in particular, and Angola to the northwest.

It was felt that if the South Africans had at least a credible short-range thermonuclear deterrence that it would contain Soviet interests in Africa, which it certainly did.

You can see this *vis-a-vis* the 1975 situation in Angola when the Soviets put in technical advisers and heavy weapon systems to back one faction, and the South Africans, the Chinese and the Pakistanis covertly backed UNITA, the other faction.

UNITA is still backed by the same combination of powers today as it was more than twenty years ago. Little has changed. However, the policy was successful, and the Soviets were forced to withdraw.

This was an example of cooperation between the United States, China and its mutual client states pursuant to this "Colby China Doctrine," containing Soviet expansionism in all spheres of influence and in all theaters simultaneously.

This famous South Africa-to-Israel-to-other-destination military transfer points worked very effectively *vis-a-vis* getting weapons to Iran in 1985, and later the following year, getting weapons to Iraq.

People tend to forget. They look at Iraqgate as being a 1988-1991 thing, when in fact weapons transfers and weapons sales to Iraq had begun as early as 1986. It was one of the policies of then-interim DCI Chief, Bobby Gates.

To conclude on the South African-Israeli connection, it should be noted that this connection in itself proved profitable to the United States *vis-a-vis* the mutual military relationship established by Israel and South Africa.

South Africa provided the State of Israel with nuclear weapons technology and also sold Israel artillery pieces, particularly the very high quality Bofors guns and self-propelled 155 and 175 mm artillery pieces.

In exchange for these, Israel began to sell South Africa jet fighters, principally the Israeli Kafir, which was essentially a knock-off of the American F-5 at a time, when the South Africans were looking to rebuild their air force, which had become very old.

This was also a time when the United States could no longer either overtly or covertly sell such weapons system to South Africa due to the various economic, political and military embargos placed on South Africa after 1979 because of their apartheid policies.

Filtering Iran-Contra into this equation for a moment — who was the principal conduit between the US, South Africa and Israel regarding weapons transfers to Iran and Iraq in 1985-1986?

It was the infamous Michael Harari, a senior Mossad agent who operated closely with Manuel Noriega.

The policy towards arming China began to change in 1986, when relationships between the United States and the Soviet Union began to thaw to some degree. They continued to thaw in the years thereafter.

Some of my fellow cohorts knew — for instance, in discussions I had with Elliot Abrams in 1986 (he was the Assistant Secretary of State for Latin American Affairs) — what the bigger picture was.

The Republicans within the Reagan-Bush regime knew as early as 1986 that there was a potential scandal brewing, if the extent of indirect weapon transfers to the People's Republic of China in exchange for Chinese money ever came out.

This became an increasing detriment due to the shift in global strategic policy from a hardline towards the beginning of a thaw between the US and the Evil Empire of the Soviet Union.

By this time (1986-1987), the Chinese began to be regarded as a destabilizing force geopolitically, whereas before they had been considered a stabilizing force.

The Soviet Union had not been particularly concerned about our weapons transfers to China for twenty years (from 1966 to 1986) insofar as Chinese strategic nuclear weapons had all been concentrated around the facilities where China produced nuclear weapons, namely Lop Nor.

By 1986, however, much to our chagrin, Chinese strategic assets had been well dispersed throughout the country in mobile launchers and in silos.

We also became increasingly aware that the bulk of Chinese strategic forces was in fact aimed at the United States, not at the Soviet Union, as had been commonly presumed earlier — and as the Chinese had informed us earlier.

Therefore, there was a period from 1986 to 1990 where weapons technology transfers and sales to China via intermediaries were temporarily scaled down, just as the Soviet Union began to convert from a communist country to a capitalist country.

However, when it became apparent in 1990 that the Soviet Union was effectively unraveling, we returned to the situation that we were in previously. This time it was for a different reason. It was that Russia was now a destabilizing factor because of its own internal political chaos.

Therefore, a renewed effort with China to bolster Chinese technology and to bolster the production of strategic systems in China was looked at as a restabilizing influence against Soviet internal instability instead of external adventurism, as it had been ten years prior.

In 1991-1992, at the very end of the Bush administration, technology and weapons transfer to China was ramped up again, which served Mr. Bush well in terms of the amount of Chinese money that came into his 1992 presidential campaign.

However, this is not to say that the Chinese didn't hedge their bets.

They had traditionally given money to both parties for years through a variety of artifices. Before 1992, the bulk of political campaign contributions had always been given to Republicans.

In 1992, even the Chinese sensed there was a shift coming. They made sure, for the very first time, that the Democratic National Committee started to get six-figure Chinese political money.

Fast forward to today, that amount of money has increased. The policy of covertly arming China has really not changed. As Larry Klayman at Judicial Watch is correct in pointing out, we are "Japanning" China. And I wonder how many Americans really understand what that means. What he's saying is that by allowing China, ostensibly a hostile nation, to have "most favored nation" status with the United States regarding trade policies, we are allowing China to exercise a $3 to $4 billion a month trade deficit with the United States.

Most of this trade deficit is then used to purchase weapons, which are used to build strategic thermonuclear weapon systems pointed at the United States.

The long and short of it is that the American citizen acting in his capacity as both a taxpayer and a citizen is essentially arming China to point weapons at the United States.

And that is the real nub and the real sizzle of the scandal.

Klayman knows it. And you can tell by the way Klayman talks on the political talk shows, he tries to grind in the "Japanizing" of the connection, since we allowed Japan to run trade deficits with the United States for years in order to purchase US goods, principally weapons.

You can imagine that Klayman says this is the biggest potential scandal of the century — a covert policy that has existed for over twenty years. This cannot be disguised or colored for geopolitical or geomilitary purposes because in the public's mind, it is so much about money.

Even in the politician's mind, it is now really a relationship about money. There are no longer any geomilitary or geopolitical concerns.

This budding scandal, which is now starting to be investigated by the Department of Justice, as I have said, is the next big scandal.

For twenty years, this policy has existed.

There have been millions and millions that have come into both political parties' national committees in exchange for weapons going out the back door.

These are weapons that the American people, both as taxpayers and consumers, have financed to have pointed at themselves.

You can imagine that this is one hell of a scandal if it gets packaged up the right way, which is exactly what Klayman is attempting to do.

We've discussed the previous geopolitical, economic and military implications of this policy — why this policy was framed to begin with and why it continues to this day.

What we have not discussed is the money coming through a variety of Chinese agents. The crossover between the Republicans and the Democrats vis-a-vis surreptitious Chinese political money coming into the national committees of both coffers has been worked consistently over twenty years by the same intermediaries.

That is what has already been publicly revealed about Charlie Trie and John Huang, for instance, and the 147 other Chinese that commonly mentioned in the media as being "The Gang of 147 " identified by Congress.

The banks, which are the root of the money, start from the Bank of

China and filter out through the Hong Kong branch of the Hong Kong and Shanghai Bank, the Industrial Bank of Indonesia, and the Riady family.

The notion of Clinton's closeness to the Riady — this isn't new. None of this is new. The Riady family was also very close to the Bush people. It's just that when the money for Republicans left the Industrial Bank of Indonesia, it simply took different routes.

It is Chinese money (and this is little known) that principally caused the formation of the Nugan Hand Bank.

When that fell apart and became exposed and some people in Australia died to make sure it stayed covered up, there was simply a new artifice created for Democrats.

Money from the Riady group was coming directly into Arkansas banks, principally through the Stephens Investment Group. It was simply a different artifice when the money went from the Orient to the United States.

When it got to the Democrats, it was simply a different set of banks and a different set of brokerage firms. In Republican times, the money had often been filtered through Merrill Lynch.

Now the money is filtered through Stephens Investment Group and other smaller brokerage firms close to Clinton or other Democrats.

What has come to light recently is the Democrat side of the equation. This includes the connection of Ron Brown, the DNC, Chinese weapons and licensing by the Commerce Department for export of armaments and high-technology weapons, which were winding up in China being mislabeled and so forth.

You start to understand the role of Ron Brown in all of this. And you start to understand why he had to go.

Ron Brown suddenly died at the very same time the FBI received conclusive information that John Huang and Charlie Trie and a few others were not only just Chinese businessmen, but were in fact reserve officers (not just in the PSB) but of the MSS, the Chinese Ministry of State Security.

If this were to become publicly known (the FBI already knew it and had leaked some of this information, but not the proof to back it up, to Burton's committee), FBI Director Freeh has recognized the political implication.

This would constitute treasonable conduct by the Clinton administration.

The notion of treason has been put forth by Klayman, Charlie Smith and others. Enough has been leaked out publicly that you can start to connect the dots of why they're using the word "treason."

Chinese money is coming in from Chinese brokers. Some of these Chinese brokers are not only closely connected to the government in China, but in fact they're Chinese intelligence officers.

The Department of Commerce, under Ron Brown and continuing to this day, is allowing false bills of lading for exports of forbidden weapons that it knows are going to wind up in China.

Ron Brown had already begun to leak some of this publicly before he died. I imagine this is one of the reasons he did die.

Chinese weapons merchants, who are also Chinese intelligence agents, are being allowed such access to the Redstone Arsenal in Huntsville, Alabama.

Many of the Chinese arms merchants and Chinese people identified as having been at weapons auctions at Redstone, or having been at certain military parties with two- and three-star generals are also the very same people who are on this List of 147.

Perhaps it becomes more obvious why the Klaymans of this world are invoking the word "treason" because if this is all put out the right way, and the dots are all drawn in, it does represent treasonable conduct by the Clinton administration.

It also represents treasonable conduct by the Bush administration. I imagine that's why certain Republicans aren't all that enthralled about investigating it.

Look at the Republicans who are the most reticent in supporting a new and expanded probe into Chinese money for Chinese weapons. They are the very same Republicans of the old Bush group who were very close to the defense industry before and continue to derive much money from the defense industry.

It struck me with some humor that the members of the Congressional Select Committee investigating this includes the second most senior Republican member. It's none other than Congressman Porter Goss, who has the distinction of having received more defense money from Loral and Hughes Electronics than anyone else.

So if anyone is looking for any astounding revelations from the select committee, or even the Defense Intelligence Oversight Committee, which is also loaded with Republicans close to the defense industry, I wouldn't bet on it.

There's an ancillary point to this, and that is the Chinese hedging their bets.

In a separate probe, there was a gentleman who was revealed to be acting as an intermediary, laundering Chinese government money to both recent Bush gubernatorial campaigns — both in Florida and Texas.

It was also discovered how that money was being used by their campaigns, and then getting laundered back to Republican National Committee, principally through members of GOPAC.

It is exactly the same Chinese money route that existed in the 1980s. Nothing has changed.

The way the Democrats are getting the money is almost exactly the way the Republicans have always gotten it. It just involves a different series of banks, once the money leaves the Orient and gets to the United States.

But more and more of this is going to come out, and more and more of it is going to be provable because there was never a large effort to cover it up.

The Clinton administration had begun to scramble, and you can tell this is getting closer to home. Republicans were also becoming increasingly concerned about previous liability.

Why else would it be that Israeli, South African, and Brazilian so-called "Agriculture Trade Delegations" have all shown up at the Redstone Arsenal in Huntsville, Alabama?

This United States military institution has nothing to do with agriculture. It's the same old connection. It's really the South African-Brazilian connection and that's a separate issue.

You may remember some of the comments in the media and the little scandal that had been created by the revelations of George Sr., and George Jr., and Jeb and Neil's connections with a certain Brazilian named Amaro Pintos Ramos, who was heavily in the Brazilian nuclear program and how nuclear materials left Brazil and went elsewhere.

That's a whole different sub-connection.

However, the only reason I happened to mention it is because of all the South Americans that showed up in these trade delegations.

Simply look who the people were from the past. It isn't hard to understand what the probable text of the discussions was.

This was called a "cover your ass" meeting which involved Israeli, South African and some South Americans, as well as some senior military officers, mostly two- and three-star generals, who got their initial appointments (their initial stars) in the Reagan-Bush administration.

What's going on in Huntsville now is essentially a Republican effort to cover your ass at the source.

An interesting little double feature of this on the Republican side is how they're making money three ways to Sunday on this thing.

In 1991, the first people who set up export companies in the Soviet Union were all part of the Old Bush Gang.

Frank Carlucci and Dick Armitage set up an export company, Blackstone Investment Group, operating ostensibly for the CIA to purchase potentially wayward nuclear materials out of the Soviet Union. This also involved some technology that people aren't aware of.

The stuff was getting repackaged and then surreptitiously sold back to China.

In other words, how can you can sell the same nuclear components and technologies five different times in ten years and keep selling them to the same parties back and forth?

It's incredible. But, as I've said before, you could write a separate book on this.

Certainly, that's what Larry Klayman and Charlie Smith will ultimately do. He and Smith will collaborate with a few others, and you'll see a book attempting to expose all this as much as they can. Unfortunately, they probably don't know half of what I know, but they'll try.

Anyway, I think I'll end it here because otherwise if I start getting into the banks, it's just endless — following this Chinese money around. And then how it gets looped into deals in the United States and looped into transactions that are so far removed, you would never believe that they originally extended from Chinese money.

They get guaranteed from all sorts of esoteric little agencies that don't have anything to do with the Department of Defense.

It is almost laughable.

Chapter 15

MORE IRAN-CONTRA STORIES: BOTH HUMOROUS AND SALIENT

I WOULD LIKE TO DEVOTE some time to both humorous and salient narrative stories about myself and my involvement in Iran-Contra, as well as other illegal and covert matters of state in the 1983-1986 time frame.

I think it's important to not only have raw information, but also narrative stories, true stories in a non-fiction, narrative sense. I'd like to do a series of narrative stories, a combination of stories that are not only true, but are also humorous and yet salient.

These stories will be in no particular chronological order. They are going to be as I recount them from my own head. Actually I can do a better job that way rather than having to sequence them chronologically.

They will involve characters such as Oliver North, Richard Secord, Jeb Bush and a host of others.

One interesting story that comes to mind is my meeting with Jeb Bush at the end of the second week of February 1986, ostensibly to discuss the text of my upcoming grand jury testimony.

In this meeting with Jeb Bush, I intended to reveal to him in a backhanded manner how I intended to play my cards and to see what his responses were.

In this discussion, I had mentioned the recent assassination, only a few days before, of Barry Seal.

I said to Jeb, "Isn't it convenient that Barry Seal was assassinated when he was? And now suddenly all the information and documents he had have gone missing?"

Jeb had a rather broad smile on his face, and he concurred that it was convenient. He added a little snicker — as he often had a tendency of doing.

Also little beads of sweat formed around his forehead, as when he gets nervous. It's something you can notice when he's on television. He still has a tendency to have little beads of sweat around his forehead, when he's either lying about something, or he's nervous about what someone else is saying.

My conversations with Jeb at this meeting were overheard by the two Secret Service agents who were always assigned to Jeb when he was in his office at 1390 Brickell Avenue in Miami.

I had intimated that if certain parties in Washington were not prepared to come to my aid pursuant to my grand jury testimony, that it would be entirely possible that certain details of a certain meeting occurring in September of the year before might be leaked out to the press.

Jeb asked me what I was talking about.

I specifically mentioned a September meeting of the Dade County Latin American Chamber of Commerce, which Jeb chaired, and which, of course, was not used as a Chamber of Commerce meeting at all. It was essentially used as a political meeting for covert operational planning pursuant to Iran-Contra.

As I've said before, Oliver North, Richard Secord or Dewey Clarridge or, in a few cases, even Sam Watson and Fred Ikley himself, would show up at these meetings.

Anyway, I had recounted to Jeb, as if he didn't know what the text of that meeting was that he chaired — the conversations he had with Oliver North and Richard Secord and Dewey Clarridge, all of whom attended that meeting.

Dewey seldom attended the meetings, but this time the four of them were discussing the assassination of Barry Seal and how it was to be carried out, since Barry was becoming an increasing liability.

I had told Jeb that I had substantial corroboration of that meeting. And I think Jeb understood what I meant.

I could certainly place him into a conspiracy to assassinate a CIA drug runner for the sake of political expediency.

When I was through speaking, Jeb became quiet and his demeanor became serious and changed. He became flushed, as he often does when he's frightened.

Jeb responded by telling me that it would be most unfortunate if I were to do that, since I might wind up like George Morales or Johnny Molina.

What he was referring to, of course, was that, a number of months earlier, George Morales had been set up on a cocaine charge — to distance what Morales was doing from the CIA.

As any serious student of Iran-Contra would know, Morales absolutely screamed "CIA, CIA."

But ultimately he was convicted.

He was bound and gagged in the courtroom before the Republican Judge Hoover, who allowed him to present no CIA defense. He couldn't mention any Bush names, or North, or Secord, or anything.

He got the standard fifteen-year sentence for cocaine trafficking. At the time, in the State of Florida, you had to serve six years nine months mandatory.

Jeb then went on to mention to me about Morales. He said "Of course, Morales will never leave prison alive."

Fast forward to the time when Morales was due to be released from prison in early 1992.

The day before Morales was to be released, he did, in fact, slip on a bar of soap in the prisoner's shower and supposedly died as a result of the fall.

The following day, Morales was due to be picked up at Miami International Airport by a Congressional charter flight arranged for him by Congressmen Alexander, Rose, Brooks and Gonzalez. He was to be taken to Washington to have a detailed discussion with them and their investigators about his knowledge of Iran-Contra.

At that moment, the threat that Jeb was making to me — the sublime threat about not wanting to wind up like Johnny Molina — really didn't mean anything to me because I knew as of the day before that Molina was still alive and well.

I didn't think anything of it until the next day when I got into my office and opened the *Miami Herald*.

I read that Mr. Molina had in fact "committed suicide" that evening in the parking lot of a restaurant in Pensacola, Florida.

He had "committed suicide" by discharging an entire twenty-round clip of a MAC-10 into his own body.

Of course, by the following day, the body had quickly been cremated — before his family was notified and before an autopsy could be done.

It's the same old story.

It was interesting to note that Jeb had issued that threat at that meeting which was held at about 10:30 a.m.

Molina "committed suicide" at about 9:30 p.m. that evening.

I found the connection rather humorous, but also salient in that Bush knew what was going to happen a number of hours before it actually did.

A second interesting and humorous story I can relate from that September meeting was not only the discussion of Barry Seal, but the general discussion of narcotics, wherein Jeb was talking to Oliver North.

Dewey Clarridge and Joe Fernandez were there and Jeb was whining about how they were importing so much cocaine for the purposes of maintaining illicit covert revenue streams that, in fact, they were depressing the street value of the price of cocaine.

Revenues were in fact diminishing.

And North chuckled, and said that he had already made arrangements, that he, Dewey, Fred Ikley and Clair George had made arrangements.

What they were referring to by "arrangements" was the opening of the so-called sea routes to substantially increase the amount of cocaine that was being imported.

Jeb Bush said to Oliver North, "All you would manage to do is to further depress the price of cocaine."

North's attitude was, "Well, we'll simply bring in more and more of the stuff to maintain revenues."

As it has been pointed out in the past, CIA-assisted enterprise narcotics trafficking managed to depress the street price of a value of cocaine from $30,000 in early 1985 to $12,000 by mid-1986.

Later in this conversation, Jeb, wanting to be helpful, threw out a suggestion regarding the separate Guns-For-Drugs Operation being run out of Mena Airport in Arkansas.

He suggested that North start changing the fraction vis-a-vis the Contras.

Instead of one M-16 rifle, 1,000 rounds of ammunition, and the full field kit in exchange for one kilogram of cocaine, Bush suggested that North inform Enrico Bermudez and Eden Pastora that henceforth it was going to be two kilograms of cocaine for the same weapons delivery as it had been in the past.

North rebuffed this suggestion, reminding Bush that the one M-16 rifle, ammunition and field kit cost them a total of a $1,000 net delivered and the value of the kilogram of cocaine was still $17,000 or $18,000.

The third and final salient highlight I'd like to point out about that meeting (which was an important and pivotal meeting) is that General Secord had mentioned to Jeb Bush — and I was standing not two feet from him — that some of Jeb's hangers-on (some of the old Cuban Bay of Pigs crowd that were Jeb Bush hangers-on *vis-a-vis* Jeb wearing his hat as a scamscateer and a money launderer) were beginning to have big mouths.

And Jeb asked, "Who?"

Secord specifically said that it was the infamous Manny Perez, who was a very close ally of Jeb's and had been for a long time. Perez used to act as a straw at various fraudulent deals for Jeb. He transported cash. He wired money into accounts he controlled through a variety of other straws. He was also very close with Jeb at Eagle National Bank in Miami.

Jeb asked General Secord what he, Jeb Bush, was supposed to do about it.

And Dick Secord said, "Well, your father controls your show and he's got to clean up his own mess."

History records it wasn't that long after that an article appeared in a certain major newspaper about Manny Perez.

Evidently Manny's body was found floating in a canal in West Hialeah, and his death was duly declared a "swimming accident."

Perhaps the reader can better understand the phone call I received the day after the November 1998 elections when Jeb Bush won the governorship of the State of Florida.

On that very same evening, I got a phone call from Neil Lewis in Miami, an attorney who had previously represented both Jeb and me, and who had acted as a conduit for people like me to Jeb and Dick Secord and a variety of others.

Neil told me that he had a direct message from Jeb stating that if I wished to continue to be a resident of this state and to remain at large and with life that I best not reveal stories such as I have revealed here.

When Neil relayed the threat to me that evening, I told Neil that when he talked to Jeb the following day (which I knew he would because he wanted to know what my response would be) to tell Jeb that I was aware that my former close colleague, Larry Hamil, prior to the November 1998 elections, had been involved in a political campaign money laundering scheme, wherein Mr. Hamil laundered certain monies of Chinese origin to certain Republicans (not Democrats, but Republican candidates) including the gubernatorial candidacy of Jeb Bush.

Neil laughed and said, "Are you certain you want me to relay that?"

I said, "Yes," and I didn't talk to Neil after that.

I can only presume Neil did, in fact, relay that message because the next morning when I got out of bed, I was greeted by a view (outside of my bay windows) of two unmarked cars parked directly in front of my townhouse. They were of the sinister variety I'm used to — dark Chevy Caprices, darkened windows, black-wall tires, four or five aerials coming out of the back of them, Washington D.C. plates.

There was enough sunlight that I could see two men sitting in each vehicle.

And that's all they did.

They simply sat there and looked directly at my unit. They stayed for a few hours in that position and then drove off.

I had one of my neighbors record the D.C. plates on the car and upon checking them out later in the day, I was informed that no such plates existed.

But nonetheless, the message was sent.

Recently I have not gone forth attempting to bang the drum on the issue of Chinese political money coming into Republican candidates in 1998, particularly Jeb Bush.

I would also like to add an adjunct to what I just said — for the naive and the uninformed — about the type of lives people like me live. When I say people like me — there may be four or five hundred left that in my category.

It is the sinister looking cars with the darkened windows and aerials with Virginia or Washington D.C. plates that trace back to nowhere.

It is the binoculars and the parabolic rabbit ears, the obvious telephone taps, the loose surveillance, and having the local or county police drive slowly past your home in the middle of the night and shine their spotlight on your windows.

This is the way signals are sent to people like me (when we are playing the game of chess we are forced to play every day in order to exist) that we're getting too close to the proverbial line in the sand that exists for all of us.

If we, by this manner of more subtle intimidation, do not take a step back from the line, but rather decide to be obstreperous and take another step closer to the line, then the pressure, harassment, intimidation (whatever you want to call it) will increase in some manner.

Then the knock on the door will come.

And suddenly you'll be arrested for the umpteenth time under some obscure charge that you never knew even existed and held in some county jail.

God knows where you're going to wind up being booked under an assumed name.

There's a progression of pressure the closer you step to the line with the truth about your former colleagues in Washington.

If you step over that line, there is only one end and final result — as about 400 of us have learned in the past 12 years.

And that is death.

On a personal note, this is the type of life I, and others like me, have to lead, the few who are left now 15 years later, who have yet to be classified through the proverbial strainer, as I have mentioned before.

Those of us who are left are still in this state of limbo. We still have a line drawn for us in the sand, a line we did not draw, but that others drew for us.

The others are those who know too much about those in power to both draw and enforce that line. And what pisses me off about Jeb Bush — and why I have a particular dislike for him — is how he ground into me in subsequent periods when I had some contact with him again through Neil Lewis, when I was trying to work something out in 1992.

He said, "Al, there are no heroes, and there are no tooth fairies."

That comment will stick in my craw and it will do so forever.

The reason it sticks in my craw is because he's right.

What he was referring to was the life I have to lead.

I have to say enough. I have to use enough of my information in order to earn a living without stepping too close to that line.

And yet I remain in the jack box into which others have put me in — forever consigned to this fate.

What he meant to imply, when he said "There's no heroes or tooth fairies," is that there isn't anyone on the other side of the coin that would ever pull me out of the jack box.

There's no Good Samaritan. There's no member of the public, no member of the media, no public interest group that's going to say, "Al, we'll pull you out. We'll pay you what you are owed. We will help protect you, and in exchange you will tell us everything you know."

That doesn't exist.

How could such a thing exist?

The truth is not profitable. You cannot eat it. You can't live on it. You can't deposit the truth in the bank.

The truth, in the last analysis, is not only a zero sum game, but it is a dangerous thing to possess. And don't I know it.

By that last comment, I mean, if any outside observer were to look at what has happened to me in the last 12 years, to look at what I've been put through — the level of harassment, intimidation, unrelenting pressure, imprisonment after imprisonment after imprisonment under charges that either no one ever heard of or don't know anything about — or in some cases not being charged at all...

Just being held endlessly — forty-five-day FBI hold for "suspicion," "violation of various national security acts," esoteric little clouded acts.

Being intimidated with that section of the U.S. Title Code 18, wherein it can constitute a felonious act to reveal an illegal act of government should such revelation prove injurious to the national security (also included in this part of U.S. Title Code 18) or "the political stability of the State."

All the cards tend to be stacked in these people's favor, who have something to hide and who have the money to ensure that their dirty laundry remains hidden.

To close out my personal comments on this subject — Jeb Bush and the various meetings — I've tried once before when I was debriefed by Rebecca Sims.

It took ten hours of tapes simply to tell all that I knew about Jeb because I have such extensive notations about all these meetings in my own logs — who was there, who said what to whom, what happened as a result of the meetings, and so forth.

But to close this out on a personal note and to lead me into the next story, I've often thought that I had two opportunities to defect to the Soviet Union.

"Defect" is perhaps too strong a word.

I had two opportunities to work with the Soviets and/or other eastern intelligence bloc agencies during the Iran-Contra period, which may have very possibly led to my ultimate "defection."

As it turns out, I would have been better off.

I would have been further ahead today financially.

I would have been treated better — had I betrayed the United States by revealing certain illegal covert operations of the United States government to the Soviets — than the way I was treated by remaining loyal to my former colleagues.

200

There's something very wrong with this.

This will lead me into my next narrative story, in which I will reveal some things I have never revealed before, i.e. my flirtation with east-bloc intelligence groups in 1985 and 1986.

I have been obviously reticent to discuss it because I would potentially face continuing legal consequences today if I were to tell the truth.

I tend to suspect, as my attorney agrees, that I never would be prosecuted however. It would be politically impossible to prosecute me for anything because nobody wants those doors reopened a second time and no one wants to have a flashlight shined on what is behind those doors a second time.

So with the passage of time, I've become a little less reticent.

As I am a middle-aged man, I have worked or been involved in illegal covert operation of government all my adult life.

How many others in my age group can say that they have personally known in their adult lifetimes almost 400 people who have died under clouded circumstances?

The common thread among the deaths of these 400 people was not anything they did — but what they knew.

I wonder how many others can make the same comment about their lives.

It's an indication of the type of life I've led.

Even what I've revealed thus far — it isn't a tenth of what I know. And it is such a task. That's the type of life I've led and what I know. I hope that the flavor of this comes out of what has happened to my friends, those I've known, who became inconvenient to their superiors and who died to maintain the deniability of others.

The egregious nature of the conspiracy surrounding their death goes to a level that becomes virtually humorous.

When Jeb Bush, Oliver North and Dewey Clarridge once spoke about an individual, North laughed and said, "Well, we haven't decided how we will rule his demise yet — whether it will be accident, natural causes, or suicide."

And these are true stories. These things actually happened. You can prove that these meetings took place. I can prove it. There's enough substantive proof existing that the meetings took place. There's enough substantive proof of the conversations and the people that were discussed.

Look what happened to them three months later, six months later and so forth.

Anyway, I wanted to make that comment as setting the stage for this next part.

It is now late January - early February 1985.

To put this in context of my life and Iran-Contra, I was in the process of severing my relationship with Larry Hamil since Hamil was becoming an embarrassment.

He had taken his mandated ability to commit fraud and gone way beyond that and created so much liability that frankly Richard Secord and others were getting tired of covering up for him all the time.

It was at this period I was deciding what to do.

I was now moving without Hamil. I was moving into having more direct relationships with my ultimate superiors — Richard Secord, Oliver North, etc.

I really could not describe Jeb Bush as my superior. It would be more on the actual "Enterprise" side, and it would include guys like Aderholt, Secord, North, Terrell and so forth.

At that time, I was becoming increasingly nervous about what I was doing and what "we" were doing as a group — "The Enterprise," "The Cause," the "Government Within a Government," as it has been verily described.

I became increasingly interested in "hedging my bets."

I made my move at one of the Saturday lunches at the Czechoslovakian-American Club (I was a member and active in the club), the club which served almost as an intelligence clearing house.

It was chock full of Czechoslovakian and Hungarian intelligence agents, as were most Eastern European social clubs in the greater Miami area. They essentially acted as quasi-intelligence gathering posts, useful as a place to recruit people.

This is true in Eastern European social clubs wherever there was concentration of Iran-Contra activity. This has been discussed before, but the East Germans and the Czechs and ultimately the Russian masters looked at this as a prime recruitment opportunity.

They knew people like me would want to hedge their bets. And when you want to hedge your bets, and you're involved in illegal covert operations of State that have international implications (and a direct policy implication towards an enemy like the Soviet Union), there's only one place to go to hedge your bets.

It's called somewhere south of Moscow, hopefully.

It was at one of the Saturday roast duck lunches, at the

Czechoslovakian-American Club, which were always excellent since they had a Czech cook there named Bobby Urban, who could cook a roast duck in brandied cherry sauce. It was wonderful.

I used to sit with him every Saturday as a matter of fact and throw back shots of Chert washed down by glasses of Urquell. I had discussed with Alexander Petrovic, whom I knew was a Hungarian intelligence agent and had been in the United States a long time operating under the cover of a real estate agent, mortgage broker, that sort of thing.

He had never mentioned anything to me about it, but I had said to him that I would like to hedge my bets.

And when I said that, he knew exactly what I meant. No further explanation was necessary.

He simply asked me, "How can I help you?"

And I said, "I don't want to know anybody's name. I don't want a pre-arranged contact. And I don't want to talk to anybody within the United States."

He then said to me, "What would you like to do? What are your intentions?"

And I said, "Well, shortly I intend to take a trip quietly to Germany under the guise of a skiing vacation. And you know the reputation that I have, that I've carefully crafted with my superiors in Washington and Miami, this reputation I have of being a pretty heavy drinker and life of the party, and the first guy with a quick witticism has made me very popular within Republican cocktail circuits that frankly were way above my station."

"But I am looked at as, 'Hey Good Ole Non-Threatening Al.' And liquor loosens lips, and I know a lot and I hear a lot. I hear a lot more that goes way beyond what I'm directly involved in. And I think what I hear would be of interest to others."

And Petrovic understood what I was saying exactly.

He didn't ask any questions at all. And under the parameters that I discussed, I would like to be in Germany and I would be in West Berlin for awhile.

It wouldn't be considered unusual if 'Hey Good Ole Al' went out with a couple of good lookin' blonde-haired, blue-eyed frauleins and got half in the bag and the next morning woke up in some hotel in East Berlin.

That story would go down real well with my superiors, particularly Richard Secord and Oliver North who knew me personally.

They knew what I was like. And that story would sound very plausible and would be just like water off a duck's back.

My loyalty to "The Cause" was unquestioned. This time period, late January-February 1985, was also an ideal time for me to embark upon such a venture since I had not yet been looked at in any other context other than my position, which was a guy on the money-end of Iran-Contra, who essentially sold bogus limited partnerships in concert with my superiors to raise ongoing covert revenue streams pursuant to the mandate that had originally been given to me.

I was not looked at in any other context despite my association at these Eastern European clubs.

It was known that I spoke many of the languages and enjoyed the food, and I wasn't considered any kind of a threat. But I knew based on a general heightening of tension overall between the Soviet Union and the United States that it wouldn't be long before people like me would come under some scrutiny.

Only two or three months later, I was proved to be correct, when I got that visit from a certain agent from the FBI CI-3 division.

I arranged surreptitiously in February 1985 (I've not revealed this before publicly) to fly to Switzerland, which I did using one of my alternate passports, shall we say. And I did in fact enter Germany. And I did in fact stay in Berlin.

This was all under the auspices that I had told General Secord that I hadn't had a vacation in years and I wanted to go to Switzerland skiing.

I am after all, of Germanic extraction. I have friends of the family there. And I was intending to do a lot of drinking and a lot of whoring around.

He just laughed and said, "Have a good time." And that was exactly the impression I wanted to give him.

As a result of this trip, I did wind up in West Berlin, and as a further result of this trip, I did wind up in East Berlin at a certain hotel.

I won't mention the name, but anyone in the intelligence community would know that there is one particular hotel in East Germany, which happens to be the best hotel in East Germany, where every single room reserved for foreigners is bugged by the East German intelligence.

This is a hotel where the East Germans conduct intelligence operations against the west. It's a hotel which has a reputation for people from both sides to get together and discuss things. And that was my specific intent in staying there.

Now, mind you, I had no names. No contacts. Nothing. That's the way I wanted it. I wanted them to come to me.

I came up with what I thought was a rather ingenious plan. I don't really know how ingenious it was, but it worked.

I am sure that Petrovic must have said something. They must have known I was coming, or they had some general idea about me or something.

I wasn't particularly concerned about our own people noticing me in East Germany because I wasn't a high priority guy. It would take a couple of days before Secord found out about it.

And when I got back, I could always say, "Well, General, I'm sorry. But I wound up getting drunk in West Berlin and I woke up in a hotel room in East Berlin with a couple of naked frauleins next to me the next morning with a hangover."

It was a perfectly plausible story. If I had to use that story, Secord would have swallowed it hook, line and sinker.

Anyway, it's February 1985 and I am in a hotel room in East Germany, assuming, correctly, that the room is bugged.

What I do to draw attention to myself — I had a microcassette recorder with me and I made a tape. I just talked into a tape recorder. I pretended that this tape was for Dave Lyons, my friend, the senior investigative political reporter at the *Miami Herald*, to whom I had leaked stuff in the past.

I pretended that the tape was for him. And I pretended I had established an elaborate scheme to get him this tape. I revealed to him in this tape why I was in East Germany, that in fact, I wanted to explore a relationship with the East Germans because of their known competency in the intelligence world.

I also mentioned the reputation the KGB has in Washington of being little more than blindfolded moles in a china closet.

On this tape, I went on and on, "Well, Dave, you know who I am and what I do. And I have picked up substantial miscellaneous intelligence."

More importantly, my motivation, which was quite genuine at the time was that not only was I seeking to hedge my bets, but I did have a genuine motivation (that was my belief as I explained on this tape and as the East Germans heard) that what we were doing — Iran-Contra, "The Enterprise," "The Cause" — had gone so far beyond what it was originally intended to be, the diversion of money from an Iranian operation to arm Contras.

As a cover story underneath, there would be narcotics trafficking, fraud, weapons, things like that to generate a certain number of billions of dollars to replenish the proverbial coffers.

But in fact, we've gone way beyond that, and North was even now talking about this Operation Orpheus — what would happen if everything fell apart and everything was to be revealed.

What the public reaction would be to the enormity of the fraud, of the narcotics and weapons trafficking so that as George Bush later said the people would have chased everyone in Washington and lynched them all.

With North being the Chairman of the National Programs Office (NPO) and the NPO building up sizable assets of its own covertly, North was talking about Operation Orpheus, which included potentially instigating an incident with the Soviet Union to divert U.S. public attention should our involvement become known.

This was very dangerous in an era of heightened tensions, particularly with North being as powerful as he was.

Being so far out of the loop, taking naps through meetings, Reagan had no real effective control at the time.

North, Casey and George Bush. They were "The Three." And they were it.

With god-like powers, they could act with absolute impunity.

And God knows what these guys would have done to protect themselves because had Iran-Contra become revealed, policies going back decades may have also become revealed in the interlinkages and that would have just been one hell of a problem.

To even start a limited thermonuclear exchange with the Soviet Union, I would not have put that past "The Three," as they call themselves.

I thought it was important that the Soviets know their intentions.

As I was to find out later, they knew a lot more than I thought they did.

Also I wanted the Soviets to know, in the event I needed their assistance and should I subsequently become some sort of Iran-Contra scapegoat, that the only information I was prepared to supply them with would be information concerning illegal covert operations of the US Government I was familiar with.

Also I could tell them what I had learned about the Star Wars programs around the Beltway Cocktail Circuit, that in fact, it was all a big fake out and that it was all fictitious. The Soviets, I found out, already suspected that. Only two or three of the actual fifteen weapons systems worked. The rest were pie in the sky — 20 or 30 years and a trillion dollars away from development. That even included the ASAT program.

I had learned that there was going to be a test in 1985 of the ASAT program that the Department of Defense intended to dummy up.

The thing didn't actually work yet and it wouldn't work for a number of years. But this was under the guise of fooling the Soviets and increasing pressure on the Soviets and so on.

The Soviets, as I would later discover, actually bought a lot of this ruse out of Washington.

It really wasn't until 1985 or early in 1986 that the Soviets actually began to figure out how much of it was a ruse — that it was just the same old Republican thing — hundreds and hundreds of billions of dollars on pie in the sky weapons for unaccountable black projects.

The money disappears into Republican coffers and black holes and nooks and crannies and offshore corporations. The same old deal. This time it just involved a lot more money with a supposedly appealing political motive to cover it up.

Anyway, this would make a great story in itself — a great novel, although it's true.

This is a true story and it includes all the things people like — sex, money, deception, selling out, and backstabbing.

Chapter 16

CHINESE MONEY FOR ILLEGAL US WEAPONS SALES

THERE IS CERTAINLY nothing new about the concept of Chinese money coming from The People's Republic of China (PRC) and flowing into Republican coffers in exchange for 1) political favors, 2) the continuation of Most Favored Nation status, and 3) not seriously pressuring the Chinese regarding human rights issues — all in exchange for high-technology weapon sales to China which are illegal.

Recent allegations of Chinese money flowing into Clinton coffers (for the first time into Democratic coffers) are certainly nothing new or unusual, since the Chinese were reasonably convinced that Clinton would win the 1996 election — and survive a second term in office.

The Chinese money connection must be understood and be put into a context of the southeast Asian theater, or protocol, or whatever words you wish to use.

This significantly predates PRC money coming into the United States for political purposes. It is well known that in the early 1950s, at the beginning of the Eisenhower Administration, a series of secret protocols were established with various southeast Asian nations — Japan, Korea,

Taiwan, Hong Kong — for those countries to funnel monies surreptitiously into Republican campaign coffers in the United States.

These countries would then allow favorable treatment and entrance into their markets by certain U.S. corporations, like Texaco and Hewlett Packard for example. In the late 1950s it would have been Tidewater Development. In the 1960s, it was Zapata Energy.

One need only look at the major stockholders and the officers, principals and directors of these publicly-held companies to understand the Republican connection.

Much of this has been written about before in widely dispersed articles. But certainly, there was, by the late 1950s, an entire scheme developed which became literally a covert protocol of the United States to funnel money from these countries, most notably Japan and South Korea, into Republican coffers.

We have mentioned previously why in Republican administrations the ambassadors to Japan, the ambassadors to Taiwan and the ambassadors to South Korea have invariably come out of the CIA and have acted as a control feature, or a control mechanism, in the past.

That was extremely evident in the Reagan Administration. The most prime example of that was Colonel Donald Gregg (after the Iran-Contra scandal in which he was significantly tarred) became Ambassador to South Korea, despite rather strong objections from the Democrats because of his covert and illegal role in Iran-Contra.

Overall, the *quid pro quo* is reasonably easy to understand. Namely, the Republican administrations, since the days of Eisenhower, have acted to prop up right-wing dictatorships or near-dictatorships in southeast Asian countries in exchange for those countries essentially giving campaign contributions to Republican coffers through a variety of disguises.

Until about 1980, this had been traditionally handled by the CIA.

When the Church Committee found strong indications that Chinese PRC money had flowed into the coffers of President Ford (some of the investigative footnotes in the 1977 Church Committee hearings mentioned this), it was duly noted that there was a strong suspicion that then-DCI George Bush had made the arrangements to launder those funds through two very infamous proprietary Agency cut-outs, Mongoose Enterprises, Ltd., and the Interfax Gold Corporation.

They were both infamous and much has been written about them in the past. These were two proprietaries that George Bush helped create when he was briefly DCI in 1976.

These companies also had a relationship to other CIA notables, such as Frank Snepp and the infamous Col. Jack Terrell. The Interfax Gold Corporation, which Jack Terrell ran for a period of years while he was very close to the Marcos Regime in the Philippines, was initially set up to aid Marcos in his illicit gold bullion dealings.

Later on it became a conduit for gold bullion coming out of southeast Asia, monies that principally went into CIA coffers in the United States. But this would be another story and a whole book could be written just on this topic.

To get back to the Chinese money the connection — during the Reagan Administration, it became much more obvious with the Chinese using Indonesian surrogates, which had been done previously.

Again, there is a George Bush connection to these Indonesian surrogates, all controlled by President Suharto, a long-time ally of George Bush, who was essentially kept in power all those years by Republican interests in the United States.

Even as early as 1958, the late liberal Sen. Fulbright tried to complain publicly to The New York Times about these connections, but The New York Times wouldn't print them.

Remember Sen. Fulbright's comments in 1973 when he said that there is an illicit and covert protocol. In essence, he said we are propping up inefficient right-wing dictatorships in southeast Asia, and eventually it's going to come back to haunt the whole world because these economies, at some point, will collapse because they are being raped and pillaged by a gaggle of right-wing, tin-horn dictators supported by political and corporate Republican interests in the United States.

Although the goodly senator has long since expired, in recent months, his predictions have come true.

It is also interesting to note the talk about Bill Clinton's closeness to the Riady family of Indonesia and the Riady's own bank and real estate holding group.

Mohammed Riady was the long-time President of the Industrial Bank of Indonesia, the largest bank in Indonesia, which acts as a *de facto* central bank for Indonesia.

If we think back only fifteen years, there were similar allegations about George Bush's long-time relationship with the Riady's and the Riady's laundering PRS Chinese government funds through their various enterprises and having that money laundered through the Industrial Bank of Indonesia into other offshore entities, like The Hong Kong and Shanghai

Bank, where George Bush was a long-time Director. That's not widely known.

And then it was done through the Stephens Offshore Investment Group, which had an office in Hong Kong.

They never had an office outside the United States, and all of a sudden a medium-sized regional brokerage firm starts to open up offices in Hong Kong, in Sydney, Australia, and in Jakarta.

There was a reason for this and it had very little to do with the securities business. It was essentially to launder money back to Republican interests here in the United States.

There was an interesting instance in which one of the Riady sons, Mahmoud Riady, was linked to a rather large shipment of heroin into California in 1983. He was arrested and, in fact, incarcerated for seven or eight hours.

The CIA then marched into the Sheriff's office, took him out, and put him on the next plane back to Indonesia.

But it was Mahmoud Riady who subsequently befriended Bill Clinton. He was the very same son who helped launder Chinese PRC money to Bill Clinton and to the DNC twelve years later.

I find it interesting and humorous. It's the same old connections and the same old schemes, really.

There was that photograph released of Mahmoud Riady and his wife having dinner at the White House with Bill and Hillary, yet Mahmoud is technically still a wanted fugitive in the United States.

He seems to move around very freely under his own name in this country, despite his so-called fugitive status. He must have an angel on his shoulder somewhere in Washington.

A more recent example of this is Col. Lan Chin, otherwise known as Lannie Chin, who's on the CIA's list as being a foreign intelligence officer in the Ministry of State Defense of the People's Security Bureau of the People's Republic of China.

Even so Chin is allowed to travel freely in the United States without any of the usual restrictions placed on foreign intelligence officials. Also, he has a Class 1 license to bid on Department of Defense so-called surplus and high-technology weapons auctions.

Chin is also able to transport these weapons outside the United States very readily, without any customs checks at all, despite the fact that he's a known foreign intelligence agent of what is potentially a Class 2 country, meaning a potential foe of the United States.

The odd part is that it is now substantially easier to uncover information about this so-called Chinese money-for-weapons, or money-for-political favoritism connection.

Nobody makes a secret of it anymore, and it's pretty well out in the open.

Of course, what the Clinton Administration desperately hoped to avoid was any notion that the media would start to announce that both political parties in this country were foregoing the future military security of this country by arming China in exchange for covert political money.

Furthermore, they allowed China to have, as part of this covert policy, Most Favored Nation status, despite the fact that Clinton said he wouldn't renew it.

Clinton has renewed it four times with the understanding that there would be increased pressure on China regarding their human rights record. This was a bone to Clinton's own left-wing constituency. Of course, Clinton talks up a pretty good game. But that's all it is.

Now the Chinese, as any economist could tell you, have been allowed to run huge trade surpluses with the United States, rivaling the old trade surpluses of Japan.

These trade surpluses essentially get kicked back to the United States by covert political donations and by the very same money used to illicitly purchase high-technology U.S. military weapons — weapons that are, in turn, targeted back at the United States.

I know for a fact that the Clinton Administration is scared shitless of anyone putting it together this way in the media because no matter what the complacency of the American people, if the truth came out this way, the American people wouldn't stand for it.

In the recent State of the Union Speech, Clinton said one of the bills he has proposed in the past is campaign finance reform. But if one looks at the proposed campaign finance reform legislation he's proffered before, you will see in the fine print, that there are specifically worded exemptions. It becomes immediately apparent then that these exemptions are targeted at the American defense industry — to ensure that the defense industry is not limited in its so-called soft money contributions to political parties, political action groups, and political think tanks and committees, which are exempt from existing limits as it is.

To date, what has been revealed to the American public about the recent Chinese government contributions to the Democrats in the United States is about Charlie Trie, John Huang and a host of others.

We do not hear about all of the others, the one hundred and seventeen listed by the Federal Election Committee. All one hundred and seventeen conveniently left the United States in very quick order.

What has not been revealed (because the media won't go after it because it considers it too tedious) is how this money is getting here.

What banks are being used for its laundering?

When one looks at the Chinese money connection in that respect, one sees that the names of the banks involved are the same old banks that have been involved in this for twenty years.

That's not only with Chinese money, but Southeast Asian money in general. Illicit campaign contributions in the United States have come through the Industrial Bank of Indonesia, as we've already mentioned, and the Hong Kong and Shanghai Bank.

In Europe, it's been Credit Lyonnais, Banque Paribas, and Union Bank of Switzerland.

And with smaller banks, it's the same old deal — The Swiss-Italian Credit Corporation, and The Jarlska Bank of Copenhagen, the largest bank in Denmark which operates very secretly and has operated for years as a conduit for foreign government money going to places it shouldn't be going.

The implication of what I'm trying to say is that there is nothing new in all this.

This information nowadays is not difficult to obtain compared to the way it used to be because it is done much more in the open now — under the guise that the American media will cooperate by not telling the people the truth.

Under the notion of a good economy, the American people have become even more politically apathetic than usual. The best way to put it is they go from their normal apathy to a state of being virtually moribund.

The only reason the issue of Chinese money for favors, specifically weapons, is being kept alive despite an ongoing investigation at the Department of Justice is because of a handful of small alternative publications that keep real issues like this alive — *The Village Voice, The Boston Phoenix, The Rocky Mountain Gazette, Conspiracy Nation, Covert Action Quarterly,* and so forth.

These are some of the publications where you will find some of the best information ever printed and revealed to the people. Every time these publications come out with something that is genuine, truthful and hard-hitting, they are immediately slammed by the major media for being con-spiracy theorists or disseminating information that they do not have first-sourced.

And in some cases, they're right. This information is not first-sourced because of the age-old problem — alternative publications do not have the money to properly investigate and get first-source information.

In order to fight back, what the alternative media does is employ the little arcane quotes of notables from the past to defend themselves.

Any subscriber of *Covert Action Quarterly* would know in recent years, that Lou Wolfe, the editor has adopted the slogan on the front cover of his magazine (at my suggestion no less), which is the famous Henry Kissinger quote, from 1977, in which he said "The fears of even the most paranoid conspiracy theorists can sometimes be justified."

Kissinger was speaking in the context of misdeeds of State when he made that quote.

The ongoing Department of Justice investigation into this Chinese money connection will be concluded and a preliminary report will be issued.

Reno, of course, will not recommend the appointment of an Independent Counsel to further investigate the matter and you will see absolutely no political pressure from the Republicans for her to do so. This will be done under the guise of collateral political liability.

Already you can see how quickly this issue has been buried, and how the Republicans have not made any use of it. They have not attempted to use it as any kind of political lever or score any political brownie points. It is because they are hamstrung for the same reason that the Democrats find themselves hamstrung — both sides of the aisle have received Chinese money in the past.

The only thing that warrants further investigation is what I have men-tioned before — Larry Hamil's recent involvement in developing a scheme to launder money for the gubernatorial campaigns of Jeb Bush and George Bush, Jr. in the 1998 elections.

Now, granted, this is a small connection. But, as always, it is a way to back-door this whole thing of Chinese money-for-weapons. It is a little episode, a little scenario that I happen to have a lot of information on.

The Chinese money-for-weapons connection is really not my forte. I only have one or two files full of information about it, and it was nothing that I was ever involved in directly.

The Hamil episode, however, is easily flushed out, easily looked at, and easily explained. The banks are all known. The corporations are all known. How the Bush brothers got the money and through what corporations it was laundered.

That would be a way of back-dooring this. And certainly, it would be a way of hurting Jeb Bush and George, Jr. by tying them to Chinese money.

I think this Hamil-Chinese Money-Governors Bush Connection is something that should be investigated.

I think it would be a mistake, though, to attempt to launch a general investigation into the Chinese Money-Clinton-Democratic National Committee Connection

I honestly think that's a quagmire, and I doubt that any organization would have the resources to make a real effective effort in that direction since there are so many people involved, so many banks, and so many records.

It would be a task beyond the resource limit of most organizations. Therefore, I would suggest, as I have done before, that any group, if it's interested in continuing this investigation regarding Chinese money-for-weapons-political favoritism, should try to back-door the issue.

The Hamil Connection, in fact, would be an excellent back door.

Chapter 17

US GOVERNMENT NARCOTICS TRAFFICKING (PART II)

S O FAR, WE HAVE explored six principal CIA-connected cocaine traffickers active during the Iran-Contra years; three principal Bahamian cases involving well-known Bahamian ministers of state; Barry Seal and some of his partners, including Buddy Young, who subsequently was appointed a regional director of FEMA in the Clinton Administration.

And there has been an overview of CIA and DIA operations at the time as it related to the importation and distribution of narcotics for the maintenance of covert revenue streams.

Now we will further explore these connections and examine six other prominent cases of CIA-connected dopers.

The first case deals with another Barry Seal associate — what used to be called the "Jewish Threesome."

These included Eddy Singer, a cocaine trafficker and his partners, Yoram Ettinger, then a member of the Israeli Knesset, and Lt. Col. Ari Klein, a retired Israeli intelligence officer who had been Mexico City's station chief for the Mossad until his retirement.

They operated extensively through Mexico from 1984 to 1986 and they were partners with Barry Seal.

Barry Seal tends to be the common link between cocaine traffickers and the CIA. His name comes up in virtually every connected dope case that was filed in the mid-1980s. More were filed, when it became convenient to do so, after Barry Seal's murder on February 10, 1986.

The Singer case, which I think Dinnerstein worked on, was interesting because it showed the connections between the CIA and the Israeli intelligence service regarding the transportation, trafficking and narcotics. This was very overlooked at the time and it was never mentioned in any subsequent congressional hearings.

Nobody in the press, for obvious reasons, really went after it for fear of embarrassing Israelis or whatever.

But I think it's a case that should be looked at again. There has been some recent interest in the media, particularly non-Jewish aligned media.

The Singer case has been mentioned in the last six months in a variety of congressional forums still dealing with Iran-Contra. The reason this case was brought back to the fore was the new activities of Yoram Ettinger and his recent travels to Huntsville, Alabama, as well as his new business in trafficking weapons and technology and acting as a broker for the Chinese and the Russians on the illicit transfer and sale of high technology US weapons and weapons design.

That's what brought the Singer case back to the fore. But I can tell you at the time, getting back to the narcotics aspect of it during Iran-Contra, that Singer was a substantial dealer in cocaine, perhaps trafficking a thousand to twelve hundred kilograms a month, which came through Mexico.

By the way, this was one of the sensitive cases that the DEA agent who was murdered, Enrique Camarena, found out about.

And I have often speculated that one of the reasons he was murdered (although he was murdered by the Mexican Federal Police and they had some complicity with the CIA who were desperate to get rid of this guy) was that the CIA knew he had discovered the Singer Organization in Mexico.

Singer's connection because of Ari Klein also connected to senior Mexican government officials at that time, including a past Mexican President, Ernesto Portillo, who was later indicted in Mexico for fraud, narcotics trafficking, weapons trafficking, etc.

The connections for Israeli narcotics trafficking in Mexico had been essentially set up in the 1970s by Ari Klein and Rafi Eitan and others.

218

The Israeli government was very friendly with the former Mexican dictator, Ernesto Portillo. You may remember there were subsequent fraud cases involving bogus oil deals, oil leases, and oil schemes that didn't exist.

Those who are well-educated on Iran-Contra would remember the great effort that was made in 1986-1987 to keep George Bush and his two sons out of the Mexican indictment of Portillo on the oil fraud because this was a fraud in which Zapata Corporation, Tidewater Corporation and Harken Energy had all participated in.

There was a desperate effort by the Reagan-Bushites to keep Bush's name out of that indictment, which was successfully done.

What has also not been known is that in 1986 the CIA was very nervous about DEA activity in Mexico. The CIA was very concerned that it would be exposed through its connections to corrupt Mexican officials.

There was some speculation after the Kerry Committee hearings, particularly in the Hughes Committee hearings, about whom the CIA was trying to protect within the Mexican government, particularly the Mexican Federal Police.

They were trying to protect the CIA's hand picked guy in Mexico, Gen. Raul Medina, Chief of the Mexican Federal Police. Medina actually ordered the death of Enrique Camarena at the urging of the CIA.

After Camarena died, another renowned DEA agent operating in Mexico, Celerino Castillo, found out. He knew about the connections and the orders, how it was done, and how Camarena's killers were protected.

Of course, when Castillo tried to go public, he was immediately discredited and dismissed from the DEA.

Another prominent CIA doper I wanted to mention is the infamous Michael K. Palmer, who operated out of Detroit.

Palmer was another minion of what I would classify as the "Barry Seal-CIA-DIA-Southern Air Transport Narcotics Organization," which is literally the way it was at the time.

I think it's the best way to look at it. Although I haven't seen him in years, I knew Palmer personally at the time. He used to be in Miami a lot. And when in Miami, he would always stay at one of Southern Air Transport's corporate suites, provided for him at the Intercontinental Hotel.

Palmer had a Southern Air Transport Guest Membership Club Card to the Jockey Club, the Ocean Club and the Turnberry Club — the three most exclusive clubs in Miami at the time.

And I used to drink with him. He was a drinking friend of myself, Gen. Secord, Jim Langton and Bill Mason, the President and Vice President respectively of Southern Air Transport.

He would be in and out of Miami quite frequently, although he did operate out of Detroit.

The reason I wanted to mention him is because Palmer was one of the keys in what was then known as the "Canadian Connection."

When thinking of Iran-Contra narcotics trafficking, we tend to think of South America, Central America, and the United States. We forget all the other points of entry and all the other places that cocaine trafficking routes existed, including through Canada.

Narcotics were coming through what is a very porous border. Palmer had owned a couple of aircraft hangars in a little complex on the outskirts of the Detroit airport. As a matter of fact, the cocaine would simply come by truck, the Canadian border was so porous. By air, it would get reshipped to New York or San Francisco or wherever it was going by Polar Aviation.

This is also a little known fact. This fact was contained in the Brad Ayers Report when Ayers reported back to his superiors at DEA the connection of Polar Aviation, which is a wholly owned subsidiary of Southern Air Transport, and it still exists to this day.

It's headquartered somewhere in Ohio. But Polar Aviation was a little known subsidiary of Southern Air Transport, as it had once been a subsidiary of Air America.

Polar Aviation gets its name by flying mostly northern routes, particularly in the tundra and very cold countries. Anyway, this fact was suppressed to a huge extent during the Kerry Committee hearings when Kerry himself and even Lee Hamilton, the co-senior counsel on the committee, attempted to just write "Southern Air Transport" on these reports all the time, instead of the different divisions of Southern Air.

Southern Cross Air, for example, was involved in narcotics trafficking through the Pacific and into the desert southwest of the United States.

There was a conscious effort to keep Southern Air Transport sort of in one vein — and that was simply flying narcotics up and weapons back *vis-a-vis* the Caribbean and Central and South America.

Nobody, including the Democrats, wanted to blow this thing up and really tell the American people the much bigger story beyond Iran-Contra — the cocaine and heroin trafficking, how long it had been going on, how many countries, and how many ports of entry were used.

That would not have done either political party any good at the time.

Another government official who knew about Palmer's cocaine trafficking (particularly in the northeastern corridor in the State of Maine and into Nova Scotia) was the Customs agent, Peter Videnieks, when he was stationed as a Customs agent in the Portland, Maine office.

Customs had intercepted some freighters full of cocaine. It was the incident where a lot of people died after it happened. Reports were destroyed, and Videnieks's career was ruined. He was forced out and discredited the same way as DEA agent Brad Ayers.

Ayers and Videnieks were personal friends before this happened, despite the fact they were at two different agencies.

I had talked to Videnieks at the time, and he did have some sympathy within Customs, particularly from Billy von Raab.

Billy von Raab was Customs chief in Miami for a long time and he actually came very close to blowing the whistle on how Customs had been told by the Vice Presidential Task Force to allow certain planes and certain aircraft into our territorial waters and air space without looking at them.

Of course, von Raab was later dismissed and discredited and almost charged with a variety of bogus crimes because he wouldn't keep his mouth shut.

But Videnieks's real downfall came in that report he submitted which became pretty famous because of Southeastern Regional Customs Commissioner George Weiss.

Weiss was part of the "Home Team," as we like to say. And Weiss made sure that report went no further, and, as a matter of fact, got put through a shredder.

The long and short of it (and the way everything works) is that Videnieks was pushed out and discredited.

Weiss, because of his loyalty to the Administration, by keeping his mouth shut and destroying reports, was ultimately elevated to Customs Commissioner of the United States

Recently he retired from that position and moved to the Caribbean and now lives off some unknown income in some offshore bank accounts that no one can quite explain how he got.

But Palmer was a pretty big player, a real key player, in what was called the "Canadian Connection."

It was speculated later on why such resources were committed to cover Palmer's ass after things fell apart in the post-1986 environment.

It's because Palmer could have exposed the connection between the

CIA and the Canadian Intelligence Service, the Royal Canadian Police External Intelligence Division, now known as CEPIS.

He could have named names and faces and agents. And that was a sensitive connection that the CIA and the Canadian government went to great lengths to hide, including those two Canadian intelligence officials who now live comfortably under assumed names in the Caribbean.

A lot of resources were committed to protect Palmer.

Palmer was subsequently indicted in Miami and was facing a forty-year to life sentence. He pled guilty, served 117 days in the Federal Metropolitan Correction Facility in Miami, and then was quietly relocated to Honduras in further aid and execution of investigations of the United States Government.

We know how that story works. I have no idea where Palmer is now. I know he uses Honduras as a home base, but I have no idea frankly where he is.

The other fellow I wanted to discuss is Bill Duncan.

Bill did a real good job in the mid-1980s in his position as an investigator with the Arkansas State Attorney General's office. He was able to document activities in Mena, Arkansas but he went much further than people commonly presume.

He documented connections between the Clinton Governorship and what was going on in Mena through Barry Seal, through Clinton's brother, Roger, through Buddy Young and so forth.

He documented connections with the State Police that Tommy Goodwin had already known about.

Unfortunately Tommy had a heart attack before he wanted to say anything.

But I always felt bad about Duncan because we all know what he went through — the absolute shit this man got put through because of what he knew, particularly when he started to get some press exposure.

The Attorney General's office felt that they obviously could not fire him since it would only increase his prominence.

But what he went through — the harassment of having his phone tapped and his home broken into — the harassment he went through was horrendous.

I think the Attorney General's office wisely elected to allow him to continue with his position, until he had enough time in for his pension and then he retired immediately.

He sold his home, and now lives discreetly in a cabin in the Ozarks under an assumed name, by the way. He's not easy to reach anymore.

This is a good case of someone who got burned out on the truth, particularly when all the major networks wanted him, when he helped everybody and made a lot of noise in Congress.

He didn't realize that the bigger scheme of things was that nobody was going to ever bring out the whole truth.

Another interesting Iran-Contra/CIA narcotics trafficking connection, not extensively discussed at the time, was the trafficking points in Nevada and Arizona.

Also there were the flights coming in through the Pacific, from Southern Air Cross, a division of Southern Air Transport, which was technically based in Australia. It was a foreign domiciliary in Australia at the time.

The Australian Supreme Court judge, Murray Fahrquar, was brought down by the Southern Air Cross investigation in Australia, when he attempted to leak documents the court had indicating a relationship between Southern Air Cross, the CIA, and the Australian intelligence organization.

Fahrquar was charged with a variety of crimes, and ultimately he was brought down. He was impeached and imprisoned, as a matter of fact. He got set up on some bogus charges.

This was widely reported in the Australian press. As a matter fact, *Four Corners*, the Australian equivalent of *60 Minutes*, did a piece on this. It was Peter Brown who did the piece before Peter went to the Australian Broadcasting Corporation and became head of their Washington office.

There had been some discussion about this and there was quite a bit of reporting in *The Arizona Republic* and *The Phoenix Gazette* and so forth. Several reporters went after it.

You may remember that Gary Webb also tried to go after this. Frankly, anyone who has gone after this connection in the past hasn't made out so well.

One of the reasons, this connection (which wasn't a big connection in terms of volume of narcotics) is so sensitive is that it would have exposed the relationship the CIA had with various American militia groups, particularly the Arizona and Nevada Militias.

It would also have exposed relationships the CIA maintained with the Hell's Angels and exposed how militia groups and the Hell's Angels were used for the distribution of narcotics. That's what was extremely sensitive.

Also the fact that Lone Star Trucking had been used by the CIA for a long time to transport narcotics was a sensitive issue.

Had that fact been revealed, it would have significantly embarrassed George Bush insofar as his family had a stock interest in Lone Star Trucking's parent.

The Bush connections, especially the financial connections, would take a lot of time to explain, since the boards of directors, officers, and principals had been used by intelligence services or were proprietary cut-outs of intelligence agencies before becoming public companies.

In the Nevada connection, Governor Miller was dogged with allegations for years about Iran-Contra profiteering.

Eventually, it got to the point that Miller decided not to run again for Governor of Nevada.

An interesting connection into all this is that Nevada is a place similar to Florida — but on a smaller scale. It's a place where government-sponsored cocaine trafficking and government-sponsored fraud meet because of Nevada corporation laws.

It's where a lot of shell corporations were formed. In order to do this, George Bush had to have control of the Nevada Secretary of State's office. And it is so patently obvious.

Before becoming governor of the state, Miller was the Secretary of State of Nevada. He was dogged with allegations about missing corporate documents, when Congress tried to subpoena them.

When Miller moved into the Governorship, look who becomes the new Secretary of State of Nevada.

The infamous, sinister, dreaded Frankie Sue Delpapa, a longtime minion of George Bush. One of George's personal secretaries in the past, DelPapa, who was considering running for Governor, was then forced to withdraw from the race under renewed allegations of Iran-Contra involvement *vis-a-vis* certain fraudulent entities in Nevada — the substitution of corporations.

She personally substituted corporate records and actually substituted officers, principals and directors in the Hellenic Seafood Corporation case and the Cosmos Investment Group case.

The fraud was egregious. The problem is that it was regarded as a regional issue. Some of the alternative papers like the *Contact* newspaper did an extensive exposé of this and documented how Miller linked to DelPapa, and DelPapa's linked to the Republican National Committee and to George Bush.

Also there were the underlying links of the corporations in question to George, Jr., Jeb, and Neil. They did a wonderful exposé of it.

But nobody in the mainstream media would pick it up, since it was considered as a minor regional issue within the greater Iran-Contra picture.

It's still a choice area of investigation today if somebody wanted to get in there and dig and put together the Nevada story *vis-a-vis* Iran-Contra. You bring in narcotics. You would drag in the CIA. You would drag in Naval Intelligence as well because it was one of the prime sites for the ONI's involvement in Iran-Contra narcotics trafficking.

That's something that was only looked at around the edges — those Medford, Oregon to Nevada routes they used.

Another interesting item would be the Arizona connection and Iran-Contra narcotics trafficking into Arizona through Fire Lake, Nevada, where the Office of Naval Intelligence maintains an airstrip and facilities.

These have been specifically used for the transportation of weapons and narcotics in the past.

If you followed the Evergreen Airlines case, in which the now retired Major Gary Atel tried to be a whistle-blower. He subsequently filed a civil case and one of the political fallouts in Arizona was when Barry Goldwater found out about it in 1987.

Goldwater said he was aware that the CIA was trafficking narcotics *vis-a-vis* Iran-Contra operations in Arizona, and that he was going to tell George Bush to stop it.

Goldwater made that comment publicly and embarrassed George Bush with that comment.

Another prominent Republican casualty of Iran-Contra activity in Arizona was Governor Fife Symington.

You may remember what happened and the involvement in that real estate scam he had, which also involved General Secord and General Singlaub and a host of others. Fife got indicted for bank fraud and was eventually forced out of the governorship. He was prosecuted and eventually imprisoned.

But the corporation, Cosmos Realty Corporation, was also mentioned in the Hughes Commission as having been involved in narcotics trafficking as well as CIA operations.

One only has to look at who the general partners were in that deal to get some idea of who was involved.

Frank Snepp, a former senior retired CIA agent and Iran-Contra notable, was a general partner of the deal.

When North was asked by Senator Inoue in the committee hearings if he ever had any contact with any United States militia groups or fringe groups, he said no — and that was an out-and-out lie.

I have pretty good records — places and dates of where he was and whom he had met.

More specifically, I have the exact place and date and the text of the meeting he had with Dave D'Adabo, who is now head of the Arizona militia and another meeting with Jimmy Johnson, head of the Texas militia.

There was also a third meeting in which North flew directly to Carlsbad, California to meet with Gary Burke, then head of the national association of Hell's Angels.

I have a pretty good text of what their conversation was *vis-a-vis* narcotics distribution. This is a very, very key point.

People tend to dismiss it as something very minor, but it's not like North meeting with Manuel Noriega or something. Actually, this is very important because it begins to connect the dots and fill in the gaps that have existed so long.

There is a huge body of knowledge about CIA involvement in narcotics trafficking during Iran-Contra to provide illicit covert revenue streams.

There is a substantial body of knowledge about that in terms of where cocaine came from, particularly in Central and South America, the routes used, the aircraft used, the weigh points in the United States, the landing points, the air fields, which government officials were involved.

However, when I refer to the gap, what I mean is — how did this cocaine get distributed? How did it get sold? Who bought it?

It's one thing to be able to prove that they brought it into the country, and that the intention was to provide covert revenue streams, but how did it get sold?

One of the ways it got sold was through a distribution system using the Hell's Angels and through various militia organizations in the United States, which in turn had contacts with all sorts of fringe groups.

They acted literally as subcontractors for the distribution of this cocaine.

The only people in Congress who ever really expressed an interest in this was not surprisingly the Black Caucus. Maxine Waters actually talked about this publicly, the connections that North had with the militias and the Hell's Angels and so forth.

But they simply did not have the resources to pursue it. I think it is an interesting connection for someone to get into if they ever wanted to dig around and bring that back because it fills in the gap — not completely, but at least it's a beginning.

It begins to fill in the gap of the entire route whence the cocaine came and ultimately how it was sold, how the money was laundered and so forth.

The next question, as always, is — how do we put people in the picture, put them in the frame? How do we connect the dots?

One way of doing that (the way I have always preferred) is look at the corporate connections. For instance, Michael Palmer's principal corporate artifice that he operated under was Carben Industries, S.A. of San Jose, Costa Rica. Look at the officers, principals, directors, board of advisers, and so on. You will see names like Oliver North, Richard Secord, CIA Costa Rican Station Chief, Joe Fernandez, to name a few.

Then look and see where they did business. Carben Industries, S.A. had hangars at Detroit. They had hangars at Mena, and ultimately in Miami, which is the ultimate weigh point.

Where did they do business in Miami? That's one of the keys to connecting them to everybody else. They had facilities at Opa Locka Air Station. People forget that, although it is a naval air station, over two-thirds of the Opa Locka Air Base is leased out to private industry.

Carben Industries, S.A. had four hangars at Opa Locka.

How do you then make the connection between Carben Industries, S.A. and Southern Air Transport?

You do it through little known facts.

The fact that Carben Industries, S.A. used the same limousine service that Southern Air Transport used in Miami.

The fact that Carben Industries, S.A.'s billings were billed for the use of that limousine services directly to Southern Air Transport.

The fact that all of Carben Industries, S.A.'s facilities in Miami (hotel suites, corporate charge, travel agency) were all exactly the same as Southern Air Transport's.

And more importantly, they were all billed directly to Southern Air Transport.

These are the little things. They don't seem important on their own, but this is how you build connections between people and organizations and what they did.

Banks are another way to go. Look at where everyone had common accounts. Then find out, of the officers, principals, and directors of those

Iran-Contra friendly banks, how many of them were officers, principals, and directors of corporations registered in Panama and Costa Rica?

Another thing that I've worked on extensively in the past — it is tedious work that people don't like to do. It is not sizzle. It is the steak. And it is certainly something you wouldn't see on 60 *Minutes* because it is steak.

They're not going to get up there with a bunch of complex charts and graphs that show all the interconnections. But this is the way you have to do it to connect the dots, which is what I have done the last thirteen years on behalf of others.

Another thing I've been asked before is — how do you connect active United States military personnel and facilities to Iran-Contra cocaine trafficking?

I'll tell you one way it's done, and this is overlooked.

You have to have some technical understanding. I imagine that's why it is overlooked. One of the ways to do it is by radio transmission and frequency.

You only have to go to the FCC and find out in the Aviation Section, the designated transmission codes of all these little nickel and dime airlines, or corporations that controlled four, five or six Fairchild 123's or something used for cocaine trafficking.

Find out their signal codes because when they respond to signal codes overseas, there are records kept of corresponding signal codes received.

For instance, Carben Industries, S.A. and Palmer Aviation, a subsidiary of Carben Industries, S.A., had the authorized transmission code of HTR585, actually transmitted as Hotel Tango Romeo 585.

Hotel Tango Romeo 585 is the exact air transmission of United States Air Force forces then stationed in Honduras and El Salvador.

These little things are actually not that difficult to find out. But they are how you go about building a case.

Another way — one of the classical ways of doing it — is to draw the dots through the lawyers. Look at the commonality among the lawyers and the law firms.

We will see in Iran-Contra connected corporations, no matter what the corporate artifice did, Iran-Contra connected banks and so forth, that there is really a very small nub of attorneys, perhaps three or four dozen very notable attorneys (Bob Becker, Tom Spencer, Phil Bronner) who tend to represent everyone, including individual defendants, not only corporate defendants.

All the attorneys, all without exception, in this group are former government counsels, mostly CIA or Treasury counsels, a few State Department counsels, mostly through the State Department's Internal Security Section, who left and went into private practice.

The law firms tend to be all the same — Shaw, Gardner, Anderson; Steptoe & Johnson; McMillan, McClain; and so forth. These are notorious Washington law firms with intelligence connections.

One could simply say, "Well, that's all coincidental. So what? They all have the same attorneys. These attorneys were all former government counsels, mostly within intelligence agencies."

Well, the obvious next step then becomes to compile a compendium of how Iran-Contra connected corporations and individuals were treated, when they became criminal or civil defendants versus how non-Iran-Contra corporations and/or defendants were treated in similar circumstances.

And it becomes quite glaring.

There are those, in cocaine trafficking or bank fraud or securities fraud, who received ten, twenty, or forty year sentences, who were gone three or four months later.

Corporations that should have been fined and put out of business were allowed to operate.

Bank accounts that should have clearly been seized and were not seized despite court recommendations in some cases to the U.S. Treasury that the accounts be frozen which the U.S. Secretary of the Treasury refused to freeze.

There's another cute trick: The U.S. Treasury freezes the account the day after all the money was wired to another offshore bank.

This is another area I worked on extensively and which is quite glaring and it's a reasonably easy way for the informed armchair Iran-Contra sleuth to put some things together.

The lawyer angle leads into another very primary post-Iran-Contra investigation in terms of a certain agency of government and division — namely the Treasury Department, which has been significantly overlooked.

There has been much focus on the CIA, the NSA, the DIA, State Department and so forth, but very little focus on Treasury's activities vis-a-vis Iran-Contra — particularly in the post-Iran-Contra or Iran-Contra coverup era.

The obvious question (and this is another area I have investigated in the past) is why hasn't FARCO, the Foreign Asset Recovery Control

Office of the United States Treasury, acted to seize offshore accounts and accounts in foreign countries, which it has the power to do?

It has the power to freeze them and then petition for return of the monies.

Why is it that *all* whistle-blower complaints submitted to them about discreet Iran-Contra related accounts in the post-Iran-Contra environment have been ignored and the accounts have not been seized?

Or, if an account had been seized, why is it that the whistle-blowers never got the percentage the U.S. Treasury promised in writing they would get ?

Then we find out, through the few whistle-blowers who had the financial wherewithal to press forward with a lawyer, in several cases, that the U.S. Treasury did in fact seize sums and then in discreet court filings and arcane jurisdictions gave the money back to the principals from whence it was seized.

Then you see the names of the people who got money back from the U.S. Treasury, and it includes people like General Richard Secord, for instance.

Surprise. Surprise.

I think it should be mentioned here that the only little crack in the Treasury wall about Iran-Contra was back in the early 1990s when Richard Newcomb, then head of Treasury's FARCO office, was secretly indicted by the United States Attorney's office for Washington, D.C. under these very same allegations.

As a matter of fact, other certain accounts were not frozen when Treasury had evidence from other agencies that said accounts should be frozen.

Newcomb was secretly indicted.

Eric Holder (I have a file on this guy six inches thick) was then the US Attorney for Washington, D.C., and he personally presented the case to the grand jury.

An indictment was issued and then put under national security seal.

Newcomb was eventually unindicted, forced out and retired.

Holder had previously been an Assistant United States Attorney in Little Rock. He was a very loyal Republican under then U.S. Attorney, now Senator, Asa Hutchinson, investigating links between narcotics trafficking, Mena and the Clinton administration in Arkansas.

Holder then moved up to US Attorney, and zealously participated in all manner of Iran-Contra coverup.

And where is he today? Eric Holder is the Senior Assistant Attorney General of the United States.

If you look at his career and the cases he was involved in, Holder is a good example of how a Reagan-Bush coverup specialist became a Clinton coverup specialist.

Holder's career route (the cases he prosecuted, or unprosecuted as the case may be) figure in subsequent allegations he faced in the early 1990s during the Alexander probe of Iran-Contra coverups.

It's a real classic example. It also sets the mold if one ever wanted to do a study on all of the people held over from the Reagan-Bush Administration and put into the Clinton Administration. There were over 1,100, as we mentioned before, an unusually high number.

But look at who the people are. Look at the commonality between them.

Over two-thirds of these 1,100 people had been alleged, during a congressional hearing or some lawsuit, to have had involvement in the Iran-Contra coverup, the destruction of documents, or the manipulation of witnesses and so on.

Holder is a real sneaky son of a bitch. Not only is Holder a Senior Assistant United States Attorney General, but guess what else he's in charge of?

Holder is in charge of Iran-Contra whistle-blower filings.

I wasn't even aware of that until about eighteen months ago, when Dinnerstein and I made a whistle-blower complaint on that account in Belize.

We got back a letter from Treasury saying that $16.6 million had been seized and that we were due a $623,000 finder's fee.

Of course, a subsequent letter denied that finder's fee to us claiming that there was a previously existing file claimed, to which we have no access. We also aren't entitled to any information about it.

The subsequent letter of denial was signed by Eric Holder himself.

Speaking of whistle-blower complaints pursuant to Iran-Contra monies, it would be an excellent idea to approach all of the Iran-Contra whistle-blowers.

When it comes to money or accounts, you will see that they have all been denied the fees that were originally promised, finder's fees originally promised them after the money was supposedly recovered by the United States Treasury.

Under the section of law that gives them the right not to tell you who the previous claimant was, they don't have to prove it. And you don't have any right to that information. You just have to take their word for it, and that's the way it is.

Match that with the actual account holders, corporate or individuals, when the money is supposedly seized and find out how many of those people got the money back from the U.S. Treasury.

This is a real interesting connection. It would sure as hell help a lot of starving whistle-blowers who found out that telling the truth will get you broke.

Of all the various Congressional committee, subcommittee, and permanent committee reports on Iran-Contra investigations — there were a lot of little gems in the Alexander probe.

Of course, it discredited Congressman Alexander and ultimately ended his career in Congress — thanks to Bill Clinton who personally pressured him not to run and supported his Democratic challenger after the two men had been friends and political allies for twenty-five years.

But that Alexander Committee report is full of little gems.

One of the overlooked gems in it regarding the actual distribution of CIA-imported narcotics in the United States was that exceptionally long series of depositions given by Dick Brenneke before the committee.

Dick was a friend of mine. We had worked together during Iran-Contra and although what he did and what I did were two different things, we knew each other and were friendly.

Brenneke was very familiar with Mafia distribution of CIA-imported cocaine. And this was very true with the New York mob. In those depositions, Brenneke did a real good job of detailing it — the names, dates, places, meetings, connections, who met with whom and so forth.

He spelled it out pretty well, which was what unfortunately led to the subsequent discreditment of Dick Brenneke — those depositions.

That combined with what he had to say about the Venezuelan government, the Venezuelan army's connection, their helping CIA cocaine out of Colombia through the Caribbean and so forth — I think those two things together probably ended Brenneke's credibility because there was such an effort to discredit him after those depositions were made public by the Alexander probe.

It's a good place to look if one is interested in that gap — of cocaine coming into its ultimate street distribution and if one wanted to look at mob involvement with the CIA pursuant to the distribution of narcotics. That's a good place to start.

Another overlooked area, in which I am reasonably knowledgeable, is the CIA's involvement during the Iran-Contra period with foreign intelligence agencies for the importation of cocaine into certain foreign nations and its distribution as part of the overall CIA scheme to produce an ongoing covert revenue stream.

I have discussed this before publicly. Unfortunately, there have been very few who wanted to proceed further.

Some foreign media people have wanted to proceed, and it's another good area to get into. Look at the connections at the time, 1984-1986, the meetings, dates, and places. These were meetings that mid-level CIA officers, and even Oliver North himself, had with ranking members of the British MI-6, the French DST, and the German BFI.

Those intelligence organizations collaborated with the CIA in aiding the importation of CIA cocaine into their respective countries and its distribution.

Note how these foreign intelligence services and certain individuals within them profited. How certain conservative political parties in Europe also profited the same way the Republican Party profited in the United States.

There has been quite a scattered body of work done on this. If you didn't maintain a clipping service at the time, it would be hard to put it all together.

The London Times did a lot on this at one time. The *Economist* did quite a bit. *Le Monde* did quite a bit. It's not like it's unknown and nobody's gone after it before.

But nobody's ever really tried to go after it hard and really cement the connections.

I can tell you that those who did try to go after it hard, particularly some of the guys at the BBC that I used to deal with, they were immediately kicked out of the BBC and they never worked in media in Britain again.

Paul Sappan would be a very notable case. Paul Sappan was a senior BBC producer I worked with on this very subject matter, and Sappan's career was absolutely destroyed because of it.

But it is another area that I think bears out investigation. There is a body of work on it already, and it would be an interesting thing to proceed with.

We see how sensitive in the late 1980s and early 1990s the British, French and German governments became to these allegations, and how quickly they acted in their own countries to clamp down on these allegations.

There were some cases, like the case of several French DST officers who were actually murdered by their own people to keep it quiet.

I do have information about that. I think it's an interesting area to proceed. It's part of the overall puzzle, and it would expand the horizons of the puzzle. It's something that needs to be done.

Speaking of foreign intelligence agencies' involvement in Iran-Contra cocaine and weapons trafficking, it still remains an overlooked area, as is hostile east-bloc intelligence agencies' knowledge of CIA narcotics trafficking and western European intelligence agencies duplicity.

Also how East-Bloc intelligence services attempted to recruit Iran-Contra players, particularly when things were falling apart in 1986. How they attempted to use for political gain the knowledge they had about CIA narcotics trafficking and other misdeeds and how that backfired on them in some cases.

That would be a great subject for a book in itself — to look at what the Russians, Czechs, and East Germans knew. A lot of that is public knowledge now.

What happened to the agents who actually knew it?

Some are dead. Others, particularly colonels and generals live quite comfortably in the United States now and receive a fat check from Uncle every month for keeping their mouths shut.

There are still many in the mid-level of former east-bloc intelligence services who were not treated so well.

Yuri Shvets is a prime example. He wasn't treated very well, particularly after he wrote the book, *Washington Station*. There are still a lot of those guys I know who live in the United States, who would be prepared to talk, but no one ever tries to talk to them.

It isn't as if there isn't any information available. I think it's a great way to expose knowledge because these people have credibility by virtue of the fact that they were serving field officers of foreign intelligence agencies at the time.

These are people with real credentials mostly stationed covertly in the United States. I'm familiar with them. I did business with a lot of them. The United States did business with them, and even Richard Secord did business with them.

This is an area we should really go after in the future.

Chapter 18

IN HIDING AGAIN

H ERE I SIT — on Wednesday afternoon, June 9, 1999 — in hiding again.

Although I was not going to include this as part of the overall story, I think it would be good to have it for the reader's edification.

This is to explain about those who have the unfortunate situation of knowing too much of the truth, what I and others like me are put through endlessly.

So here I am — in hiding again for the umpteenth time.

The current round of pressure against me started last Monday, June 7th, when I noticed a strange car in front of my place.

Nothing unusual about that. I notice them all the time.

The cars are always a dead giveaway — typically white, blue or gray Ford Tauruses or Crown Victorias. Always with blackwall tires. Always with tinted windows. Always with a lot of aerials coming out of the back of the boot.

I noticed a well-dressed man, suit and tie, about forty, sitting in the automobile. Of course, the other giveaway is that it was brazenly apparent through my binoculars that it was a J.C. Penney special. He obviously smacked of government. I also noticed he had a clipboard with some forms on it.

He was simply sitting in his car, curiously looking at my residence, writing down notes.

It would appear that he was simply updating a file, probably making physical description of my residence, possibly hoping I noticed he had a camera with a telephoto lens in the back seat of his vehicle.

He was probably hoping to get a good quality photograph of me, a new recent photograph for a file.

This wouldn't be anything unusual. However, as I have learned in the past, I've been forced into hiding so many times through this kind of pressure, that what this man was doing is generally a precursor to me, let us say, being reinconvenienced for the umpteenth time.

It means someone is updating a file, tagging me, checking and making sure where I am, looking at where the entrances and egresses to my property are.

Upon further investigation I found out (the last two days being in hiding which gives this a more sinister twist) that the Polk County Sheriff's office had absolutely no idea what this man was doing.

I found out that he ran my record at 9:10 a.m. on Monday, the 7th, using his secure passcode, but the Sheriff's office has absolutely no idea what he's doing, and there is no active file with my name on it in the Sheriff's office.

Nor is there an active investigative file with my name on it, or even my name mentioned in any file within the Polk County State Attorney's office.

It turns out this guy is one of those nebulous sort of guys that every State Attorney's office has in Florida. Although he is technically employed by the Polk County State Attorney's office, he is invariably on loan to different agencies.

As of right now, he is on loan to the statewide prosecutor's office, which is a division of the Attorney General's office of the State of Florida located in Tallahassee.

As it turns out, this man was a functionary in both the 1994 and 1998 gubernatorial candidacies of Jeb Bush in the State of Florida.

Prior to that, he was an official in the 1992 presidential State of Florida Bush campaign committee. He obtained his job as a political appointment. It has become obvious through my investigation and through inquiries I've made that he is operating directly under the Governor's office.

He simply bypasses all of his supposed superiors. This should not strike the reader as unusual, though, particularly in the State of Florida, where there is always at least one state attorney in each county directly under the control of the Governor's office.

This is done for political purposes — to protect the Governor from people like me, who might know too much about them.

Governor Jeb Bush most certainly does not want his Iran-Contra past thrown up in his face, especially while news is beginning to leak out that there will be allegations that both he and his brother George Bush Jr., the Governor of Texas, accepted Chinese Government campaign money during their most recent gubernatorial bids.

Fox News just broke this the other evening, and I suspect there will be more coming out about it because Fox News, which has been the vanguard of this issue, would like to expand it to include Republicans taking money.

So that's why this man was here — because a list is being compiled of anyone who can throw Jeb's past back in his face. Or anyone who can make connections to Jeb's past about what he's done with the Chinese money.

The reader should understand that in these various conspiracies and cover-ups (Iran-Contra, Iraq-gate and now, Fox News is calling this one PekingGate), the places and the dates change, but the names behind these operations, in terms of movement of weapons, laundering of money, and the people receiving the money, don't really change much.

Consequently, people like me who may have known about certain Jeb Bush connections in the mid-1980s — these same connections are being used today *vis-a-vis* Chinese weapons, or the facilitation of transporting American weapons to China through third party countries.

In terms of money laundering, Chinese Government contributions have used exactly the same character as before — namely my former superior, Larry Hamil.

It became quite obvious to me what this tactic was — surveilling me and trying to tag me, as the jargon goes, within the community.

Then I became aware that there was one state attorney in all the sensitive counties (the word "sensitive" implies counties where Iran-Contra activity took place) like Polk, Dade, Broward, Palm Beach, Hillsboro, Orange County, that were doing exactly the same thing as this "watcher."

These are Florida counties, known for the shipment of narcotics or weapons, money laundering, as well as being the headquarters of fraudulent corporate entities.

The "watcher" had been provided with a list of names. I don't know how many names are on that list, but it's a list of obviously sensitive names of people residing in the county.

Other names on this list included Marty Greenberg, Dennis Raditsky, and Louis Champlaign.

Frankly, I know these men but I haven't seen them in years. I didn't even know if they were alive or not. But if those three men were on a similar type of list, it gives me a pretty good idea what's happening because the one thing those three gentlemen and I have in common is Jeb Bush.

We have a connection to Jeb Bush — either transactions with Jeb Bush and a knowledge of Jeb's Iran-Contra activity. That's the one thing we all have in common.

Another thing we all have in common is that we tried to talk about our knowledge of Jeb Bush to different congressional committees or through newspaper articles or whatever during the post-Iran-Contra environment.

Therefore, it becomes patently obvious that there is some sort of a hit list that's being drawn up a second time.

Undoubtedly, as the Chinese limelight, shall we say, in the media starts to get a little closer to Jeb Bush and his brother, individuals such as myself will be contacted by the media and will be asked what we know about the past to help connect the dots.

Then we will most likely be reinconvenienced to dissuade us from doing so — as has happened to me in the past.

Just a little thumbnail description of the other three fellows.

It's a pretty diverse lot. Marty Greenberg and I actually did business together during 1984-1986. Marty was a syndicator for Atlantis Securities, headquartered in Denver. It was one of the legions of Denver penny stock houses that participated in raising Iran-Contra connected money in Florida.

Marty used to syndicate real estate deals, principally small airport developments and secure warehouse facilities around airports. He put them together in limited partnerships, most of which never panned out anyway.

But Marty, surprisingly enough, also used to market Jeb Bush real estate product during this time frame. In fact Marty's one very sensitive connection was the fact that Jeb Bush was on the Board of Directors of that West Palm Beach Airport development deal where all those supposedly ultra-secure warehouses were going to be built around West Palm

Airfield, way out in the western section which the military still controls there, or did at the time.

What those warehouses were going to be used for was the storage of narcotics. That was the intent. And Oliver North was directly involved in that West Palm Beach Airport deal.

Ollie, for instance, was at the due diligence meeting for this offering held on the second floor of the Intercontinental Hotel in downtown Miami.

To show you how close the relationship was, Greenberg was staying in a corporate suite paid for by Southern Air Transport.

Greenberg also had a plane given to him, or had access to, a Lear jet that belonged to Southern Air Transport.

He also used Southern Air Transport's limousines and other corporate charges.

The relationship was pretty close. Greenberg would have the ability to put Jeb Bush directly into having knowledge of that development, of profiting from the development financially, as well as knowledge of what that development was when Oliver North and Jeb Bush sat down at a dinner on the second floor of the Intercontinental Hotel in Miami talking about it.

I don't know how Jeb could possibly deny it, since much of that meeting was recorded by a variety of sources. The *Miami Herald* was there. There were some other people that commonly covered due diligence meetings.

Unfortunately, they weren't investigative reporters. They were business reporters. And a lot of what was said didn't really mean anything to them. They didn't really tape record what they should have in my opinion.

Dennis Raditsky, another interesting guy, was a very flamboyant CIA-connected doper at the time. This is what we used to call a "navta-doper," instead of an "aero-doper." In other words, he ran dope out of high-speed boats.

Dennis had a customized marine shop on the Ft. Lauderdale River just behind the Pier 66 development, just down the river a bit.

It was a custom marine shop that built high-speed racing boats and repaired boats, engines, and high-speed engines.

That was what he used as a cover. But Dennis had worked for a long time with some much more infamous dopers with CIA connections such as Jack DeVoe, Tony Fernandez and Bill Blakemore and so forth.

Dennis was squeezed very, very hard after Iran-Contra fell apart because of what he knew.

Dennis had this very unfortunate knowledge (and I say it's unfortunate because many times it is unfortunate to know the truth) that there was a connection between Jeb Bush and Don Aronow.

Aronow was the famous boat builder in North Miami Beach, who built the Aronow speed-boats and who was subsequently murdered a few days before he was to testify before the Hughes Commission hearing.

Anyway, Dennis was one of the very few people who knew — because of his relationship with Aronow. They were both in the same business — building speed boats.

Dennis was supposed to get a piece of that contract. You may remember the $5 million contract Noriega gave Aronow through Oliver North at Magnum Marine (the name of the corporation) to build five gunboats for the Panamanian Navy.

Dennis was supposed to get a piece of that, and he was very familiar with the negotiation of that contract because he was in Aronow's office at the same time Oliver North was there.

It was North who was supposed to steer this piece of business to Aronow, and Aronow was supposed to give him a percentage of the money back as a kick-back for, as North would like to say, "The Cause."

The problem was that North had mentioned to him that Jeb Bush was also aware of this transaction and that Jeb was going to get a piece of it as well.

Jeb was extremely familiar with what these boats were actually used for, that although they were going to be gun-boats for the Panamanian Navy, they were actually going to be used for the transportation of narcotics.

Despite his professionalism, North never hesitated to tell you who else was involved in something that he let slip out. And Dennis remembered that. And he made notes of it when he was there because he realized what he had heard was dangerous information.

Ollie essentially screwed Don Aronow and kept the $5 million for himself — well, not for himself, but for "The Cause," as Ollie liked to put it.

Eventually, of course, it went into other people's pockets.

But Aronow got fucked out of the money and he's sitting there with a signed contract saying, "I can't deliver these gun boats without the money."

For those who think Ollie is such a wonderful guy, he is a cold, steely, calculating killer. No more. And that's what the man is.

He is a zealot who would do anything to advance the cause he believed in at that time — the prevention of a communist beachhead in Central America — and he didn't care what means had to be used, whose pockets had to be enriched and so forth.

North told Noriega (at the discussion with Nestor Sanchez and Fred Ikley, Deputy Director of the Defense Intelligence Agency for Central and Caribbean Theatre Operations held at one of the lunches of the Dade County Latin American Republican Club, which Jeb Bush chaired) that Aronow simply absconded with the $5 million which was a lie.

North kept the $5 million himself.

Aronow didn't have any contact with Noriega, not that I know of. I don't believe he ever did, but the long and short of it is that Aronow started to get pressured from the Panamanian government to deliver these boats he's supposedly been paid for.

He started to talk about it, particularly to Sydney Freedberg at the *Miami Herald*.

That's how a lot of this came out. You may remember that very shortly thereafter, within two or three weeks, Aronow was murdered. He was machine-gunned in front of his office by the ubiquitous and convenient Colombian drug lord gangs. What a convenient excuse that was in the mid-1980s in Miami for every political assassination that came down and for every Iran-Contra-connected murder that happened.

Invariably, it was blamed on the mythical Colombian drug gangs or drug lords.

Only later, it was discovered that the shooters weren't even Colombians. They didn't have anything to do with the Colombian drug lords. Of course, Aronow's killers, in this case, were never found — quite conveniently so.

This is part of the case that involved Rolando Sojes and Freddie Fernandez and some others who themselves were subsequently murdered.

We've discussed this before with Sydney Freedberg when she switched from the *Wall Street Journal* to the *Miami Herald*. She was the one who interviewed Sojes' wife after he had died in that helicopter explosion. Then Sojes' wife was murdered the next day.

The Miami Metro Dade Police Sergeant tried to leak it to Mike McQueen at the *Herald* that she had two bullets in her head, but there were three shots fired. They went directly through her head.

There were three shots in the wall, yet only two bullets were missing from the .38 she had in her hand.

Where'd the third shot come from?

Before Sydney and I (this is when they retained me) could go to see the sergeant, he was found dead in the morning the day after, floating in the canal in back of his house. He lived in an area of Miami called Hialeah Lakes which fronts a series of canals.

His death, of course, was ruled a "swimming accident."

There was also a connection in the sequence of all these deaths. It involved a guy named Johnny Elesquary. His real name was Warren Elesquary and he was the brother of Omar Elesquary.

I was the one who originally told the Metro Dade Organized Crime Bureau about who Omar Elesquary was. In fact, he was a Cuban intelligence agent, a DGI agent, who was slipped in here through the Mariel boat lift in the early 80s.

The *Herald* tried to go with it once before but it got closed down in a hurry — this concept of Castro sneaking agents into this country during the boat lift.

Anyway, that's another story, but an awful lot of people died in this sequence of events, a lot of people, at least seventeen that I knew of.

Sydney Freedberg, of course, finally realized what she had done, that she had been unprofessional. She had kind of a loose mouth and she didn't believe people. Then when everyone died, she wigged out.

She took a sabbatical from the *Miami Herald*, supposedly to go the University of California. She has never come back. She has never returned phone calls, and to this day, she says she doesn't want to hear the word Iran-Contra again.

The third individual on this list of names is Louis Champlaign. Louis lived in West Palm Beach. He was Dr. Barbouti's right-hand man.

The very infamous Barbouti from this so-called West Palm Beach "Cherry Syrup Deal," which always struck me funny — the way this thing got labeled in the press when it fell apart.

The Iran-Contra afficionado would certainly remember Barbouti's name because when this deal was exposed, it became a sizeable scandal.

"Cherry syrup"? What was being shipped was chemicals for chemical weapons labeled as "cherry syrup." That's where the name came from.

The *Miami Herald* and *The West Palm Beach Post-Gazette* both did a lot with this story and it was done nationally as well. This was a company in West Palm Beach that Oliver North had a part interest in with one of his partners, Imre West, whose real name as we mentioned before was Imre Vida.

The third partner was the infamous Dr. Mansour Barbouti.

It didn't fall apart, until after most of the so-called "cherry syrup," which I've forgotten what the exact chemicals were, but they were chemicals used in the making of chemical weapons, when most of this stuff had gotten shipped to Iran.

Yes, Iran.

Not Iraq.

We're not talking about 1989 Iraqgate. We're talking about 1985 and the shipping of chemical and bio-chemical weapons components to Iran.

This has always been overlooked. Very little has been done with that because Iraqgate tends to steal the limelight.

Louis Champlaign — what he knew that was a problem with Jeb Bush is that Barbouti didn't speak English very well. He spoke with a British accent. He was educated somewhere in England, but he didn't really understand English as well as he let on. So he would take Louis with him everywhere.

Louis was the Plan Supervisor for West Palm Beach, but he also acted like an interpreter for him as well because Louis spoke both a little Arabic and a little Farsi.

So consequently, the infamous doctor would take Louis along to all sorts of meetings. One of these meetings Louis got taken to was a meeting at the main office of the Great American Bank and Trust in West Palm Beach, then founded and chaired by the infamous Marvin Warner.

At that meeting, not only was Warner there, but so was, of all people, Jeb Bush.

Jeb is recommending that Great American Bank and Trust extend the fifty million dollar line of credit to Dr. Barbouti's organization for the building they had to complete. They had some more building to do, something to do with his chemical complex that Barbouti owned. He needed some more financing for it, so Jeb personally recommended it. He personally went through an infamously cooperative Iran-Contra bank with an infamous chairman and personally recommended that the bank lend Barbouti money.

What Barbouti didn't know, however, but he what found out later on, was that Warner was paying Jeb commission fees for steering loans to him.

That's why Jeb was there so strenuously recommending it. Jeb had told Warner (and Louis was there when this was said) because Warner was concerned about the chemicals that were involved and all the various licenses necessary for chemicals.

Jeb told Marvin not to worry because the good doctor had a very special relationship with Washington — and that there was no problem in transporting these materials or anything else.

Warner knew exactly what Jeb meant because, of course, since Warner and Jeb were pretty tight.

Great American Bank and Trust, after all, financed a lot of Bush Codina property deals that later on fell apart. That didn't make any difference to anybody. It was just the taxpayers that had to eat it in the end. No one cares about them, certainly not Jeb Bush.

Lord knows, his deals cost the taxpayers enough money. I think the estimate was $156 million or so. That's from one of the congressional estimates at the time. But no one cares about that, least of all Jeb.

Anyway, that's why Jeb has a continuing problem with these guys, Louis Champlaign and Dennis Raditsky and Marty Greenberg. These guys weren't big players.

One reason I spend a lot of time on this is because it's a good example of how little guys get liquidated as time goes by.

These are the little guys that only have a very few pieces of the puzzle. But these pieces of the puzzle continue to be quite germane, particularly when the limelight that swirls around all the time on the latest scandal, which is invariably connected in some fashion to the scandal before that, which in turn is invariably connected to the scandal before that, and so forth under the guise that the names and the faces don't change.

You take out these little pieces of the puzzle and suddenly it gets harder to put together the bigger pieces of the puzzle.

It's unfortunate about guys like this because these guys were nowhere near my level.

We're talking about guys who were eighth or ninth string on a one to ten.

But unfortunately, they have a few pieces of the puzzle that could severely embarrass Jeb Bush by bringing up and doing something that Jeb does not want to do if the Chinese limelight gets a little too close to him.

He doesn't want the past brought up in his face — his own Iran-Contra past – because then we start to see the same names and connections that will connect him to Chinese money 15 years later.

There are still many in the media who don't like Jeb — particularly in the major Florida media — the *Miami Herald*, for instance, and *The West Palm Beach Post* and the *Tampa Tribune*. There are many who don't like him and would love to throw the past up in his face again at the first opportunity.

Jeb certainly knows this, so we come full circle to me sitting here in hiding, for God knows the hundredth time since the day after Thanksgiving 1986.

The pressure is relentless. It never ends.

People like me are always monitored, particularly people like me on the fourth string. It shows that the fourth-stringers like us have not been forgotten, and we are never forgotten, particularly when the limelight of the most recent scandal threatens to illuminate one's past and somebody's got something to hide, or somebody's got a career and a pension, or any ill-gotten offshore account to protect, or whatever.

Suddenly people like me become quite inconvenient again. And we are put through a never-ending cycle of harassment, intimidation, pressure, and surveillance.

Yes, it's not constant. It's intermittent. And we always know when it's coming.

All we have to do is watch the news, and we can tell when it's coming. We know what we know, and we know the minute someone that we know something about from the past starts to seep into the media a little bit, then a few words, a few connections, and suddenly people like us are put under the gun once again.

And this never ends.

The only way this ends for me, for someone in my position as a fourth-string player, frankly, is to write a book and see it published. I don't really care how many copies it sells, but to see it published, with the media I can garner, I can stand up there with this book and say, "This is Al Martin's story."

And the people have the right to know. The people should know my story, what I have done in the last twenty years, or what I did the first ten years for our government, all of which, of course, was illegal, covert, surreptitious or illicit, and what happened to me the ten years thereafter during the ensuing coverups.

It would be an eye-opener for all those that think the government is just lovely and doesn't do these things and just follows the rules and treats everyone wonderfully.

The truth has got to be told about me, I think, not only for my long-term survival, but for the edification of the people. And certainly, my book would sell. The reason why my book would sell where others' might not is not only because of my name, but the fact that my book is not exclusively an Iran-Contra book.

My book is my entire experience, my life, what I've done with Uncle Sam and those in the immediate shadows. Therefore, it's not exclusively an Iran-Contra story.

That's been the problem in the past with me. I tend to get pigeonholed as an Iran-Contra player and that's it. People tend to forget that I was also involved in the subsequent Iraqgate scandal and that I had a relationship with BCCI and Banco Nationale Lavoro.

Prior to Iran-Contra, I was involved in illegal Dominican sugar transactions and I was also involved in illegal transactions in Argentina to smuggle credit cards, an operation directly fronted by the CIA at the time.

My story is a continuous story from Vietnam on. And I am in a good position to do what many can do but obviously wouldn't do because they were on the right side of the door of liability as these various conspiracies collapsed.

I can paint a continuous picture from Vietnam, from my service in Vietnam, all the way to Iraqgate and even beyond.

I can show how Air America becomes Southern Air Transport, which then divides into Southern Air Cross and Polar Aviation and on and on and on.

The continuous connection of the military and CIA behind it, for instance — this is just one thing. But there are many things I can show as a long continuous conspiracy because it's all the same names and the same people. I worked with the same people literally from 1972 to 1986. It's all the same people.

And then, when I got back into the things briefly in the late 1980s and early 1990s, again, it was the same people doing the same thing — transporting illegal weapons with the government's approval, or importing cocaine, or laundering money or whatever.

I think it may become obvious that I have a tone of exasperation in my voice.

I always do when I'm in hiding.

I think to myself, I'm definitely getting too old.

And the idea that Iran-Contra is passe is so wrong. That notion in the media hurts people like me because we don't have the same ability to elicit media coverage we once had, yet we face the same pressures that we've always faced during the coverup phase of Iran-Contra.

Iran-Contra is not dead.

There are still congressional hearings about it to this day.

Unfortunately, every time I am in hiding, I think I get a bee in my bonnet to talk a lot and to try to make a push to complete the book because I see it as really the only way for my long-term protection.

Otherwise, the rest of my life is going to be the same — intermittent harassment and intermittent hiding and pressure. This will never end until the last son of a bitch that I know something about, that's got something to hide, is out of the government.

Since a lot of these guys were my age, or in some cases even younger, it's likely to last the rest of my life.

And people want to say, or the naive will say, "Well, so what Jeb did fifteen years ago? You know, yeah, he ripped off Broward Federal Savings and Loan for $4 million. Who cares about that shit now?"

The reason why people would care (not necessarily that they do care now) is that people like me will come along and connect the dots. And suddenly we start to get a little media attention, particularly at the same time the limelight of a new scandal, which relates to the past is shining around the individual in question who has something to hide.

That's why the past is still pertinent today because things do not change.

The players do not change.

The government acquiescence does not change.

On a more personal note, it is days like this when I am in hiding, particularly the nights when I can't sleep, when the faces come back to me from the past — all those I've known who have been murdered.

Sure, it didn't come out that they were murdered.

They died in "swimming accidents."

They "committed suicide."

They "died of natural causes."

But no one's being fooled by that. Not even anyone in the media was ever fooled by that.

Deaths of convenience.

I think of the faces of all of the men I've know that have died so very conveniently.

Within a few days of going before a congressional committee.

Within a few days of testifying in an Iran-Contra-connected civil or criminal suit.

Within a few days of meeting with a reporter or a congressman.

It is all so very convenient. And it's the nights, when you're under pressure, and you know the knock could come at the door at any minute, as it comes for everyone like me.

The knock at the door eventually, you know, will come. Because eventually the pressure and harassment will turn into an outright termination.

Because it will become cheaper to have me eliminated than it would to have me surveilled, harassed, pressured, intimidated, which the people who actually do that have to devote more resources.

Termination is cheaper.

One bullet. One time. And that's it.

And the only reason I am still alive as many reporters, friends of mine, and my own attorney often says, is that I'm still just a little too well known.

It's called the conundrum of being on the fourth string.

You're just a little too well known.

You've submitted just one too many depositions or interrogatories or affidavits to congressional committees.

You've given just a little too much testimony in a variety of Iran-Contra or Iraqgate, whatever-connected, civil or criminal suits, to which records are still public.

Your name has appeared in print just a little too often.

There are still just enough guys around in the mainstream media that like me, so if something happened to me, there'd be questions raised. Probably even some new articles written and all the names and dates would all be connected from the past again.

That's what keeps me alive.

I doubt it will do so forever.

I have to take the offensive and the only way I can do that is by getting my story out and then getting myself under the proverbial rock for a while, which is the way others have done it.

All this takes a pretty common theme. Just as I know what's going to happen to me, I know I'm going to be harassed, intimidated, and pressured. I know the routine that takes. I've been through it before.

I also conversely know what I have to do to defend myself against it in the future. All of this is play.

This game, surprisingly enough, between those who are charged with maintaining a coverup and those who would potentially expose that coverup — the game is played by a certain set of rules in a way.

You know that when the limelight shines the right direction, you're going to get pressured, harassed and intimidated.

You're going to get thrown in jail for thirty or forty-five days on uncountable circumstances.

You might be declared persona non grata quietly and forced out of the country. But this is the way the game is played.

And then you retaliate by going to the media again, by rattling the cage again, by going to your friends in Congress again, which in turn forces the response for those who are charged with maintaining a coverup.

It's a never-ending circle. Because people like me simply want to get on with the rest of our lives. We have to have the financial resources to do that. The only way those resources can come is by what we know, by marketing what we know.

That's the way everyone does it, even those who are charged with maintaining coverup, or those who would attempt to discredit us and prevent us from garnering those financial resources just to live quietly. Because if we, those who could threaten the coverup, all had the ability to do that, we'd have a tremendous upper hand. Because we couldn't be controlled financially. We could sit out there and say, "We have enough resources to live quietly the rest of our lives."

So the information we get, our information, what we know now becomes our own sword of Damocles that we control, and not someone else controls us, because they can control us financially by preventing us from earning a living.

Anyway, I'm dwelling on this point, and elaborating on it in great detail because I want this to be not only a book about information, but about one man's life, one man's story.

It's not simply a dry nonfiction book full of names and dates and places and bank account numbers and who did what.

Those kind of books, non-fiction books which have been written that way *vis-a-vis* Iran-Contra, have never sold. And the reason they've never sold is because they've been such dry reading.

They've really been like a journal of factual account. That's not what people want. They want to read a story that is interesting with a character they can sympathize with.

They might not be able to sympathize with me in the beginning, but at least I can say I did so to help my country, which was the truth. And to line my own pockets. But so did everybody else.

In terms of what happened to me afterwards, I can elicit the readers' sympathy, and certainly it is a story that will maintain the readers' interest because it's full of everything that people like. It's full of spies, sex, intrigue, and large amounts of money — all that we like to read.

This is just going to be in an autobiography of my life, full of near misses, chases and long walks off of short piers, multi-million dollar sums of money in briefcases and voluptuous blonde-haired, blue-eyed women in hotel suites, and Lear jets. That's what my story is about.

And I think it's a story that the public will be interested in reading. It's a story that they should know because interwoven in this story will be literally (although it will be done subliminally) "Here's the way the world works." Because look what happened to me.

And there's a regular routine. I'm harassed, and I'm pressured.

The guy next to me is liquidated, but that's the way it goes to maintain a coverup.

This book is about conspiracy and coverup woven into the story of my life.

I hope I've gotten my point across, so I've got to get back to downing more Rolaids and taking more Tagamet and nervously looking out the window, looking for the car and waiting for the knock on the door.

However, I do have a home shredder and to end this on a humorous note, I can take solace in the words of George Bush, Sr., who once said, "The greatest reliever of stress is shredding documents."

Chapter 19

GOVERNMENT FRAUD, CORPORATE FRAUD AND MORE FRAUD

NOW I'D LIKE TO FILL IN some of the gaps regarding fraud and weapons and narcotics.

To present this information, I will draw from summaries of my own files, logs, notes, tape recordings, surveillance photographs, journals, as well as very hard to find court transcripts and other court submissions that have been made in the past in relevant cases I worked on.

In my fraud files, I have a summary I labeled a "Master Iran-Contra Fraud File," which includes all substantive frauds committed between 1983 and 1991 during the Iran-Contra and the post-Iran-Contra environment,

In this file, which includes 543 names, I have detailed and broken down the fraud into various categories. These categories include real estate fraud, oil and gas fraud, gold bullion fraud, bank fraud of many different varieties, securities fraud — all the way down to charitable contribution fraud, brokerage fraud, i.e. aircraft and luxury yacht brokerage fraud and diversion schemes.

This is all under the Iran-Contra banner.

Some of the significant names you will find as principals in these frauds include, but are not limited to, George Bush, Sr., George Bush, Jr., Jeb Bush, Neil Bush, and George Bush Sr.'s daughter, Dorothy Bush's husband who is Jimmy Le Blonde, Jr.

His father is the famous Colonel Jimmy Le Blonde of Air America and Iran-Contra fame.

By the way, Col. Le Blonde held a congressional record for invoking the phrase, "I don't recall," 117 times, when he was asked questions about Southern Air Transport's involvement in Iran-Contra cocaine and weapons trafficking.

Anyway, those are some names at the top.

Other names include Frank Carlucci, former Assistant Secretary of State, Elliott Abrams, former Assistant Secretary of State, Bernard Aronson, former Under-Secretary of State, Lawrence Eagleburger, and former Assistant Secretary of State, Richard Armitage.

Involved in fraud on the CIA side of the ledger, the list would include former Deputy Director of Operations, Clair George, Assistant Deputy Directory of Operations, Allan Fiers, a variety of CIA station chiefs that there's no sense in going into at this point, and CIA Internal sub-director, Dewey Clarridge.

On the military side, I have divided the "scamscateers" into both active and retired.

The retired group is quite substantial. In the fraud file, there are names like, but not limited to, Maj. Gen. Richard Vernon Secord, Maj. Gen. John K. Singlaub, Brig. General Harry C. Aderholt, Col. Sam Dutton, Col. Richard Gadd, Col. Robert Steele, Lt. Col. Jack Terrell, Lt. Col. Duke Rome, and Maj. John N. Piowatty.

You may remember Piowatty, of course, in his connection with Southern Air Transport in the testimony he was forced to give in the 1990 Hasenfus civil case, and some of the articles that were written about him in the *Wall Street Journal*.

The officers I just mentioned are all retired, and of course, they are notorious Iran-Contra figures. They are often, however, just placed into their involvement with Southern Air Transport and its subsidiaries with regards to the trafficking of weapons and cocaine and the liaison facility these men provided between the NSC and the CIA, *vis-a-vis* the Honduran armed forces, the El Salvadoran Air Force, the Colombian and Venezuelan Air Forces, etc.

They are seldom looked at in the context of fraud, which they were involved in to line their own pockets. This was fraud committed under the banner of Iran-Contra and fraud for which they were never prosecuted.

In these frauds, you'll see very often there are companion links to other corporations controlled by one of the Bushes. That is the common link that runs throughout these frauds. This is particularly true in real estate, oil and gas, banking and securities fraud.

Some of the more minor frauds that were committed — the gold bullion and the charitable donations frauds — those were undertaken directly by Gen. Singlaub, who is quite notorious for those types of frauds.

In terms of active military officers participating in Iran-Contra fraud, they would also include Lt. Gen. John Gavin and Lt. Gen. Michael Collins.

Also included in the notable list of retired officers in Iran-Contra fraud are Adm. Elmo Zumwalt and Adm. C. Garrett Henderson, former Deputy Chief of the Office of Naval Intelligence.

In the real estate fraud, which is the most extensive of the files, segmented into regions, I have also linked all the real estate fraud and cross-referenced it with the banks that were involved, which were of course all Iran-Contra friendly banks.

Otherwise, the fraud would not have worked.

I have cross-referenced these frauds insofar as 80% of them involve so-called busted out HUD property, or so-called busted out bank deals that had been previously been syndicated and broke down for one reason or another. That was the most common underlying theme in these real estate frauds.

My former associate Larry Hamil's recent activity, his most recent fraud was the $11 million fraud he committed in the State of Florida, which also involved busted out HUD properties.

The schemes literally continue to this day, although not to the monetary extent they once did. The only reason is because there isn't the availability of busted out property deals like there once was.

And, of course, HUD is under significantly more scrutiny than it ever was before. Or else, if the properties were available, these frauds would reach the same magnitude they did in the mid 1980s during the Iran-Contra period.

There are two real estate frauds I haven't mentioned — two out of the many in my file of about 137 major frauds. You have to understand I didn't make records at the time of every nickel-and-dime $10 and $20 million fraud. It just wasn't possible.

In my personal logs at the time — based on my own business affairs and my interaction with others, particularly selling these fraudulent products, I used the cut-off line of $100 million in the real estate fraud category.

Another larger fraud I think is worth mentioning is the Phoenix Development Fraud, which involved a combination of busted out HUD property and busted out Lincoln Savings and Loan property.

It got lapped up into a limited partnership and resyndicated by the general partners, including Gen. Secord, Gen. Singlaub, Col. Gadd, Col. Dutton, Jeb Bush, Neil Bush, Walter Bush, the then-Vice President's nephew, Prescott Bush, the then-Vice President's older brother, and Prescott's son.

Prescott himself became one of the problems in this fraud later on.

It involved busted out HUD property bought surreptitiously through loans at Lincoln Savings and Loan for anywhere between ten and twenty cents on the dollar.

These were very expensive residential developments in Phoenix, wherein Lincoln Savings and Loan had a collateral guarantee against the original loans used in the HUD property.

It also provided bridge financing to build the developments. Lincoln Savings and Loan finally sold out to this partnership at about seventeen cents on the dollar and simply wrote the rest off.

What was not commonly known is that Lincoln Savings and Loan through another loan to Stanford Technologies Overseas, Ltd. actually provided the capital to purchase the property from Lincoln Savings and Loan at an eighty-three cents on the dollar loss.

Ultimately, the loan itself by Stanford Technologies, a $17 million bridge loan, was also defaulted on.

Stanford Technologies' two principals were Oliver North and Richard Secord — Secord, being the primary principal. Ollie was just a director of Stanford Technologies Overseas, Ltd., but this is one of the few links.

To link Ollie North into fraud, to get him away from the narcotics and the weapons and to link him into fraud — the best way is to link him through Stanford Technologies Overseas, Ltd., or Intercontinental Industries, S.A. of San Jose, Costa Rica, in which he was the principal and Richard Secord was the director.

These two are the most common ones. Intercontinental would often front as a money-laundering organization for disguised loans from other Iran-Contra sympathetic banks in the Caribbean. A good example of this would include the Banco de Popular, more specifically the Santa Domingo branch.

Intercontinental Industries would launder proceeds from what were essentially illicit loans back to Stanford Technologies, who would in turn direct these proceeds by purchasing interest in fraudulent real estate limited partnerships, to wit the Phoenix Group Development.

Another example would be a large fraud like The Boulder Property, Ltd. series of limited partnerships, in which Neil Bush, Bill Walters and Ken Good were all general partners in the deal. The only difference in that deal was that the principal financing came from Silverado.

The underlying property, which was bought very cheaply, had originally been HUD property bought by MDC Holdings Corp. of Denver. And this gets into the Denver cast of characters — Phil Winn, Steve Mizel, and Leonard Millman.

Millman is the principal of MDC Holding Group. There is a tremendous interlinkage in this MDC Holding Group fraud through MDC's subsidiary, M&L Industries, Inc., which in recent years has been indicted several times.

Its principal, Robert Joseph, is currently in the Colorado State Penitentiary as a matter of fact. He was offered a deal — if he would admit what Millman, Mizel and Winn's involvement was and how they profited by it. But he refused to talk and received about a seventeen-year sentence.

It's quite humorous that one of the consequences in the Phoenix Development Fraud was that Gen. Secord, Gen. Singlaub, and George Bush all wind up owning homes together on the same cul-de-sac in Phoenix near the country club — for which they paid nothing. These homes are appraised between $400,000 and $800,000. And it cost them absolutely nothing.

Further up the street, Col. Jack Terrell has a home. This fraud is really blatant. People have tried to look at it in the past, and they've been hit with a blizzard of paperwork.

If you weren't there from the beginning and weren't involved in it from the beginning as I was, it's tough to connect all the dots because there are so many of them.

But George Bush, Sr. would invariably be given a piece of everything, of every fraud that was done, because he was at the very top of the pyramid, and much of this fraud could not have been committed without either his protection or his influence. So he winds up with this house on a certain cul-de-sac in the Riverdale development of this Phoenix project.

Although naturally it's not held in his own name, it's held by an entity known as PHB Trust, Ltd. The PHB stands for Prescott Herbert Bush, Sr. who is George Bush, Sr.'s father.

The way that these real estate frauds work was all inside of a neat circle. For instance, the limited partnerships themselves were marketed by J. Walter Bush Securities in Phoenix, which had a rent-free office in the Lincoln Savings and Loan complex.

J. Walter Bush is George Bush's nephew.

In turn, another entity that would raise money for these deals was Prescott Herbert Bush, Jr. Investment Banking Firm of New York.

The frauds were all kept in a very small circle — MDC Corporation in Denver, a publicly listed company which still trades on the American Stock Exchange, would raise money for the same deals through their National Brokerage Group subsidiary.

Then National Brokerage Group winds up buying an interest in another firm, at one time, the largest penny stock firm in the United States, Meyer Blinder, which later became Blinder Robinson before it was closed down.

In turn, MDC owned pieces of penny stock houses throughout Denver — Balfour McClain, Atlantis Securities, Singer Island Securities. The list goes on and on, and you will see that most of these corporations in turn had offices in Florida, Nevada, and Texas, states where security regulations were rather lax.

Also these were states where there was a lot of Iran-Contra control features because these state governments were very loyal to George Bush. Consequently the ability to control liability within the various state securities or state bank examiner's offices was really remarkable.

The reason these frauds were able to operate for so long and rather discreetly — in some cases, some are still extant and operating fifteen years later — is because no individual investors' money was ever used.

There wasn't a series of warm bodies that bought one hundred thousand dollars worth of these partnerships that got burnt.

The people who ultimately got burned were banks and securities firms, and, of course, by extension, the American taxpayer who had to bail them out.

Another individual who was involved that you don't often connect with Iran-Contra fraud was Malcolm Forbes and his son, Steve Forbes.

I have extensive information on one of the direct frauds they actually postulated — the Forbes River Development deal in the Ozarks, financed by Twin Cities Bank of North Little Rock, Arkansas.

Again, Twin Cities comes to the fore.

Bridge loans were provided by another renowned Iran-Contra friendly bank, Beach Federal of Kingsville, Texas.

That was an out and out fraud, and that deal did get busted out. Unfortunately, Forbes had to come up with money out of his own pocket to hush everything up. He wasn't very good at it. He was the only guy I ever knew that went into fraud to make money, and it wound up costing him more money in the end.

But I have all the original information on that deal. It was very slick and glossy and it was well done. It would have been a good fraud had Forbes actually known how to turn it into a fraud.

But that's what you get when you have that idiot, Jonathan Flake, in charge.

Flake is the former president of Twin Cities Bank of North Little Rock who was subsequently indicted and named in civil actions filed against the bank by Congressman Alexander.

Alexander got whacked out of $3 million from that Boulder Property Limited series of partnerships which Twin Cities Bank of North Little Rock cosyndicated and acted as a sales manager in Arkansas.

These were the Boulder Property, Ltd. Partnership Series Six and Seven which got used for a very sinister purpose.

The purpose was to specifically defraud certain targeted individuals, and those individuals were hostile congressional Democrats. This has been mentioned before. They were offered lucrative deals, no cash down, all recourse notes that had tremendous tax leverage and so forth. These guys literally couldn't resist it.

The people who got hurt in these deals were Steve Solarz of New York, Congressman Dellums of California, Senator Boren of Oklahoma, Congressman Alexander of Arkansas, Congressman Hughes of Ohio — and on and on and on.

Look who got hurt. They were all leading congressional Democrats who were banging the drum about Iran-Contra. This was a way to control them.

And, boy, did it ever control them because it bankrupted every one of them. All of these congressmen got suckered in.

It was the classic bait and switch. They were all offered small investments, which they made out of their own pocket — usually $20,000 to $30,000 in various real estate developments.

They were bogus pyramid schemes, but designed so that these guys would get their money back and show a huge profit. Then they would be very susceptible to signing up into a much more major fraud later on. That's the routine that was used.

In Alexander's case, he was offered a partnership interest in Marine Research and Development Corporation in Boca Chica, Florida, which was a division of the Boca Chica Development Corporation, Ltd., whose principal was Jeb Bush.

Another point that can be made through close scrutiny of Iran-Contra fraud is to link seemingly minor players into major players.

For instance, if you wanted to link George Bush, Sr. directly into Iran-Contra fraud (I mean, his name on a piece of paper), then the corporation at the top you're going to be looking at is, of course, Lone Star Corporation.

That's Lone Star Development, Lone Star Cement, Lone Star Trucking. It's a publicly listed firm, in which Bush was a substantial shareholder, as well as a director at one time.

Lone Star has been mentioned many times *vis-a-vis* Iran-Contra fraud, the transportation of narcotics and weapons, Lone Star Cement's involvement, and other real estate frauds, etc.

The one deal that links him directly is to start with M&L Industries in Denver and go through Brodix Manufacturing in Mena, Arkansas.

You may remember Brodix Manufacturing as one of the deals set up by the infamous Mena player Freddie Lee Hampton and Hubbell's father-in-law, Seth Ward.

Brodix received letters of credit from Madison Guaranty, which in turn were hypothecated to Lone Star for a bogus real estate development outside Paris, Texas, which in turn is rehypothecated to the Victoria National Bank in Texas and so on.

If you put it all in front of you, you can see how George Bush directly profited from this fraud. It gives you tremendous ideas about where to go *vis-a-vis* George Bush, Sr.'s connection with Lone Star.

Lone Star is also the starting point to connect George Bush, Sr. into fraudulent transactions with E-Systems Corporation of Dallas, Texas.

Another fraud (not specifically real estate, although it was partially a real estate fraud) was the medical equipment fraud that links George Bush, Jr. directly into illegal Iran-Contra profiteering — the International Medical Corporation (IMC) deal in Miami.

It was the infamous Miguel Recarey who was the head of IMC. Jeb Bush was a director of the corporation and a major investor in it through the $4 million he borrowed — and later defaulted on — from Broward Savings and Loan.

Jeb was pretty crafty though in trying to cover his ass in that fraud by forming that shell corporation in the Bahamas and having Col. Duke Rome and Col. Lanny Thorme head that shell corporation, International Medical Overseas, Ltd.

That's how Jeb siphoned money out of IMC and consequently out of Health and Human Services. You see IMC got most of its money from HHC in fraudulent billing through all of its clinics in Little Havana and so on.

When that deal fell apart, Thorme got nailed, but Thorme would never talk. He was one of those guys who was going to swing in the wind.

Jeb Bush's two bagmen and gofers, Manny Diaz and Manny Perez, were prepared to talk about the deal and, in fact, they had made arrangements to talk to Jeff Goldstein of the Kerry Commission.

Unfortunately, Manny Diaz died in an unusual car accident before he could be deposed.

Perez also unfortunately died in his swimming pool before he could be deposed.

You may just remember the names Diaz and Perez. Sydney Freedberg did quite a bit on them at the *Wall Street Journal*.

They were Jeb's bagmen *vis-a-vis* Jeb's dealings with Eagle National Bank in Miami.

People in the media often ask me to give them examples of frauds that began in Iran-Contra and continue to this day, albeit under different names.

It's essentially the same fraud and the same cast of characters.

The examples I always give (about which I have substantive information, since I was involved in all three of the original frauds and also involved in marketing some of the partnerships for the secondary fraud) are the Ocean Reef Development Group, Ltd., the Omni Development Group, Ltd., and the Tri-Lateral Investment Group, Ltd.

Who were the common players who are links between all three deals during Iran-Contra?

They are Frank Carlucci and Richard Armitage.

When Frank Carlucci and Richard Armitage left government service immediately after Iran-Contra (they literally had to leave in order to avoid being subpoenaed as part of the overall coverup), they become principals with Pete Peterson, the infamous Republican player and

GOPAC money launderer, in the Blackstone Investment Group, which is a big organization.

Then they simply continued the same real estate development frauds which were begun under Iran-Contra.

This time all the original deals went bankrupt. A certain set of banks got burned. The property reverted to them, and then they refinanced the property again through Blackstone.

Subsequently they entered into an arrangement with another similar sounding company (there's always been some confusion) the Capstone Development Group, which was also a post-Iran-Contra creature.

They are two separate organizations.

Some people will try to claim that Capstone was simply a subsidiary of Blackstone.

It is not. It is a separate company. Look at the directors. They are none other than Larry Eagleburger and Bernie Aronson, former co-workers of Frank Carlucci and Assistant Secretary of State, Richard Armitage.

However, the real estate frauds continued essentially until the early 1990s. It's interesting to note how former government officials who were in the Reagan-Bush Administration during Iran-Contra profit by subsequent frauds, post-Iran-Contra frauds if you will.

For instance, in 1994-95, there was the great Mexican Diversion Fraud, when Blackstone immediately opened an office in Mexico City to take advantage of American taxpayers' money being lent to Mexico vis-a-vis the OCED and OPEC and other United States lending and/or guaranteeing agencies.

The opportunity to commit fraud against the United States Treasury during that Mexican bailout was just like a walk in the park.

You buy a busted out Mexican company for pennies on the dollar, pump it up, make it look nice, make sure you've got your hands out for a twenty or thirty million dollar loan from somebody else, like the IMF, or a direct United States lending agency, and you would be given Brady Bonds which could then be rehypothecated.

And it was such a scam.

Dinnerstein alone documented $320 million of fraud committed by former officials of the Reagan-Bush Administration during the "Great Mexican Turkey Shoot" as it became known.

And then what happened?

The Russian bailout.

Blackstone suddenly opened an office in Moscow and promptly proceeded to do the same thing again. This time they were raping and pillaging the American taxpayer with the same corporate schemes to get money out of U.S. agencies and/or collateral guaranty or fidelity instruments that could be rehypothecated.

It's exactly the same scheme.

It was another $38 million of fraud according to our estimates at the time.

To follow fraud from the Iran-Contra period and to continue to do it to this day — just look at where the Blackstone Investment Group is opening up offices in the world.

You can usually tell what the next place is going to be, where there's going to be a fraud.

There's something that I haven't revealed until this time, and that's the fact that I had the opportunity to become involved in a Mexican diversion scheme with some of my former chums and other government hangers-on.

I probably could have made several hundred thousand dollars or more.

Unfortunately, the position I was offered was the position of front man — meaning my name and my signatures would be on everything.

Of course, people like me learn that being a front man means very simply that you make the least money.

And you're also the most expendable later on when something goes wrong and everyone else is looking to cover their asses.

I therefore declined the offer to become involved.

Chapter 20

THE REAL STORY OF OPERATION WATCHTOWER

D EPARTING FROM FRAUD, I'd like to discuss the other two legs of the Iran-Contra — namely weapons and narcotics.

Something we haven't discussed before is my knowledge of Operation Watchtower — the most coveted of all Iran-Contra operations.

When I say "coveted," I mean that information regarding Watchtower was coveted by journalists in the media as well as Democrats in Congress at the time.

There has been much printed about Watchtower in the alternative media — some of which is correct and some which isn't. There's even been some mention of it in the mainstream press.

To clear up the confusion, first of all, the dates about the installation of Watchtower are incorrect.

Operation Watchtower was originally developed and built in 1976 by an elite Air Force group under the command of the Defense Intelligence Agency known as Task Force Hawk.

It was commanded by Brig. Gen. Harold Abrams, later to become Maj. Gen. Harold Abrams, retired, who, in turn, was very friendly with

Richard Secord. He would often get used in Iran-Contra in a role of relaying messages and as a mediator.

There has been much speculation about this so-called "Cutolo Affidavit."

Col. Cutolo's affidavit is correct and it's not correct, since Cutolo didn't realize what they were doing in Panama at the time when they started to build the thing.

Abrams knew. Cutolo didn't. Abrams was Cutolo's immediate superior officer, by the way.

Watchtower was simply a series of radio towers that were first built in Panama, which was the hub of it, because they needed the radar relay capability of the 16th Southern Expeditionary Force, then billeted in Panama.

It was run operationally by the 407th Intelligence Unit of the 16th Southern Expeditionary Forces, then under the command of Maj. Gen. Collins.

Later it was put under the command of Lt. Gen. John Gavin.

Although the 407th Intelligence was nominally part of the 16th Southern Expeditionary Force, it reported directly to the Defense Intelligence Agency and was effectively commanded by the Defense Intelligence Agency.

More specifically, it was commanded by Assistant DIA Director for Caribbean and Central American Theater Operations, Fredrick C. Ikley.

Watchtower was a series of very powerful radio transmitters on towers with beacons on the end of them, built from Andros Island off the coast of Colombia all the way up into US air space, essentially transversing all of Central America.

These beacons would emit a frequency which was changed from time to time for security reasons.

Aircraft could triangulate a position from them. The beacons in essence created a corridor. It was a so-called "safe corridor."

In other words, all aircraft flying in that corridor would not be intercepted.

On the United States end, aircraft transmitting the correct frequency were not to be inspected by Customs.

What's not known (it has been a source of great speculation) is what the response transmission code, or aircraft code, was for the Watchtower signal.

I think I'm one of the few people living who knows it, by the way.

It was HTR585, or in military parlance, Hotel Tango Romeo 585.

And that was the correct response code for an aircraft flying within the corridor to be recognized.

The corridor was created originally for the same purpose it got used in later on in Iran-Contra — to provide a safe corridor for the shipping north of narcotics and the shipping south of weapons pursuant to authorized narcotics and weapons transactions.

The deal had to have the approval originally of then-Panamanian dictator, Gen. Omar Trujillo. He agreed to it for a certain fee that went into a Swiss bank account every month.

I believe it was $50,000. I have quite a bit of information about it.

Trujillo later complained about the deal because he wasn't getting enough to spread around to the Panamanian G2, and then he got assassinated and up pops Noriega, a guy who would do what he was told.

But that was the essential function of it.

In 1983, the command structure of Watchtower did have to change a little bit, and the control had to move away from DIA, particularly on the United States end.

The reason this was necessary was because there were starting to be leaks in the press about Watchtower. There were little references about what it was and what it may be used for and so on.

It's this decision in 1983 to move the command structure on the US end away from the DIA, which was one of the reasons that led to the implementation of the so-called Vice Presidential Task Force on Drugs in 1983.

This essentially took over the liaison function the DIA previously had in terms of being a relay communication point through a secret radio compound in Homestead Air Force Base.

The Vice Presidential Task Force on Drugs in Miami was actually located on an entire floor. They had an entire floor in a Customs building. They also had a secret radio transmission center at Homestead Air Force Base. That's how the messages would get relayed back to Miami Customs or various Customs offices in the southeast so that certain aircraft were not to be touched, not to be inspected, and so forth.

Another reason the Vice Presidential Task Force on Drugs was created was because of sea routes.

The CIA had this idea in conjunction with the DIA to transfer weapons shipments from aircraft to freighters. So now we needed sea corridors, very similar to Watchtower providing an air corridor.

The sea corridor started at Swan Island, Honduras, and went all the way up to Haiti, through the Bahamas and into the United States.

We see the relay points were all Iran-Contra sensitive areas that were mentioned in the press later on, for instance, Cap Haitién and North Andros Island in the Bahamas.

The links were there for anyone, who had a little understanding, to see.

One of the trip wire links could have been the leaking of that FBI Internal Memorandum 12B-151, which leaked out in 1985.

It mentioned the flight from North Andros Island by George Morales, including Assistant Deputy Director Allen Fiers and 332 kg of cocaine in the back seat.

That was one of the tip-offs for anyone who really knew what they were looking for at at the time.

Some of Watchtower became vulnerable, and this is when you started to see a lot of people die.

This is when the tide turned against Noriega and suddenly some of the senior colonels in the Panamanian G2 were found assassinated because as Trujillo had gotten greedy, so did Noriega who wanted a bigger slice of the pie because of everything that was moving through Panama.

After all, Panamanian airports had to be used.

His own G2 had to be used, and they wanted a cut of the action.

Noriega began to complain that what he was getting per kilogram (or per M-16 going the other way) wasn't enough money.

He threatened to talk and to start letting some stuff out. That was evident in the December 10, 1985 meeting at the Hotel Intercontinental in Panama City between Noriega and Assistant Secretary of State Elliott Abrams and Bill Walters who also attended the meeting.

In this meeting, these exact matters were discussed.

Also attending that meeting (although it is not recorded in the upper right-hand corner of the memorandum I have, but I know through independent sources that he was there) was Maj. Gen. Joseph E. Stilwell, Jr. whose father everybody knows.

Stilwell, as we mentioned before, controlled the Guatemalan corridor, including the Watchtower corridor in Guatemala, for which he was also responsible.

Later in 1986, Stilwell briefly became Assistant Secretary of Defense before conveniently retiring just before the formation of the Kerry Committee hearings.

Of course, when Stilwell was going to be subpoenaed by the Alexander probe in late 1991, he conveniently died of a heart attack — three hours before he was due to give a deposition.

But I just wanted to mention that much of what has been said in the alternative press about Watchtower including a lot of technical details were actually correct —transmission codes, frequencies, things of that nature.

But other information was not available — exactly where the radio towers were, the mobile radar sites in some cases, the exact linkage into a central control into Panama, and the role of active United States military forces in maintaining this operation, their linkage to DIA and CIA — because very few people know it the way I know it.

I have all the names, all the officers, and who the contacts were. In some cases, I even have the sat-link telephone numbers which went into the clearing house at Homestead Air Force Base.

I had one of the very same numbers in 1985, which was an emergency number to reach Oliver North.

There had been articles, such as in the *American Spectator*, in which the media has tried to say that Watchtower was an Iran-Contra baby, but that's not true.

Watchtower had existed six or seven years earlier. It wasn't until late 1983, when Watchtower got ramped up in terms of personnel. Coincidentally at the same time, Oliver North was appointed Director of the then-secret NPO, or National Programs Office.

I think this linkage led to a lot of sinister inference *vis-a-vis* Watchtower. The inference was that the NPO, in the event of a national disaster, would be the agency in charge of Watchtower. That was certainly one of the reasons North was appointed.

What is true about Operation Watchtower is that it had originally been established by US military intelligence units and that a lot of people died to keep the thing secret.

A lot more were discredited, imprisoned, ruined, or forced into exile to keep knowledge of the thing quiet — how it was established and what its intent was.

The pressure continues to this day. As we discussed earlier, Gene Tatum wound up dead on a beach in Guatemala, and although this is not generally known, there's a lot of speculation in the alternative press and on the Internet why.

It didn't have anything to do with his knowledge of that FBI operation in Haiti. The reason why is because of what he knew about Watchtower.

What has been the common link of people who have been killed in the last three or four months?

The common link has been their knowledge as serving military officers during Watchtower. Suddenly all these guys suddenly wound up dying on beaches and falling out of windows.

It's an extant operation to clean up liability *vis-a-vis* Watchtower because it is one of the premiere Iran-Contra operations.

If Watchtower were to be explained to the American people in one continuous article, feature or book, that its purpose was to provide a safe zone for the illicit transportation of "authorized" narcotics and weapons (funny — authorizing that which is illegal), I can imagine there wouldn't be a good reaction about it among the people.

It's been said that the American people would just yawn, even if the whole truth was told to them.

I don't know if they would or if they wouldn't because there's one part of it that the American people don't like, and that is the concept of loyal American citizens, particularly military officers, being liquidated or discredited or imprisoned because of their own loyalty or because of what they knew.

It wasn't anything they might have done. And that's something that does raise the ire of the American people. That is the part of Watchtower to go after. It's not what Watchtower is, or what it did, but who had to die, or who is still languishing in prison, or who is living in Africa in hiding today because of it — because of what they know.

I'm a pretty good example of what can happen. The only time I ever publicly mentioned my knowledge of Watchtower was in that *in camera ex parte* deposition I gave before Federal District Judge Eugene Spellman in Miami Federal Court on Friday, March 21, 1986

I mentioned Watchtower and what I knew about it — not all I knew, but some of what I knew. And when that seal was broken and that information surreptitiously got into the hands of Washington, all sorts of shit happened to me.

Of course, it all ultimately wound up leading me to a twelve month jail sentence, which I could have gotten out of, if I simply told them what I knew and offered to keep my mouth shut, which was something I refused to do.

And who was the guy that was put in charge of the Watchtower coverup?

It was the infamous, sinister and dreaded Lt. Col. John K. Berglund and his adjutant Maj. Karl Wahl. They were the ones who intimidated Judge Spellman and got the transcript out of the judge's safe.

It is these two guys who have shown up everywhere, when there's been a problem with Watchtower and the conspiracy to cover it up. These two guys intimidated my own attorney, for instance. They are two of the most sinister fucks you ever want to meet.

These guys, Berglund and Wall, come in the middle of the night, bearing identification from any agency. One day they're the FBI. Then they intimidated my attorney by showing up with Secret Service credentials. You never know what agency they're going to be coming from the next day.

But what they were originally were the commanding officer and the adjutant commanding officer of the 407th Intelligence Unit, then seconded to the 16th Southern Expeditionary Forces, although under the technical control of the DIA.

Their immediate superior was that asshole Fred Ikley.

Fred Ikley is the man I used to sit next to at many functions in Miami at the Dade County Latin American Chamber of Commerce, and the Dade County Latin American Republican Club. I used to have lunch next to him because he would often show up there.

Next I would like to do more about Watchtower — not so much about the technical specifications of the project. That's pretty well known. But the coverup of what's happened — that has not been well disseminated — and I think it should be.

Especially the number of people who were hurt, killed or imprisoned because of what they knew about it. That's a story that should be told.

And in the story of the coverup, you can draw all the higher links to individuals in the various agencies.

Chapter 21

IRAN-CONTRA: KGB & EAST GERMAN INTEL ACTIVITY IN THE US (1985-1987)

T HE KGB AND MOST of the major Eastern European intelligence organizations were extremely active in the United States in the 1985-1987 period.

This activity was prompted by two developments: 1) the initiation of the Star Wars project (the Strategic Defense Initiative) and what the KGB hoped they could learn by turning US citizens who had knowledge of the project or worked on the project; and 2) the KGB wanting to exploit Iran-Contra

The KGB looked at this as a prime opportunity to recruit people. They knew they would not have to approach anyone, that people who were involved in Iran-Contra (such as myself) would, in fact, approach them.

It became evident by late 1985 that what was to be called Iran-Contra was falling apart and that there would be some sort of a hit list accumulated, as there is just before a covert operation falls apart.

That hit list would include all of the fourth, fifth and sixth string players, so to speak. These would have to be inconvenienced, or liquidated, or exiled, or whatever, to maintain the deniability of their superiors when the inevitable Congressional investigations began.

The Soviet intelligence officer who handled the Iran-Contra file for the KGB at the Soviet Embassy in Washington was Major Yuri Shvets.

Shvets was the number three man within the KGB operation at the embassy. In intelligence circles, the embassy was called the KGB Washington Station.

Shvets later wrote a book entitled *Washington Station: My Life as a KGB Spy*.

Unfortunately, he couldn't reveal all he wanted because immigration authorities were hanging his immigration over his head like a sword of Damocles.

Shvets was frankly scared shitless about being sent back to the Soviet Union, and therefore, he could not reveal all he wanted in that book, particularly about his own activities.

Most of that book was written about what he knew about the activities of others, and much less about his own activities, or the activities of eastern European intelligence services in the United States regarding Iran-Contra which he nominally coordinated.

It was fortunate for Shvets, although his superiors in Washington didn't agree with him. His ultimate superior was Gen. Alexander Karpov, then head of the KGB's North American desk.

Karpov was probably one of the smartest people the KGB ever had on its North American desk, and his strategy was exactly the same as what Shvets had recommended, namely, to put the word out through various means, and the word was often put out to eastern European social clubs.

For instance, it was a very common practice in certain bars and restaurants where it was known that KGB officers hung out. So the word was certainly put out in 1985 that the KGB would be sympathetic to people who wanted to talk to them and hedge their bets.

Karpov understood the situation exactly. He knew they weren't going to get a flood of Iran-Contra operatives coming around and begging for their help. They would, however, get information from individuals who were looking to hedge their bets. Exactly like me. People who were in my circumstance looking to hedge their bets regarding the future.

What happens when an operation like Iran-Contra falls apart is that, all of a sudden, all these personnel are suddenly put on the short end of the stick because we suddenly become politically inconvenient.

That is the way Karpov saw it, and it's the way General Marcus Wolf saw it.

Wolf was then the head of the East German Intelligence Service and one of the brightest people in the intelligence field ever.

In this time frame (1985-87), the CIA and the FBI Counterintelligence Unit (otherwise known as CI3) was aware of the increased Eastern European and Soviet intelligence activities in this country.

They were also aware of what information the Soviets and their client states were interested in. However, there was a great deal of confusion among CIA and, particularly, within FBI Counterintelligence, about what the KGB was doing.

This effectively allowed the KGB to obtain much more information about Iran-Contra than they would have otherwise. It was a classic case of the right hand not knowing what the left hand is doing, as is so often the case in the Beltway.

This time, however, it was done on purpose, that is, FBI Counterintelligence was kept out of the Iran-Contra loop to a large degree. Consequently, they didn't know names and faces of people like me, although they did maintain a file on me, as we subsequently discussed, giving me the code name "Red Beard," which I always found rather humorous.

The FBI was put in the predicament that they didn't know who I was, or what I was really doing. They thought — when I was around a certain money deal or weapons transaction in which my name was involved — that this was a straight case of espionage or of treason.

What they didn't realize was the substantial connections that those in the shadows of government maintained with the Eastern European intelligence services during the Iran-Contra operations to facilitate weapons transfers to the Contras or to purchase weapons, particularly AK-47's and other eastern European-produced munitions.

As Oliver North had discussed in one of the bi-weekly meetings at the Dade County Latin American Chamber of Commerce, which Jeb chaired (Jeb was there for that meeting and I have extensive notes about that meeting), you certainly didn't want the Contras winding up with thousands and thousands of American-made M-16 rifles. Because when the media got a hold of that, they'd know exactly what the story was.

Therefore, the specific intent became to arm the Contras with Soviet weapons, East Bloc weapons, or weapons generally identified with East Bloc countries, to give the United States some deniability. In other words, they could plausibly say that they weren't arming the Contras.

During this time period (particularly 1985-86), it was also frustrating for CIA and FBI Counterintelligence efforts to deal with the numerous spy cases in the United States — the Pollard case, the Walker case, the Korcher case, the Ross case, etc. The list goes on and on.

These were all very embarrassing cases for the CIA and more particularly, for FBI Counterintelligence, because they were the people actually on the ground doing the surveillance, or following people around.

Although the Walker case bore fruit for them in terms of political brownie points, they didn't catch up with Walker until after the damage was done.

In the Korcher case, Carl and Hannah Korcher, the famous Czechoslovakian husband and wife spies, were able to get out of the United States cleanly, with what they had come for — Project Ivy Bells, that underwater listening device the Defense Intelligence Agency, in cooperation with the ONI had placed on an underwater Soviet communications cable that ran across the Kamchatka Peninsula.

It essentially relayed messages from Moscow to the eastern Russian Rocket Command. The Soviets had a separate command for rocket forces.

Even I knew Carl and Hannah Korcher and had met them once, as a matter of fact, in Miami. They were often in Miami, and when they were, they would always be hanging out at the Czechoslovakian-American Social Club, like most intelligence operatives. It was a good place for them to exchange information, where they wouldn't necessarily stick out.

That's one reason why the FBI in Miami assigned an agent to the club and why, later in 1985, FBI CI 3 in Washington actually sent an agent there to monitor suspected intelligence activities out of Miami-based eastern European social clubs.

The agent in question was one who visited me, Anna Maria Mendoza, who I believe, is still with the FBI in Washington. She's still with Counterintelligence, as a matter of fact.

But to wrap it up, the Korcher case (which I kind of chuckled at because it severely embarrassed the FBI) was the one in which Korcher, as husband and wife, were able to operate so openly. Hannah, in particular, was able to obtain information using her feminine wiles.

These people knew how to operate. They were very, very slick, and a very handsome couple as well. She was an absolutely gorgeous woman. But it was a joke at the time, how they were able to operate so openly that even I, who really didn't have anything to do with them, knew of their activities.

The FBI was consistently one step behind them all the way.

When they fled Washington, the FBI was about nine hours behind them. Of course, that didn't work out, if you're nine hours behind.

And Ivy Bells did wind up in the Kremlin.

This was the incident which led to the subsequent retirement of Jack Verona, then Director of DARPA (Defense Advanced Research Projects Agency).

Then there was the Ross case in 1986, which was certainly the most embarrassing case the FBI ever handled.

Ross was a National Security analyst who probably did more harm to this nation's security, certainly political security, than had ever been done before.

That's why the Ross case, to my knowledge, was only shown twice on network news at the time. Even though Ross was in his home in the US Southwest, Arizona or New Mexico, and the FBI had him under very intensive surveillance (cars out front, the helicopter overhead, the whole nine yards) he, his wife and two children, with the help of two KGB agents, were able to get out of the house the night before he was going to be arrested.

It was a very dark, moonless night. They were right on the edge of a desert, where the house was, and they were able somehow to get them out of the house, right under the FBI's nose.

Twenty-four hours later, this guy shows up with his wife and kids in Moscow.

It was extremely embarrassing for the FBI, which is one reason I think they didn't give the media a lot of details — or at least that was the common presumption at the time.

Normally an intelligence assessment is done and made available to certain Congressional committees — and there's always someone who leaks it out.

There's almost no way to keep an intelligence damage assessment report secret.

But in the Ross case, a damage intelligence assessment was never done, and it's the only instance of a spy who was able to leave the country successfully, wherein a damage assessment was not done.

The reason it was not done is because Ross was able to obtain information that went far beyond the National Security Agency.

One of the items he was able to obtain in 1986 was a list of about 500 names. This was the Preamble, although it wouldn't be called this until six to nine months later. These were 500 people, including myself. My name (I was able to subsequently discover) was on this list. These were people who would most likely be liquidated, discredited, inconvenienced or whatever — after Iran-Contra fell apart.

That was a very sensitive list, and it was very valuable to the Soviets because it gave them — should they wish to approach people, or should they wish to encourage people to approach them (which they often did since it was their normal strategy) — a list of exactly 500 names.

If they had been successful in getting the cooperation of all these 500 people, God knows what the political repercussions would have been in the post Iran-Contra environment.

The Soviets would have sat back for awhile, waited until there was a Congressional hearing, then started to leak things out and put witnesses in — the way they've done it before.

I've often wondered and speculated what the political ramifications would have been.

From December 1985 till about March or April of 1986, Oliver North and Bill Casey came up with the idea, later named "Project Reassurance."

They knew that people like me were having some contact with eastern intelligence services. They correctly presumed that we were hedging our bets, so later we could not be put on the short end of the stick.

That was a correct presumption on their part. And that is why, by the way, Oliver North was so active, traveling around so much throughout Miami and parts of Florida from December 1985 to April 1986.

What he was doing (he also enlisted the help of Richard Secord and Jeb Bush to aid him) was meeting with people like me.

They met with me on December 20th to reassure us that we were still part of the team, that we'd be taken care of, and everything was just wonderful, that we would be paid all what we were owed, and so on and so forth.

And Ollie was just peaches and cream.

But this was done to prevent us — or certainly to give us pause — from continuing any relationship that we might have based on initial contact with any Eastern European intelligence groups.

The problem for me?

I swallowed the bait.

Although I did have subsequent contact with the East German Intelligence Organization, I didn't give them as much as I intended and I didn't establish as deep a relationship, a defensive type of relationship, as I intended because of North's sweet talking.

It was a very smart tactic.

And I was not the only one approached. Dick Brenneke was approached. Harry Rupp was approached. There was a list, and I've got the list somewhere of everybody who was approached at the time.

It was maybe 40 or 50 people on the fourth string who were approached. They were the first ones to be first approached because they (we) were the ones — it was correctly assumed and the East Europeans also correctly assumed — who were just one step too low on the rung of the ladder when the proverbial door of liability slammed shut.

And, of course, that is what happened.

I kick myself in the ass every day for having swallowed North's line at the time. Because if I didn't, I would have formed a deeper relationship with the East Germans because they were the most professional of any of the Eastern European intelligence services.

They had the best network in the United States. They had the ability to get you out in a hurry if you needed it. And they had a fabulous support system for people who would help them.

How I knew, by the way, that Jeb was involved in this Operation Reassurance (I later call it "Operation Massage" in court) was when I had gone to Jeb's office for a meeting with him in February 1986 to discuss my upcoming grand jury testimony in March.

Jeb had mentioned to me that he was aware that Ollie had already talked to me — and he just continued the line.

He wanted me to rest assured that Attorney General Ed Meese was informed of the situation, that Deputy Attorney General George Terwilliger, who was then in the role of a Suppressor for the Department of Justice regarding political liability concerning Iran-Contra, would be contacting my attorney and that everything would be straightened out.

Everything would be fine.

I would be rehearsed and told what to say. And no problems.

Of course, it didn't quite work out that way.

In February 1986, what I should have realized is that I was being set up.

Looking back on it, the signs were there, but North had put stardust in my eyes.

And this set-up which subsequently happened was being done with the duplicity of my own attorney, the infamous Michael Von Zamft.

Von Zamft was a well-known attorney in Miami, and he was one of the very few attorneys who handled national security/intelligence matters.

As I have described before, he pulled the rug out from under me after my grand jury testimony.

And then there were all of his own personal problems. He was facing a money laundering charge because of one of his clients, a conspiracy charge, and a perjury charge.

Then suddenly all of his problems disappeared — when he cooperated in pulling the rug out from under me.

Through Steven Dinnerstein, I was subsequently able to understand the whole story of what happened.

I didn't know just how close Jeb and Von Zamft were, but they were much closer than I thought. To illustrate this, you have to understand that most of the clients Von Zamft had were people connected with Jeb Bush.

I knew about George Morales and a few others, but I didn't realize that Von Zamft's principal business was indeed people connected in some manner to Jeb.

As subsequent history recalls, this Operation Reassurance was enough for people like me. Unfortunately it was one of the very few successful operations ever undertaken during Iran-Contra.

And I wasn't the only one that fell for it.

Brenneke and Rupp both fell for it because North had the psychological edge, I think.

North would show up in uniform, with those silver square-rimmed glasses he used to wear, a trench coat over his uniform, and he would just talk to you.

And essentially you do not want to "betray" your country (people like me have a loyalty to this country) unless you're absolutely forced to by circumstances.

Were we really "betraying" our country by giving the Soviets information about covert illegal operations of our own government?

I never quite figured that out in my head.

That's a pretty fuzzy area.

For instance, some of the federal judges I was involved with when the government came after me made a similar comment, Judge Spellman said that this gets to be a real gray area here. And legally, it certainly was.

But I'm discussing "morally" the decision to make.

Therefore, North's plan was very successful, I think, because of that edge.

After my grand jury hearing on Friday, March 21, 1986, the following Monday, I had gone down to see Von Zamft at his office in Coral Gables.

One of the things I discussed with Von Zamft was how I didn't like the way North treated me, that the assurances he had given me, particularly the financial assurances which were not yet forthcoming.

He had promised them within a certain time frame, and then I was issued other promises, and it simply wasn't happening.

What Von Zamft said (and I thought this was another trap and that's the reason I never did what he suggested) and what he wanted me to do (and apparently unbeknownst to me the arrangements had been all made) was he told me, "Look, you do business with Eagle National Bank. They're involved..."

He said, "Simply borrow two hundred thousand dollars for one of your corporate subsidiaries. Do a little artful bookkeeping and subsequently collapse the corporation and default on the loan."

Then Von Zamft promised, "There will be no repercussions."

He had told me he was making the same arrangements for others who got nicked out of money during Iran-Contra, who were owed money.

Later on, of course, I discovered what a large scheme it was.

This way North or nobody else had to dip into the well.

You simply defraud the banks for what you were owed in something that was illegal to begin with. There was sufficient control of the banks.

Someone as well connected as Von Zamft, someone who had direct access to the Attorney General of the United States, could certainly make that assurance.

I was tempted by it.

But I decided against it very quickly, because my first thought was that it would be some sort of a set up down the road — to get another sword of Damocles over my head.

In some cases, in 1988 and 1989, when there was renewed Iran-Contra investigative efforts, both in the media and in Congress, there was an effort to control people who had borrowed money that way and then subsequently defaulted on the loan.

When I say people, I mean people like myself in the fourth string, the people who were forced out and put on the short end of the stick.

Now, Jeb Bush was able to successfully default on all of his loans, but of course, that's because he was on the right side of the door of liability.

People like me were not able to do that. In hindsight, I'm honestly glad I didn't take Von Zamft's suggestion. I really am. It would have just been another sword to hang over my head later on.

Because of the confusion among the CIA and the FBI, particularly the FBI from 1985 to 1987, people like me (because of what we knew) were put under investigation.

We were being told that — from the very same people we were associated with in Washington, or our contacts within the very same FBI field office. This gave us an advantage because we could have collectively — all the people on the fourth string — blown it all out of the water, a year before Iran-Contra actually fell apart.

We could have simply told them the truth — these agents assigned to investigate us and establish case files on us.

I could have said to Agent Ross Gaffney (who was put on my tail through the FBI's Miami field offices) "Hey, you want to know who I am and what I'm doing? Ask supervising agent Paul Miller in your own field office. Or ask someone else."

I could have given him the list of all the names of agents in his own office, who actually understood what was happening.

This gave us some ability to protect ourselves.

However, when the government started to come after people like me in the post Iran-Contra environment, particularly after Congressional hearings had cooled off, it made it much more difficult for us to defend ourselves because there was always a lot of speculation and innuendo built into these files. That I was a suspected Soviet agent. That I was a suspected Czechoslovakian agent. That I was suspected in weapons and cocaine. And on and on and on.

Obviously, those who actually knew the real story were not going to help us.

You'd get nothing if you attempted to subpoena someone in the FBI, who actually knew what was going on and knew what you were up to, and most importantly, knew that what you were doing was authorized by the U.S. Government.

But they realized you had a certain connection with those in the shadows of government. Naturally, when you would try to subpoena those people, the subpoenas can't be delivered. Or the agent in question is on assignment somewhere else, so nobody can seem to find them.

You'd be put through the paperwork rigmarole and ultimately, you wouldn't get to subpoena anyone who could actually help you and actually knew who you were.

Yet there were always people there, particularly from the U.S. Attorney's office ready to shit on you.

And what always piqued me, so to speak, was the fact that the man who later came after me was the same Assistant U.S. Attorney, William Richard Scruggs, I had previously dealt with in 1985 and 1986, the Miami field office's man on the inside, so to speak.

So that was a pretty good set up. It worked out pretty well for the government. They would take these cases marked Iran-Contra. They would secretly bring you before a select group of Republican-appointed judges. Then the judges would deny every one of your defense counsel's motions to present a so-called CIA Defense.

It was very convenient for the government and very bad for people like us.

This confusion came back to haunt us later when there were subsequent efforts in late 1991 or early 1992 to deal with me.

My attorney, Marc Sarnoff, had made an arrangement with his friends in Washington, so there was an effort to deal with me, to pay me what I was owed and to get me back into the woodwork.

Then at the last minute, an admiral from the Office of Naval Intelligence, shatters the deal.

In other words, there would be lingering suspicions in different agencies, besides the CIA or the FBI, suspicions in NSA, DIA, or ONI about me.

In late 1991 or early 1992, when Sarnoff was negotiating to get me back into the woodwork, he got a real eye-opener regarding how many government agencies had really been involved in Iran-Contra.

Agencies I had not been directly involved with would suddenly pop out of the woodwork and put the kibosh on the deal because they were nervous about what I knew or what I might know.

To finish this story, I thought that all the arrangements had been made, that I was going to go to Germany, and simply lie low — and not be put on the shelf — because I was pretty well out, but there was too much suspicion of me.

I was going to be paid and go to Germany and simply disappear, which would have been fine with me.

But in the eleventh hour Admiral Lawrence Pauley came out of the woodwork from the Office of Naval Intelligence and actually met with my attorney secretly at the Ramada Inn in Miami.

They were concerned about what I knew. Sarnoff said, "Look, my client wasn't involved with your agency at all."

And Pauley chuckled at this and said to Sarnoff, "Not to his knowledge, he wasn't."

What Pauley said to Sarnoff was true. This became the Golden BB scenario. He said, "We're not concerned about what Martin knows. We're concerned about what he knows that he doesn't realize he knows. And we're concerned that at some point in time, he will get sufficient information from other sources to put it together, to put together all the pieces in his puzzle bag that don't seem to fit in his own puzzle, that there's always the threat that he will be able to put these pieces together. And that would be a real problem for us."

Pauley said that it wasn't the amount of money to pay Martin off and get him back into the woodwork, which was $200,000 to $250,000. But if he put together these pieces in his puzzle bag the right way and understood what they were, Pauley said, "It would cost a fortune to deal with this guy, Martin. We would have to pay him millions to keep his mouth shut."

And what Pauley said — the words resonated to me.

So they failed — all three efforts to get me back into the woodwork and pay me what I was owed. I don't even use the word "pay me off." I wasn't asking for anything more.

It was the same concept that consistently foiled the plan in the eleventh hour — always in the eleventh hour — the suspicion that I would someday be able to figure out what it is I have that I don't realize that I have.

No one seemed concerned about what I had that I knew I had, and that they knew I had.

It was what I had that I didn't realize the connections.

That was always the problem. And it continues to be a problem for me to this day.

Even now, those who like to say Iran-Contra's long over, are wrong.

There are still Congressional hearings about it today that we don't hear much about because they're behind closed doors, but there is still media interest in it.

There are still many people within the government who can still be hurt, and they are in even higher positions than they were then. That's why it remains sensitive.

Certainly, I have learned, and noticed, that even now fifteen or more years later, every time I try to make a move, every time I try to talk or do a radio show or get quoted in a newspaper article or something is mentioned about me in a book, all of a sudden my lawyer gets a call, and says, "Hey, we didn't know your man was active again. You'd better tell him not to become active again."

And I get threatened, pressured, and harassed and surveilled and my phone is tapped and all sorts of other shit happens. Then of course, once in awhile, when I refuse to go back into the woodwork, and I step over the line, then I'm inconvenienced with a forty-five day stay in some hell hole of a county jail under an assumed name.

After the March 21, 1986 grand jury session for me was over, and after we came out of Judge Spellman's chambers, Special Agent Gaffney gave me a ride back to my office. I had taken a taxi downtown. My office was 600 Biscayne Tower Building and the FBI's old Biscayne Boulevard Headquarters Building was only about a hundred yards away.

So Gaffney offered to give me a ride. I thought, "Well, why not?"

I didn't mind the guy, so I took it. And on the way up, I said, "Ross, let me ask you a question. What's the story here? Why is it that you've taken this great personal interest in coming after me?"

I said, "Ultimately, we work for the same people. We're both on the same side. The only difference is that the services you perform for the government are overt and legal, and the services I perform for the government are covert and illegal."

And he looked at me and said, "Well, I don't know anything about that, pal. I just do what I'm told."

I went to say something else to him, and he said, "I don't want to hear it. I'm much more interested in protecting my rice bowl than I am in hearing the truth."

And boy, if that wasn't saying a lot in a few words.

Gaffney knew what was going on. He might not have known, but he suspected what was happening, and like legions of federal minions, he was just interested in protecting his pension and his little slice of the pie.

I was just informed that Gaffney has submitted his retirement papers. He is taking early retirement. He has built a very expensive home in the Bahamas and no one is quite sure where the money came from.

But, Mr. Gaffney is retiring.

Chapter 22

THE WOMAN IN RED (AND BLACK)

I ALSO WANTED TO ELABORATE on something I mentioned before — my two days in East Berlin. I said very little about it. I've never revealed the whole story to anybody. But now I think it's time to do so because it would make interesting reading.

This can't be just a dry dissertation of places, peoples, dates and facts, and bank account numbers. This is an interesting story that people want to read.

Unbeknownst to anyone, I had secretly made arrangements to go to West Berlin in the spring of 1986 — after the so-called secret deposition I had made before Judge Spellman on March 21st had been secreted out of his office and transcribed.

I was concerned that, even though most of what I said was a lot of gobbledygook, which I said on purpose, I figured it was wise not to say the truth at the time.

If I had told the whole truth in that deposition, the minute that deposition had leaked out the next day, I wouldn't have been alive.

So I was concerned. At that time, I decided to approach the East

Germans more directly instead of the way they had always approached me, which was fronting the Czechs all the time.

The Estoppel, the Czech Intelligence Service, was pretty strong in south Florida. I told this girl I knew (she was the bartender at the Czechoslovakian-American Social Club in Miami on 133 Arch Creek Road.) I have no idea if she is still there. Her name was Tanya. And she was a beautiful girl, very striking, flaxen hair, brilliant blue eyes. I thought she was a Czech. As it turned out, she was a Russian. She had asked me if I would talk to the Colonel.

We kept referring to the Colonel, a Czechoslovakian intelligence agent who held the rank of Colonel in the Czech Estoppel, who operated through that club in Miami.

They were willing to make arrangements for me to meet somebody in East Berlin. I said, "Frankly, that would look too obvious. I'm concerned about leaks in your own organization, and if somebody gets needled the right way, that would come out and the whole thing would look real obvious. Too obvious."

I said, "I want this to look like a chance encounter." And she understood right away what I meant.

So the only information she would give me is that when I got to East Berlin that I would stay in a certain hotel. That's the only information I was given. A certain hotel that is quite infamous. I mean, everyone in the intelligence community knows it and it's no secret. Let's put it that way. Everyone knows that this hotel was used for intelligence contacts in East Berlin.

It's an odd looking hotel. The Stadt Internationale with the big tower and the strange stainless steel bulbs on it that you can see directly across the Brandenburg Gates. It had all sorts of microwave dishes and everything. It was essentially used to spy on West Berlin.

In fact, I did go to West Berlin and I crossed into East Germany as a tourist with no problem. I wasn't really concerned about any of our own people in East Berlin noticing me because one of the advantages of doing something or operating for one's government in a covert and illegal capacity is that one never has to be concerned about official investigations or official inquiries.

I knew if my picture had been taken in East Berlin, it would have gone back to the East German desk in the Agency. They would have discovered that they didn't have a copy of my photograph. They'd have no idea who I was. They would circulate it to other departments and other people within the Agency. Eventually, the photograph would get to somebody who did know who I was like Deputy Director Clair George or Allen Fiers.

They would have not informed their own East German desk who I was for obvious reasons, given my capacity of doing something illegal.

Rather, when I returned, there would be an unofficial visit from a bunch of guys in blue suits asking me what I was doing there. But I was prepared for that.

Anyway, I registered in this hotel. Of course, immediately they take your passport and everything. I had brought a cassette tape recorder with me and some files. Nothing hugely sensitive, but stuff I intended to give the East Germans anyway about certain illegal money laundering operations and precise details on illegal CIA narcotics trafficking, weigh points, other government officials, foreign officials, things like that.

I used the excuse because I knew it was an excuse that everyone would buy. The persona I maintained at the time was good ole drunken Al Martin. You know, always well-dressed, well-coiffed, the first guy to become three sheets to the wind at every Republican cocktail party, the first guy with a witty joke, the first guy with a martini in his hand. And everyone loved me. And I was well thought of. But I had that persona of, "Good old innocuous Al. He's harmless. He's over there on the sixth martini telling somebody a dirty joke."

I knew I could get away with it, and I planned it this way on purpose, so if I were to be asked any questions when I returned, I had it all planned out. I'd say, "I was in West Berlin. And I got into the martinis and met a couple of broads, and the next thing I know it's the next day and I wake up in a hotel room in East Berlin with a couple of half naked broads with a hangover."

And I knew that story would sell because I knew the persona I had and everyone else believed it.

And any direct contact I had with the CIA, it was obvious that that's how they thought of me. I was just innocuous and harmless and the first guy with a martini and a joke. It was such a plausible story, so I knew it would be bought.

That's why I didn't really have any fear of being in East Berlin.

So there I am in a hotel room, which was actually kind of nice by the way. I wouldn't exactly call it five star, but it was pretty close. Very modern. A lot of leather furniture and expensive carpets, done in sort of a gray tone. (When you're in East Berlin, you see just about everything in a gray tone.)

The first operation of business when I was there was obviously how to draw attention to myself without making it appear that I am doing so. There was a desk in the hotel room and writing paper. I simply took out my microcassette recorder and talked into it, as if I was making a tape.

My friend, Dave Lyons at The *Miami Herald*, their chief Iran-Contra investigative reporter, was one of the very early guys in 1985, who had pretty well figured out what it was all about.

I used to leak things to him on purpose. A lot of us did that just to hedge our bets. So I pretended that I was making a tape for him.

I said, "Here I am in East Berlin and I intend to have direct contact with the East Germans here. I intend to make some plans. I intend to tell them more than I have told them in the past via the Czechs. And I intend to establish a relationship with them."

I made sure the tape was very heartfelt.

I made my voice sound as if I were nervous about the enormity of what I was potentially doing.

And I interjected into this tape — to make it sound more plausible — a lot of personal commentary about women, my fondness for martinis, my life, that sort of thing.

I even interjected in it that I had been thinking of my mother recently. I hadn't thought of her in years. You know how it's said that when a man is under stress, the first thing he thinks of is home and comfort of mother. You know, I was trying to make this sound real.

And I talked about Tracy, my secretary for those two years when I ran Southeast Resources, Inc. as my Iran-Contra front. I said things in this tape which, of course, Dave already knew because he and I used to get together for a drink down at the bar in the Hamilton's sometime because they gave away free hor d'oeuvres.

I mentioned how good Tracy looked in red and black, in that red dress she used to wear and that wide black leather belt and black heels.

I mentioned I had always had a weakness for women dressed in red and black. And he, of course, already knew that.

Anyway, I finished the tape and put it in the brown envelope and put it in my briefcase and addressed it to Dave Lyons. As a matter of fact, it had his actual address and suite number and everything.

Before I did so, the last passage I had made on the tape was that now I was going to take a shower and go down to the bar.

I had seen the bar in this establishment and it looked real nice. And it was. And hopefully, I said, "You know, I need the comfort of a woman right now. The psychological comfort of a woman. And hopefully, I will meet some attractive young gal dressed in red and black."

You know, that was the key.

I had to say that on purpose so that whoever was listening — since I knew all the rooms were bugged — somebody would know how to approach me.

And sure enough, I did take a shower, and I did go down to the bar and ordered a martini.

And it wasn't maybe five to seven minutes before a woman walks in, gets off the elevator.

You can't see the elevator from the bar. You have to walk around the corner. But it's very dark. The whole place, the hallways and everything, were dark because of the color scheme.

But this woman walks in and she was not Tracy's size, who was six feet. This gal was maybe 5'10". Beautiful blonde hair. Brilliant blue eyes. Milk white skin. Dressed in a red dress that fit her real nicely.

Let me tell you. With a black belt and black stockings and the whole nine yards. Just as I had described on the tape.

And that part was true. I always did have a weakness for women dressed in red and black. I wasn't putting that on when I made the tape.

That part was the truth. And this woman comes in and doesn't sit right next to me. As a matter of fact, she sits four or five chairs down from me on the bar. The bar chairs were very nice, very plush and comfortable, by East German standards.

And I looked at this woman and she looked at me.

I had the bartender send her over a drink and she came over and sat next to me and we started to talk.

I mean, she didn't tip her hand or anything and I did not tip my hand because I was not supposed to know.

I mean, the way I had set this thing up was that I wasn't even supposed to know that the room was bugged.

So the charade had to work.

And it wasn't long, as you can well imagine, four martinis later, we wind up back in my hotel room. Let's put it this way — what a lover this woman was. She knew her business. And she was obviously a trained intelligence agent, but as a woman, she knew her business. What a lover.

When I woke up the next morning, I thought I must be in a coma after spending the night in bed with this gal. I mean, that's how good she was. She was sexually relentless, I think this is the way to describe this gal. Her

289

name was Greta. Well, who knows what her real name was. But that is what she told me anyway.

The next morning, I was sitting on the edge of the bed. She was still in the bed on the other side and I pretended to look nervous. And she bought it and she asked me what the problem was.

And I sort of just acted. I could always get tears in my eyes on cue. I've always been able to do that. And I just poured it out. I hugged her and poured it out and said, "Look this is who I am. And I'm considering betraying my country possibly, lest I myself be betrayed."

I just told her the whole story. And this woman is well trained. I mean, so sympathetic and so on and so forth.

And anyway, she had an uncle (I love this story). She had an uncle that I just had to meet who would absolutely want to see me and could help me, Uncle Bruno. And that's actually the name she used — Bruno.

And when I met this guy, his name was Bruno Becht.

But who knows what this guy's real name was. He did appear in an East German army officer's — rank of colonel — uniform.

We had made arrangements to meet in a certain building (if you know where the Stasi Headquarters used to be in East Berlin).

Stasi also had a small office building, although modern, which was about four blocks down where they used to meet people in. And it had a very discreet entrance. You could go in the parking garage on the other street and go underground and come up underneath this building without being seen.

I had heard of the building's existence, but here I was inside of it. The rooms were all soundproofed and they had all sorts of electromagnetic pulse detectors and signal detectors and everything. I mean, it was impossible for the building to be penetrated electronically. It had real darkened windows.

Anyway, I wound up talking to this man for two or three hours and he was just as sympathetic as could be. I told him what my situation was and that my motivation was to protect myself and I wasn't really interested in any financial gain from the relationship other than what I really wanted was in exchange for any information I could provide is a place to go if things started to fall apart for me.

Because I said, "I'll be good and goddamned if I'm gonna be a scapegoat."

And I pretended not to know certain language and protocols commonly used in the intelligence world and said to this guy, which was essentially the truth, that I was a little more than a glorified money launderer.

I told this man every capacity I had been in before, and what I had done on behalf of the government of an illegal nature (which was unfortunately everything I ever did was) and I gave him some of the names of my immediate superiors and what they were involved in.

And I got a feeling he knew a lot about this already.

We talked about Miami a lot. And he wanted to know what access I had. I told him that I attended the bi-weekly meetings of the Dade County Latin American Republican Club and the Dade County Latin American Chamber of Commerce and who was there — and you could tell he was real interested in that.

I gave him lists or names of people who would regularly show up, what was discussed, the nature of the operations. And they were quite interested in that. That was obvious.

They asked me what other type of intelligence I have access to and I said, "You know, it's strange you should ask. Because I'm not in a position to ask for anything, but lots of times, information just simply comes to me by the way. Because I get invited to a lot of meetings that only peripherally concern me or what I am doing where many other things are discussed. And I get invited to all the Republican cocktail parties where liquor loosens lips and you'd be surprised what slips there are."

I proceeded to tell him some of the slips I had heard in the past year for instance, about the Strategic Defense Initiative.

The minute I mentioned SDI, his eyes lit up.

Anyway, I told him the cover story.

He wanted to know what cover story I used in the event that I had been here, and he got a chuckle out of it. But he said, "We'll help you with that when you leave." And they did.

I told him I couldn't stay in East Berlin very long. Frankly, I wanted to leave the same day. And he wanted me to meet with someone else and I said, "Look, I want to be out of East Berlin today. If you want to meet with me, arrange for one of your people to meet with me back in the States. Because I am growing nervous about being here and the cover story I laid is only going to be believable if I'm only here for one night. If I'm here for a second night, it ain't going to be believable."

When I crossed back into West Berlin and went back to the hotel, they arranged for me to have a couple of women in the car who appeared a little drunk, and I made sure I appeared a little drunk. Of course, these were

East German women who probably did a little make-work projects for the Stasi or whatever.

I dropped them off before you get to the East German checkpoint. You know, you have to come around that corner. When you're in East Berlin, coming back the other way, there's that corner and the stone wall on the end.

Well, I dropped them off there, but within sight of the American sector and then made it appear that I was half in the bag.

I wanted the story to work. I would have believed the story, had it become necessary.

Fortunately, when I got back to the States and back to Miami, it was obvious to me that I didn't raise any concerns. No one ever said anything to me. I expected that the minute I got back, Secord or maybe even North himself or somebody would be at the airport. No problems.

So apparently, I was either unobserved, or the connection was never made. Or I was observed, which was more likely, but the connection was never made. Or if the connection was made, no one said anything to me about it, which would have been the smarter thing to do, and then try to monitor my activities.

That's what I would have done. But it appeared that no one had seen me, although, I think that's unlikely.

Bruno Becht did provide me with a contact name in Miami. And it just so happened it was somebody I knew and I had met before.

I didn't even know they were German. I thought they were Hungarian. But it turns out they were German. And it is a man I had regularly met at the Czechoslovakian-American Club.

I would subsequently meet him sometimes at the German-American Club. I had always assumed he was Hungarian. His name was Alexander Petrovic and he operated a little real estate agency.

I had always assumed, when I had talked to him, that this man was much more than he seemed, because he seemed to know the intelligence world and he seemed to be the type that had been around it for years and years.

As it turns out, he had been around for years. I mean, this man's story is a whole different story. I didn't realize what he had once been — how high up in the East European world this man was at one time. But that was my contact, and we had subsequent conversations and it never really amounted to anything because I never made the decision to go forward.

I made sure that all of the information I gave them was information about the United States government's illegal covert actions.

I did not give them any information other than what the United States was doing which was illegal — not that it would have made any difference in my prosecution. That statute, I think, is 432 of U.S. Title Code 18. It doesn't make any difference if you're giving information about an illegal operation or not. It still constitutes espionage. The only difference is that it's awfully hard to get prosecuted for it.

Chapter 23

THE BUSH FAMILY: CORPORATE, REAL ESTATE AND BANK FRAUD

I THOUGHT IT WOULD BE worthwhile to once again touch upon Iran-Contra fraud, more specifically, real estate fraud — and even more specifically, real estate fraud connected to the Bush family.

As I've said before, Iran-Contra can be divided into three categories — fraud, narcotics and weapons. Fraud can also be subdivided into numerous categories.

The principal categories of fraud would be real estate fraud, insurance fraud, banking fraud, securities fraud, and oil and gas fraud.

There were many other types of schemes, but these are the principal frauds committed.

I've been asked on radio shows and in newspaper articles and interviews, "How could this have taken place — this level of fraud? Billions upon billions of dollars that the American people were defrauded of?"

The enormity of the conspiracy is such that only those who lived it, who were really involved, can truly understand it.

Otherwise, it boggles the mind.

Real estate fraud is a prime example. Obviously, you needed the cooperation of an Iran-Contra sympathetic bank as well as an Iran-Contra sympathetic insurance company.

In some cases, when these fraudulent real estate deals were marketed as public securities, you would in turn need the cooperation of an Iran-Contra sympathetic brokerage firm.

The real estate fraud, for example, acts as a cascading fraud through all the components that were necessary to make it work.

And there is a completion of a circle in these frauds.

When one takes a fraud and follows it from A to Z — and more importantly, follows the money — the money will tell you how large the conspiracy is and its State-sponsored (or at least State-acquiesced) nature that allowed the fraud to exist.

That's why I have consistently called it (and I know it has been confusing to some in the past) Iran-Contra Real Estate Fraud or Iran-Contra Banking Fraud.

These were, in effect, *de facto* State-sponsored schemes. It could not have worked any other way unless there was State-sponsorship or at the very least, State-acquiescence.

These real estate deals were certainly investigated at the time (particularly when they became public deals) by a panoply of State and Federal regulatory bodies.

It was obviously necessary to garner the cooperation of these bodies insofar as the frauds were often not that sophisticated. It wasn't that difficult for anyone to ascertain that they were frauds.

Very seldom were all the T's crossed and all the I's dotted in the commission of any of these frauds because we knew, in terms of my marketing these frauds, that we faced no real scrutiny. Certainly, we faced scrutiny — but no real scrutiny, because the proverbial fix was in.

Also these frauds could sometimes be marketed in a rather sloppy way because we never had any fear of repercussions. We never had any fear of punishment for breaking the law because we knew that none of us would be prosecuted.

After the falling apart of Iran-Contra in late 1986, then there were some prosecutions. But those prosecutions were only those where it became politically expeditious to do so, in order for certain parties on the upper rungs of the ladder to maintain their deniability *vis-a-vis* their involvement in the commission of these schemes.

In some cases, the more common reason to prosecute was to discredit somebody.

The Bush family was intricately and intimately connected to Iran-Contra fraud, particularly in real estate fraud which is probably the most notable because there have been the most newspaper articles written about it and the most public revelations have been done in this realm.

Banking fraud, insurance and security frauds which drew in the other Bush brothers have not been as closely examined as the real estate frauds. The reason why is because there was always more public information available about real estate fraud. This is very true on the HUD angle.

When busted out HUD properties were bought and repackaged (fraudulently purchased, fraudulently repackaged, and fraudulently resold), it left a much larger and more easily discernible paper trail to trace these frauds.

Although Jeb Bush and his younger brother, Neil, are the two Bush boys most commonly mentioned in the same breath with Iran-Contra real estate fraud, they are mentioned because they were more visible. Their names appeared on so many documents and so many corporate names.

But George Bush, Jr. and George Bush Sr., as well as George Bush, Sr.'s brother, Prescott, and his son, Walter, were very much connected to the very same real estate frauds. It's just that it's much harder to find their names and signatures on documents than the other two brothers. And often the fraud was segmented. By that, I mean that Neil and Jeb would formulate the initial deal — the initial deal that would become a real estate fraud.

George, Jr. (this has been mentioned before) would often come in on the insurance end. He is most notably connected to Iran-Contra Insurance Fraud, *vis-a-vis* his relationship with American Insurance General and American Re and other large insurance companies as well his ability to produce essentially bogus guaranty fidelity and/or guaranty instruments from insurance companies which often stood by to back fraudulent real estate deals.

These were then used to obtain fraudulent bank loans, which were then used to finance fraudulent securities deals, using the fraudulently obtained real estate as the supposed asset.

George, Jr. also becomes connected again on the fraud end, particularly in the realm of securities fraud.

Rolling Stone magazine did a good piece on George Bush, Jr. and three of his oil and gas companies which failed. But the article didn't go far enough. It did not go really into Harken and Tidewater and other public corporations which George, Jr. was involved in and in which securities fraud was committed.

He was able to neatly skirt the laws, or should we say, deflect the shit away from himself through a whole series of contrivances. The way he was able to do this, by the way, was to post these essentially bogus fidelity and guaranty instruments, so the deals wouldn't be scrutinized until long after they had collapsed.

This was one of George Jr.'s specialities — and I did this myself, by the way. It was a common tactic in Iran-Contra Securities Fraud.

As the expression goes, it was to "back in" fraudulent assets, normally of a real estate nature, to back in fraudulent assets into a public shell.

More commonly, they were known by their regulatory names in those days as a Reg D offering, or a Reg 501 or 505, or an S1, S3 or S18 offering.

These were the common euphemisms used in the day.

This is, of course, Security and Exchange Commission language, or "SEC speak" as we used to call it, for various types of offerings, which govern how large these offerings could be, how many states they could be "blue-skied" in (meaning how many states they could be sold in), the total amount of money that could be raised, the market making regulation that was necessary to maintain a market in the shares thereinafter.

Anyway, a very common securities fraud was the use of 144 stock.

144 stock refers to Rule 144, or Restricted Shares (shares that are not free to trade under the two-year restriction rule).

Often a company that would nominally have ten million shares outstanding could issue a hundred million shares of 144 stock that would then be sold at a steep discount to the market price.

If you had a stock trading at a dollar, you would issue scads and scads of 144 stock, and you sell it for twenty cents a share.

This stock would get bounced out into offshore bank loans, principally through the Union Bank of Switzerland, but also through a whole host of offshore banks through the Caribbean.

The large French bank, Banque Paribas, for instance, was notorious for this because of George, Sr.'s relationship with the bank.

What would happen is you would raise an enormous amount of money, but you would also have an enormous amount of restricted stock, out of which at some point, the letter (what is known as the restriction or the letter) would come off that stock, and that stock is going to come bouncing back at some point to the market makers.

Because the scheme was at the banks, this was only meant to be interim financing.

We are now talking about cooperative banks who were not meant to be burnt. They were just meant to provide bridge financing. This was very, very true with Union Bank of Switzerland, Royal Trust of Canada, and Imperial of Canada, Banque Z of Curaçao, Banco de Populare.

These were banks that you did not burn. These banks just acted as facilitator banks. But you have to make them "whole" in the end.

Now, if you bury them under a pile of 144 stock, how did you make them "whole" in the end?

How you made them "whole" is by pumping up the deal as the letter began to expire on the 144 stock that was out.

You would pump up the shares artificially in the marketplace and begin to bleed the stock back through your market makers at forty or fifty cents on the dollar.

You would make money again.

You had originally borrowed twenty cents on the dollar. You perhaps would bleed the stock back into the marketplace at forty cents on the dollar by the tactic of what is known as "back-dooring" the stock to your market makers and dealers, and issuing certain guarantees to them that they in turn would be made whole.

The ultimate bagholder in these deals, of course, are the people that bought the hype, the people that bought the endless press releases, most of which were all bogus.

In some cases, we would have to make the representation that Company A has a tremendous new product or that it just has a contract with the International Monetary Finance Corporation.

And boy, this is just going to be the greatest since sliced bread.

Of course, what the prospective hypee didn't know is that the International Monetary Corporation was in fact a shell that had been formed by the very same people who had perpetrated the original fraud.

It is the only way you could keep control of the hype.

So you would have one bogus company signing a contract to purchase ten zillion widgets from another bogus company. Not only did the widgets not exist, but both the companies themselves were essentially worthless.

In this way, you could pump up the price of the shares and be able to create enough liquidity, enough excitement in the shares to distribute all of the stock, all of this 144 stock that you had bouncing back.

Since the problem was obvious, you would vastly expand the flow to the shares — in some cases, by a factor of ten.

There were previously, let's say, 10 million shares authorized, but usually there was 300,000 or 400,000 shares that were actually out.

The rest of it was buried in the hands of dealers or constituted restricted stock.

So what would happen is towards the end, when the deal would falter, you could always give the deal a second shot by instituting a reverse stock split, which would bring the stock back up to a level where penny stock investors and speculators felt more comfortable, and also back to a level where the shares would then again meet certain regulatory hurdles, thus making it easier to distribute the stock.

You took the stock that was originally done and pumped it up to a dollar. In order to maintain it at a dollar and absorb all the stock, you needed a constant flow of hype.

When the shares eventually sank (because the distribution began to back up on the dealers a little bit), you would give the stock a secondary chance by instituting a reverse stock split.

That would boost the price of the shares back up to where they were, usually even higher. Of course the spreads would widen out, and as anyone knows in reverse stock split penny deal, the spreads always get very, very wide.

But you simply disguise those spreads.

The dealers can very easily disguise those spreads by either not posting Bids and Asks on the pink sheets, or just posting so-called nominal Bids and Asks which would give the appearance to the would-be investor that the stock was substantially more liquid than it was.

But the reverse stock split was always the last link in the chain of the fraud of the underlying deal. Because the last time you would pump it up would be through this artifice, this device using a reverse stock split.

It wouldn't be long thereafter that simply the deal would fall apart, and you could distribute the stock all the way back down to a penny bid, three cents offered, which we did on a lot of deals.

Once the broker/dealers were out — or were "whole" financially — as well as your other market makers and specialists, once you had made them whole financially, because you had so severely discounted the stock to them to begin with, then there would always be 30 million or 40 million shares left over.

And the Bids and Asks would quickly go to like a penny bid, three cents offered, but with that, you would get a whole new crop of potential investors.

You would keep a little bit of hype there. You'd keep a little bit of activity and spread on the sheets. And there's a whole lot of people that will buy 10,000, 20,000 shares of a two or three cent stock in hopes that it might be a twenty or thirty cent stock.

You do open yourself up at a penny — making a market of one and three cents — you open yourself up to a whole new crop of speculators that will be sellers of a deal at twenty cents, not buyers of a deal at twenty cents.

We use to call these type of penny speculators "green feet." We used to delineate them by where the stocks traded, on what sheets, in other words.

For instance, a pink sheet speculator is someone who bought higher priced penny stocks and shares that traded in the low dollars. Of course, when the stock fell down below the pink sheet regulatory level, it would be kicked down to the green sheets.

That's where you find the one cent, three cent, five cent stocks.

When they could no longer be maintained at that level, they would be kicked down to the yellow sheets.

That's where you would sometimes see stocks trading in mils — so many mils bid, so many mils offered.

As long as there was still somebody willing to buy it, a market could be maintained, particularly since the stock, by this point, did not cost anything to the broker/dealers or those who initiated the fraud.

Everybody was out and clean and made their money, and public shareholders were the ultimate bagholders.

But you could actually keep these deals floating and alive for a long time before they absolutely fell apart.

How were we able to accomplish these frauds?

How could they be pulled off?

Let's take a fraud apart. As a for instance, I was thinking of using this deal, which I marketed in 1985 known as United States Securities, Inc. (Tape symbol was USSI).

The deal's long since gone. It had been either a Utah or Nevada shell. Most the shells were Utah because Utah's security laws were extremely favorable toward the formation of shells, particularly Regulation 501 shells. But it had been a shell deal.

The nature of this was a machine similar to an ATM. There was supposed to be a whole chain of them and it was a cash-dispensing machine.

You could get cash through your credit cards and things like that. And naturally, it was never really done. I mean, four or five prototype machines were actually built and installed for promotional purposes. That always had to be done. But everything else was bogus. Everything.

How were the shares able to trade? Because the market makers were all conspirators with the officers, principals and directors of the corporation itself.

The banks who provided some of the original financing were themselves conspirators. It is a complete ring of conspiracy.

As these deals were obviously, at least, acquiesced to by the U.S. government, they had to pass scrutiny. But look at how many local and regional SEC commissioners retired quite handsomely. And how many people within the Office of Thrift Supervision and the Comptroller of the Currency retired quite handsomely.

Those who tried to talk or blow the whistle, like Rebecca Sims, were summarily dismissed and immediately discredited. People forget what Rebecca originally did for a living, but she was an auditor with OTS.

The same thing happened to Bobby Mullins, the Comptroller of the Currency, when he tried to talk

Obviously, these deals had to be at the very least State-acquiesced. The entire chain of conspiracy could not have worked otherwise because there would have been the fear of inevitable prosecution if the thing fell apart.

In order to alleviate that fear, people had to know that the state (either the individual state or the federal government) had actually signed off on the deal — and that in fact, everybody got a piece of the action.

You know, Oliver North was approximately correct.

Few believed him at the time. But he was approximately correct when he had said in deposition before the Kerry Committee hearing about Iran-Contra fraud, how he was personally frustrated by it because in his estimation ninety-seven cents out of every dollar was going into other people's pockets, and only three cents on every dollar was being used to illicitly support the Contras and North's other pet projects.

But of course, North was no businessman. I mean, I knew him and I met him several times, and I understood what his role in everything was.

But frankly, he wasn't a businessman.

He never seemed to understand that in an extremely complex conspiracy, it's necessary that almost all of the money has to go out, elsewise the conspiracy does not work. Because there are so many people involved in these conspiracies that have to be taken care of.

Therefore, there is very little left over to fund what these conspiracies were essentially set up to originally fund. That was the whole original idea — that money would be diverted from various frauds to support the Nicaraguan Contras or to create deep operational accounts for further illegal covert operations of State.

That was supposed to be the original mandate under which all of us operated.

But greed being what it was, the amount of money available to fund the Nicaraguan Contras and the amount of money that went into deep operational accounts, from 1984 to 1986, became less and less as greed took over.

This was particularly true when people like myself in late 1985 sensed that the end was coming, that things were beginning to unravel.

Then it was essentially a cash grab.

Every conspirator grabbed as much as he could and hid it all in offshore accounts and went back into the woodwork and waited for it all to unravel.

One of the problems later on, after Iran-Contra had fallen apart (and I had mentioned this to Jeb several times in early 1986 when Jeb and I were still on the same side, so to speak) was that not enough money had been put into the deep operational accounts to manage the ensuing coverup.

He didn't seem concerned about it. But I could plainly see that that was going to be a problem. The enormity of the conspiracy would mandate an enormous and expensive coverup.

And I had questioned whether there was going to be enough money available to maintain such a coverup. The coverup consequently was of course maintained, but sometimes it was done in a very dramatic fashion.

Certainly, more people died and more people had to be liquidated than probably would have had to have been otherwise — had there been more money available to pay people off.

That was what kept Iran-Contra going for so long in the coverup stage, and what keeps it alive today — the fact that there's an awful lot of aggrieved people out there, including myself. Because in the end, there simply wasn't enough money to go around to maintain the coverup, because it had been botched from the very beginning. Because people like Bill Casey and George Bush underestimated the resources that would be necessary to cover this thing up later on. Because they never envisioned it would grow to the enormous proportions that it grew.

In the original addendum to the white papers on Operation Eagle (the birth parents of Iran-Contra), Casey originally envisioned only $20 billion to $30 billion worth of fraud being committed pursuant to the maintenance of a surreptitious covert revenue stream.

He never envisioned that what he was creating would grow to a $350 billion fraud over time and that essentially it would become much more difficult to manage.

It was originally envisioned that there would be only 500 or so people involved in the fraud end of Iran-Contra, not the 5,000 that were ultimately involved.

Now, let us take a look at an Iran-Contra Real Estate Fraud since I got a little sidetracked with securities.

A good example of an Iran-Contra Real Estate Fraud that can be followed from A to Z is the infamous Destin Country Club Development deal in Florida.

Destin Country Club Development was located in Destin, Florida, which is between east and west "Nowheresville."

It was originally envisioned as a $78 million residential community with championship golf course and swimming pools and the clubhouse — a typical Florida gated community, although this was going to be a very large development and very upscale where homes would start around $199,000 and sell up to maybe $499,000.

This was top-end development for the time, and it was specifically meant to appeal to Republican money types. They were the first people offered equity in the deal or offered the ability to purchase equity in the deal.

You will see that many of the so-called investors were members of GOPAC who wound up getting land sites for five cents on the dollar.

The general partners of the deal was Gulf Stream Realty, controlled by Neil Bush and his infamous partners, Bill Walters and Ken Good, who also were involved as co-general partners with Jeb Bush through his Bush Codina realty.

George, Jr. was on the Board of Trustees of the deal and had an equity interest in it which of course he had for nothing. Like all the Bush boys.

The original financing came from Silverado. It was the original $50 million bridge loan to start the development. Of course, the development was designed as a fraud. In other words, it was never meant to be built.

The only thing ever built was a couple of models and a sales office and a few other things on site. And a little bit of the land had been cleared so it would pass some sort of scrutiny if someone actually came to look at it.

I don't know anyone who actually ever went there to look at the place.

I had the brochures and everything because I was one of the people marketing the deal. And naturally, the brochures of what the place was going to look like were just absolutely wonderful. Like all the fraudulent deals we marketed.

As usual, the underlying land that was going to supposedly comprise this development was never actually bought.

The only thing that was ever bought was an option to purchase the land.

You will see that pretty consistently throughout bogus Iran-Contra real estate deals, when something was supposed to be built, the underlying land would be very seldom purchased. Only an option to purchase the land would be obtained. And that's what happened in the Destin Country Club deal.

The Bushes paid $9 million for an option to purchase the land, a three-year option at a certain price. And there was $41 million left out of the loan after the option was purchased. But there were obviously other expenses. There were legal costs in printing up the limited partnership and the memorandums and red herrings. And there was some actual cost of the properties and the whole deal, the fraud, cost about $13 million to set up.

It was a good investment, since ultimately people profited to the extent of about $350 million.

What is different about Destin Country Club Development is that it was one of those feel-good payback frauds, wherein sympathetic individuals in Congress, sympathetic congressmen, senators and governors, suddenly wound up owning equity in this deal which they supposedly paid for with non-recourse notes.

Theses were the infamous non-recourse notes that would be issued by Iran-Contra friendly banks.

The principal issuer of these notes (for individuals to obtain bogus equity on essentially bogus notes) was American Bank and Trust of Pensacola, Florida, a little tiny one-horse bank owned by BCCI.

They issued ultimately about $153 million of non-recourse notes.

To give you an example, there was Congressman Porter Goss of Florida in whose jurisdiction Destin was located and Senator Paula Hawkins of Florida (before she lost her reelection bid in 1986), Senator Graham, and Senator Mack of Florida. They were all involved.

Despite the fact that Senator Graham is a Democrat, he was one of the conservative Democrats quite sympathetic to Iran-Contra fraud and he was able to profit handsomely himself on the series of transactions he did with his own land in Florida with the Swissco Management Group.

Graham was essentially given that deal on a platter as, should we say, his reward for turning a blind eye on some of the committees that he chaired in Congress.

He, of course, co-chaired several regulatory committees in Congress. It was later reported that he made a profit of about $57 million. That was the estimate by the *Miami Herald* in that Swissco deal.

Swissco Management was a company in Miami set up by the infamous Chilean arms dealer, Carlos Cardoen. It did little more than act as a clearing house for real estate fraud, banking fraud, securities fraud and money laundering. It was essentially set up for money laundering, but the guise to launder this money would be a variety of Iran-Contra related frauds.

Not to digress (which I always do because I can't help but digress since there's so much information) but that Swissco Management is a humorous story.

After Carlos Cardoen was indicted on weapons charges, the FBI finally raided their offices. You may remember Carlos Cardoen. They used to call him "Mr. Cluster Bomb." Or "Mr. Fuel Air Bomb."

The FBI raided his offices. Of course it was FBI agents who were the ones not in the loop in Miami. Sixty-eight boxes of records were seized and taken to the U.S. Attorney's office in Miami.

Then US Attorney Leon Kellner immediately put all the boxes under seal in their special secure room. And it was the infamous Assistant US Attorney William Richard Scruggs, their man in the CIA at the time, who went through all those boxes of documents and picked out essentially all of the Iran-Contra sensitive records and financial files and information.

What blew the whistle on this was a lowly secretary named Kelly Hanson. She was not in the loop. She's just a lowly secretary who noticed that there were supposed to be a lot more boxes in the US Attorney's office than what wound up being there.

And the cover story (I love the cover story) was that they had completely run out of storage room.

This was when the FBI still had their old building on Biscayne Boulevard which admittedly was rather small. Their document storage room on the third floor (I had been in there several times) — you couldn't cram another box full of stuff in that room.

So what happens is the FBI in conjunction with the U.S. Attorney's office as well as Immigration and Customs, wind up renting some document storage warehouse facilities out by the Opa Locka Naval Air Station on the other side, the west side of Miami.

As the US Attorney's office is transporting forty-three of these Swissco Management information boxes (they got them on a truck) they're transporting them across town because they think, "Oh, we don't have enough room to keep this."

The only thing that was kept were the files that weren't sensitive. So as this truck is going across town, it miraculously manages to catch on fire before it reaches their auxiliary document storage facility.

And wouldn't you know it? All forty-three boxes of documents burn up in this mysterious truck fire and no one seems to know how it got started.

Back to the Destin Country Club — Silverado had provided the initial $50 million bridge loan to get the deal underway.

What happened then is Bush and company went to Marvin Warner at Great American Bank and Trust, another Iran-Contra sympathetic bank, which had its main office in West Palm Beach, Florida.

They proceeded to borrow another $17 million as a continuing financing loan. The partners — Jeb, Neil, George, Jr. and a host of others — then begin to take their personal general partnership equity and pledge that to loans.

For instance, that's how Jeb was able to get that $4 million loan at Broward Federal Savings and Loan, which he later defaulted on.

It actually became a political issue later on because he did it in kind of a sloppy way. Broward Federal Savings and Loan was owned by two brothers who themselves were subsequently indicted for bank and securities fraud and because of that, they talked about the bank's relationship with Jeb Bush and others.

It very nearly became a problem for Jeb.

Of course, one of these brothers somehow died under unusual circumstances before going to trial, and the other brother simply pled guilty and nothing further was ever said.

The bank simply went into receivership. But it's an example of how the general partners would take the general partnership interest in the deal and rehypothecated that to bank loans personally.

And they'd put the money in their pockets. It wouldn't be much. Three or four million dollars per deal, usually. But it was a way of extracting more money.

Ultimately, that Destin Country Club Development deal got hypothe-cated through a total of 53 banks worldwide. That's how far the scheme went with the rehypothecation of fraudulent interests and refinancing of fraudulent interests.

When you started with the core banks that have to be protected, you would need further bank loans to pay off the existing bank loans from your core banks that had to be protected.

So you would go to your second ring of sympathetic banks, wherein you knew the loans didn't have to be paid off.

And the whole scheme was to ultimately allow those banks — there's about 140 of them on my list — to go into receivership anyway.

Orange State Bank of Miami, Ocean Bank — the list is endless of these little banks that went into receiverships with $200 million or $300 million outstanding on their books.

How did these congressmen, governors and senators get money out of the Destin Country Club Development deal?

It was very simple. They were non-recourse notes they had supposedly borrowed to begin with.

A deed equity interest would show that Goss in fact paid, let's say, $7 million for his equity interest in the deal, when in fact he didn't.

He perhaps paid $3 million, put the other $4 million in his pocket, and ultimately defaulted on the loan. He didn't even have to pay the interest on the loan.

The Destin limited partnership paid the interest on his loan for about eighteen months before it defaulted. As a matter of fact, the many defaults of congressmen and senators for Destin Country Club Development loans forced American Bank and Trust of Pensacola into liquidation.

Of course, they also took a $26 million hit on the original loan they had given Topsail Development Group, Ltd.

As a matter of fact, when the bank was finally scrutinized by the comp-troller's office of the state of Florida, they didn't even realize that the bank was ultimately owned by BCCI.

Of course, that's what they claim. But you must remember that Gerald Lewis, the longtime comptroller of the state of Florida, was Marvin Warner's second cousin.

Lewis was later implicated in kickback schemes in these very same deals. He lost reelection and then quietly left the country. He now lives quite comfortably in the island of St. Lucia, in a $350,000 cottage with a fifty foot Hatteras.

Nobody ever asked the question — how is the man able to afford this on his state pension of $24,000 a year?

Of course, the Destin Country Club Development deal doesn't need a huge amount of rehashing because so much has already been written about it.

It's been written in little one-story pieces, here and there, over the years. But if you were to gather all that has been put in print about this Destin Country Club Development deal, you would get nearly the whole story.

People have just divided the story up. There were the initial stories of how the fraud began.

There was an excellent series of articles written by Mary Fricker and Steve Pizzo. This was after Fricker and Pizzo separated from Sims in 1991 in *Mother Jones* Magazine. It was a good series of articles that pretty well laid out the whole development of the fraud.

Then as the fraud moved along into its different components, there were different pieces written in the *Tampa Tribune*, for instance, and even in far-flung newspapers such as the *Rocky Mountain News*.

But you never see one article that spells out the fraud from A to Z, and you will find nobody in the mainstream media who would ever write such an article, as it has never been done on an Iran-Contra fraud — spelling out that fraud from A to Z.

Because as my friend, Bill Plante at CBS News once told me, "It is not possible for us in the mainstream media to spell out the fraud that way, lest the American people get the right idea."

He also used to chuckle and say. "It gets far too close to the way everything works, and what it's really all about."

And that serves nobody's interests — including the public's.

There was this fear after Iran-Contra, in shall will say, intellectual media circles of the Walter Pincus, the Hugh Ainsworth, Pulitzer prize-winning journalists' and the old timers' variety.

There was always a fear of this idea of putting all of Iran-Contra together under one roof, and spelling it out for the American people.

The fear was — what would the people's reaction be?

Would it actually prove to be politically and economically destabilizing to the nation for the people to know the truth because of the way the people may react — the negative way people may react, and the consequential loss of confidence that would come from the people knowing the truth?

Frankly, I've always agreed with that idea, that it's better for the people themselves not to know the whole truth. I've always thought that.

And it is that very notion that has allowed the fraud to happen. It allowed it to go forward. It allowed it to expand.

It's what George Bush had said to me privately once when I was at a dinner with him in Miami in late 1985.

Jeb was there and Felix Rodriguez was also there — the whole cast of characters.

But George Bush, Sr. always said that his concept of government, what he believed in, and how he had always operated, was on the Big Lie principle.

Of course, we all know what the Big Lie principle is.

Essentially it's what allowed Iran-Contra fraud to happen and to foster other frauds — to increase into enormous amounts of money, way beyond what was envisioned.

Because if it all ever was put together under one roof, the people would be much less likely to believe that such an enormous and intricately woven conspiracy could ever exist.

It's much easier for people to believe one $300 million deal was bogus over here and another $400 million deal was bogus over there than to understand that there was a chain of conspiracy between all these deals.

And, of course, the public are the ultimate bagholders.

Speaking of Iran-Contra Real Estate Fraud, another interesting angle that has not really been looked into is the international component of these frauds (not all of them, of course) but the international component in some of these real estate frauds, particularly the larger ones.

The media's never been keen on piecing the international components into these frauds because of the obvious limitation of space, of column inches, it takes to put in a lot of factors. A lot of components. A lot of operations internationally.

Also there's this generalized fear that if you start talking about the international aspects of these frauds and involvement of foreign banks and foreign real estate companies and the conservative politicians those companies are linked to in their own nations, then you start to get into that Big Conspiracy that everyone likes to shy away from.

But in fact, I will devote more time in the future to the foreign connections.

A good example in Iran-Contra Real Estate Fraud was the connection between Olympia & York Development Group in Canada and its U.S.

subsidiary, The Cadillac Development Group, headquartered in Miami, which was very closely aligned with Jeb Bush.

You will see that many of Jeb Bush's fraudulent real estate deals also involve the Cadillac Investment Company and this was particularly true of busted out HUD deals, which were always the most profitable of all.

These were the so-called Section 8 busted out HUD property deals that could be refinanced endlessly — and on a tax-free basis, no less.

Or they were virtually tax-free because of the tax incentives offered on Section 8 property.

That was the most common way of repackaging of HUD property — Section 8 development deals. That's why you would see Bush Codina or Cadillac Investment Group real estate signs in the worst sections of major cities — the Black areas, the Latino areas, and places where there was a lot of Section 8 HUD housing.

In Section 8 housing, there was never a lot of scrutiny. Those deals were designed, so that they could be set up very easily, financed very easily, and they wouldn't be scrutinized that much.

That was the original pre-Iran-Contra notion as a matter of fact — how to entice money into low income housing. There was horrendous fraud committed within that Section 8 housing. At least half of all of the repackaged HUD deals I marketed for others were busted out Section 8 deals that were being picked up again and refinanced.

HUD had already wiped it off or taken the loss and they would essentially transfer the property a second time for fresh money. What would happen is there would a secondary default, then a tertiary default, and on and on.

For instance, there was a development in Miami, a HUD Section 8 development, which is a huge complex. It was over 830 apartment units spread all along the Overtown, Hialeah border. It was mixed Black and Latin low income.

That one deal was busted out and picked up seven times from 1984 to 1986 and refinanced seven times. The same piece of property. Not one penny was ever spent to improve the property.

Ultimately there was $83 million sucked out of it seven different times. And HUD took it on the chops each time.

But it's a great deal to look at.

It was called Blackbird.

The name of Bush's deal for it was the Blackbird Investment Group, Ltd.

Blackbird. Get it?
Guess who one of the general partners were?
Who had the codename Blackbird?
Richard Secord, of course.

Chapter 24

IRAN-CONTRA REAL ESTATE FRAUD

I'D LIKE TO BREAK DOWN frauds by regions, to give the reader a better idea of how Iran-Contra fraud, weapons trafficking and narcotics, was principally undertaken in so-called Iran-Contra-friendly states.

These are states which had very solid Republican governors and very solidly Republican bureaucracies that could be controlled.

When hearing about Iran-Contra states, we tend to immediately think of Florida or Texas or Nevada or Arizona — the better known Iran-Contra states.

One seldom thinks of Connecticut or Illinois, where there was extensive Iran-Contra activity, particularly in real estate and banking fraud.

And speaking of Connecticut, a serious student of Iran-Contra would remember the Jeb and Neil Bush instigated real estate fraud in Connecticut involving the Mohawk Indian tribe, which later became known as the Carrollton Development Swindle.

That was the proposal Jeb and Neil had become involved in — to build a casino under the Indian Rights Act in concert with the Mohawk Indian tribe in Connecticut.

The long and short of it is, of course, the Mohawk Indian tribe wound up getting swindled out of approximately $4 million before the deal fell apart.

Subsequently, they did try to squawk about it a great deal.

The *New York Times* became involved, and did several pieces on it pointing out the fraud.

One of the Indian leaders, in fact, did go talk to Congressman Jack Brooks who was then Chairman of the House Judiciary Committee.

Of course, nothing was ever done because the Mohawk Indian tribe understood that if they were to continue to push their complaints regarding Jeb and Neil's activity in swindling them, it was very likely that the State of Connecticut would have revoked their charter rights to build casinos and bingo powers and that type of thing.

So frankly, the Indian tribe just walked away from it and took the $4 million hit and kept its mouth shut after that.

Another interesting fraud state to look at is Illinois.

I was extensively involved in marketing Illinois-based deals, and marketing to people in Illinois. This was under the guise of marketing to the "right" people as it were — not just average investors.

Illinois at that time was controlled by Republican Governor Thompson, who is very closely aligned to the Bush faction. And certainly, he profited quite handsomely from Iran-Contra fraud in many of the oil and gas frauds perpetrated in Illinois.

For instance, I was present at the Whitehall Hotel on East State Street in downtown Chicago when the Governor was paid a bribe in cash.

Not a bribe. That's the wrong word. He was paid his "percentage," shall we say, for a series of deals involving Dr. Keller and that slimy Republican-connected promoter in Chicago, the famous CPA, Al Barrish.

In Chicago proper, you tend to think of Cook County as being solidly Democrat. But it never has been. That was particularly true in the mid 1980s.

There was a very small, but well financed and cohesive, cell of Republicans that operated within Cook County. These Republicans were led by a Cook County judge named Harold Gordon, who bird-dogged deals for me in Illinois. And he was very good. Very well-spoken, and naturally the title of Judge helped.

So every time I was in Illinois, he would lend credibility to transactions by being there and he did quite well for himself.

How we paid him off consistently, by the way, was by giving him cheap stock all the time in deals that we were pumping up. We let him buy stock for, let's say, twenty cents a share in some penny deal, and then we'd let him get out at eighty cents a share. This was a common way of paying people back because the transaction seemed perfectly legitimate.

Gordon made a lot of money — in the hundreds of thousands of dollars because of us. He was personally friendly with Governor Thompson and knew many Republicans in Cook County. The very same Republicans who were GOPAC members were involved in supplying us with money by investing in these fraudulent deals.

Another large Iran-Contra profiteer in Illinois was Congressman Henry Hyde, who profited enormously on that Oak Brook Savings and Loan series of transactions. They were known as the Glenwood and Glenbrook Realty Limited Partnerships.

Jeb, Neil and George Jr. all had a piece of it, and, of course, those Glenwood and Glenbrook deals were just out-and-out fraud. I mean, you can't put it any other way. There wasn't even any pretense to make these things look legitimate. It was just out-and-out fraud.

The Oak Brook Savings and Loan took it on the chin for $8 or $9 million dollars in that deal. He personally profited by a million dollars. And of course, Hyde was forced to disgorge some of it and had to pay $800,000 in congressional fines when he was secretly censured because of this transaction.

Pursuant to Iran-Contra activity, Chicago worked the way Miami did. There was one FBI officer who was in control of political liability suppression later on, and who monitored all of these deals. The same split faction. That is, you had a faction that didn't know what was going on, and then the faction within this FBI office that did know what was going on. And it was not the FBI's own office in Chicago, but it was a small ancillary office in Mt. Prospect, Illinois which handled the suppression later on.

You will see that the subsequent indictments — after Iran-Contra fell apart —generated out of Illinois, came from that Mt. Prospect office.

All of the subsequent investigations during the Iran-Contra cover-up (so that those investigations could be controlled and where they would lead to could be controlled) were generated out of the Mt. Prospect, Illinois office.

Chicago is also notable in my mind insofar as most of the Iran-Contra Caribbean-based real estate fraud (of which there was much) was based out of Chicago.

The reason this was the case, by the way (people often speculated why Chicago) is because most of those Carribean development frauds were run by two guys, Peter Green and Bill Lucher.

Lucher, of course, was a very close friend of Ollie North. Both Secord and North often had disguised interests in Iran-Contra Caribbean-based real estate development fraud, like the North-controlled Intercontinental Industries, SA and/or the Secord-controlled Stanford Technologies Overseas International, SA.

One of the deals that stands out that I had helped to market was that St. Lucian development deal, which was a fraud. We were able to successfully market a lot of that deal through GOPAC members.

That deal only fell apart when it became evident that the St. Lucian government never intended to grant the building permits for the development because the land that had been optioned to supposedly build this luxury townhouse community and yacht club (the typical fraudulent Caribbean development) was in an environmentally sensitive area of St. Lucia.

There was no way the St. Lucian government was going to issue the permits to build this development on the land. The land, as a matter of fact, wasn't even suitable. You couldn't build anything on it. It was swampy sort of land. But we kept that deal going right until 1986. That was a nice choice fraud — about $13.5 million was raised from that fraud.

Richard Secord profited directly, I would guess, by a half million dollars or more.

North probably profited to the same extent through his Intercontinental Industries, SA, although as it has been noted before, it was not North himself.

North never really profited personally from any of these transactions, unlike Secord. North, in some cases, used money from the Intercontinental Industries to finance illicit covert operations in Central America, as well as the purchasing of weapons. This was particularly true after early 1986 when congressional money dried out.

Of course, to get away from real estate fraud for a minute, Illinois was also a choice area, particularly southern Illinois around Alni, Illinois, where there was some oil production on the border of Kentucky.

That whole area was used for Iran-Contra oil and gas fraud.

Our principal guy in Alni was named Royce, who owned a little public shell called the Royce Development Group, which was later changed to the name on the pink sheets of Dutch Creek Petroleum. That's when we tried to pump it up again.

Carl Royce was the individual behind it. He was subsequently indicted and got, I believe, a ten-year sentence for fraud. He was made the designated fall guy, shall we say.

But we pumped up that Dutch Creek Petroleum deal from about eight cents a share to maybe sixty or seventy cents a share before we pulled the plug on it.

We sucked a lot of money out of that fraud, and Al Barrish, as a matter of fact, was the guy that would package this stuff up into highly leveraged oil and gas partnerships — three to one or four to one write-offs, this type of thing — so that "investors" could actually pull their money out of the deal within two years — before the deal fell apart, with the tax incentives.

We see in the 1990s that the IRS reversed a lot of these oil and gas tax shelters that had enormous tax leverages in that there were hundreds and hundreds of limited partnership deals. And people had to pony up some pretty big tax money because of it.

But look at the deals that were not reversed — they had extreme leverage. That tells you where the politics of the situation were. Of all the deals I marketed, not one was ever reversed by the IRS.

We see deals that were reversed were often deals that had been marketed by larger security firms that were in fact genuine deals — not a politically oriented transaction to raise illegal covert monies. But I marketed over 300 deals and not one of them was ever reversed later on.

Also, I wanted to mention another Iran-Contra state in terms of fraud — not only real estate fraud, but also mining fraud — Nevada.

People have often asked me why there was so much corporate fraud concentrated in Nevada. It's because of the control that Bush had within the Nevada Secretary of State's office.

After all, the Secretary of State was a very close associate of George Bush — the infamous Frankie Sue DelPapa. She was later investigated umpteen times in the late 1980s and early 1990s, but no charges were ever proven against her.

She was investigated for having substituted corporate records, which in fact, she did. That's one reason she was there. She made corporate records disappear, and she did substitution of corporate records.

The Bush faction had such incredible control in the State of Nevada that you could literally commit fraud with absolute impunity. When you have a sympathetic Secretary of State who's prepared to destroy corporate records, or alter corporate records, or actually substitute corporate records and steal other people's corporations, which DelPapa did, it's incredible what you can get away with. And what we did get away with.

In the Nevada series of mining property deals that we did, they were mostly sponsored under the Glory Hole Master Limited Partnership Development, which was actually Colorado-based, but extended deals also into Nevada.

Students of Iran-Contra would remember that the Glory Hole mining properties were controlled in Colorado. The control was through retired CIA and FBI agents — all of the Board of Directors, the Trustees — everybody was either retired CIA or retired FBI.

To make those deals work, it involved a lot of Republican judges. There was Judge Ed Barnes, who was a state district judge in east Texas, Judge Barnhill in Colorado, and Judge Nottingham in Colorado.

These judges were subsequently investigated. None were ever indicted, but they were subsequently investigated for surreptitious investments they made, actually paper investments they made in certain mining deals and reaped just enormous rewards for monies that they had never actually invested — except on paper.

Speaking of judges, this borders on another subject that we haven't really got into and that's judicial involvement in Iran-Contra frauds.

The connection between U.S. Attorney's offices and certain federal judges, and even State Attorney General's offices and certain state, district or circuit judges wherein Iran-Contra sensitive criminal fraud cases would be consistently investigated by the same parties within those state or U.S. Attorney's offices.

These cases would consistently wind up in the jurisdiction of certain Republican-appointed judges to make sure that the outcome was what everybody wanted to see the outcome to be.

You'll see there were plea bargains in these cases.

In cases where the designated fall guy didn't like the idea of being the designated fall guy and wanted to put on some sort of so-called CIA Defense (which of course has much broader implications than just the CIA), you will see that the people who tried to do that didn't fare so well.

They received very long prison sentences, and often the judges (it's particularly true in Miami) would close their courtrooms to the media when there was an uncooperative designated scapegoat. They would either close the courtrooms or attempt to close the courtrooms.

This finally stopped in 1988 when there were increasing howls from the Democrats on the Hill and increasing media agitation about this consistent use of "National Security" in Iran-Contra sensitive fraud cases to keep out the media.

Frankly, the practice was politically untenable after 1988.

In the Nevada properties, there had to be at least the semblance of reality, particularly in the mining deals. All of the mining deals I marketed in Nevada, including the Helena Mining deal and the Cosmos Development deal — it was similar to the oil and gas frauds.

In other words, the oil and gas frauds were based on old beat-out limestone pumpers that pumped one barrel a day perhaps and had been pumping a barrel a day for fifty years.

Give them a shot of acid every ninety days, and they'll pump fifty gallons of water and one gallon of oil a day. But you just do manipulation of the logs and meters. You make that one barrel a day appear like three hundred.

The mining deals were mostly the same way. In Nevada, all of the mining deals that I marketed — the gold, silver, platinum mining deals — were all what's known as open pit leach mines. And they did, in fact, produce precious metals, but nowhere near the production we were actually claiming in these deals.

Let's put it this way. People familiar with mining would know that in leach mining, you have to move an incredible quantity of earth. You have to build these enormous pools, which almost look like swimming pools. Then there's the acid and solution and electrolytic zinc rods which attract the metals from the sands.

But frankly, to make a leach mine profitable, it has to be an incredibly large operation. Anybody with any brains who visited these sites would have known that there wasn't anywhere near the amount of metals coming out of these mines that what we claimed.

Thanks to our Nevada friends in the Bureau of Natural Resources in Nevada, which was very solidly Republican controlled, we could easily manipulate it to make it appear that much more was coming out of these mines than there actually was.

The final Iran-Contra note I wanted to make about Nevada was the egregious swindle that George Bush Sr. himself instituted in concert with Frankie Sue DelPapa on that Cosmos Development deal.

The scenario in question later became known as the Peruvian Gold Certificate Swindle, where DelPapa actually substituted corporate records.

Bush had formed a corporation with a very similar sounding name.

This was so commonly done — mimic corporations with similar sounding names.

You simply substitute the records and it was an out-and-out swindle of the Durham family. This is the scenario that the famous California conspiracy theorist, E.E Eckert, got involved in.

Of course, he pounded away on this conspiracy for years in that paper he printed, The *Contact*. And he actually presented a pretty good case of it. We're talking about a man and his staff of about three guys who spent years investigating this fraud. And they did have it put together awfully well.

But it was such an egregious fraud, an out-and-out theft by George Bush.

What Eckert did was connect this fraud to ever larger frauds. He connected this gold certificate fraud into big money, tens and hundreds of millions of dollars in bank loans at Banque Paribas, Credit Lyonnais, Union Bank of Switzerland.

This is also part of the National Bank of Greece swindle that was instituted by Prime Minister Papandreou and George Bush together.

As a matter of fact, Bush's attorney, C. Boyden Grey, flew to Athens.

You would see his travel records to the same places all the time — to Paris, Zurich and Athens.

Eckert did a good job of pointing out who he met — the President of the National Bank of Greece, for instance. This wound up being an enormous swindle in the end and this is what is called the Grade One Swindles in Iran-Contra. These are the swindles that nobody is ever going to want to look at because it gets far too close to the way everything works and what it's really all about.

For a long time Eckert tried to get the major media interested in it. And they would bite. ABC bit a couple of times on it. As long as the fraud could be contained, to say, "Well, it's just a small $75 million fraud, and Bush was connected to it."

But the minute Eckert was able to show that this was up in the clouds. This is one of the frauds in the clouds that makes the world go around, that ultimately were to involve Daiwa Bank and Sumitomo Bank.

It's an interesting example. They had hired me at one time as a consultant to provide some further information for them, which I did. They needed some connecting pieces of the puzzle.

But this is a very interesting fraud about which an entire book could be written. It's a fraud that starts out with a $50,000 investment by

George Bush, and ultimately it grows into a $2 or $3 billion international bank fraud.

How? By simply rehypothecating loans and/or borrowing ever greater amounts of money, using proceeds to pay back the old loans, or in some cases to partially pay them back, which was more common.

Then the corporate entity would go bankrupt. Credit Lyonnais was one of the very few banks to ever admit that it lost money, that it had in fact lost about $68 million on this fraud. Of course, they would have no comment when they were asked about George Bush's involvement with this fraud.

But Eckert knew and the *Financial Times* of London knew that Bush's signature was on loan papers at Credit Lyonnais.

You may remember this famous scenario. FT London revealed that Credit Lyonnais had a fire in their reserve document storage facility in Paris and (wouldn't you know it?) there were three or four file cabinets that got burned up, including all of the Bush documents.

I had wanted to discuss Colorado to some degree because it tends to be misunderstood in terms of Iran-Contra fraud. When a student of Iran-Contra hears Colorado, they instantly think of HUD because Colorado was the center for HUD fraud in the west.

That's how Colorado tends to be looked at, but what is always less looked at is the huge amount of securities fraud that was run out of Denver.

Denver, after all, was really the chief place for Iran-Contra-instigated securities fraud because so many penny brokerage firms were located in Denver. They had by 1985 much common ownership through the National Brokerage Group, which at that time was run by the infamous Dick Brenneke.

National Brokerage Group had equity interests in Blinder Robinson, for instance, which was the largest penny house in the country. But they also controlled many smaller firms — Butcher & Singer, Trotter & Company, Marco Island Securities, Atlantis Securities. We could go on and on.

You would see that it was these small broker/dealers — the same fourteen broker/dealers — that appeared on the pink sheets for all of the public penny deals that I marketed.

Their officers, principals, directors, trustees and boards of advisors consisted of individuals such as Oliver North, Richard Secord, Jeb, Neil or George Bush Jr. Or people like Colonel Robert Steele, Colonel James

LeBlonde, Colonel Dutton, famous Iran-Contra names in the securities part of Iran-Contra fraud where many names can be pieced together with the actual commission of fraud.

If we group Iran-Contra fraud into the subtexts of real estate, banking, insurance, securities, mining, aircraft brokerage fraud, charitable foundation fraud, and so forth, we find that securities fraud has been the least investigated to this day.

Documents are significantly harder to get out of the SEC than many other federal agencies because, for such a long time into the post-Iran-Contra coverup, the Republican Party had such control at the SEC that they were able to deny access to documents for a very long time.

Documents to which they could not deny access could very quickly wind up in a court case in which a Republican-sympathetic judge would place them under seal. Therefore, documents were either unavailable or under seal.

The media will quickly lose interest because of the time, effort and resources that had to be devoted in any thorough investigation of Iran-Contra securities fraud.

This is an area that I thought should be further explored.

Who is going to explore it? I don't know because it would be cumbersome, tedious and difficult, although the documents *vis-a-vis* Iran-Contra securities fraud, are usually more easy to obtain because criminal cases and civil cases involving the SEC regarding these brokerage firms and the penny deals they proffered are more readily available today than they were before.

I'll preface this by saying that many had thought that the securities fraud aspect of overall Iran-Contra fraud was rather minor. It wasn't as minor as people thought. As serious students of Iran-Contra know, the SEC did a very comprehensive review in 1992, in the waning days of the Bush Administration to try to quantify Iran-Contra securities fraud.

After going through all of its field office and regional office records, the SEC was surprised to learn that their own estimate was that public shareholder losses (the ultimate bagholders, the public) amounted to some $3 billion through Iran-Contra fraudulent penny stock deals.

I don't mean to imply that any of these were legitimate because they weren't. However, to get back to Colorado, we see the chain of holding of these various security groups.

National Brokerage was, of course, a division of MDC Holding Group.

MDC was controlled by none other than the famed Republican player in Denver, Leonard Millman and his associate, Steve Mizel and former ambassador to Switzerland, Phillip Winn.

Their corporate counsel, by the way, was Norman Brownstein.

Brownstein had been a former CIA counsel. And although Brownstein did mostly criminal work, he was corporate counsel in Denver in the securities and real estate deals. They all have Iran-Contra connections.

Students of Iran-Contra would remember how Brownstein became involved in representing people in many Iran-Contra/CIA sensitive narcotics cases.

You can point some of these Colorado deals to the naysayers.

It is good ammunition to counter the Iran-Contra naysayers.

Some would like to say Iran-Contra is long over. There are no entrails. There are no further connections.

Read my lips.

Iran-Contra is not over. It's as alive as it ever was. The same people, the same banks, the same firms. It's as much alive as ever.

And you can demonstrate this by looking at the people that were involved in deals in the 1983-86 timeframe.

Look at the same people today. They continue to be in the news.

In Colorado this is very true. There's the US Attorney's office in Denver, the Norton and Griffin affair *vis-a-vis* Federal District Judge Zita Weinshank, their active covering up of certain HUD cases, and the involuntary scapegoats, such as Don Austin.

The relationships are still cozy to this day. When Norton is forced out of the US Attorney's office and ultimately the US Attorney is forced out, a Democratic appointee, Henry Solano, comes in.

Although he's a Democrat, Solano then starts to do the same political control feature that had been done before.

Solano owes his political patronage to Congressman Henry Gonzalez. He's the one that originally got him the appointment, under the understanding (and I got this directly from Gonzalez's investigator, Dennis Caine) that Solano was going to be more forthcoming with documents that Gonzalez wanted — Iran-Contra-sensitive banking and security fraud documents that Gonzalez's committee was interested in.

Then Solano completely pulled the rug out from under Gonzalez.

There really isn't anything that Gonzalez could say or do because it was sort of, shall we say, an off-the-cuff type of deal to begin with. I can tell you Gonzalez was really pissed off about what Solano did to him.

HUD Secretary Federico Pena did exactly the same thing. Pena really got his position because of Gonzalez. And this is the little Mexican Democratic cabal that these guys are now.

Pena wouldn't give him any HUD documents.

But to get back to Norton — Norton acts as a control feature within the U.S. Attorney's office in Denver pursuant to HUD prosecutions.

This is all under the guise of Iran-Contra coverup. And then Gale Norton becomes Attorney General of the State of Colorado and acts in exactly the same capacity for cases that are getting kicked out from the federal jurisdiction to the state jurisdiction.

Recently Gale Norton resigned under pressure from her position as Attorney General of the State of Colorado and became a senior partner in Norman Brownstein's law firm with the infamous Phillip Bronner, another former CIA counsel.

We could go on with the story. It just shows you how cozy the relationships continue to this day, and that Iran-Contra activity is still both extant and the ensuing coverup is still extant.

The last frauds I wanted to mention — speaking of Dick Brenneke — are crossover frauds. That is where Iran-Contra Frauds cross over into Iraqgate Frauds and/or weapons schemes and/or narcotics.

Brenneke started the infamous Wa-Chang Trading Group of Albany, Oregon, which is well known to any Iran-Contra and Iraqgate students. It later became known as the Zirconium Diversion Deal, wherein the principle was to help Iraq surreptitiously build up its nuclear weapons program.

We have to examine who is on the Board of Directors and Advisors of that deal. That will give you an enormous clue of just who in the United States Government wanted to see Iraq helped in building its nuclear weapons program in 1986-1987.

Chapter 25

MORE CHINESE-MILITARY CONNECTIONS

THE CONCEPT OF THE Chinese Government contributing large amounts of political monies to both parties in this country is nothing new.

When we say "Chinese Government," of course, we are referring to the PRC or People's Republic of China.

I was involved in a very similar scheme in 1985 to launder money for the Republican National Committee. That became known as the CARI-COM deal, and very little was said about it at the time. It's strange. One reason why there wasn't a lot of interest in the media at the time is because it was regarded in 1985 as being old news.

But these connections had actually existed since the mid-1970s and the entire notion of illicit Chinese money going into U.S. political coffers was nothing new. The schemes really had never changed, and the reasons behind it have never changed.

The Chinese are giving this money for two reasons: 1) to buy political access, and more importantly, 2) to buy weapons and technology access.

What is happening today and what has happened in recent months is absolutely no different than what has happened in the past.

I would like to take this time to explain some of the people who are involved.

We have heard on the major media, principally the Fox Network, which is on the cutting edge of these Chinese revelations, all kinds of names being thrown out to the American people — General Ho, Colonel Liu. But they're just names.

There was never any effort to tell the people who these individuals are. And I thought I would take this time to explain it.

Gen. Ho is Lt. Gen. Ho, Chief of the North American Desk of the Chinese Ministry of State Security, Foreign External Operations Branch.

His equivalent, for instance, in the KGB would have been Lt. Gen. Alexander Karpov, Chief of the North American Desk of the KGB.

His American equivalent would be the operational chief of any large country desk or continent desk. It is certainly no small position.

We have also heard much about his daughter, who was consistently referred to as Miss Ho. Her actual name is actually Yu-Fen Ho, which means "beautiful flower." She has been intimately connected with passing money to Al Gore. She is married to Col. Liu. His full name is Col. Lang Liu.

Of course, what I don't like about the way these revelations come out is that there's no context for who these people are.

Col. Liu is married to Gen. Ho's daughter.

Col. Liu is also Gen. Ho's adjutant at the Ministry of State Security.

Col. Liu's immediate subordinate is Lt. Col. Lan Chin. Chin's immediate subordinate (he travels with him in the United States) is Major Wei Pong.

Lan Chin, more commonly referred to in the United States by those who know him, including myself, as Lanny Chin, operates under the cover of being a Chinese arms dealer, when in fact he is an officer of the Ministry of State Security.

This is known by the CIA and it has been admitted by the CIA — they know he is an officer of the Ministry of State Security.

And yet he is not required to be registered as a foreign intelligence officer in the United States with the Central Intelligence Agency, and thus faces no traveling restrictions whatsoever. He moves very freely in the United States under his own name.

In recent months, he was in Huntsville, Alabama. He has a very high security clearance with the Department of Defense which allows him access to secure facilities of the Department of Defense, particularly in the realm of high technology, especially military technology involving thermonuclear and energy discharge weapons.

Of course, this is not all that unusual. There is nothing new about foreign intelligence officers operating in the United States. Many have not been required to be registered with the CIA — as is required by law.

In the past, all foreign intelligence service officers operating covertly in the United States, who have not been registered, have always been involved in something the United States (at the very least) tacitly approves of.

Therefore, that is why they're not registered and given such freedom of movement. It's actually to facilitate their illegal transactions in the United States, which in the past have always been done and are presently being done with at least the acquiescence of the US Government.

For instance, it became obvious in the series of meetings in Huntsville, Alabama recently. One reason Dinnerstein became involved in it was that it became obvious what Chin's function was in terms of being a liaison officer between the CIA and the Ministry of State Security and other foreign intelligence services.

This explains Chin's meetings in Huntsville, Alabama. Sitting next to him at dinners, for instance, were agents of other governments — Yoram Ettinger, for instance.

Although originally Ettinger was an American citizen, he gave up his citizenship, went to Israel, and became an Israeli citizen.

Subsequently Ettinger became a member of the Israeli Knesset and a member of the Israeli Armed Services Committee. He subsequently left the Knesset under some cloud of suspicion for his Iran-Contra involvement, amid allegations of CIA-sponsored money laundering and arms trafficking, along with his partner, Eddy Singer.

But Ettinger is now acting in the capacity he once acted in before in the 1980s, essentially as a *de facto* state arms merchant for the Israeli government.

Also attending this meeting were representatives of the Russian Federal Security Service and the West German Federal Security Service.

The principal person there who was representing West German interests in a series of weapons transactions that we have previously discussed, wherein China acts as the principal front, was Rupert Von Braun. He is the son of the great General Von Braun.

And General Von Braun is, was, and still is Chairman of Braun Industries in Germany.

You see their products advertised on American television. He was also for many years on the Board of Advisors to the Siemens Electronics Group. He represented Siemens military operations here in the United States for many years.

Interestingly enough, he owned the *Frankfurter Algemeine* newspaper, which is the second largest newspaper in Germany.

You may remember General Von Braun's name, if you've ever seen the movie about the famous West German whistle-blower, Gunther Waltrop. The part was played by Jurgen Prochnow.

Von Braun's name was featured prominently in that movie in terms of what he did to whistle-blowers who attempted to expose Siemens, Univac and other German corporations, and their longstanding relationship with the CIA and US Department of Defense regarding their shipping weapons components from the United States, as well as Germany, to certain third-party countries, principally Israel, Iraq and Iran.

To illustrate how far back some of these connections go — General Hasso Von Braun is the nephew (and namesake) of his very famous uncle, Lt. Gen. Graf Hasso Von Manteufel.

Manteufel, of course, escaped the Nuremberg Trials due to the personal intervention of "Wild" Bill Donovan, Chief of the OSS and later the first Director of Central Intelligence.

Manteufel became a very important agent for the OSS and the interim capacity they played until the formation of the CIA in 1947.

Manteufel also became an important asset for them in Germany because of his connections in East Prussia, Ludendorf and what subsequently became East Germany.

Another representative who also met with Lan Chin, a person who was seen in Chin's company in Huntsville, was Marcel Dassault, Jr. Of course, we know who his father was — the founder and longtime Chairman of Dassault Industries in France.

Dassault is the major military contractor in France. They make the famed Mirage jet fighters, and the equally renowned Exocet missiles.

It is interesting to note here the further duplicity of the United States *vis-a-vis* the French and Chinese governments, when the United States conveniently turned a blind eye to a transaction between Dassault Industries and the Chinese People's Army, wherein a quantity of Exocet missiles were shipped from France through the United States directly to China.

Afterwards the Chinese People's Army began to manufacture a cheap knock-off version of the Exocet, which recently showed up in the 1999 Paris Arms Show.

The Chinese designation of the missile is the Swan II, which costs about a tenth of what the Exocet does. It is being marketed by the Chinese government's chief foreign marketing representative who is none other than Sarkis Soghanalian.

I know it sounds like I'm digressing from what is being called "The Chinese Connection," but I'm really not.

In all fairness, the Chinese connection must be looked at globally and as to how it relates to other nations — not just the United States.

A fuller revelation would take more time but would illustrate just how old these relationships are, how cozy these relationships are, and just how meaningless "non-proliferation laws" are, and how meaningless the U.S. customs and export laws are when it comes to a State-acquiesced policy of what the United States actually wants to see done to maintain tensions in certain parts of the world.

And this is the whole key — the purposeful maintenance of global tension.

The average reader may not understand this concept, but I think the more sophisticated reader would understand that it is in certain parties' best interest — within the CIA, the Department of Defense, the defense industry, and their political allies on both sides of the aisles in Washington.

It is in everyone's best financial interest within this little circle that tensions be maintained in certain parts of the world and that certain proliferation of weapons be allowed to exist.

This isn't the Nixon-Kissingeresque policy of the 1970s anymore when this started in order to maintain supposed balances of power between sub-spheres of influence.

It isn't done that way. And nobody cares about that anymore.

The world is changed. It's just all a matter of money now. And that very simply is what it comes down to.

There is no higher state policy that can justify this anymore.

It's just a matter of greed and money.

When we get down into the lower rung of this so-called "Chinese Connection" into what I would call the "bag men," these are names that we've all been saturated with — Johnny Chung and Charlie Trie, etc.

These men are consistently portrayed in the United States media as being small businessmen or restauranteurs, which always strikes me funny.

Nobody in the media ever bothers to find out who these guys really were or are, or what even their real names are.

For instance, I have not heard on any news broadcast anywhere that Johnny Chung is a former officer in the People's Army.

I have not heard anywhere that Trie, actually more interestingly, is Vietnamese.

Charlie Trie is billed as a nickel-and-dime Little Rock restauranteur, but his real name is Trang Qua Trie. He's a former captain of the Communist North Vietnamese army during the war. His father, Trang Wa Trie, was a general in the North Vietnamese army.

As a matter of fact, during the war, Trie acted in a liaison capacity with the People's Army, pursuant to the supplication of Chinese weapons for the North Vietnamese during the war.

And yet, Charlie Trie gets billed as a "little restauranteur."

I have consistently said this to Fox News, which is on the cutting edge of this, and Matt Drudge in particular, that some effort should be made to actually investigate who in the hell these people are and how they're all connected to each other in the past.

If somebody would do that, it would be much easier to put together a broader picture of this Chinese Connection — how long it's been going on, how many people are involved, and approximately what weapons systems and technologies have been transferred because of it.

How much money has been brought into the United States and gone into U.S. political coffers?

The first step in ascertaining this is to find out who this cast of characters is — who they were in the past, how they interrelate, and their connections to people in the present.

It's like we say "Iran-Contra." "Iran-Contra" activity continues to go on today. In some cases, it's the very same names and faces. In other cases, it's a newer, younger generation of names and faces. But the narcotics, weapons and fraud aspects still continue to this day.

The same facilities are used now that were used then. It is no different with the Chinese Connection.

As always, it's the little things that get overlooked.

- The fact that Charlie Trie's restaurant in Little Rock is actually in the Worthen Bank Building.
- The fact that Bill Clinton and Charlie Trie have eaten at his restaurant together with Johnny Chung many times.
- The fact that Trie, Chung, Clinton and James Riady, Jr. have all eaten dinner before at Trie's restaurant in Little Rock.

If you continue connecting the dots higher and higher, it is these little things that give you much better clues as to the reasons behind what is going on today, and how some of the connections are made.

This so-called Chinese Connection Scandal will grow into a major scandal. There are many more revelations to come. We are not to the point where somebody has come to me and asked me to piece it all together on a six by nine foot chart for use in a court room. But that will come.

Somebody will come to me eventually, particularly when this scandal gets to the point that the designated bag of scapegoats start to get indicted and prosecuted.

It reminds me of the six by nine foot graph I did for Noriega's counsels in 1989.

We are already getting to what I call the "silly stage" in these scandals. They all have their own life, and we're now at the "silly stage," the bumbling stage.

Some of it's actually humorous. For instance, when the FBI had Chung and Trie under surveillance and they saw them walking out of the National Bank of China's agency office in Washington with briefcases that they could hardly carry.

FBI Director Louis Freeh was subsequently asked why the FBI didn't stop these guys to find out what was in the attache cases that they were taking out of the bank.

And Freeh said, "Oh, well. We didn't have any probable cause because we weren't certain what might be in the attache cases that they had just come out of the bank with."

And Matt Drudge immediately responded by saying, "Well, Mr. Director, don't you mean that you didn't want to know what was in the briefcases?"

This embarrassed Freeh.

But this is the silly stage.

We'll get past this, and there will be more revelations to come. Anyway, this was only meant to explain who some of these characters were, and some of the humorous and salient revelations that have occurred so far.

In the future I will do a fuller revelation. I have pulled up, as it were, all my Chinese files, which admittedly are scant.

I really didn't have many dealings with them in the 1980s. But I do, as always, have the ability to find out more.

I can't do a fuller revelation until such times as I am engaged either individually, in concert with Steve Dinnerstein or in concert with others to mount a more thorough investigation, at which time I will probably connect the dots even more.

Certainly, the revelations yet to come in this so-called Chinese Connection Scandal will tend to broaden the scandal out as these scandals tend to get broadened out. In the new series of revelations that are coming, we'll begin to connect the Chinese to the Israelis to the Germans to the Russians in terms of arms shipping, who the ultimate recipients are, and how the United States seems to turn a blind eye to all of this.

This will come and there will be a fuller definition and a broadening of the scandal. The Chinese Connection will not be looked at so narrowly as it is now. And maybe at some point, the American people will begin to get the idea of just how big of a cabal this deal actually is —- how things work, what happens, and what are the motives behind it.

That is certainly, I believe, the direction that this thing is going. I'm aware of some of the revelations yet to come. And I think this is a good and healthy thing, so that the people can see for themselves just how deep and old these conspiracies are.

Chapter 26

ONI, CZX AND OPERATION ORPHEUS

I WANTED TO MENTION the awesome power of the Office of Naval Intelligence (ONI). When I have been interviewed for newspaper or magazine articles on Iran-Contra, people have always asked me, "Where does the real power lay?"

And of course, everyone's first answer would be the CIA, the DIA, and the NSA.

And I would always say "No, the real power is in the ONI." It always has been. They virtually have god-like power. Their mechanism to control liability is absolutely unparalleled.

And this has been a subject which has not been discussed much in Iran-Contra. Certainly pieces have been written on ONI's involvement in Iran-Contra, particularly in the area of weapons and narcotics trafficking.

There have been about 4,500 articles written about Iran-Contra in all publications from the *Frankfurter Algemeine* to the Tokyo *Asahi Shimbun*. But there have only been six articles that go into any detail in terms of ONI's involvement in Iran-Contra.

I would like to discuss that, although it is diverging a little bit.

Most of the ONI operations are in the west — and always have been. It is generally well known that they control their air facilities out of Medley, Oregon in that little air strip that used to be called "Mena of the West."

ONI's principal controlled cut-out was Evergreen Airlines.

One of the very few people to stay on Evergreen Airlines in an investigative capacity was Major Gary Atel, United States Army Major, Retired, who has testified before congressional committees investigating Iran-Contra.

I know Gary very well. I've bought information from him in the past, and he has purchased information from me.

He has a continuing civil action on behalf of the United States people against the now-bankrupt Evergreen Airlines, which is very revealing.

Unfortunately, Gary has been persona non grata in the major media for some time. He wasn't so in the beginning, but he is now.

Part of it is due to the ONI's ability to intimidate. Their power is such that the largest media organization is frightened of them.

The group of admirals I was familiar with at the time included Admiral Henderson, Admiral Pauley, and Admiral Collins in connection with Retired Admiral Elmo Zumwalt. They were all mostly retired ONI admirals, or in some cases still active but they constituted a group known as the "Goal Oversight Development," which was the name of their group — the initials GOD, which I think they did out of some humor.

But their powers are virtually god-like — their ability to assassinate people, to make people disappear, to make documents and entire files disappear anywhere, anytime, and their ability to corrupt judicial proceedings. It is simply enormous.

I had a taste of their power once before, in late 1991 and early 1992, when my attorney was attempting to work out a deal for me. If they don't want a deal being made by certain quarters within the CIA to happen, then it ain't going to happen. And if they want to get rid of somebody, they do.

What separates them, I think, from the CIA is that in the past the CIA has acted to get rid of certain journalists. Even the CIA itself doesn't really dispute that much. The journalists the Agency has gotten rid of have been well known journalists at well known mainstream publications.

Bill Moyle would be a good example of the caliber of journalists that they have successfully gotten rid of in the past.

However, within the ONI, they will even go after and eliminate nick-el-and-dime journalists from alternative conspiracy publications, or alternative publications of all types.

Witness the termination of people like Paula McCollum, Keith Wickenham, John Lear, and Lars Hansson. These guys were nothing really. They were nickel-and-dime journalists for nickel-and-dime alternative publications. None of the publications probably had a circulation of more than seven or eight thousand.

It was all within the conspiracy theorists community. But even these guys were all subsequently liquidated.

What was the common theme? What were they all working on?

They were all working on the very same thing — ONI involvement in Iran-Contra. Now they're all dead.

But it's interesting to note the extent that the ONI goes to cover up its dirty laundry. They act in a very brutal and final capacity. They never deal.

You cannot deal with them in terms of a payoff or in terms of getting somebody back in the woodwork that might know too much and helping them out financially. They never deal that way. They only threaten and they liquidate. That is their only way of keeping their own laundry clean. That's the only way they know how to operate, and it's the only way that I've ever known them to operate.

Even now when I am approached by those interested in reinvestigating or ONI involvement — even now, I'm very hesitant because their ability and power has not diminished.

And the mode in which they operate, their ability to intimidate has not diminished. I still remain in fear of them as does anyone who wants to stay alive.

Certainly, I was aware at the time (1985) of ONI's narcotics operations to the western corridor. They had a corridor and trans-shipping facilities for narcotics that were completely separate from the CIA's.

They operated out of Spokane, Washington and Medford, Oregon and down into Fire Lake, Nevada, which is another big ONI operation. It's in a place called Fire Lake, Nevada. They also have air and transportation facilities outside of Phoenix.

They operate principally through Mexico and Evergreen Air was their principal cut-out. It had been a CIA cut-out originally, which the ONI took over.

They imported a significant quantity of narcotics into this country to fund their own covert operations, the same type of deep offshore accounts arrangements that the agency has had, but the ONI did it completely themselves for what they perceived to be their own jurisdiction — their own little Admirals Club or Retirement Club, as we used to say.

How many of these admirals retire in million dollar homes and own private jets on their pensions?

Anyway this is a subject that I think should be further reviewed. It is a subject about which a small body of information already exists, although not much.

Atel has probably garnered more information about it than anyone else. Why he is still alive? I don't know. I think he's in the situation I am. Atel is probably on the same level as I am, and perhaps it's a case that he's just a little bit too well known for something to happen to him.

The ONI has inconvenienced this man in every way possible. This man has been pressured, threatened, intimidated and harassed in every way imaginable. But he still stands up to them pretty well.

It was really Atel's investigation and subsequent lawsuits that threatened to reveal ONI involvement which forced Evergreen Airlines into bankruptcy.

Evergreen Airlines has plenty of money. That wasn't the problem. But they were forced into bankruptcy and they were able to claim that since we have existing litigation out, certain documents cannot be disclosed,, the court was sympathetic to them and so forth.

But this was a bankruptcy by convenience to disguise documents and make it more difficult for others to get documents and information from them.

This has been a common Iran-Contra tactic in the past, by the way.

People don't commonly realize what protection a corporation is afforded in bankruptcy in terms of disgorging with information, either oral information from its principal officers and directors, or paper documentation.

But this trick's been used repeatedly and has been quite successful.

And speaking of ONI, I wanted to mention one of the operational cut-outs called CZX Productions, about which 60 *Minutes* did that piece, but it was very half-assed. They thought it was just a nickel-and-dime airline with connections to the CIA and others transporting narcotics. They didn't realize just how large it was.

CZX Productions Ltd. actually stood for Casey, Zumwalt, X-Files. Of all the Iran-Contra operations undertaken, this was probably the most secretive and sinister of all the operations. *60 Minutes* was quite desperate to do the piece. I spoke to Steve Croft about it a couple of times, and Leslie Stahl called me about it. I said, "Look, you want information about CZX, it's going to be big money. It's gonna cost you big money." They weren't prepared to pay it. And when they started to get an inkling of what it was all about, they didn't want to go any further.

But CZX Productions is directly related to Oliver North becoming Chairman of the National Programs, the then-secret NPO (National Programs Office) in late 1983, and the very sinister Operation Orpheus.

As an extension of Operation Orpheus, money was poured into the envisioned resurrection of the CILF units. The Civilian Inmate Labor Facilities. Very sinister sounding. And it was. What they envisioned was very sinister indeed.

I was asked before about this, how I knew. I was asked, as a matter of fact, in several congressional committees, and the only thing I've ever said publicly is, "Well, it's just things I heard from little quips I picked up from North and Secord and others at the time."

That's not exactly the truth. What I'm about to say I've never revealed publicly before.

The reason I know so much about this was a meeting I attended in late 1984 in Miami. It was one of the regular bi-weekly meetings which Jeb Bush chaired. But in this meeting, Oliver North was present. This was one of the very few meetings that Donald Gregg himself was present, and Frederick Ikley and his sidekick, Nestor Sanchez.

These were all the top people. Gregg was the National Security Adviser to the Vice President. His aide, Lt. Col. Samuel C. Watson, Frederick C. Ikley, then Deputy Director of the Defense Intelligence Agency for Caribbean and Central American Theater Operations, etc.

In this meeting, North gave an extensive speech about the Orpheus Operation and how monies were being diverted from narcotics operations to rebuild, reinvigorate, and to refurbish these various Civilian Inmate Labor Facilities, most of which had been built early in the 1970s under the guise of housing Iranian-Americans should there be a problem down the line. North, Casey, Zumwalt and others envisioned a much more sinister use for that. These facilities, of course, had been allowed to deteriorate, until money started to be poured into them in 1984 to build them back up again.

Now there has been some media exposure — very, very little, but there has been a little written about this. Of course, it will only appear in the alternative press. But there have been some articles written, particularly about the big Civilian Inmate Labor Facility in Kings County, Washington, and the other big one in Paris County, Texas. There's another big one in Lake Charles Parrish in Louisiana.

The monies that were put back into these things? The big one in Kings County, Washington has the ability to house one hundred thousand civilian people, minimally incarcerated.

Orpheus was this idea that, if what later became known as "Iran-Contra" fell apart early and everything spilled out publicly, it would have been potentially necessary to institute a silent coup against the Government of the United States.

Obviously, it would be done with the tacit support of said government, in which case Oliver North would have become a prominent member of the new post-silent coup administration He would then control political fallout, which would have been tremendous, if all of Iran-Contra fell apart and became revealed to the public. But it went beyond that.

Orpheus actually went to the point, where if the liability could not be controlled, it would be necessary for Casey, North, and George Bush to secretly formulate and potentially launch an outright coup d'etat against the Government of the United States. These were the three principals involved. Zumwalt wasn't a real principal. He was only a principal on a certain end within naval intelligence and other intelligence circles.

There would still have been some tacit support, but this would have been an outright coup. It was envisioned that George Bush would become acting President of the new Provisional Military Government of the United States.

In order to do this, the pretext was going to be a limited nuclear exchange with the Soviet Union, wherein we would create a situation, a catalyst as it were, a military confrontation, that would lead to a limited nuclear exchange. This would be in cooperation by the way with certain hardline elements within the Soviet military. That was the whole idea of the Orpheus Project.

That's why there was so much contact between North and senior Soviet military people, particularly within the hard line. This contact was oftentimes disguised under normal types of meetings that a senior staffer in the National Security Council may have with his Soviet counterparts in certain discussions.

Some of the contact was disguised under this idea of purchasing weapons for the Contras from Eastern European countries which acted as a pretty good blind. What I heard at that meeting was quite frightening as a matter of fact. It was quite frightening what North and Casey and Bush were actually prepared to do to cover up what they were doing. They understood the egregiousness of what they were doing.

They also understood that if Iran-Contra fell apart, then everything else fell apart that came before it.

All of the preceding conspiracies and coverups including the post-war conspiracies and coverups might also fall apart. That's what they were actually frightened of. And the temerity of this was such that it would require a new government with an iron fist.

It would also require the cooperation of the Soviet Union because there were many hardliners who were also very interested in getting rid of the new and tender Gorbachev. The hardliners in the Russian military saw him as a tremendous threat. So there became commonality between hard line interests in both the United States and the Soviet Union to maintain the status quo.

The status quo of the Cold War was very good for business, and it was very good for the maintenance of old power structures and cabals. Those who had benefitted from it on both sides didn't want to give it up. They saw the end of it potentially coming.

The Civilian Inmate Labor Facilities were also built for those American civilians who would be incarcerated. They would essentially become forced labor incarcerees. These were a combination of citizens who knew too much and citizens, whom they felt would be difficult to control under a provisional military government.

Liberals envisioned that liberals would be housed there — and a lot of members of the media. Liberal members of Congress would be put there and so forth. This is just an overview, but I heard it in pretty good detail, and I made extensive notes about it afterwards.

It's a funny thing about this meeting. This is the only meeting I actually attended, where I was actually searched to see if I had a tape recording device on me. We were not allowed to make any notes at this meeting. But fortunately I did make extensive notes about it directly afterwards, and I hid those notes over the years. I recognize the temerity of the situation.

But can I absolutely prove that this meeting took place?

I don't know. Yes, I can prove it secondhand, so to speak, because everybody else would have to disprove it. I know where certain individuals were on a certain day, where they were, and what was said. They would then have to try to prove that they were somewhere else on those days. Oliver North has tried to prove that before — and unsuccessfully — thanks to me in some cases.

When I make full disclosure and full revelation of all that I know about the Orpheus Project and its sister project, Project Sledgehammer (which shows the vanity of North, to name a project after one of his own code names, Sledgehammer), if only 5% of the American people believe it, there will be hell to pay. When I reveal all of this, the public opinion polls are on my side.

We've seen some of the big polls done by NBC recently, in which 66% of the American people claim to be extremely distrustful of their government and are much more prepared to believe in deep dark conspiracies of State than ever before.

And I believe that Orpheus, Sledgehammer and associated contingency projects and operations are probably the most sinister operations ever undertaken by minions within the people's government.

Why? To hide all conspiracies that existed before. To start a limited nuclear engagement in which it was envisioned, as North himself said, that there would be 50 to 70 million American casualties.

North let it out before and people didn't listen. When North was once asked the question, "How many people must be killed to maintain the coverup? One? Ten? Ten thousand?"

North said, "It's all semantics. Numbers." I mean, he was giving you a clue when he said that. But anyway, I will reveal all that I know about this meeting.

It was a very extensive briefing in detail, how these operations would have proceeded in every phase; the cooperation of the Soviet Union; Gorbachev would have been overthrown. The hardliners would have come in. The Soviets would have suffered just as many casualties.

The political orbits would have hardened after these events had taken place. That's what was envisioned. Essentially, it was a reslicing up of the pie between the New United States and the Evil Empire.

By the way, I've noticed in the past when I've even mentioned Operation Sledgehammer on radio shows and the few articles I've done or mentioned anything about what was envisioned, just these few words have provoked an immediate reaction against me.

I've been arrested or severely pressured, or harassed, intimidated, whatever. But it has provoked a very quick reaction. You can tell how sensitive people still are to these revelations. Because I maintain segregated notes pursuant to projects and operations, it certainly makes it more tedious to put all this back together later on. But I did make some notes of who had mentioned details of this project before. Everyone who has is dead.

Anyone who crossed a certain threshold subsequently died under clouded circumstances.

Even Congressman Brooks noticed this. Brooks was personally interested in this. Sharon Matts, one of his investigators who is very good, had begun to notice people who would talk too much about this, they would cross a certain line and what would happen to them later on.

That would be another part of the story that I would like to detail.

Anyway, just to wrap this subject up, I want to mention in full disclosure of what I know. This was not simply the United States and the Soviet Union. Some of our allies, as North had mentioned, had also been consulted about this. The Thatcher government and the Kohl government — they were going to become part of this because they had exactly the same concerns.

From what I heard, it was obvious that this involved the long-term post-war cooperation between deep right-wing elements within our allied governments and their concerns that conspiracies of the past would potentially come back to haunt them.

This is really a big story. As a matter of fact, I don't know if I even dare tell it. As you pop open layers — and the layer above keeps expanding — all of a sudden we get into something that's considered conspiratorial — that there is, in fact, literally a global, deep right-wing conspiracy with connections that make certain things happen, so that certain policy objectives are met and certain geopolitical, economic and military spheres interact.

This might get a little too philosophical though.

It's probably just better to stick with the facts.

THE CONSPIRATORS

SELECTED COLUMNS: BEHIND THE SCENES IN THE BELTWAY BY AL MARTIN

Published on Al Martin Raw (http://www.almartinraw.com)

What Will It Be Like With George Bush Jr. As President?

What will it be like with George Bush Jr. as president?

It will be a return to the "Bush" form of government — namely a government of shadowy cliques, secret commissions and *de facto* star chambers.

The new Bush Administration will probably accelerate the pace of re-arming China to make China the new boogeyman because nobody makes any money unless there's a boogeyman.

The Bush Administration will then use that as an excuse to pump up defense spending, to wit, all defense contractors have given very generously to the Republican Party. Consequently, years later, a new Bush Administration will institute tax cuts for the wealthy and try to eliminate estate taxes which Bush has talked about in the past.

By the end of the first term of a new Bush Administration, all the surplus which is supposed to be used to reduce the national debt and repay the money his father swiped from social security would in fact be absorbed in new spending and tax cuts.

You have to look at the entire Bush Family in this context — as if the entire family ran a corporation called "Frauds-R-Us."

Each member of the family, George Sr., George Jr., Neil, Jeb, Prescott, Wally, etc., have their own specialty of fraud.

George Jr.'s specialty was insurance and security fraud.

Jeb's specialty was oil and gas fraud.

Neil's specialty was real estate fraud.

Prescott's specialty was banking fraud.

Wally's specialty was securities fraud.

And George Sr.'s specialty?

All of the above.

The Gotti-Cuomo-Bush Scam

And what about all the heat regarding the National Heritage deal recently profiled on *60 Minutes*?

It's another fraud. The genesis of the fraud is that a partnership was formed to purchase Heritage Life Insurance for $4 million. This partnership involved all of the Bush Brothers, including, by the way, John Gotti. John Gotti was also a member of the partnership.

How did it happen? On a Friday night, this partnership purchased Heritage Life. They proffered a check for four million dollars. The check was worthless. It was no good.

Over the weekend Heritage turned over the keys to its offices in Boca Raton, Florida, all its files. Everything. Over the weekend this new partnership proceeds to transfer $4 million dollars of Heritage Life's reserve capital into its own accounts to cover the check that it had written to buy it.

It's a true story. Then they proceeded to turn Heritage Life into a fraud center. They perpetuated a variety of fraud, specializing in and concentrating in HUD fraud. They would buy busted out HUD properties for $500,000, then list their value on the Heritage books as $5 million dollars. The other four and a half million dollars would simply go into the partnership's pockets. And they did this repeatedly.

Andrew Cuomo, through his father Mario's influence, was hired on as a consultant to the corporation. He was also a member of the Board of Trustees of Heritage Life at $50,000 per year.

When Andrew became Director of HUD, Andrew helped cover up Heritage's scams *vis-a-vis* HUD. Heritage in turn not only buys up HUD property, but it also becomes its own insurer of HUD property. For example, it would claim that the insurance premium on XYZ property was $1 million a year, when in fact the insurance was only $100,000 a year.

Heritage Life insurance Company was part and parcel of Heritage Financial Group, Heritage Credit Group, Heritage Securities Group, Heritage Banking Group. It was much more than just an insurance company. Heritage was a consolidated financial group involving securities, banking, and insurance.

One of the principals of the company was John Gotti. Among the directors was George Sr., George Jr., Jeb, Neil, etc. These were the directors of the holding company called Heritage Group International.

Because of the relationship (Gotti's involvement) Richard Brenneke and the National Brokerage Group become involved in selling Heritage policies and securities.

Richard Brenneke was very close to John Gotti and more importantly was very close to Gotti's superior, Paul Castellano. When it came to pass, Brenneke was head of National Brokerage Group, which had a primary securities relationship with Blinder Robinson, Meyer Blinder, the old con artist. National Brokerage Group in turn marketed Heritage product, Heritage insurance, Heritage annuities, Heritage securities and Heritage partnerships, etc.

Andrew Cuomo may become another Samuel Pierce, another scapegoat. The missing $59 billion dollars from HUD coffers is probably a record, but only in terms of public disclosure.

DoJ: The Old Conspiracy and Cover-up Crowd

The *Wall Street Journal* article, ("At Justice Department, a Conservative Takeover Looms" by David S. Cloud, Dec. 26, 2000) attempts to portray DoJ's Public Integrity Division Chief Lee Radek as some sort of left wing lackey. I find this completely ludicrous. It should be noted that Lee Radek like many others in DoJ's Public Integrity Section has come out of the CIA. And the CIA is not known for producing left wing lackeys.

The Public Integrity Section came into its own in the mid 1980s to give the appearance in the post Iran-Contra environment that the Government was cleaning up its act. Actually it was part of a DoJ Control Mechanism pursuant to an Iran Contra Cover-up.

And what is a "Control Mechanism"? It suppresses information. It's a mechanism which harasses and intimidates those who know too much. It's a mechanism which is used to subvert Congress vis-a-vis congressional investigations. It's mechanism to seek out and destroy documents.

The Public Integrity Section's real purpose is to act as a unit within a much larger political liability control mechanism within the Department of Justice. The Public Integrity Section also acts to coordinate the management and suppression of information and the management of political liability with other federal agencies.

Lee Radek has been Chief of the Public Integrity Section for a very long time. He has acted with his confederates within the DoJ, namely Dave Margolis, then Chief of the Domestic Criminal Section and Mark Richards, then Chief of the International Criminal Section of the DoJ. These three men, operating under the auspices of Deputy Attorney General George Terwilliger, essentially managed the Iran-Contra Cover-up for the Department of Justice.

I have talked with Dave Margolis several times. The only thing he ever did was he threatened me. He would say to me that if I revealed anything to congressional committees, or if I leaked any thing out into the press, that I would be subject to all sorts of unpleasant things. Everything was "national security" with these guys.

The Department of Justice informed me via Jeb Bush in February 1986 that in the grand jury testimony I would be giving on March 21, 1986, I was told by my counsel Michael Van Zamft through Attorney General Ed Meese that I was authorized to invoke reasons of "national security" for refusing to answer questions during those proceedings. Then when I did invoke "national security" as a reason for my refusal to answer questions, the Department of Justice claimed publicly that I was not authorized to invoke such.

They left me flapping in the wind. This is the incident I write about in my book. It all comes back to Radek. Miami was the key place that had to be controlled. It was where most of the liability vis-a-vis US Government involvement in Iran- Contra occurred. As I said at the time — which the *Washington Post* began using — "Washington was where the misdeeds were thought up and Miami was the place where the misdeeds were executed."

Radek, Margolis and Richards were the three top control guys in the Department of Justice. They were nominally under George W. Terwilliger. Margolis had the function of liaising with the CIA pursuant to the Iran-Contra Cover-up. His contact in the CIA was then CLO (Congressional Liaison Officer) Thomas Rinehart. This position actually involves much power. This person at the CIA is the officer who ultimately clears all the requests for documents the congressional investigating committees make to the CIA. The CLO will often manage a pan-agency cover-up and will often be the CIA's chief guy in liaising with all the other federal agencies, in this case, the Iran-Contra Cover-up.

During the Grand Jury testimony, I was questioned by Miami Assistant US Attorney Scruggs, who was accompanied by Miami FBI Special Agent Ross Gaffney, who was completely out of the loop. He wasn't aware of the real story. I was prepared to plead guilty in order to protect the deniability of others. I then would have been compensated for any time I spent in prison.

Gaffney in concert with FBI CI-3 Anna Maria Mendoza, daughter of the famous Colonel Robert Mendoza of CIA black ops fame, investigated me during that time. She was under the impression that I was a Russian spy codenamed "Redbeard".

Gaffney worked for the WC-1 (White Collar) crime division of the Miami FBI Field office. Mendoza, who came into my office once, actually tried to infiltrate my former wife's jazzercise club to get information from her. My wife had been previously married to a prominent Iranian dissident, who had been liquidated in 1979 by SAVAK, the former intelligence unit of the Shah of Iran.

By the way, Special Agent Ross Gaffney was suspected of misstating his academic credentials on his employment application with the FBI.

However, under Rinehart's control were two of the CIA's most notorious henchmen, the infamous Lt. Col John Berglund and his equally sinister cohort Major Karl Wahl. I was the one who exposed these men. These men were dispatched by Rinehart after my *in camera* and *ex parte* testimony before Federal District Judge Eugene Spellman on Friday, March 21, 1986.

After I gave testimony, the Judge ordered the testimony sealed for ten days. On the eighth day, the Government suddenly and inexplicably dropped its request for the material to be unsealed. The reason why is that on the preceding Wednesday, two men in military uniform bearing insignias of the Judge Advocate General's office showed up at the judge's chambers. These men then talked to the judge's secretary, Judy. As it turned out Judy also worked as a part time secretary for the CIA-controlled Dade County Latin American Chamber of Commerce, chaired by Jeb Bush.

Judy let these two guys into the judge's chambers when the judge wasn't there. She also had the combination to his personal safe where my testimony was kept. They took the transcript out of the judge's safe. That's why the Government suddenly dropped the request. They already had a copy of what I had said.

These two men were under the impression that the judge's secretary was sympathetic, since she worked for Jeb Bush. Jeb Bush told her to let these two guys in. She later admitted this in an affidavit submitted to the renowned Iran-Contra private investigator Steve Dinnerstein, then under my employ. She knew what day they were coming. She was playing both sides of the street. She was paid by Dinnerstein to help us on the day these two guys in military uniform were coming. She didn't even know their real names.

On that day Dinnerstein arranged one of his guys, a former Hollywood Police Department officer in the intelligence unit, who worked on the fourth floor of the Justice Building, to take pictures of them with a miniature camera. He was there under the guise of being a maintenance guy. He had a broom and a pail of water.

Later I exposed these two in the *Washington Post* as henchmen for the CIA. They would appear in various places in Miami bearing credentials of the Secret Service, or the FBI, or BATF. They would also attempt to intimidate attorneys representing Iran-Contra whistle-blowers, including my attorney.

Radek was the guy at the Department of Justice who acted to screen and quantify Iran-Contra whistleblowesr. It was his job to identify people like me and find out exactly what we knew and then to recommend a course of action *vis-a-vis* control.

Radek reported to Terwilliger, and Terwilliger reported directly to the DCI, the Director of the CIA. He didn't report directly to Ed Meese to maintain his deniability.

This is the direct deep connection that the Deputy Attorney General represented with the CIA. This has been going on for a long time. It's the standard operating procedure of those charged with the responsibility to maintain cover-ups and their interconnections when the Department of Justice has launched a cover-up of government wrongdoing. Then Attorney General Ed Meese was aware of these things, but he professed to be out of the loop.

This is the operational framework for the internal control mechanism of the Iran- Contra cover-up, the largest cover-up ever instituted by the US Government.

Also, Rinehart would try to get whistleblowers to spy on various congressional investigative committees by promising people like me that the CIA would help us and that our grievances would be addressed, if we helped them.

Those in my position didn't believe that story for one minute. I tape recorded every conversation I ever had with Rinehart. I then sent the tape to the chief investigators of the various Committee Chairmen — Henry Gonzalez, Jack Brooks, Charlie Rose — and they then leaked the tapes to the *Washington Post*. Rinehart was actually attempting to recruit people to suborn Congressional committees, and that ended Rinehart's career.

After this revelation Rinehart was transferred to "unspecified classified foreign duties" and he could not be contacted through the Agency. This is how the CIA gets rid of people because it gets them out of the way of any Congressional subpoenas and it also prevents any media access to them. His replacement was Dan Moskowitz who was one of the CIA's specially trained clean-up people.

I will take credit though for helping to end Rinehart's career.

Below the level of Radek, Margolis and Richards, there was a control mechanism that filtered down to the local US Attorneys' offices. This existed everywhere Iran-Contra activity occurred — Washington, Atlanta, Miami, New Orleans, Little Rock, etc. How it works is that in every US Attorneys office, there is always one AUSA (Assistant US Attorney) who has a significantly higher security clearance than the US Attorney himself.

The control man in the Miami US Attorneys Office was none other than Assistant US Attorney William Richard Scruggs, who reported directly to Chief of Domestic Criminal Section, Dave Margolis.

There's actually an official title, Cover-up Operations Field Manager. You will see in the "pink cable" traffic — restricted cable traffic between the US Attorneys offices and the Department in Washington, a coded designation for the guy managing the cover-up within the local district.

Scruggs was one of the 1,100 Reagan-Bush holdovers brought into the Clinton Administration specifically for that reason. They are the C&C Crowd, the Conspiracy and Cover-up Crowd. They control conspiracies and their ensuing cover-ups. These are the ones who are held over from administration to administration.

Scruggs was one of the "Miami Boys" that Reno brought with her to Washington. He rose to the rank of National Security Advisor to Attorney General Janet Reno, while at the same time being under indictment for kidnapping in Costa Rica.

Radek, Margolis, Richards and Scruggs were all involved in the so-called Reagan- Bush kidnapping policies that started in 1986 and were extant until 1991. It involved kidnapping both US and foreign citizens on foreign soil. After the US Supreme Court in its 1986 landmark decision gave the administration the right to use "extralegal" procedures to bring foreign fugitives before American courts. There were 22 in all who were kidnapped, mostly those who were under indictment for cocaine trafficking in the United States. The commonality is that all of these cocaine traffickers were controlled by the CIA. In their own defense, they had all begun to leak out information to Congress and the media about their connections to the CIA. That's why they were targeted for kidnapping.

It all fell apart when they tried to kidnap a cocaine trafficker named Israel Abel form Costa Rica in 1991. And how did it fall apart? Someone tipped off the Costa Rican government — when, where, and who the people were.

Gee, I wonder who that could have been!

Scruggs was actually stupid enough to go along himself and the Costa Rican government nabbed him. He got indicted for violating Costa Rican national sovereignty and other felonies. The US Government exerted pressure against President Oscar Arias Sanchez to return Scruggs and so he got returned.

Then the Costa Rican Attorney General's Office proffered a bill of indictment with the US State Department seeking the extradition from the United States of William Richard Scruggs to stand charges in a Costa Rican Court of Law pursuant to these crimes.

On a humorous note, sometimes I would get friends of mine in Costa Rica to send a postcard with a picture of the Costa Rican penitentiary on it to Scruggs. The note would read, "Wish you were here."

Scruggs is still being sought by the Costa Rican authorities.

The Secret Life of Gale Norton: A Republican Party Apparatchik Also Rises

Gale Norton, the Bush Secretary of Interior appointee, was Attorney General of Colorado from 1991 to 1999. She was brought in after her predecessor Duane Woodard was forced to resign because of his involvement in illegal political contributions. Incidentally Woodard through his involvement in a series of partnerships and corporations had borrowed over $70 million from the infamous Silverado Savings, which he never repaid. He was recommended for these loans by then Silverado Director Neil Bush.

At the same time, Robert Gallagher, the Arapahoe County District Attorney, was appointed to investigate MDC Holdings Corp., a publicly traded company on the American Stock Exchange, controlled by the infamous Republican cabalist Leonard Millman. After an SEC investigation, MDC plead guilty in 1991, paid a $1.5 million fine and was under SEC supervision for three years.

Then Judge Richard G. Matsch (of the Oklahoma City Bombing Case fame) was assigned to the MDC Holdings case. Denver US Attorney Mike Norton (no relation to Gale) was the prosecutor. Prior to his US Attorney appointment, Mike Norton ran for the Senate, and his campaign manager was the Chief Executive Officer of MDC Holdings, Larry Mizel. The Assistant US Attorneys in the case were Joseph Mackey and Greg Graff, whose brother, Robert Graff, was also an MDC Holdings Director.

Because of public and media pressure, the US Attorneys office indicted several of the vice presidents of MDC subsidiaries, including Richmond American Homes, one of the nation's largest builders. They plead guilty.

At that point, Judge Matsch made a statement in open court that he was tired of the prosecution bringing in low level vice presidents before him and because of the serious evidence he expected the prosecutors to vigorously prosecute those who were at the top, David Mandarich and Larry Mizel, and that he would vigorously sentence those involved. Within days, his daughter was dead.

The bizarre circumstances involved her "falling" into a volcano on Hawaii during a trip there with her boyfriend. An inside source claims that the boyfriend was planted on her. He supposedly met her in a grocery store, wined and dined her and had been dating her for about a month from the time Judge Matsch was assigned to the case.

Then because of the death of his daughter, the MDC case was reassigned to the Chief Judge of the Tenth Federal Circuit Court, Judge Sherman Finesilver. Finesilver accepted a $1.5 million plea bargain from MDC and acquitted Mandarich while Judge Matsch was in mourning.

At that time, Robert Gallagher was appointed Special Assistant Attorney General by the Governor of Colorado to investigate the alleged political contributions of MDC Holdings. Colorado Attorney General Woodard was named one of the recipients of illegal campaign money and he resigned.

With Woodard gone and Gallagher's investigation completed, Gale Norton, the new Attorney General, took the investigation report and doctored it, eliminating evidence of wrongdoing by MDC Holdings and its officials, especially Larry Mizel.

And how was Gale Norton paid off? She was allowed to hire six new attorneys for her staff to interface with Colorado state officials, congressmen and senators. Eyewitness reports have described only two attorneys on staff in the basement offices and the other four attorneys were never seen. Evidently the notorious M &L Business Machines, a subsidiary of MDC Holdings, had laundered the attorneys' payroll checks for Gale Norton's benefit. In fact, M & L Business Machines president Robert Joseph testified before a US Federal Grand Jury that the payroll checks for Gale Norton's phantom attorneys were indeed laundered through M& L Business Machines. Assistants to Gale Norton were further advised and evidence was turned over to them about their boss's criminal activity and obstruction of justice.

Later when allegations of corruption concerning Silverado Savings and Loan and Denver International Airport appeared on an official report, Gale Norton again rewrote the report omitting any accounts of wrongdoing by her real bosses, Leonard Millman and the Denver Boys.

When Gale Norton left the Attorney General's office, she was rewarded, given a partnership at the infamous Denver-based Brownstein Law Firm.

So here are some of the connections. Norman Brownstein was on the Board of Directors of MDC Holdings, parent company of Silverado S&L and Richmond Homes, as well as MDC's corporate counsel.

Brownstein was also on the Board of Directors of Chubb Securities, the insurance company, which paid for Bill Clinton's impeachment defense, the Paula Jones lawsuit damages, and other legal expenses.

Brownstein was on the Board of Directors of AIMCO, one of the largest apartment landlords in the US, which owns properties formerly stolen from HUD.

Other MDC Directors include illegal campaign money and narcotics money launderer Larry Mizel, HUD scamscateer Phil Winn, recently pardoned by Bill Clinton, as well as Clinton's personal attorney, James M. Lyons, who was also involved with the Whitewater Development Fraud and illegal campaign money laundering related to Clinton's 1992 presidential campaign.

M&L Industries was controlled by MDC Holdings Group, which is Leonard Millman. Gale Norton then was given the lucrative partnership with the law firm of Norman Brownstein.

By the way, Brownstein, a former Bush-era CIA counsel, made his claim to fame in representing Republican-connected scamscateers and CIA-connected dopers in the past. Brownstein was also co-counsel for the defense of Jack DeVoe. DeVoe was the largest CIA-connected cocaine trafficker during Iran-Contra. DeVoe received sentences totaling 117 years and spent 22 days in jail. Then he was allowed to leave the United States and take up residence in India, of all places.

When the SEC asked Norton to investigate the Boulder Properties Limited Partnerships, she dragged her feet and again came up with a clean report. The assets of these limited partnerships was simply defaulted HUD property picked up by Leonard Millman, appraised for twice its value, and also formerly owned by Millman himself. The financing for it came from a loan from Silverado S&L personally approved by Neil Bush. Neil Bush then was put on the Board of General Partnership of the Boulder Properties Limited Series.

The intent of the Boulder Properties Limited Partnerships was to market them to potentially hostile Democrats in Congress for the purpose of compromise and control. Congressman William V. Alexander, Democrat of Arkansas, for example, purchased one of them through Jonathan Flake, an officer of the selling agents, Twin Cities Bank of North Little Rock, Arkansas, and a cohort and close business associate of Oliver North.

Alexander made the purchase for $3 million dollars. No money down. Just recourse notes. Then in 1992, he was approached by Flake and asked to stop his Alexander Commission's Iran-Contra probe. Alexander refused. The notes were pulled and made full recourse. Since the partnership was not paying out any cash dividends anymore, Alexander had no choice but to declare bankruptcy. Congressman Alexander formally complained to Colorado Attorney General Gale Norton. Again Gale Norton undertook no action.

For the record, Gale Norton also used her authority as Attorney General to fight any increase in mining and mineral lease fees in the State of Colorado. which had not been raised since 1872. She was also involved in keeping prices down on grazing fees, since her patron Leonard Millman, a large landowner, was on the Colorado beef marketing board. She continued to serve Leonard Millman by allowing the sale of BLM property at below market value. Millman's companies, Richmond Homes and Red Hawk Homes, as well as Venrock and Phoenix-based Olympic Corp., were the beneficiaries of her fraud. As US Secretary of Interior, Gale Norton will be able to orchestrate the continuing cover-up pertaining to sales of BLM land at below market value.

Gale Norton should probably also be tested for drugs. Doreen Bishop, the infamous Denver political gadfly, involved in Woody Harrelson's campaign to legalize marijuana, claims that she supplies Norton with high-grade sinsemilla. According to an inside source, she grows very high quality marijuana on her property, which an eyewitness reports "look like trees." She claims she sells the marijuana to all the politicians, including the former Colorado Governor, Gale Norton and "all the Denver crowd." She said even Denver Mayor Wellington Webb's wife came over and picked some up for him.

The eyewitness also said that "this is the only gal I know where the FBI goes out to her house, stares at her marijuana plants and says, 'Wow, I didn't know they grew this big.'"

Incidentally, Norman Brokaw, the head of William Morris talent agency, is Doreen Bishop's uncle. Her cousin is Tom Brokaw of the NBC Nightly News.

Doreen Bishop also admitted that Oliver North was "taken care of" to the tune of $40 million. Of course, North, formally represented by William Morris, has claimed that any payments made by William Morris were for his book or for appearances.

It's well known that Ms. Norton frequents a certain Denver drinking establishment which caters to a female clientele of a certain sexual persuasion. There is also a prominent Denver area woman involved in politics who has publicly revealed the nature of her relationship with Ms. Norton to a prominent political investigative journalist with the *Rocky Mountain News*. Since this column is devoted to serious political matters, perhaps it would be in the domain of the tabloid press to pursue these well-documented allegations.

Fraud-As-Usual at the Redstone Arsenal

Redstone Arsenal in Huntsville, Alabama — where illegal foreign arms merchants enjoy sumptuous lobster and prime rib lunches at US taxpayers' expense.

The Huntsville, Alabama complex is one of the four United States National Arsenals. It's also the headquarters of the United States Central Missile Production Command, where most of the United States missile systems are produced and tested.

During the last year, there have been reports in the media about two congressional investigations, one by the US Senate Defense Oversight Committee and the other by its companion committee in the House, regarding illegal sales of extremely sophisticated US military technology and weapons systems to embargoed foreign countries.

When a country is embargoed by the US Defense Department, US defense contractors can not sell them weapons because these countries constitute a potential threat to the United States, or they constitute a potential threat to destabilizing US influence within a certain region of the world.

The principal weapons, illegally sold through the Redstone Arsenal, have been components of highly advanced missile technology. Through a circuitous shipment route, then, the end user or recipient has been the People's Republic of China.

These shipments have been disguised under the Freedom Space Station Program, as well as through the cooperation between the thirty-six nations which are contributing to this program.

In fact, Congress passed a specific law, a little-known waiver for the Freedom Space Station Program, wherein the United States could ship certain embargoed technology (dual use) to other countries which were participating in the building of the space station.

It is this loophole that is being used to ship weapons components which have nothing to do with the program.

China is a partner in this deal. Over the past year (2000), this fraud has expanded into selling many other types of restricted high technology US weapons systems. This is often accomplished through the weekly meetings at the Redstone Arsenal by certain individuals known as "The Group."

This Group consists mostly of foreign arms dealers, principally German, Russian, and Chinese brokers. These brokers are almost exclusively foreign military officers or retired foreign military officers. Often they even show up in uniform.

Their US counterparts are mostly retired US Air Force senior officers, who have formed arms companies themselves, or they act as paid agents or distributors for US defense contractors.

That in itself is not against the law, as long as they do not sell this technology to any embargoed country. There is, however, already an artifice in place to break that embargo.

The foreign arms merchants oftentimes either own their arms companies or they work for foreign defense contractors. Most of the Germans there, for example, come under the auspices of the Siemens Group.

In other words, the Siemens Group is being used as a front to broker weapons with the Russians to the Chinese.

How they're doing it, by the way, is by disguising these transactions. They have weekly auctions. However, what the auction sheet lists as the items being sold are in fact not what the items are.

Even my inside source, the Friendly Colonel, tried bidding on a lot. It was described as "Miscellaneous Department of Defense Used Office Furniture and Equipment." That lot was number 103 on the August 19, 2000 auction. It sold for $354,000.

The man sitting at the table next to him was the infamous Chinese arms dealer, Lan "Lanny" Chin. It should also be mentioned that he is a colonel in the Chinese Ministry of State Security.

The lot in question, actually contained a number of landmines. These landmines happen to be the most sophisticated landmines in US military inventory.

These landmines are all made of non-metallic components. They have automatic proximity alarms and differential frequency alarms. They also automatically send out their own radar signal. These are the most sophisticated land mines produced in the world today. They're so state-of-the-art that the United States itself hasn't even deployed the system yet.

And what happened then? This lot of landmines was then shipped from the military airfield in Huntsville, Alabama to the government of Mexico. They were listed as "Crates of Eggs."

The Mexican Government, actually the Mexican Army, acted as a trans-shipper. From Mexico, they were shipped to Ecuador. From Ecuador, they were shipped to Peru. From Peru, they were shipped to Pakistan. And from Pakistan, they were shipped to China. That was the route taken by these particular "Crates of Eggs.

What we got then was $354,000 of the Chinese People's Army money for weapons that cost the United States $13.4 million.

Remember — these weapons were sold from the manufacturers to the US Department of Defense for $13.4 million dollars. Mr. Chin was able to purchase them for about $354,000.

By the way, Mr. Chin has diplomatic immunity from the Chinese embassy to operate in the United States as a "commercial attache."

However, there are, or should be, normal security restrictions to his conduct as a known intelligence operative of the People's Republic of China.

For instance, he is not supposed to travel more than fifty miles outside of Washington without contacting the FBI. Yet Mr. Chin is able to travel with impunity in the United States, without his military credentials, and he's given unfettered access to a highly restricted US military installation.

By the way, the FBI Counter Intelligence Section (FBI CI-3) is the agency that lets him get away with it, but someone else is obviously telling them to do it.

Other people who appear at The Group's weekly auctions include Russian arms dealers who are also active duty Russian military officers.

The Defense Oversight Committee has supposedly been investigating this for the past eighteen months. So has the GAO.

Interim reports have been released, but now these Republican-dominated committees in anticipation of a George Bush win have suddenly slowed down their investigations.

What will eventually happen is that there will be some fall guys from the Clinton people within the Department of Defense. Anybody who will be a scapegoat will be a "Clinton person."

The problem was that the GAO's interim report of September 2000 began to link US defense contractors. They found lots of records and details about which defense contractors were selling which defense systems at which prices. These wound up in the Redstone Arsenal inventory fraud auctions. They in turn were then sold for five to ten cents on the dollar to illegal arms dealers.

The investigators started to find a lot of Bush connections — into E-Systems, Honeywell and Loral Corp.

It should be noted that Loral was one of the principal providers of missile component systems to the US Air Force. It was mostly Loral technology and Loral produced components that got sold to the Chinese. Of course, we know that the Bush family is intimately connected with the Loral Corporation. It's well known that Loral CEO Bernie Schwartz was a big fundraiser for the Clintons, but the deep connection is with the Bush Family.

The Bush Family Trust is a very substantial shareholder in Loral. The connections between the Bushes and Loral Corp. have existed since the time of the old man's (George Bush Sr.'s) father, Prescott, Sr. It was one of very first stock acquisitions they made, as a matter of fact, and they still own a substantial amount of shares in Loral Corp.

Rockwell, Lockheed Martin — the usual cast of characters are all involved. You have to remember that this was extremely high technology that was being sold — so high tech in fact that some of it is still experimental.

One of the devices sold to Lannie Chin was an experimental hand-held high-energy discharge weapon, which is powered by a very complex chemically actuated fusion power cell.

The device is rectangular, about the size of a telephone pager. The demonstration of the device was in a testing field directly in back of the dining hall, the commissary, where they have lunch.

There's a big building there that they use for blowing stuff up. A US Air Force colonel was holding onto this device. They had towed in an old beat-up 1975 Chevy station wagon. This car is built like a tank. The colonel points this thing at the car at a distance of 200 meters. He pushes a button and out from this little square box shoots a yellowish-bluish bolt of light. When it strikes the car, it's completely destroyed, blown to pieces. The car exploded like it was an incendiary explosion, like a ball of fire.

The colonel then told Lannie Chin that the devices were available for $200,000 a piece.

How does it work? It's been known that US defense contractors have been experimenting with them for a long time. In fact, the military has even begun to field some of these devices. The problem with energy discharge weapons, however, as always been the miniaturization of the power cells.

We have already developed miniature thermonuclear power cells, but the problem is that they're obviously not safe. Apparently, rather recently, we have invented a chemically actuated fusion power cell.

Fusion, unlike nuclear fission, can also be created chemically. For instance, in cold fusion, it's a chemical reaction and the process is quite simple. The problem has been the miniaturization of the components — how to make it safe and small enough and powerful enough.

This device itself is a deep matte black with digitized red letters on it: EFW-1. When asked what it stands for, the Friendly Colonel said it stands for "Experimental Fusion Weapon."

Investigations of these activities are heating up once again.

One measure of this is the more than ten-fold increase in the personnel at the FBI office in Birmingham, Alabama.

The question that should be asked is this — is the buildup of FBI personnel in order to investigate these activities?

Or is the buildup of FBI there to help cover up this ongoing military fraud?

After all, it's business, or should we say, fraud-as-usual at Redstone Arsenal...

FBI Angst & the Ongoing Redstone Arsenal Fraud Saga

Alas! The record manpower buildup at the Birmingham, Alabama FBI field office has been short-lived.

The FBI angst level about the previous revelations in this column regarding fraud at the Redstone Arsenal have since declined as FBI agents are being moved to Florida.

We've also been informed that FBI agents have formed Al Martin Raw Fan Clubs. We have word from numerous field offices that the FBI has become very concerned about field agents who are clicking on to the Al Martin Raw website to find out the truth about their own bureau.

In fact, a confidential memorandum has evidently been dispatched from Washington to all field offices, forbidding agents to click on to the Al Martin Raw website unless it's for official business. It should also be noted that an agent in an FBI field office has stated that the Al Martin Raw website is the only way that agents who are out in the boonies can find out what their own bureau is up to.

There has also been an increasing number of younger FBI agents who have said that reading *The Conspirators* has opened their eyes to the bureau's past involvement in illegal covert operation of state. They applaud this book because it is "the only source of truth they have had about their bureau" versus the propaganda they get jammed down their throats at their training sessions at Quantico. The word among younger agents to read the book is spreading.

"It really opened my eyes," says one agent. After the training at Quantico, he continued, they get fed a line of propaganda, to wit, that the FBI works for the people and is there to enforce the law. And the FBI never gets involved in any illegal covert operations of government. And they always tell the truth. And they never shred documents.

Since the FBI had surreptitiously set up multiple surveillance cameras during the Super Bowl, there had been a substantial number of matches, including many people wanted for questioning, regarding allegations of espionage, terrorist activities, as well as a large assortment of escaped felons, parole and probation violators, etc.

Some high-level prominent politicians were also caught on camera, including Jeb Bush with an unknown attractive woman — not his wife. In this latest scandal, the FBI has a problem because they're afraid that one of the women has threatened to file a lawsuit to obtain copies of the tape. The girlfriend is evidently asking for some hush money, after becoming aware that she and Jeb were photographed by the FBI. As you can imagine, the FBI is in a quandary.

Also it has been learned that the Tampa field office of the FBI has extra help from the Jacksonville office and they've been moving these people around like it's nobody's business.

The FBI has, of course, denied publicly that there were any matches made with anyone who had any criminal history.

The remaining agents in the Birmingham, Alabama office are desperately trying to keep the FBI out of the limelight regarding recent revelations about illegal weapons sales at the Redstone Arsenal. They have instituted a new operation aimed at identifying those in the Redstone Arsenal and its accompanying military complex who are known to have been involved in arms trafficking and those who are known to be double, triple and quadruple dippers.

So, in a desperate effort to take the limelight off themselves, the FBI is said to be ready to raid Redstone Arsenal employment records. However, they don't seem to be too concerned about the actual fraud and continuing illegal high tech weapons auctions to agents of foreign governments.

By the way, double and triple dippers include retired military officers, who, while drawing a check from the Department of Defense, may also be drawing one or two or more checks from other federal agencies as well — checks to which they are not entitled.

Apropos this story, the Friendly Colonel says that a retired female federal civil service employee he met at the supermarket in Huntsville was very indignant that her husband's checks had stopped coming. She was complaining that her husband's two federal checks, one of which she wasn't entitled to, had recently been stopped — despite the fact that her husband had been dead for four years.

Even though he was dead, the husband had evidently been promoted, thereby increasing the woman's pension check. Then, when he was demoted — while he was still deceased — the widow got upset.

In other words, he was promoted after death and then demoted after death. Plus she was getting two checks from Uncle, one of which she wasn't entitled to.

You have to understand. She's not getting the widows mite. She's getting the guy's actual check — as if he were alive. She went to the base commander at Huntsville and complained about it. Her checks were then restored. The Brigadier General told her in essence that the dead husband was a loyal federal employee who kept his mouth shut his whole career about illegal things he saw the government doing. Therefore, you are entitled, she was told. "Just because your husband is dead is no reason why you shouldn't be getting your checks."

Federal employees who work for sensitive agencies, like the Department of Defense, the Department of Justice, the FBI and so forth, tend to accumulate a lot of information throughout their careers, information that passes across their desks and information regarding illegal activities of government.

Instead of turning that information in to somebody, they simply save it. This has always been the routine. As a reward for not revealing that information to any prospective congressional committee or any outside investigating committee, they in turn expect to receive a very generous pension. Or even two.

Oftentimes, if they know enough sensitive material, they are given extra rewards by being given a pension from GSA or GAO, a pension to which they are not even entitled. Or they might be given an early social security disability check. This is another way to take care of people and it was commonly used in the post Iran-Contra environment. These people know they've kept their mouth shut all their lives and they expect to be rewarded in the end with spurious pensions.

This is common knowledge among retired FBI guys. When some of them had not been given extras when they retired, they would sell the information they had. These were the guys who were considered less reliable or they were simply on the outside and not part of the inside loop.

They figure they've kept their mouths shut over the years, so they're "entitled." It doesn't make any difference — even if the person has been dead for four years.

The current level of morale at the FBI is believed to be extremely low. Not only is the morale low, but they're completely disorganized. The Friendly Colonel adds that everybody is suspicious of the FBI and their cases fall apart in no time at all. He reminds everyone of the Waco Debacle — that everybody but the FBI was calling the shots.

However, there is hope for the future. When younger FBI agents, who are not aware of the Bureau's checkered past, read *The Conspirators*, they will learn to be wary and watch out for internal skullduggery and the odd midnight shredding party. Otherwise they too might become a target.

Huntsville: Corruption City, USA

The Friendly Colonel has recently reported that the Redstone Arsenal and its surrounding military complexes, the Missile Command Center and Test Center, etc. are in a complete state of turmoil.

Senior FBI agents, who know too much, are retiring, and there are a lot of colonels and generals who have also suddenly taken early retirement.

In addition to this turnover, the GAO has a new investigative team at the Redstone Arsenal looking at missing weapons components and missing monies. The problem was that they sent down a bunch of accountants. After the audit, the GAO found so much material missing without any payments to account for the losses.

The audit, completed last year, showed discrepancies, which were so vast as to be mind-boggling. The "discrepancy" at the Huntsville military complex was over $16 billion.

Now the GAO is looking for new information. They are looking at senior military officers and their offshore accounts and this new investigation is making an awful lot of people very nervous.

As a humorous aside, the Friendly Colonel reports that the FBI had evidently sent a fresh-faced lad from the Memphis office, newly indoctrinated in the halls of Quantico, who believes the FBI can do no wrong. Sent down to infiltrate the arsenal complex and see what he could find, he was offering to buy information. On his first day he was able to purchase five separate disks containing classified US military information, including a disk, which detailed the location of all secret military supply depots within the United States. The young FBI agent was surprised to find that the average cost per disk (the kid couldn't get over it) was less than a hundred dollars.

Everybody in Huntsville knows that things are falling apart very quickly. They've been informed that there will be new congressional investigations and everyone is looking to cover their asses. Consequently there has been a surge in retirement applications from senior FBI agents, and from colonels and generals. Everybody is just looking to make as much money as they can to augment their offshore accounts, etc.

Of course, there is nothing new in all this, but what is new is the turmoil with which it's being conducted so that everyone is looking over their shoulder. And the prices that information is being sold for is such that you can tell it's like the Last Days of Pompeii. People are just trying to grab what they can before it all falls apart.

Most of the leaks are evidently coming from retired military people. Every day the base has more traffic in and out from retired military than it does have regular guys, including a new 300 lb retired major general desperately attempting to fit into his old uniform. They have meetings there every couple of days. These are retired colonels and generals who have become arms merchants or who now work for defense companies.

This is the heart of the whole scheme to sell weapons to embargoed countries through a variety of artifices and cut-out nations, as has been previously described. Most of this is being run so the military can maintain deniability as these deals have always been run, as Iran-Contra was run — by retired military officers. This has been ongoing for twenty-five or thirty years.

You must remember that we were selling weapons surreptitiously to China in the 1970s. There is really nothing new about any of this. The only thing that is different is the turmoil, frenzy and paranoia among senior FBI agents and senior military officers.

The reason the FBI are in a frenzy is because the FBI Inspector General is being pressured from various congressional committees and the GAO to look at senior FBI agents' offshore accounts and offshore property holdings etc. and that's making them crazy.

This is going to reach all the way up to George Bush. What's going on now is an effort to draw the line of liability at a certain place, lest it go any higher. It's a liability control mechanism and they're trying to draw the line before they lose control of everything and it gets back to Washington, and into the White House, and into the Department of Defense. Then it would get real sticky for everybody.

They will try to draw it within the senior echelons of the FBI and the senior echelons of the military, but try to keep it away from the Department of Defense and away from the White House. They've done it before. It was done quite successfully during Iran-Contra. You blame it on all the generals and colonels, but you keep it away from Washington by circling the wagons.

Things have progressed to the point where somebody in the White House or somebody in the Department of Defense is starting to draw up a list of scapegoats. That's what's generating a lot of nervousness. The senior FBI guys have to leave their office and go to a payphone to call their offshore banks and to move their money around.

A lot of people wouldn't believe it, but what's going on in Huntsville is the true essence of the way everything works in this country in terms of the federal government. Nobody cares about the law or enforcing it. It's all about money, simply augmenting your retirement the best you can, before whatever it is you were involved in falls apart.

Word has also leaked out that the Department of Defense is trucking down a batch of their turbo shredders. And that is an ominous sign that the end is near.

When the Department of Defense brings in their turbo shredders that means that the whole thing is going to fall apart pretty soon and they want to get as much stuff shredded as possible.

By the way, the young FBI agent told the senior FBI agent that he actually met a major who told him, "Hell, for $10,000, I'll give you every god-damn military secret in the United States."

This is just business as usual. Nobody cares about the laws, regulations or mandates. It is a good example of the way the US Government works. It's all about yourself and lining your own pockets and covering your own ass. And there are cabals within cabals within cabals. And the higher up the ladder you go in the federal government, in any bureau, in any agency, you are invited into an ever higher concentric circle of cabals, where there is bigger money and bigger liability.

Parked in the corner of the airfield at the Redstone Arsenal, there were several private Lear jets, standing by, so if it gets too sticky, the retired guys can get to their luxury Caribbean homes in a hurry. After all, these Lear Jets are provided for them for free by the defense contractors.

The level of corruption and the way it all works and what it's really all about becomes unbelievable to most people. It's about the Great Abyss. Picture a canyon, a deep abyss, surrounded by high walls. And in that Abyss whirls a continuous maelstrom of fraud and corruption. At the very bottom is the Great Vortex, known as the Vortex of the Way Everything Works and What It's Really All About.

You don't want to look too deep into the Vortex. It's dangerous. Look at all the people who have looked too deeply and the consequences. The only way you survive the Vortex is to become part of it. Everyone who has attempted to expose the Vortex hasn't fared very well. But conversely, that's The Way It's Supposed To Be. That's the way everything works. It is an interlocking system of corruption and fraud that transcends and goes through all governments. It is in fact the common link that all governments share.

But to get back to Redstone – when the turbo-shredders are on the way, everybody knows that the jig is up – or it's close to being up. And everybody's getting nervous about whether they're going to be on the Scapegoat List.

The people on the Scapegoat List are always the highest-ranking people who know the least.

And the Scapegoat List is invariably drawn up from the 20% of the people who are actually honest, who actually believe in what they're doing, who actually have lived on their paychecks, who actually have to live on their retirements, those who do not have offshore accounts, or luxurious Caribbean cottages.

Traditionally that's how the Scapegoat List is drawn up — from the ones who know the least. The young and naïve. Or the old and deceived.

Appendix B

SELECTED DOCUMENTS

WINSTON BRYANT
ATTORNEY GENERAL

STATE OF ARKANSAS
OFFICE OF THE ATTORNEY GENERAL
200 TOWER BUILDING
323 CENTER STREET
LITTLE ROCK, ARKANSAS 72201

(501) 682-2007

January 17, 1991

THE HONORABLE ▮▮▮▮▮▮

Dear Judge ▮▮▮▮▮

This letter is to inform you and other interested parties that Alexander Martin has been, and hopefully continues to be, of invaluable assistance to authorities and media in Arkansas who are working to bring to light certain illicit events which occurred in Arkansas in the early 1980's.

Mr. Martin has provided, without compensation to my knowledge, information which has been crucial in exposing a sordid partnership between certain U.S. government entities and cocaine traffickers who used a Mena, Arkansas airport as a staging area for their illegal activities.

We respectfully request that Mr. Martin be given the freedom and encouragement to continue his courageous efforts in regard to this effort.

Sincerely,

LAWRENCE GRAVES
Chief of Staff

LG:ble

ALEXANDER, M.C.
ARKANSAS

COMMITTEE ON
APPROPRIATIONS

Congress of the United States

293 CANNON HOUSE OFFICE BUILDING
WASHINGTON, DC 20515
(202) 225-4076

January 21, 1991

THE HONORABLE ████████

Dear Judge ████████

For some time, this office has been engaged in investigating activity at the Mena, Arkansas airport which allegedly involved both gun and drug running in connection with the Iran-Contra supply operation run from the White House by Lt. Col. Oliver North and others.

Alexander S. Martin has offered his cooperation by providing access to information he has indicated is related to the Mena, Arkansas airport. As you might imagine, information on covert and illegal operations is not easy to obtain and all sources are extremely valuable.

Therefore, this office appreciates Mr. Martin's pledge of cooperation. We fully realize that his decision was made in the knowledge that such cooperation can certainly carry a personal risk.

There is no doubt that in furtherance of this inquiry, we will be calling on Mr. Martin in the future. Obviously, if his ability to cooperate with the investigation is impeded, it could hinder this process.

I am determine to fully investigate allegations that my state was the site for drug and gun running in pursuit of an illegal and covert foreign policy being carried out by the White House, in violation of the laws of the United States.

Respectfully,

Bill Alexander
Member of Congress

"The greatest dangers to liberty lurk in insidious encroachment by men of zeal, well-meaning but without understanding."
Louis D. Brandeis, Associate Justice of the Supreme Court, 1916 - 1939

BILL ALEXANDER, M.C.
ARKANSAS

COMMITTEE ON
APPROPRIATIONS

233 CANNON HOUSE OFFICE BUILDING
WASHINGTON, DC 20515
(202) 225-4076

Congress of the United States

November 20, 1990

Mr. Dexter W. Lehtinen
U.S. Attorney
Southern District of Florida
155 South Miami Avenue
Miami, Florida 33130

Dear Mr. Lehtinen:

Please find enclosed for your files a copy of a letter which I
sent to Attorney General Thornburgh this date.
The contents of the letter are self-explanatory.

Yours Truly,

Bill Alexander
Member of Congress

"The greatest dangers to liberty lurk in insidious encroachment by men of zeal, well-meaning but without understanding."
Louis D. Brandeis, Associate Justice of the Supreme Court (1916 - 1939)

BILL ALEXANDER, M.C.
ARKANSAS

COMMITTEE ON
APPROPRIATIONS

Congress of the Unit States
November 20, 1⁹

233 CANNON HOUSE OFFICE BUILDING
WASHINGTON, DC 20515
(202) 225-4076

COPY

Hon. Richard Thornburgh
Attorney General
Department of Justice
Constitution Avenue and Tenth Street N.W.
Washington, D.C. 20530

Dear Mr. Thornburgh:

During your first appearance before the Commerce, Justice,
State, the Judiciary and Related Agencies Subcommittee of the House
Appropriations Committee in August 1989, I mentioned that my
membership on the subcommittee had led to an investigation of events
surrounding the Mena, Arkansas airport -- relating to alleged gun and
drug running connected to the operation of the Contra rebels in
Nicaragua.

You assured me at that time that you would pursue the matter.
While we have not had further discussions, my efforts have
continued. Congressional interest in this matter has been amply
demonstrated and I would renew my invitation that the Justice
Department participate in this effort.

One potential witness I am working with is Alexander S. Martin
of Hollywood, Fla., who was associated with Gen. Richard Secord in
the Contra funding operation.

I am now informed that he is apparently facing some sort of
federal charge in Miami pertaining to information in his possession.

Since it is my intention to obtain evidence from Mr. Martin for
use in the investigation and any future Congressional hearings which
might result, I would appreciate it if you would advise me as to Mr.
Martin's status with regard to these charges, which I am led to
understand were to be filed by the U.S. Attorney's office in Miami.

From evidence I have obtained, it is apparent that my state was
used as the site for illegal activities, including drug running and
money laundering. I am determined to find out who sanctioned this
operation and for what purpose.

Yours truly,

Bill Alexander
Member of Congress

"The greatest dangers to liberty ...... encroachment by men of zeal, well-meaning but without understanding."
Louis D. Brandeis, Associate Justice of the Supreme Court (1916 - 1939)

May 18, 1993

William H. Alexander, Esq.
1425 Ironwood Drive
McClean, Virginia 22101

Dear Bill:

Pursuant to our conversation of this date, I would first like to express my appreciation for your interest in my situation. In regard to our conversation, I shall attempt to set forth for you the circumstances pertaining to monies I feel are owed me.

In late 1982, I became aware, via some of my old associates, of an Agency Operation designated "Operation Eagle" (later to become redesignated "Black Eagle"). In layman's terms, it was an operation to covertly establish, arm and finance a resistance army within Nicaragua.

Based upon my past experience, I immediately realized that the vast funding requirements for such a large-scale operation would far exceed any legitimate funding the then Reagan-Bush administration could "hood-wink" Congress into appropriating. I assumed, later to be proven correct, that a whole panoply of semi-dormant "cut-out" corporations would be picked up and given new life out of the shadows for the purpose of illicitly supplying and funding their scheme. Shortly thereafter, I took up residence in Miami -- where else, of course?

All through 1983, I established offices in Miami and a series of corporate artifices dealing in oil and gas partnerships, real estate ventures, aircraft brokers, gold bullion, offshore banking and private securities -- all of the old time "right wing" favorites for the generation of covert revenue streams.

By early 1984, I had these artifices firmly established and minimally operating, and let it be known that I wanted a bowl of this new stew cooked up by the master chefs at Langley. Lo and behold, a fellow appeared on my doorstep, one Lawrence Richard Hamil, bearing felicitation from Richard Secord. I had marginally known Hamil in the past, essentially as one of the legions of quasi-con men with deep, old connections into DOD and the Agency involved in small-scale, covert financial and weapons deals, ostensibly because of his father, the late Harry Hamil, a long-time senior DOD analyst.

Hamil, too, had developed, in conjunction with Secord and others, a series of corporate artifices similar to my own, but much larger and with more direct Washington ties: namely, the Gulfcoast Investment Group, with ties to Neil Bush's Gulfstream Realty, Jeb Bush's Gulf Oil Drilling Supply Co. with Posada Quintero Rodriguez, George W. Bush Jr.'s Harken Energy, Tidewater Development, Houston Energy Partners, etc.,

Wally Bush's J. Walter Bush Securities and Prescott Bush's investment company. All, as was to be learned later, had ties to "Iran-Contra" funding activities.

Hamil offered, and I quickly accepted, a prime marketing contract between his artifices and mine. Although somewhat leery of Hamil, whom I considered little more than a scum bag, I was nonetheless cognizant of his powerful Washington ties, and knew he could not have established such legitimized and complex artifices without Washington's help. Secord I had known peripherally for some years, back to the days of General Hang Sung's poppy fields and Marshal Nguyen Cao Ky's relieving the South Vietnamese treasury of its bullion toward the end of the war. But I did know that if there was right wing mischief afoot and a dollar to be made, Secord would be there. Although I never thought Secord was capable of organizing a Chinese fire drill, his knack for purloining the public purse was legend, and those on his coattails would profit.

So, armed with my favorite statistics as printed in The Reader's Digest, namely that 84% of all the self-made chaps worth $10 million or more in this country are right wing Republicans, I began my "Iran-Contra" involvement.

As we discussed, Bill, this letter is not being written to describe my entire involvement in "Iran-Contra," "Iraq-Gate," "BCCI," etc. -- that would fill a book. Ergo, I shall move forward.

The way our artifices worked was quite simple, similar to many others which operated collaterally to us at that time. As I describe it to you, bear in mind that these were pre-1986 tax reform days, when the top individual tax bracket was 50%, in which all our well-heeled investors were. I will use the oil and gas partnerships as an example.

We would purchase a field of old, shallow wells, pumpers usually in old Kentucky limestone formation fields that still pumped a few barrels a day, package it up into a limited partnership, and through carefully crafted meter reads, logs and runs, we would overstate production by a thousand times. We would accomplish this with help from local officials and oil companies, whose sympathies to the "cause" were already known. With generous monthly "envelopes," their cooperation was assured. Gen. Secord would provide us with lists of "investors," usually extremely well-heeled, overweight, middle-aged, right wing Republican doctors and lawyers. All of them envisioned themselves as some sort of young, thin, handsome Republican Rambos shooting communists under the American flag in the jungles of Nicaragua. Insofar as that was not possible, they did the next best thing, vicariously living out their fantasies through their checkbooks. They eagerly "invested" in our limited partnerships. They would be paid half of their investments via "royalties" before the partnerships became insolvent. They got to write off the other half on a 2:1 leveraged basis, which was perfectly legal under the tax laws at the time. The net effect of this was that they came out whole on an after-tax basis.

I was authorized to extend assurances that the IRS would not scrutinize these transactions, and they never did. The investors received what they wanted -- no net cost to them and the privilege of serving the cause, as well as the "Standard" package -- a large framed dual color photo (deluxe) of Ronald Reagan and George Bush (autographed for those who wrote checks with lots of nice zeros on the end) and a framed letter of appreciation from Col. North, informing the recipient that he would be the subject of "the undying gratitude of the true guardian of Liberty," and the obligatory toll-free phone number that rang in a White House basement cubicle, essentially to impress their drinking buddies.

Of the half of the investors' sums retained, I kept 15%, and 35% was bled off to a variety of North-Secord controlled offshore accounts having innovative names such as Stanford Technologies Overseas Ltd. and Intercontinental Industries S.A., and of course, my personal favorite, Trilateral Investment Group Ltd.

By January, 1985, my relationship with Hamil had deteriorated and I disassociated myself from him. We parted ways with Hamil having stuck me for several hundred thousand. Gen. Secord assured me, however, that I was a valued member of the enterprise team and that the monies owed me would be made good. I warned Secord about Hamil's nature, which he most certainly knew, and that the artifices he had helped Hamil create were a con man's idea of heaven and that Hamil would go forth and pillage the general populace with those schemes, creating all sorts of liability along the way that would have to be covered up. In the ensuing months, that is precisely what happened.

Henceforth, I dealt directly with Secord. However, not wanting to be tainted down the road with Hamil's liabilities, I retained a private investigator to track Hamil's and monitor my own activities.

As 1985 dragged on, my involvement grew. I was now laundering funds through many artifices that were being generated through weapons, securities and other transactions. I also began to pressure Secord. Although I was making money, I had yet to be paid what Hamil owed me.

By September, Secord was feeling the heat from me and suggested a face-to-face with Col. North, Col. Gregg and himself. Accordingly, on December 19, 1985, we met. Present were myself, Steven Dinnerstein, my private investigator, Maj. Gen. Richard V. Secord, Lt. Col. Oliver L. North, Col. Donald M. Gregg and, much to my surprise, Director Casey himself. (Despite what later history showed through these fellows' notes, I can prove where they were on this date.)

North immediately started the conversation by informing me that there would be a briefcase containing a quarter million in my office within four days as "kiss and make up money." All was sweetness and light; however, one must know what North was like: cold, steely and dangerous. Unlike Secord, who believed all people's problems could be solved with the appropriate sized "briefcase," North would constantly employ his favorite expressions when observing a similar problem: "They will be taking a long walk on a short pier." And you knew by the look in his eyes, he meant it!

I cannot and would not tell you of the complete context of the conversation that took place, as it touches upon the larger question of, God forbid, the American people learning the truth of the way things work. That, of course, will never be politically possible for either party. Col. North wanted me to help "set up" Hamil for that long walk on a short pier, since Hamil, whose star had fallen by this time, possessed far too many "problem" documents for comfort.

Suffice it to say that what Col. North proposed, and my part in it, did not come to pass and I was never paid, despite the fact, which was clearly understood, that $200,000 of the money was already owed me, and had nothing to do with what was then being proposed. Hamil, it may be noted, is still alive today, enveloped in the golden breast of the DOD, which I must admit, takes care of its own, unlike some other agencies.

What I have been put through in the last seven years in order to maintain the deniability of others, and how I have fought back through the media and a small band of liberal sympathizers on the Hill, I am sure you are somewhat familiar with.

And now on the to the present. As you may be aware, I was extended certain "assurances" by my attorney, Marc David Sarnoff, grandson of the late Gen. Sarnoff, founder of NBC and financial friends of Democrats since the days of FDR, that during the recent presidential campaign, if I just stayed "cool" pursuant to my conversation with Ross Perot and the media, who kept using the words "Clinton" and "Mena" in the same breath while pestering me incessantly for information, that a Clinton administration would "Look favorably pursuant to the redressing of my grievances." This also held true for Perot's efforts to ask me umpteen times about certain senior Democrats, most notably David Boren. I kept quiet, however, as was to be expected, Sarnoff told me in January that his Clinton cadre pals were now telling me to stick it up my ass.

I apologize, Bill, for the length of this letter, but it's not easy to condense the episodes in question. When in 1991, a well-known journalist wanted the details of my complete Iran-Contra/Iraq-gate involvement, it took five days and forty hours of tape.

I appreciate your help, Bill, both past, and hopefully present, regarding this matter.

Sincerely,

Lt. Alexander S. Martin, U.S.N. (ONI), Ret.